Anatomy of Mistrust

This book is a volume in the series

CORNELL STUDIES IN SECURITY AFFAIRS

edited by Robert J. Art, Robert Jervis, *and* Stephen M. Walt

A complete listing appears at the end of the book.

Anatomy of Mistrust

U.S.–SOVIET RELATIONS DURING THE COLD WAR

DEBORAH WELCH LARSON

Cornell University Press

ITHACA AND LONDON

135205

First published 1997 by Cornell University Press

Printed in the United States of America

Library of Congress Cataloging-in-Publication Data

Larson, Deborah Welch, 1951–
Anatomy of mistrust : U.S.-Soviet relations during the cold war /
Deborah Welch Larson.
p. cm.—(Cornell studies in security affairs)
Includes bibliographical references (p.) and index.
ISBN 0-8014-3302-9 (cloth : alk. paper)
1. United States—Relations—Soviet Union.   2. Soviet Union—
Relations—United States.   3. Cold War.   I. Title.   II. Series.
E183.8.S65L358 1997
327.73047'09'045—dc21   96-49153

♾ The paper in this book meets the minimum requirements of the
American National Standard for Information Sciences—
Permanence of Paper for Printed Library Materials, ANSI Z39.48–1984.

Cloth printing   10 9 8 7 6 5 4 3 2 1

To my parents

Also by Deborah Welch Larson:

Origins of Containment: A Psychological Explanation

Contents

Preface

For many years I have been trying to determine why foreign policy officials make decisions that result in needless sacrifice of lives and money. Studying the making of U.S. foreign policy, I was impressed with the ways in which incorrect images of the world could distort reception of accurate information and bias the outcome of even the most structured, analytical deliberation about alternative policy options. Often, no matter how systematically the president elicited conflicting points of view, analysis and debate could not overcome the tendency of officials to fit the world to their preexisting beliefs.

To understand better the influence of beliefs and cognitive processes on foreign policymaking, I read widely in cognitive and social psychology. I was particularly struck by attribution theory, which analyzes how people explain and predict the events of everyday life. In my first book, *Origins of Containment: A Psychological Explanation*, I evaluated five social-psychological explanations for the origins of the Cold War belief system. Even in a bipolar world, I suggested, the United States and the Soviet Union could have defined their relationship differently. They could have chosen to be limited adversaries, might have competed for the favors of a united Germany or might have divided Europe into spheres of influence; they could have pursued isolation or gone to war with each other. The Cold War was not structurally determined by the bipolar distribution of military power. If alternative paths existed, then perhaps the United States and the Soviet Union could have avoided a Cold War; but I did not elaborate that counterfactual. When I wrote the book, virtually all international relations theorists maintained that the Cold War would continue as long as the world was bipolar.

In this book, I show that leaders on both sides had a strong interest in reducing Cold War tensions and in managing the arms race. I identify five branching points where, if not for mutual mistrust, U.S.-Soviet relations could have taken a different path: the period from Stalin's death until 1955; the post-*Sputnik* Soviet peace offensive; the Kennedy administration; the Nixon-Brezhnev détente; and Gorbachev's accession to power. Journalists and historians often refer to "missed opportunities," but this is the first systematic study of missed opportunities for international cooperation. The theory of trust-building that I outline in this book is potentially relevant to other international conflicts, including those in the Middle East, Bosnia, and Northern Ireland.

A striking finding of this study is that the Soviet Union made more concessions than the United States did in order to achieve agreements. Characteristic features of the U.S. political system help to explain this surprising result. The president faces substantial potential domestic political opposition to his making unilateral concessions or one-sided agreements; the Soviet general secretary did not have to concern himself with Soviet political opinion. Thus, the president was more constrained in carrying out trust-building initiatives than was the general secretary.

I have been fortunate in having extraordinary reviewers. Among those who read the entire manuscript are Alexander L. George, John Lewis Gaddis, Jack Snyder, Raymond L. Garthoff, Robert Jervis, and an anonymous reviewer. George has provided wise guidance at every stage; his finely detailed and extensive marginal comments were invaluable in sharpening the analysis. Gaddis patiently encouraged me to broaden my analysis to include ideological factors and urged me to reconsider an earlier, simplistic version of this manuscript. Snyder stimulated me to develop the psychological hypotheses. Garthoff provided me with substantive suggestions, drawing on his distinguished service in government as well as his scholarly writings and long study of the Soviet Union. Jervis helped me to elaborate the psychological hypotheses and showed their significance for the study of international relations. An anonymous reviewer made extremely useful suggestions for structuring the theoretical chapter.

I thank others who offered comments on portions of the manuscript, in particular Charles Lipson, members of the Program on International Economics and Security at the University of Chicago, Clifton Morgan, Friedrich Kratochwil, Peter Katzenstein, David Baldwin, George Downs, and James Morrow.

I am also grateful for a research and writing grant from the John D. and Catherine T. MacArthur Foundation, which enabled me to take a year off and conduct extensive archival research. Support from Columbia University's MacArthur Faculty Research Program on Conflict, Peace and Security and annual grants from the UCLA Academic Senate financed research assistance and support, without which I could not have undertaken this project. My research assistants at Columbia, William Daugherty and Randall Schweller, should be commended for discovering new sources and ideas. At UCLA, I have been fortunate to have as an assistant Kristen Williams, who has excellent insights into the historical literature and the ability to summarize key points concisely.

Roger Haydon has provided me with cheerful, efficient editorial assistance and excellent comments. Kristina Kelsey ably supervised the transformation of the manuscript into a book. Charles Purrenhage provided meticulous copyediting. Melanie Turner conscientiously composed the index.

Finally, I thank my parents, Lin and Jeanette B. Welch, to whom this book is dedicated.

DEBORAH WELCH LARSON

Los Angeles, California

[1]

Distrust and Missed
Opportunities in Foreign Policy

Now that the Cold War is over, we must wonder whether the arms race and global competition that nearly bankrupted the United States and contributed to the collapse of the Soviet Union could have been better managed. We can find reason for such rumination in statements suggesting that U.S. and Soviet policymakers wanted to resolve some of their differences at the time, or at least jointly control their competition. In a letter to his friend General Alfred Gruenther, President Dwight David Eisenhower predicted that his Open Skies proposal for mutual aerial inspection of the Soviet Union and the United States would eliminate the danger of a devastating surprise attack and "yield an immense gain in mutual confidence and trust." The two states would then have a "truly realistic basis for studying disarmament." The Soviet leader Nikita S. Khrushchev, however, viewed Open Skies as an espionage plot.[1]

Khrushchev himself regretted that he and Eisenhower could not come to terms on disarmament. He later recalled a conversation at Camp David in 1959 in which the president confided that "my military leaders come to me and say, 'Mr. President, we need such and such a sum for such and such a program.' I say, 'Sorry, we don't have the funds.' They say, 'We have reliable information that the Soviet Union has already allocated funds for their own such program. Therefore if we don't get the funds we need, we'll fall behind the Soviet Union.' So I give in." Khrushchev replied that it was the same with him. Eisenhower said, "Yes, that's what I thought. You know, we really should come to some sort of an agreement in order to stop this fruitless, really wasteful rivalry." But, as Khrushchev recalled, "we couldn't agree then, and we can't agree now."[2]

President Eisenhower was depressed by the collapse of the May 1960 summit after the Soviets shot down a U.S. U-2 spy plane. He confided to his scientific adviser that he had concentrated during his last few years on ending the Cold War and that he had been making rapid progress until the stupidity of the U-2 mess had ruined everything. He saw nothing worthwhile left for him to do until the end of his presidency.[3]

In December 1961, President John F. Kennedy and Prime Minister Harold Macmillan of Britain regretted that during the test ban negotiations the United States had overemphasized what the Soviets could gain from cheating on underground testing—and in particular that the Soviets could evade detection by testing in a "big hole." Both agreed that if less had been made of the risks of clandestine underground testing, a test ban agreement could have been signed. Asked to name the most disappointing event during his first year in office, Kennedy immediately replied that it was his "failure to get an agreement on the cessation of nuclear testing."[4]

The diplomatic record of the Cold War is not entirely dismal. The superpowers signed cooperative agreements prohibiting nuclear testing in the atmosphere, restricting nuclear defenses, accepting surveillance to monitor arms control agreements, and eliminating medium-range nuclear weapons.[5] On the other hand, the United States and the Soviet Union failed to achieve a comprehensive test ban or a ban on multiple independently targetable reentry vehicles (MIRVs). Not until 1970 did the superpowers achieve a modus vivendi on Germany, and even this solution was supposedly only provisional. Nor did the two superpowers sign an agreement that actually *reduced* the number of nuclear weapons until the Bush administration, and then only to the level prevailing under Kennedy.

These Cold War transactions may have harbored missed opportunities for the superpowers to settle some of the issues in dispute, to control wasteful arms spending, or to prevent dangerous crises. Missed opportunities refer to what might have been, to possibilities that for one reason or another were never realized. A missed opportunity for agreement is a situation in which there was at least one alternative that the parties to a conflict preferred or would have preferred to nonagreement. In other words, the two sides' preferences and interests were at some point compatible and overlapping.

We can find missed opportunities for cooperation in many social and political conflicts, but the Cold War between the United States and the Soviet Union offers striking examples. Both superpowers would have liked to limit their military production and spending. Both states wanted at least a temporary solution to the German question which would have enabled them to withdraw some troops from Europe. Although they differed on who should govern Germany, neither superpower wished to see a reunified Germany meddling in the internal affairs of Central and East European countries.

To suggest lost possibilities differs from explaining why the United States and the Soviet Union failed to reach agreement. Explanation of abortive diplomatic efforts requires merely that one identify some of the conditions responsible for the stalemate. To propose what *might have been*, on the other hand, entails showing how changes in a set of historical conditions could have led to a different outcome.[6] If the superpowers' failure to achieve an agreement reflected deep structural constraints that were not mutable in the short run, such as the balance of power, incompatible objectives, the deep-seated influence of the military-industrial complex, or strategic considerations, then perhaps there were no lost possibilities. To make the case for missed opportunities entails showing that both sides wanted an agreement, that history need not be completely rewritten to end up with a different outcome—in other words, that a plausible sequence of events could have led to an agreement, and that U.S. and Soviet leaders could have cooperated on many occasions if they had more effectively communicated their intentions. I shall use historical evidence to support the claim that the United States and the Soviet Union, if not for mutual mistrust, could have reached several significant agreements on security issues and that, through sustained effort, they could have overcome such suspicions.

Scholars have proposed different explanations as to why leaders fail to cooperate in controlling their rivalry. "Hard-core" realists believe that states compete for arms, territory, and influence out of a desire to preserve their sovereignty or increase their power. A state must be wary about entering into agreements with the enemy, who could be trying to lure it into a trap or lull it into relaxing its defense efforts. In many cases, the interests of states are inherently in conflict—two states may desire the same territory or ally, or they may both want to achieve preeminence as a world power.[7]

"Softer" realists agree that states often have conflicting interests, but these derive from global anarchy and an inability to determine if the other's intentions are aggressive. States can signal their desire to cooperate and can teach the other to respond by following a tit-for-tat strategy of rewarding good behavior and punishing attempts at unilateral aggrandizement. Soft realists propose that states can enter into cooperative arrangements if each can monitor the other's performance and retaliate against any infraction so as to make cheating unprofitable.[8] Both perspectives assume that, in at least a loose sense, states behave prudently, that they accurately assess the strategic situation and exercise appropriate caution.

My position is different. I argue that states often fail to cooperate even

[3]

when their preferences overlap, because policymakers draw incorrect inferences about the motives and intentions of others, a process that can be illuminated by social psychology. In these instances, states could have reached an agreement without changing what they wanted, or at least what they were willing to accept.

Repeated failures by the superpowers to cooperate may seem to confirm the view of international relations as a struggle for power, but such failures often could have been averted. The two states' suspicions helped to generate many of their conflicts. The United States and the Soviet Union found themselves competing in far-off areas such as Angola, Somalia, and Ethiopia where they had no previous interests. Besides, enemies can sometimes overcome a legacy of conflict to reach agreement in areas of common interest. Recently, the United States and the former Soviet Union have become partners in many areas. Since the end of the Cold War, other enemies have begun to cooperate as well, such as Israel and the PLO, Britain and Sinn Fein, and South Africa and the African National Congress. Might the Cold War have ended sooner, or at least taken a different path?

Most philosophers of science believe that a counterfactual, an "if-then" statement about something that did not occur, should be supported by a theory. Otherwise, one cannot assess the reasonableness of something that after all did not happen.[9] Because international relations scholars have not given sufficient attention to trust, I have broadened my search for observations about trust in foreign policy to other disciplines which have examined and developed propositions about this key problem. Economics, game theory, sociology, and psychology offer useful insights into the nature and sources of trust. Many generalizations about trust can also be found widely scattered in the international relations literature. I present three alternative explanations for trust and distrust in foreign policy: rational choice, domestic structure, and psychological factors.

If U.S. and Soviet leaders had objectively assessed one another's interest in observing an agreement and decided that the probability that the other would comply was not worth the risks of misplaced confidence, then there would have been no missed opportunity. But U.S. and Soviet leaders did not behave in this way: they ignored or misinterpreted evidence of the other's desire for an accord and made categorical judgments about the other's aggressiveness and lack of trustworthiness. If U.S.-Soviet distrust was deeply embedded in antagonistic domestic structures and ideologies, then events could not have turned out differently until one system or the other was exhausted or defeated. Contradicting the argument that the structures were constraining, however, is the fact that U.S. and Soviet leaders were able to achieve important agreements, such as the treaties to ban nuclear testing in the atmosphere and to prohibit antiballistic missile systems.

Social psychology provides a better explanation of the superpowers' failure to reach more agreements on areas of common interest, of the length of time that it took to negotiate simple agreements, and of the severity of the Cold War. Social-psychological theory identifies and explicates the cognitive mechanisms underlying mistrust and reveals its effects on foreign policy decisionmaking. Psychological theory also provides an indication of how mistrust can be overcome.

I shall show that U.S. and Soviet leaders passed up opportunities to cooperate on arms control and on Germany largely because of mutual mistrust, based on ideological differences, historical baggage, and intuitive mental biases. These diplomatic failures were wasteful, tragic, self-defeating, and often, if not always, avoidable. Of course, each side wanted to be able to monitor the other side's compliance to its own satisfaction; and the difficulty of verifying disarmament agreements before the days of satellite photography also played a role in the failure to achieve some arms control agreements. Even during the 1950s, however, it was possible to find observable forms of behavior (e.g., troop movements and nuclear tests) that could be monitored by both sides as the basis for cooperation. Cognitive biases are like visual illusions; once the error is pointed out to you, you can see the image differently. At the time, some individuals were less susceptible to old ways of thinking than others, and they argued for probing the other state's intentions through negotiations.

I present a systematic, interrelated set of social-psychological hypotheses to explain trust and mistrust in international relations. In entrenched conflicts, mistrust is not easily overcome. Words are not enough; deeds are usually required. States may build trust by negotiating small agreements that enable them to test each other's sincerity at lowered risk. A state may also take unilateral conciliatory actions to convey its peaceful intentions, as Charles Osgood proposed.[10] Because the adversary may suspect a trick or a propaganda ploy, a state may have to take more than one cooperative action, even if the other side does not immediately respond. Images of other states as hostile or untrustworthy tend to lag behind changes in their behavior. To build trust, a state should also maintain a consistent policy, because people tend to believe that a state's actions in different areas, no matter how disparate the circumstances, reveal its underlying motives.

I shall show that the United States and the Soviet Union were able to cooperate when each trusted the other to comply, or when one side made a series of unilateral concessions to alleviate mistrust. However, a pattern of results that is consistent with my argument could be spurious if other conditions were responsible for U.S.-Soviet successes, such as the catalytic effects of crisis, the emergence of a common threat (e.g., China), domestic public pressure, or economic weakness. Greater trust might be epiphenomenal, a by-product of changes in state interests and preferences. Thus, I examine how trust was established in each case, and I consider whether factors other than changes in beliefs about the other side's intentions and motives might have altered the two sides' interest in cooperation.

Trust, we shall see, is usually a necessary (though not a sufficient) condition for states to cooperate. Further on in this chapter, we shall discuss the effects and sources of mistrust, trust-building initiatives and how they are perceived, and the use of historical case studies to determine whether opportunities were missed. Before doing so, however, we should consider the conventional explanations of why it is that states pass up chances to control the arms race and resolve disputes. In response to these conventional approaches, I then propose three alternative ways of explaining trust and mistrust between states.

INTERNATIONAL RELATIONS THEORY AND MISSED OPPORTUNITIES

For hard-core realists, states fail to reach agreement and choose to fight because they have conflicting interests and preferences. For example, states may try to acquire the same territory, resources, or allies. To defend themselves and compete more effectively, states try to acquire more weapons than their rivals. The arms race, then, reflects underlying political differences and cannot be significantly dampened through agreement until at least one side moderates or abandons its objectives, usually as a result of exhaustion or a defeat in war.[11]

Hard-core realists concede that nuclear weapons changed this situation somewhat by making it essential for great powers to coordinate their actions in order to avoid inadvertent war and by diminishing the practical significance of superiority. When each state can destroy the other many times over, numerical superiority has little utility. Realists maintain that the United States and the Soviet Union could limit the growth of their offensive nuclear weapons after each had sufficient strength to retaliate against a first strike; acquiring additional weapons did not confer any usable advantage.[12]

If nuclear superiority does not translate into influence over others, then it is difficult to explain why U.S. and Soviet leaders accumulated far more weapons than they needed to ensure their security—the United States had 30,000 weapons in 1967, and the Soviet Union had about 45,000 in

[6]

1987. Some realists blame wasteful strategic competition on "strategic myths" (i.e., the tendency to treat nuclear weapons as if they were conventional) or on the undue influence of allies.[13]

As these explanations suggest, overreaction to the other's gains and excessive competition may have psychological causes. Distrust can turn a shared interest in controlling nuclear weapons into a zero-sum game. If one state believes that the other side is unalterably aggressive, it may insist on having a safe margin of superiority. The inferior side may be unwilling to concede a lead to the more powerful state, which might use its advantage for intimidation or blackmail. Thus, mutual distrust and suspicion can drive the nuclear arms race, even when the relative number of weapons is meaningless.

Soft realists acknowledge that states have important conflicts of interest, but argue that disputes derive from insecurity and uncertainty about the other's intentions rather than from irreconcilable geopolitical interests, strategic objectives, or ambitions of leaders. Because there is no superior authority to prevent states from using force, a state's military defenses threaten others, no matter how peaceful or benign its intentions. This creates a security dilemma: a state cannot be secure without making others more insecure, thereby provoking an arms race, heightened tensions, and greater insecurity. Even if the other state does not harbor aggressive intentions now, it may have different ambitions in the future. In theory, a state could try to reassure others by choosing weapons that are better suited for defense than for offense. But in practice the other side may not be able to distinguish the primary function of particular weapons or military doctrines, or it may believe that this is a distinction not worth making. Intercontinental ballistic missiles (ICBMs), for example, can be used either to attack or to defend.[14]

Soft realists compare the problem of international cooperation to a Prisoner's Dilemma game, which is best described by a simple story. A prosecutor offers a prisoner the chance to go free in return for testifying against his partner, but threatens to throw the book at him if he remains silent while his confederate implicates him. Both prisoners confess (or "defect" in game theory) and receive a heavy sentence, whereas they could have gotten only a year or two in prison if they had cooperated by remaining silent. An arms control agreement between enemies resembles a Prisoner's Dilemma game because, like the prisoner, a state would gain most from cheating while its opponent exercises restraint. Unless a state can monitor the other's compliance with an accord and receive timely warning of cheating, it will be reluctant to enter into an agreement that could result in an adverse shift in the balance of power should the other side violate negotiated restraints. In the view of soft realists, the fear of being played for a sucker contributed to the difficulty the United

States and the Soviet Union experienced in controlling their rivalry even when they had an interest in doing so.[15]

In the 1980s, Robert Axelrod stimulated renewed interest in international collaboration by arguing that states could learn to cooperate if they expected their rivalry to continue and practiced reciprocity. Axelrod built on the works of game theorists who had concluded that players might be able to cooperate in repeated Prisoner's Dilemma games. When the game is played repeatedly, players can retaliate in future rounds against the other's defection, and in this way make cheating unprofitable. Axelrod found that the strategy of tit for tat, which first cooperates, then matches the other's move in the previous game, achieved the highest average score in a computer tournament.[16]

Axelrod argued that trust is not necessary for cooperation: "there is no need to assume trust between the players: the use of reciprocity can be enough to make defection unproductive." He suggested that the key to arms control is better verification, because states cannot make their observance of an agreement contingent on the other's compliance unless they can monitor its behavior accurately. If so, then technical problems of verification could help to explain the failure of earlier arms control efforts.[17]

Certainly, states will not enter arms control agreements unless they can monitor the other side's behavior to their own satisfaction. As Ronald Reagan used to say, *Doveryai no proveryai* (Trust but verify). The advent of satellite reconnaissance in the early 1960s alleviated mutual fears of surprise attack and made it possible for the United States and the Soviet Union to control the numbers of missiles and bombers by enabling each party to photograph the other's delivery systems.

But verification arrangements cannot eliminate the need for at least some minimal trust in the other's good faith. States can get around virtually any inspection system if they are determined to do so. What states demand of an enforcement system depends in part on their beliefs about the likelihood that the other will cheat. Without some trust, a system of monitoring and inspection for an arms control agreement might have to meet such stringent requirements that it would be infeasible or prohibitively expensive, as was often the case during the Cold War. Indeed, if policymakers believe that the enemy is determined to cheat, no monitoring system will satisfy them. During the test ban negotiations from 1959 to 1963, some congressmen charged that the Soviets would test in huge underground salt caverns or in outer space, behind the sun! Conversely, after the Cold War ended, the United States and the Soviet Union signed sweeping agreements on chemical weapons and strategic arms reduction for which the verification arrangements were hardly foolproof. In September 1989, Secretary of State James Baker proposed that both sides agree to eliminate 80 percent of their chemical weapons stockpile, even though chemicals could be easily concealed. President George Bush agreed with his national security adviser Brent Scowcroft that "this means we're kicking the can of verification down the road." Just five years earlier, Bush had argued before the United Nations Committee on Disarmament that a chemical weapons ban required that each party have confidence that other parties were abiding by it, and the U.S. draft treaty contained a complex system of verification, including intrusive on-site inspection. In START I (Strategic Arms Reduction Talks) the United States agreed to allow the Soviets to reduce the number of warheads by removing them from existing missiles, even though some defense analysts feared that the Soviets could quickly reinstall the warheads and break out of the treaty.[18]

Nor can an inspection system eliminate all of the risks of entering into an agreement. Even if the other side complies with the terms of an accord, a state may fear that its adversary will exploit a relaxation of tensions to make strategic gains elsewhere. Or an enemy might be trying to gain a breathing spell in which to build up its arms for renewed competition. If the other state does cheat, a state may have difficulty restoring the previous situation or retaliating against arms control violations. As the title of a well-known article by Fred Iklé asked, "After Detection—What?" For democratic states, the argument runs, the difficulty is not so much detecting violations, but responding to them effectively without endangering national security. A verification system may not be able to detect cheating until the other side has acquired an irreparable strategic advantage. U.S. policymakers worried that if the United States withdrew part of its forces from Europe as part of a disengagement agreement, the Soviets could readily send their troops back whereas geographic distance and domestic public opinion might delay and impede the return of American forces. Domestic public opinion may not regard the other side's minor infractions of an arms control treaty as sufficient to justify discarding a mutually beneficial arrangement. Nor is it always possible to find a punishment that is commensurate with the other's violation of an agreement. For example, the Reagan administration had difficulty deciding how to respond to the Soviets' building of a radar station at Krasnoyarsk in violation of the ABM Treaty, since the United States had no interest in building a similar radar facility. But unless the injured state imposes some sanctions, the other side will gain from cheating and will only be encouraged to continue making marginal gains.[19]

If two actors do not trust each other at first, Axelrod argues, they can learn to cooperate if they are in an enduring relationship, for two players who have no choice but to interact with each other may gradually come to appreciate the other's interest in cooperating and the greater benefits to both from doing so. As David Hume stated, "I learn to do a service to another, without bearing him any real kindness; because I foresee, that he will return my service, in expectation of another of the same kind." Trust might then be a useful by-product, not a precondition for mutual cooperation. Thus Axelrod predicted that the United States and the Soviet Union might learn to cooperate tacitly on arms control because they knew they would be dealing with each other for a very long time.[20]

Some might say that U.S.-Soviet cooperation evolved in just this way, as the two states adapted to each other's actions and learned to manage their competition more effectively. According to this view, the United States and the Soviet Union showed greater maturity over time, as leaders moderated their ideological rhetoric and acknowledged that both sides had a shared interest in avoiding nuclear war.[21] A linear model, however, does not adequately explain the ebb and flow of U.S.-Soviet cooperation, the "unlearning" of lessons by Leonid Brezhnev, and the return to the Cold War in the early 1980s. When the Cold War ended, it did so abruptly, not through gradual evolution.

So we see that even hard-core realists concede that the United States and the Soviet Union could have cooperated on arms control and security issues more than they did. Soft realists acknowledge that mistrust may prevent states from cooperating on arms control, but they put too much stress on verification and not enough on other reasons for states' reluctance to enter into agreements with adversaries, such as fear of being lulled into complacency. Axelrod's tit-for-tat strategy founders on the underlying reef of mistrust. Many arms control and other security agreements are not self-enforcing unless a very restrictive set of conditions is met. States must have warning of the other's aggressive intentions in time to protect themselves. Measures to restore the situation existing before the agreement must be politically and militarily feasible. To deter further violations, a state must be able to impose penalties on the other side that outweigh any strategic advantages gained by cheating. Unless a state can respond effectively to violations of an agreement, even the most reliable monitoring system may not suffice to mitigate suspicion of the enemy's intentions.

If mutual mistrust keeps states from cooperating even when they have shared interests, then we need to consider whether such suspicions are warranted. If they had reason to mistrust each other's intentions, then U.S. and Soviet officials did the right thing in passing up possible agreements; they may have correctly calculated that the risks outweighed the potential benefits. Alternatively, it may be that the authoritarian Soviet system promoted fear of external enemies in order to legitimize its rule or that the pluralist American political system exaggerated the Soviet threat in order to contrive a sense of unity. Social psychologists, on the other hand, suggest that mistrust between social groups often has its origins in cognitive biases and errors that lead to misperception of the enemy's actions. Each of these potential explanations for diplomatic failure has its source in a different theoretical tradition—economics, political science, and social psychology. Let us explore these varying perspectives.

Rational Choice

Many decisions in the economy depend on a calculation of whether the actor can trust someone. A patient has to decide whether to believe a doctor who orders expensive tests from which the doctor will benefit financially. Consumers weigh the reliability claims for a new car model. A homeowner interviews a contractor for a job remodeling her home. The prospective buyer of a used car tries to determine whether a particular automobile is a "cream puff" or a "lemon." Although the seller knows the value of the car, the buyer cannot rely on him for an honest description because he has an incentive to conceal that it is a "lemon." Of course, a buyer who has been defrauded can sue, but going to court is extremely expensive and may not be successful. The problem here is not uncertainty, but opportunism: one party knows more than the other and has short-term incentives to lie, mislead, distort, withhold information, or obfuscate.[22]

In some ways, entering into an arms control or other collaborative security agreement with an adversary is like buying a used car: states take the risk of ending up with a "lemon." Even if a state offers an explanation or justification for proposing an agreement, it could just as easily be lying. A state planning to cheat on an arms control treaty will make the same promises as a state intending to carry out its obligations.[23] Indeed, a state that is offered an arms control deal may be more uncertain than the prospective buyer of a used car. Car buyers can insist on having the car inspected by an independent mechanic; the owner's refusal of this standard request provides information in itself. In contrast, a leader typically does not have available a simple test of another state's sincerity.

Without some way to assess the other party's reliability, actors may not be able to enter into mutually beneficial economic exchanges. Yet, until recently, most economists neglected trust, assuming that market competition would eliminate fraud and deceit. Some economists, however, have recognized that trust is a precondition for economic production and trade in a modern economy where goods and services are rarely exchanged simultaneously. Businesspeople are unwilling to rely on market incentives to enforce contractual agreements. Business firms in a continuing relationship, such as manufacturers and suppliers, often develop informal trust relationships. The penalty for violating trust in such arrangements is both monetary and nonmonetary, the loss of a good name. Francis Fukuyama argues that willingness to associate with others outside the family is necessary in the large-scale corporate organizations that are essential for modern economic prosperity.[24]

In general, economists define trust as a particular level of subjective probability that the other will perform an action upon which the success of one's *own* decision depends and in a context where one must decide before the other's behavior can be monitored. The person who trusts makes himself deliberately vulnerable to the possibility of a loss caused by the other's opportunism or strategic behavior. Accordingly, the probability that the other will perform a certain action must be above a certain threshold, which depends on the risks of misplaced confidence.[25] The notion of trust as a probability judgment is useful because it suggests that trust is not an either-or matter and that the amount of trust required for an agreement varies. More trust is needed for large decisions, where the potential losses from betrayal would be devastating. We might unthinkingly trust someone to hold our place in line at the movie theater, but agonize about a decision to invest money in a partnership or to lend a large sum of money to a friend. Similarly, the extent to which states must trust each other to enter into an international agreement depends on how catastrophic the consequences of betrayal would be. For some treaties, leaders could live with the consequences of noncompliance and need have very little confidence in the other state's reliability. Thus, agreements affecting the relative balance of military power between two states require more trust than cultural exchanges.

An actor's assessment of the probability that the other will be trustworthy should use information about the other's interests as well as about his character. Every man has his price, as the saying goes, and even an honest person might lie in certain circumstances. A sensible person reserves trust for situations where the other has an *interest* in fulfilling his obligations. This is consistent with the realist argument that states observe treaties that are in their interest. Thus, U.S. policymakers sometimes tried to judge the Soviets' interest in disarmament or arms control. Concerning the Limited Test Ban Treaty, Averell Harriman remarked in 1963: "I know everyone feels that the Russians break all their agreements. They have kept those in which their interests are involved and I think they are going to keep this one."[26]

A state can affect the other's interests by decomposing an agreement into smaller parts. Moving in small steps increases the other side's incentive to fulfill its obligations in order to get to the next stage. Dividing up the transaction over time makes cheating in a particular instance less attractive than the benefits the parties can look forward to receiving in the future.[27]

Staging an agreement, of course, will not ensure against cheating unless policymakers have correctly assessed the other side's long-term interests: that is to say, how much value it attaches to the end product as compared with the immediate gains of reneging. But we can never know another state's—or, for that matter, another person's—interests, motives, and intentions with any certainty. When deciding whether to trust, an individual should also consider the other's reputation for fulfilling his commitments, the public record of his reliability. Consumers often prefer to deal with a business whose reputation is known, particularly when purchasing an expensive durable good such as an appliance or automobile. Similarly, a state with a history of observing its obligations can more easily persuade others to enter into new agreements. Khrushchev cited the advantages of a good reputation to explain why the Soviets would not take over West Berlin if U.S. troops were withdrawn. The Soviet leader assured Senator Hubert Humphrey that Moscow would not try to "strangle" West Berlin because "a good reputation is important." As for the Soviet Union, he said: "Our firm is a good one and we want a good reputation. It would weaken us if we violated our word or if we let others do so."[28]

But, of course, American policymakers did not believe the Soviet Union had such a reputation to lose. Not all states or individuals have a reputation that they can invoke to bolster the credibility of their promises. Individuals or businesses have an incentive to develop a reputation for trustworthiness when they know that others will select future trading partners based on their record for keeping agreements. In game theory, in order to earn a desired reputation, an actor may try to do something that would be out of character for someone who was disingenuous, deceitful, or opportunistic. Similarly, by going against another's expectations, by refusing to take the easy way out, a state invests in a reputation that can be used in the future to influence others. Just as a state may decide to intervene militarily in order to establish its resolve and deter future aggression, so may a state make a costly concession in order to transform its relationship with an adversary. A leader, for example, presumably would not reduce troops unilaterally if he planned to invade or attack another country. Thus, in 1955, Khrushchev withdrew Soviet troops from Eastern Austria in exchange for that country's neutralization. "Is there any stronger proof necessary to show that the Soviet Union does not want to seize Europe to carry on any sort of war?" Khrushchev asked. "Who would evacuate troops if he wanted to attack?"[29]

If the value of deception is great, even an aggressive state might make a costly concession as a trick or lulling device. The longer the enemy cooperates, the more likely it has passed up tempting opportunities to betray the other state's confidence. As a state continues to comply with agreements, the other side becomes more confident about its trustworthiness. Accordingly, a reputation for trustworthiness can only be established over time, as the state consistently fulfills its obligations and provides accurate information.[30]

U.S. and Soviet leaders may well have had no real interest in restraining their arms competition or in resolving the issue of a divided Germany. Indeed, at certain times and regarding particular issues such as conventional arms control, such an assessment of the superpowers' preferences is accurate. On the other hand, if we accept at face value statements by U.S. and Soviet leaders indicating a desire to cooperate with each other on arms control—and I shall present evidence suggesting that many such affirmations were sincere—then if those leaders were sensible they should have weighed each other's interest in a security arrangement.

Because having a good reputation is crucial, leaders on both sides should have taken great care to get the other side to see themselves as reliable. If these leaders had any interest in inducing the other side to cooperate on arms control, one would expect policymakers to behave in such a way as to convey an impression of seriousness and sincerity. In fact, though, Khrushchev was erratic, and Brezhnev took actions that were inconsistent with the spirit of détente, such as sending Soviet advisers to Angola.

Because the decision whether to trust the other is so important, we would expect leaders to allocate time and effort to figuring out the other state's interests. Instead, officials usually made snap judgments about the other's lack of trustworthiness. Sensible decisionmakers would have been alert to signs that the other side was interested in cooperating to control the arms race and other forms of competition. It would have been reasonable for policymakers to modify their belief that the other side was insincere when the adversary made a costly conciliatory gesture. Instead, such actions were often ignored, overlooked, or dismissed as propaganda. When decisionmakers' beliefs changed, moreover, they did so all at once, rather than incrementally in response to each piece of supporting evidence.

On neither the sending nor the receiving end did policymakers behave as we would expect, a result that can be explained only by psychology. The Soviets might have done more to convince the United States that they were serious about arms control. On the other hand, U.S. policymakers should have responded more positively to Khrushchev's costly initiatives.

Domestic Structure and Policy Legitimacy

The conservatism of policymakers with respect to adjusting their beliefs and policies suggests that their reluctance to enter into agreements derives from sources other than a strategic calculation of the benefits of cooperation compared with the risks of being exploited. Mistrust may stem not from an assessment of the other side's incentives to engage in opportunistic behavior and a lack of information about its intentions, but rather the state's domestic institutions and the requirements of legitimacy. The structure of a state's domestic political and economic system may encourage leaders to promote distrust of other states in order to legitimate their exercise of power. Even leaders of authoritarian regimes are concerned with legitimacy—the sense of obligation that citizens have toward the state and its policy prescriptions. Rulers have to spend fewer resources to secure compliance if at least some citizens comply willingly. A foreign policy needs at least minimal domestic support in order to be implemented effectively.[31]

To legitimate their actions, rulers may try to show that they are striving to achieve societal values, as portrayed in an ideology. Ideology is a system of fundamental, value-laden beliefs that explain and justify a preferred domestic political order (and often, by extension, an international order), existing or future, and that provide a plan for its attainment. Leaders may use ideological rhetoric to rationalize specific policies in terms of a desired social order, an ideal society. Soviet leaders justified their rule as a necessary step toward communism. In order to win congressional support for $400 million in aid to Greece and Turkey, President Harry S Truman used the theme of freedom versus totalitarianism in the Truman Doctrine speech. The use of such terms as "communist" and "capitalist" by the Soviet Union and "democratic" and "totalitarian" by the United States links policy goals with societal values. Ideology gives purpose and meaning to specific policies.[32]

Although some Soviet officials were cynical and hypocritical when mouthing slogans about the eventual triumph of communism, they were constrained to *appear* obedient to that ideal. To fall within the bounds of acceptance, proposals for domestic reform or international cooperation had to be phrased in terms of the dominant political culture and norms, which were shaped by Marxism-Leninism. An official who promoted détente with the West or nonintervention in the internal affairs of other states was vulnerable to criticism from neo-Stalinists as being antirevolutionary or revisionist. Marxist-Leninist doctrine described "peaceful coexistence" as a form of class struggle, not as cooperation between rival social systems for mutual benefit.[33]

Nevertheless, ideological differences did not rule out some U.S.-Soviet cooperation on arms control and security questions. Various Soviet officials and academic writers manipulated Marxist-Leninist ideology to justify cooperation with the United States and other capitalist states. Soviet officials such as Nikita Khrushchev, Aleksandr Yakovlev, Eduard Shevardnadze, and Mikhail Gorbachev were socialized by the system yet could see that the United States and the Soviet Union had shared interests.

In addition to invoking ideological values, leaders may use the image of the opponent to legitimate their exercise of internal power. Partly as a continuation of the tsarist tradition and in reaction to the isolation of the infant Bolshevik state, the political and economic institutions of the USSR mobilized all available human and natural resources to build up military power. Such a system required an external threat for self-justification. In 1927–28, Stalin helped drum up a war scare to defeat his right-wing political opponents and justify forced collectivization, purges of the party, and breakneck industrialization. Stalin created a centralized administrative command structure that subordinated all people and interests to the state. Even after Stalin died, elements of the system endured. Khrushchev made only partial progress in de-Stalinization; he ended arbitrary terror but did not try to dismantle the centralized state machinery or loosen the party's dictatorial rule.[34]

The Soviet system favored heavy-industry bureaucrats, party ideologues, and the military, whose interests lay in opposing arms control agreements with the United States. Economic planners gave the defense industry high priority for scarce investment funds and resources. The defense sector was the most technologically innovative in the Soviet economy, a fact which increased that sector's status and attracted more capable employees to it. The Soviet military had profound influence by virtue of its monopoly of information on Soviet military programs, its prestige as a victor in the Second World War, its primary role in formulating military doctrine, and its unclear relation to civilian control. In policy conflicts, ideologues could always attack proponents of liberalization or détente as being revisionist or antisocialist.[35]

In contrast to the centralized Soviet regime, the American pluralist system has numerous independent agencies that share power. Instead of deliberating analytically over the correct course of action, U.S. policymakers must often bargain with interest groups and bureaucratic agencies. Before making an arms control proposal to the Soviets, presidents have had to win the support of various agencies with different views and interests, including State, the Arms Control and Disarmament Agency, the Atomic Energy Commission, the Joint Chiefs of Staff, and the Department of Defense. The Defense Department, Joint Chiefs of

Staff, and various members of Congress with bases or national defense plants in their state often opposed arms control. Presidents sometimes had to buy off internal opponents of arms control agreements by agreeing to programs that would modernize nuclear weapons, thus heating up the arms race. Forming a consensus was so time-consuming that U.S. responses often lagged behind Soviet initiatives.[36]

Pluralist political systems tend to produce inconsistent policy as the views of diverse groups are accommodated. In the United States, presidential attempts to satisfy independent agencies and the Congress have led to small but frequent shifts of direction. Decentralization of U.S. foreign policymaking authority contributes to further inconsistency, because officials in different agencies tend to act at cross-purposes. Contradictory statements by officials from different agencies or branches of the government make it difficult for other states to read U.S. signals or interpret Washington's intentions.[37] Under these circumstances, presidents were tempted to "oversell" both the remedy and the threat in order to gain the necessary leeway to carry out their policies in the face of a fragmented and divided elite. Exaggerated estimates of the Soviet threat or of the prospective benefits of détente produced wide oscillations in U.S. policy, from threatening arms buildups to exaggerating the benefits of cooperation with the Soviets on a wide range of issues.[38]

Thus, the incoherence of U.S. policy causes foreign governments to question whether America can be trusted to keep its agreements and carry out its promises. Whereas authoritarian states inspire distrust of their motives, democratic states elicit doubts about their resolve.

The political formula used to legitimate foreign policy may also constrain a leader's ability to offer concessions to the enemy in order to diminish his mistrust. Paradoxically, while authoritarian leaders may need an external enemy to justify repression, they can more readily treat with the enemy once their authority is firmly established: they do not need to have their rule periodically reaffirmed by the electorate. The Politburo was insulated from domestic political pressure because it appointed its own members and made its foreign policy decisions in secret. Authoritarian regimes can make unilateral concessions more easily than democratic leaders, who are under pressure to show that they have not given away the store. As McGeorge Bundy observed in 1969, "neither international nor domestic political concerns could justify any American government in seeming to accept a wholly one-sided policy of limitation." The difference in the U.S. and Soviet domestic political systems helps explain why most U.S.-Soviet agreements arose not from a tit-for-tat process, but in a pattern of asymmetric concessions by the Soviets.[39] In 1955, for example, Khrushchev signed the Austrian State Treaty, recognized West Germany, closed

[17]

the Soviet base in Finland, and reduced Soviet troop strength, whereas President Eisenhower merely agreed to attend the Geneva summit meeting.

If domestic structures were indeed the most important source of diplomatic failures, then we should expect to have found such reformist Soviet leaders as Khrushchev and Gorbachev bound by the defense industry or the military or some other institution with a vested interest in maintaining the image of an external enemy. The U.S. president likewise should have confronted overwhelming opposition to arms control and détente from the Defense Department and Congress. If domestic structures were so determinative, then U.S. and Soviet leaders *could not have overcome domestic opposition even if they had tried.*

Available evidence suggests that, notwithstanding their real importance, domestic structures were not compelling. Paradoxically, the Soviet Union was a militarist state in which the military played only a minor political role. The military did not intervene directly in foreign policy issues, other than in succession crises. In 1953, Khrushchev and other conspirators had the army arrest the Soviet secret police chief Lavrenti Beria. In 1957, Marshal Georgi K. Zhukov threw the support of the army behind Khrushchev and helped the general secretary overcome a serious political challenge from the "anti-Party group." Zhukov's independence aroused fears of "bonapartism," and Khrushchev rewarded the general for his support by having him demoted from the Politburo and stripped of his privileges. After Zhukov, no military member served on the Politburo until Marshal Dimitri Ustinov in 1973. No one should underestimate the power of the general secretary of the Communist Party in those years. Repeatedly, civilian leaders intruded into military affairs, abetted by an unclear institutional division of authority. We know that Brezhnev often overruled the Soviet military on arms control issues. Even the feeble Soviet leader Konstantin Chernenko was able to fire Marshal Nikolai Ogarkov. The military was hampered in its ability to act as a pressure group by conflicting interests and political preferences, divided between support for nuclear weapons and support for conventional forces. Nor did the defense industry act as a united lobby, except for their resistance to Khrushchev's decentralization of economic planning and management.[40]

U.S. presidents also have substantial formal and informal sources of influence on security issues. Presidents control the flow of information on national security and foreign policy, weakening the ability of Congress to offer constructive alternatives. By making speeches and taking actions in certain issue areas rather than others, the president can set the agenda for foreign policy debate in the news media.[41]

[18]

Psychological Factors

Psychologists view trust as reliance on another at the risk of a bad outcome should the other cheat or renege. Being able to trust others is essential for personal and social relationships. Without the capacity for trust, we would be paranoid, unable to confide in friends, suspicious of the government, unable even to eat our food. Khrushchev recalled that near the end of his life Stalin, speaking to no one in particular, commented: "I trust no one, not even myself."[42] States must have at least a minimal degree of trust to enter an agreement when they are not confident about the other's motives or intentions and would suffer a loss if the other betrayed their good faith.

Trust is a belief that the other will be helpful, but it must be supported by behavior. In ordinary language, "trust" sometimes means mere expectation—"I trust she will return tonight." But trust goes beyond expectation because it entails placing one's fate or welfare in another's hands. If trust is breached, the trusting party will regret that she made the decision. If our expectations are wrong, we shall experience disappointment but not regret.[43]

Trust also has a normative element. When the other party violates our trust, we are morally outraged, not just disappointed. While one might not think that relationships between foreign policy leaders imply obligation, Prime Minister Macmillan of Britain found that Khrushchev was enraged when Eisenhower sent a U-2 spy flight over the Soviet Union just a week before the Paris summit. Khrushchev complained to the British prime minister that "his *friend* (bitterly repeated again and again), his friend Eisenhower had betrayed him."[44]

Trust in a psychological sense can refer to any of three different qualities: predictability, credibility, and good intentions.[45] First, trust may simply mean that we believe the other's behavior to be *predictable*. For example, a family member might comment, "You can trust Aunt Mary to complain about her health." Within society, trust is the expectation that others will carry out their roles competently, whether as plumbers, lawyers, or teachers. Such beliefs are grounded in experience, which leads us to generalize and assume continuity.[46] As the Cold War continued, the superpowers came to trust each other in that sense that they could more accurately anticipate each other's actions and reactions. One of the advantages cited for arms control was that it made both sides' weapons programs more predictable, thereby obviating "worst case" assumptions about the other state's defense expenditures and preventing overreactions.

Second, trust may mean *credibility*—that we believe the individual will live up to his word.[47] When applied to international relations, this conception of trust implies that we can rely on a state to observe treaties and to fulfill its commitments and promises. But we would not necessarily expect the other state to go beyond the letter of the agreement. Nor would we be at all confident that the other state might not take some action deleterious to our interests that is not prohibited by existing arrangements.

Third, trust can refer to the expectation that someone has *benevolent intentions* and will not try to exploit us.[48] This type of trust need not correspond with credibility. The other person may not keep all her promises and undertakings toward us, because of competing demands or circumstances beyond her control, but we nevertheless trust her because her actions and words are well intended. Similarly, the United States may trust another state (e.g., Britain) because we believe that it has essentially benign intentions and will not take advantage of us. Two states in such a relationship will still have conflicts of interest, but these should be minor issues. If the states conduct their relations well, they should be able to subordinate their occasional differences to maintaining a long-term cooperative relationship. This type of trust is less fragile. We tend to discount or overlook the other state's misdeeds or lies because such evidence is inconsistent with our image of the state as friendly.

We do not trust anyone in *every* possible situation. That would be blind faith. We might trust an individual in business, for example, but not in an intimate relationship. Assessments of a state's trustworthiness can be similarly complex and contingent.[49] The United States generally trusted the Soviets to meet their financial obligations, but not to refrain from seizing an opportunity for unilateral advantage or from moving into a power vacuum.

A person decides to trust if the probability of a good outcome outweighs the risks that her trust will have adverse consequences. The likelihood that the other will fulfill her expectations should be above a critical threshold, which is qualitative rather than quantitative, perceptual rather than concrete, and influenced by the history of her relations with the other, which gives some events symbolic value.[50] Just as people may not detect a visual or auditory stimulus unless it passes a certain threshold, so they may not trust the other unless the perceived probability of compliance exceeds a minimal level. More trust was needed for the United States and the Soviet Union to sign an agreement limiting the growth of strategic weapons (SALT I) than to sign one demilitarizing the Antarctic. Not only would there be higher costs to the United States if the Soviets cheated in the former case, but the Soviets had a greater incentive to do so. By 1987, the United States and the Soviet Union had sufficient experience with arms control that when they negotiated the agreement to eliminate intermediate nuclear forces, they were able to satisfy each other's monitoring requirements relatively easily (especially compared with the prolonged negotiations for a test ban).

As noted earlier, because the amount of trust required for an agreement varies, states can overcome the barrier of mutual suspicion by starting with small agreements where less is at stake so that each state can test the other's intentions without putting too much at risk. In this way, states can acquire information about the other's values and reliability before they move on to riskier agreements. For example, the U.S. and North Korean agreement on nuclear nonproliferation is divided into stages over a decade, with specified mutual obligations at each step. The United States will provide central components of a light-water nuclear reactor to North Korea only after that state has opened its nuclear waste facilities to on-site inspection.[51] Logically, the fact that a state carries out a minor agreement does not provide evidence that the same state will observe its obligations when the incentives to cheat are higher; psychologically, though, such behavior does carry weight with the other side.

Some observers object that trust is unnecessary in international relations, because enemies can sign agreements without necessarily trusting each other. To be sure, enemies can enter into agreements of small scope where the penalties for being betrayed are less than severe. On the other hand, if the same states *had* trusted each other, they might have been able to achieve more ambitious arrangements. For example, U.S. Secretary of State Dean Rusk assured the Senate Foreign Relations Committee that the Limited Test Ban Treaty did not "rely on an element of trust." "If we could rely on trust," he said, "we would be discussing a comprehensive disarmament treaty."[52] Similarly, in the 1993 Declaration of Principles, the Israelis trusted the Palestine Liberation Organization enough to grant Palestinians in Jericho and the Gaza Strip autonomy for five years, but not enough to transfer authority over the West Bank.

EFFECTS AND SOURCES OF MISTRUST

States decide to trust based on their estimate of the other side's intentions. Cognitive psychology holds that the labels people give to events, persons, and things shape their interpretation of information and influence their response. This is no less true of international relations. Whether states view another's action as cooperative, hostile, or neutral depends on how they construe its motives. A proposal that may superficially seem accommodative is actually aggressive if the intent is to drive a wedge into the target's alliance system, undermine its domestic support for defense spending, or lull the other state before an attack. In the 1950s, the United States viewed various Soviet proposals for German reunification as devices to divide NATO, encourage neutralism, and weaken the West.

Beliefs about the other side's character affect interpretation of its actions. In social relations, expectations strongly influence how people construe others' behavior. For example, whether we describe Jane's silence in the elevator this morning as aloof, preoccupied, cold, or hostile depends on whether Jane is a friend, casual acquaintance, stranger, or rival. Foreign policy officials also interpret another state's actions in a way that is consistent with their beliefs and images. A leader with a "bad faith" image of the adversary will ignore, reinterpret, or discount the other's conciliatory gesture as a trick or as forced upon him by weakness.[53]

Whereas the players had no choice but to interact with the other side in Axelrod's computer tournament, in the real world states can *choose* with whom to cooperate, which heightens the importance of cognitive mechanisms of categorization and discrimination. States do not have to negotiate with an adversary on security issues. Because states need not rely on each other, they may have little reason to revise their beliefs that the other cannot be trusted. A state may never be able to prove its good faith because the other side declines to enter into agreements or negotiations. A joke about peace in the Middle East illustrates the problem. A religious Jew named Goldberg prayed in the synagogue every Sabbath that he would win the lottery: "God, I have been such a pious man all my life. What would be so bad if I won the lottery?" When the lottery was held, Goldberg never won. This went on, week after week, month after month, year after year. Finally, one Sabbath, Goldberg couldn't take it any more. "God, I have been so good, so observant. What do I have to do to win the lottery?" The heavens parted and God's voice thundered out: "Goldberg, give me a chance. Buy a ticket." Until recently, the Palestinians and Israelis refused to buy a lottery ticket.[54]

Not only is mistrust difficult to disprove, but it can be a self-fulfilling prophecy. In the early 1950s, the superpowers often put forth disarmament proposals purely for propaganda because neither believed that the other was serious about reducing the number of weapons. Assuming that the United States would refuse to enter into any serious disarmament negotiations, Khrushchev had no reason to advance any proposal that had any chance of acceptance. Rather, from 1957 to 1962 he made bold, unrealistic disarmament proposals with inadequate inspection rules and an unrealistic timetable that at least might win the Soviets the support of world public opinion. Believing that the Soviets were interested only in winning a propaganda victory, the United States likewise put forth unrealistic suggestions for general comprehensive disarmament. As Secretary of State John Foster Dulles commented at a National Security Council (NSC) meeting, "Disarmament proposals are probably an operation in public relations rather than actual disarmament proposals." Until the United States could be sure of good faith on the part of the Soviets, Dulles didn't really think that the United States could get disarmament. "Nevertheless," he said, "we must seem to strive for it or else we shall be isolated in the world."[55] At the same time, U.S. leaders assumed that some genuine Soviet arms control offers were merely propaganda ploys, and the result was missed opportunities for arms control.

Actions aimed at dealing with a potential threat may provoke aggressive or hostile actions from the other side. A large psychological literature shows that behaving toward others as if they were hostile, unfriendly, stupid, or incompetent can cause them to act accordingly, thereby confirming the perceiver's original preconceptions or stereotypes. In one experiment, for example, interviewers were instructed to act toward white applicants for a position in the same way that blacks had been treated: shorter interviews, greater physical distance, more stuttering, and so forth. The white applicants performed poorly, according to independent raters who watched the interview on videotape. Two psychologists, Harold Kelley and Anthony Stahelski, found different types of personalities in strategic situations: competitors and cooperators. A competitor forces other people to defect in self-defense, yet fails to see that they are reacting to his own aggressive behavior. Competitive people believe that the world is "dog eat dog" and they cannot be proven wrong.[56]

We form our expectations about other states from previous experience, as filtered through knowledge and inherent mental biases. Characterization of the other side's actions as hostile or friendly is usually automatic. When foreign policymakers go beyond labeling to explain the other state's behavior, they overestimate the contribution of internal sources and underestimate the impact of external forces. Leaders attribute the other side's hostile or aggressive behavior to its ideology or national character, and they overlook that the other side may be responding to their own actions. For example, after détente collapsed in the late 1970s, many Soviet officials inferred that U.S. hostility reflected the aggressive character of capitalism; they did not consider that the West might feel threatened by the continuing Soviet buildup and expansion in the Third World. In August 1983, when the Politburo discussed the American installation of Pershing missiles and cruise missiles in Europe, General Secretary Yuri Andropov did not mention that U.S. missiles were a reaction to the Soviet deployment of the mobile SS-20. When the adversary does something good, moreover, foreign policy leaders are again guided by their beliefs in explaining it. They assume that the enemy's conciliatory actions were forced by external pressures or by the exigencies of domestic political weakness.[57]

People do not make the error of overestimating internal causes when explaining their own behavior. In general, people are likely to explain their own behavior as a response to the demands of the situation and to attribute similar actions by the other person to enduring personality traits or dispositions. For example, they feel that their own views on such controversial issues as racism or abortion are based on reality and are less driven by ideology than the views of others. Thus, states are apt to use a double standard in explaining their own and others' actions. In experiments conducted during the 1960s, students rated Soviet actions unfavorably while evaluating positively U.S. actions that were virtually identical.[58] Similarly, the United States supported Afghan insurgents in Pakistan and the Contras in Nicaragua while condemning Soviet support of the rebels in El Salvador. One side's terrorists are the other side's "freedom fighters" or "national liberation" force. Each sees itself acting defensively, and the other as acting offensively.

Trying to see the situation as the other sees it requires greater cognitive effort. Consequently, people who are busy trying to figure out how to behave toward the other side are particularly prone to explain the other side's actions in terms of stable personality characteristics.[59] Focusing on the other's presumably enduring personal traits is useful in social interaction because it allows an actor to predict the other's future actions more easily and to decide how to influence them. Thus, we would expect policymakers, who are preoccupied with the need to make decisions, to be more liable to this bias than staff members or academic writers, who merely analyze the situation without being responsible for operational policy.

People can surmount the tendency to apply a double standard, to undervalue the role of situational factors in influencing others' behavior while excusing their own actions as a reaction to external pressures. When people make a conscious effort to empathize with the other person's perspective, they are better able to see the situational and role pressures impinging on the individual and are less apt to make snap judgments about his personality traits. The passage of time and a greater emotional distance from an event enable people to see their own behavior from the standpoint of an outside observer and to understand how he might view their actions as reflecting personal qualities.[60]

The divergence between the way people explain their own versus others' actions may help to account for the tendency to believe that it was the other side that started a given conflict. International adversaries from the Middle East to Bosnia to Northern Ireland develop a narrative in which they have been the victim of the other's aggressive actions. Because foreign policy leaders assume that the other state's behavior is driven by internal needs, they infer that its hostility is gratuitous and unprovoked by anything they have done.

Whoever started it, in turn, determines who is to blame. People tend to perceive the initiator of a sequence of events or social interaction as "the cause." For example, when shown two objects in an experiment, subjects perceived that the object which moved first, and then touched a second object, "caused" the motion of the second object. In experimental games, subjects view the player who first defected as more "competitive" than one who simply responded to his opponent's defection.[61] If subjects insist on imposing meaning on *sequences* of cooperative and competitive moves in a laboratory—playing against an unseen opponent, without history or context—how much more so do policymakers in the real world of international relations, burdened by the heavy baggage of history, culture, and political socialization?

In the real world, not only does it matter who started the conflict, but both parties usually believe that the other cheated first. Contrasting interpretations of the history of an international dispute may hang heavily over negotiations, shading perceptions of the other side's motives and intentions. Thus, the "heavy hand of the past" keeps states from recognizing potential gains from agreements. In the 1980s, the superpowers differed over which events caused the decline of détente. As the former Soviet foreign policy adviser Georgi Arbatov recalls, "The first thing that comes to mind is the old question: Who's to blame?" For a long time, Soviet columnists and historians "heaped all the blame on the Americans." For the Soviets, the Jackson-Vanik amendment (which tied Soviet most-favored-nation status to an increase in Jewish emigration) was, as a leading Soviet analyst put it, "the first U.S. blow to détente." Subsequently, according to the Soviets, the United States supported groups opposed to Angolan independence and lured Somalia away from the Soviets by encouraging its irredentist aims in Ethiopia. For the United States, the decline of détente began as early as the October 1973 Middle East war, followed by Soviet assistance to the Cuban forces in Angola in 1975 and to Ethiopia in 1977–78, coups in South Yemen and Afghanistan in 1978, and finally the invasion of Afghanistan.[62]

People do not stop at making inferences about who is to blame; they act to restore a balance. In experimental games, subjects held a grudge and retaliated for a long time against a player who defected after having previously cooperated.[63]

A state's leadership must be strongly motivated to transform their relationship with the adversary, and they must have some confidence from previous experience that their overtures will be reciprocated.[64] Mikhail Gorbachev needed a peaceful international atmosphere for his domestic reform policies, and Ronald Reagan had already initiated a correspondence with Soviet leaders.

Strategic equality between the two sides can also encourage efforts to build greater trust. People play more competitively when they are behind, suggesting that the drive to catch up is stronger than the desire to get ahead. Khrushchev recalled that "when we formed the Warsaw Pact, Western countries had a great advantage over us in their economies and their nuclear arsenals." That "the military and economic balances have shifted to our favor. . . . makes it easier for us to take the offensive in the areas of disarmament and world cooperation."[65]

A state that wants to induce the adversary to cooperate on security issues may use some combination of *persuasion, coercion*, and/or *accommodation*.[66] The state could offer to cooperate in reducing arms expenditures or in settling some conflicts, but words have limited value as evidence of a state's true intentions. During the Cold War, U.S. and Soviet leaders repeatedly challenged each other to prove their good intentions by "deeds not words."

By issuing threats, mobilizing, or increasing its defense budget, a state may try to force the other to cooperate. Policymakers might use coercive tactics because they believe that the other state will view concessions as a sign of weakness; so they must first establish their resolve to resist aggression before offering to negotiate. A state may conclude that the only way to induce the other side to resolve a long-simmering conflict is to impose a deadline and apply pressure, as Khrushchev did in the 1958 and 1961 Berlin crises. Such coercive tactics, even if effective in the short run, may well increase the other side's mistrust. Louis Kriesberg found that not one major U.S.-Soviet agreement was ever preceded by coercive inducements alone.[67]

More likely, the initiator will offer benefits or make concessions in order to reduce distrust and induce the adversary to cooperate on security issues: positive sanctions are more legitimate and appropriate.[68] Concessions can have a variety of purposes and consequences. First, a concession may be part of the bargaining process between two states, as when a state makes a concession in order to elicit a counterconcession. Second, a state may make a concession as an indication of good faith. For example, to prove that it will carry out a disengagement agreement, a state may unilaterally withdraw a portion of its troops, as a first installment. Third, in a more extreme version, a state may make a concession in order to change its overall image as aggressive and intransigent.

In 1959, at the height of the Cold War, the social psychologist Charles Osgood proposed the GRIT (Gradual Reciprocation in Tension Reduction) strategy, which uses unilateral conciliatory initiatives to reduce mistrust and reverse the conflict spiral. Osgood argued that cognitive mechanisms such as "psychologic," stress-induced cognitive rigidity, "us versus them" thinking, mirror images, and self-fulfilling prophecies contributed to increased mistrust and tension between the superpowers. Osgood observed that negotiated agreements between the United States and the Soviet Union required prior commitments from both sides, but that neither would act first in a climate of fear and distrust. In GRIT, the state announces one by one a series of unilateral concessions and publicizes them as part of a consistent policy of reducing tensions. These unilateral acts should be moderately costly and are intended to reduce the enemy's perception of a threat. The initiating state may suggest that the recipient reciprocate, but it should not demand any action from the adversary as a precondition for carrying out the concessions. The state should continue with GRIT for a while even if the other state does not reciprocate immediately, but it should resist any encroachment by the other side on its own interests. If the opponent reciprocates, GRIT takes a slightly more risky action, creating a spiral of tension reduction rather than of conflict. Osgood argued that public statements of concessions create domestic political pressure in the adversary state to do something in return, in line with the norm of reciprocity, and that consistent conciliation gradually persuades the adversary that the state's intentions are peaceful and increases the cumulative pressure to reciprocate.[69] As Osgood conceded, GRIT can only improve the atmosphere for negotiations. More is required for an agreement—such as resolution of differences over the distribution of benefits, verifiable terms of compliance, and consultation with allies.[70]

Use of positive sanctions has its own risks and drawbacks. The target may ignore or discount a conciliatory gesture from the enemy—thinking, for example, that it is a propaganda ploy, a means to to buy time for armament, or a response to domestic opponents. Even worse, the adversary may view a concession as an indication of weakness that should be exploited.[71]

Policymakers are more likely to infer that another state's concession is a sincere sign of a desire to improve relations if the concession is relatively costly. In general, we use the cost of a favor or gift presented by others as a clue to its underlying motives: e.g., "She gave although she could ill afford it." We discount the internal sources of behavior when the behavior could be motivated by external incentives. On the other hand, if a person makes a costly gesture, which indicates that she is acting against external rewards and punishments, such a move suggests that the internal sources of her behavior must be very strong.[72]

People are more likely to reciprocate gifts and favors for which the giver has made a sacrifice because the giver is less likely to have ulterior motives. Similarly, a state can begin to prove its good intentions by making a costly concession. In September 1987, Gorbachev explained that "the new thinking is the bridging of the gap between the word and the deed, and we embarked on practical deeds." Thus, in his December 1988 speech to the United Nations, Gorbachev announced that he was reducing Soviet troops by 500,000 and withdrawing 5,000 tanks from Central Europe.[73]

A conciliatory gesture can take the form of words rather than deeds if making the statement involves some costs or risks for the communicator. For example, in his American University speech, President John F. Kennedy pointed out that the Soviets were not entirely to blame for the Cold War, and he asked Americans to reexamine their attitudes toward the Soviet Union. Congressional Republicans called the speech "a soft line that can accomplish nothing" and "a dreadful mistake."[74]

The level of cost indicates the strength of an actor's motivation. We give more weight to internal causes of behavior when the actor has to overcome external obstacles, applying an implicit equation: the more pain, burden, or risk an actor incurs, the more important the objective. As a result, we make stronger, more confident inferences about an actor's motivation the more risky or costly her behavior is. For example, experimental subjects regard black professionals as more "professional" than whites, presumably because African Americans usually have to overcome more obstacles to achieve that status than whites.[75] Similarly, when a state carries out some costly action, the other side's policymakers should increase their positive estimate of that state's motivation, for the other state must be strongly resolved to achieve some goal if the ultimate payoffs are to outweigh the short-run costs.

The cost of a concession may take many forms: the leader's image; loss of a tactical advantage; domestic political opposition; or economic or military resources. Costly cooperative signals include withdrawing troops from a strategic area, admission of wrong, lifting a trade embargo, sharing of scientific and technological information, establishing diplomatic relations with the enemy, or allowing on-site inspection of military facilities. Conciliatory actions are more costly, and therefore more credible, if they are *noncontingent, irrevocable,* and *increase the initiator's vulnerability.*[76]

[28]

When pursuing this strategy, then, the state generally should not make the concession contingent on a prior response from the opponent. The other side may regard "I will if you will" promises as a cheap attempt to get them to make the first concession. On the other hand, when the initiator announces and then carries out a conciliatory gesture, the consistency between word and deed leads to trust: one can rely on the state's leader to do what he says he will.[77]

A gesture will have greater impact on the target's beliefs if it is irrevocable, that is, if it cannot be amended, reversed, rescinded, or annulled. One reason why states distrust each other is that even if the other side's leadership fully intends to observe an agreement, no one can predict who might come to power in the future and what they will want to do. Thus, states place great value on concessions that cannot be reversed, both as an indication of a policymaker's intentions and as insurance against a policy reversal. Formal recognition is usually irrevocable, whereas cease-fires, bombing pauses, and moratoriums are not. During the various cease-fires negotiated in the Bosnian civil war, the Serbs could have resumed at any time their shelling and blockade of Sarajevo. But for Israel to recognize the Palestine Liberation Organization involved significant opportunity costs. At a meeting of the Arab Graduates Society, a Jerusalem teacher asked about the agreement on Palestinian autonomy: "What guarantees do we have that the Israelis, snakes that they are, will not cheat us?" The leader of the Palestinian negotiating team, Faisal Husseini, curtly replied: "Do you really think the Israelis would go through all this, begin to return our lands and recognize our right to self-determination only to take it away again? For what? For the fun of taking it away?"[78]

In contrast, Secretary of State Dulles was not impressed by Khrushchev's unilateral reduction of Soviet troops by over 1 million in 1956, because the Soviets had an extensive reserve and training system and the soldiers could be quickly called back into service (as in fact many were during the 1961 Berlin crisis). Dulles asserted that reducing troop strength was "meaningless" as a disarmament measure because "you might at one time have two and one-half million men under arms but you may have seven or eight or ten million standing by thoroughly trained and ready." If weapons were available, he said, an army of 2.5 million could be readily expanded into 10 million.[79]

A major concern of the Bush administration was that Gorbachev might be overthrown by hard-liners who would reverse his cooperative policies. Yet domestic liberalization in the Soviet Union reassured many within the United States that democratization and demilitarization had acquired an irreversible momentum. In 1991, Foreign Minister Aleksandr Bessmertnykh pledged to George Bush that Gorbachev's policy of *per-*

estroika would continue despite the Soviet leader's apparent shift to the right. Soviet domestic reform was a "key factor" in making possible international cooperation, Bessmertnykh said: "It has brought us to the point of trust."[80]

The initiator takes the risk that the other side will ignore or exploit a conciliatory gesture. Both theory and empirical evidence hold that making oneself vulnerable to exploitation by being the first to cooperate builds trust.[81]

The Egyptian president Anwar Sadat's visit to Jerusalem exhibited all these characteristics: noncontingency, irrevocability, and vulnerability. Sadat made the dramatic gesture of going to Jerusalem and accepting Israel's right to exist because he wanted to break through the wall of mutual mistrust that was blocking peace. Israel's main excuse for not withdrawing from the occupied territories was that the Arabs refused to recognize Israel's right to exist within secure borders. After the 1973 war, the Arab states hinted at possible recognition, but they would not give up their principal bargaining chip without assurances that the Israelis would withdraw. Thus, mutual mistrust led to a stalemate in the peace negotiations; neither side was willing to move first. In order to remove psychological and political barriers to peace, Sadat went to Jerusalem, addressed the Israeli parliament, and declared "no more war," a promise that was not contingent on any Israeli commitment to withdraw from the Sinai. Sadat's unilateral concession opened up a rift among the Arab nations and aroused domestic protest in Egypt, including the resignation of Foreign Minister Ismail Fahmy, who argued that a secret meeting with Prime Minister Menachem Begin of Israel would not have exposed Egypt to such high costs and risks. Sadat's strategy changed the attitudes of Israeli officials, drew in American involvement, and generated domestic pressure within Israel to reciprocate the Egyptian concession.[82]

RECEPTION OF THE CONCILIATORY SIGNAL

Inconsistent state rhetoric and actions act as "noise," interfering with the other's reception of a conciliatory signal. A state that wishes to prove its good intentions in one area should be careful that its actions elsewhere do not muffle the message. When a state's leader uses combative rhetoric aimed, say, at a domestic audience, or when a state carries out hostile as well as conciliatory actions, the target state must extract the conciliatory message from the surrounding noise. In his first letter to Reagan, Gorbachev cautioned him against inflammatory language, "for trust is an especially sensitive thing, keenly receptive to both deeds and words. It will not be enhanced if, for example, one were to talk as if in two lan-

[30]

guages: one—for private contacts, and the other, as they say—for the audience."[83]

Consistency is essential because we cannot get inside someone's head to observe his or her motives or intentions *directly*. Instead, we look for patterns in behavior as a clue to underlying motives or personal traits. If the individual's behavior stems from stable goals or personality traits, then we expect his choices to be similar in different situations and to be relatively stable. People also assume that recurring patterns in a state's behavior reflect its national interest, political culture, or character. U.S. policymakers thus found it difficult to believe that the Soviets wanted to cooperate when the USSR was supporting national liberation movements throughout the Third World.[84]

Mixing signals—that is to say, combining coercion and accommodation in an uncoordinated, ad hoc fashion—can undermine the credibility of both signals.[85] President Kennedy's initial attempts to pursue both arms control and a strategic arms buildup caused the Soviets to view his cooperative policies as insincere. "Noise," in short, reduces the impact and the credibility of conciliatory actions.

How the other side responds to a state's conciliation depends on how that state's actions are interpreted. People will not reciprocate gifts or favors if they believe the donor has ulterior motives or is trying to manipulate them to do something that is contrary to their interests.[86] Similarly, if a state perceives that another state is pursuing a deceptive strategy, it will be reluctant to acknowledge the gesture or to reciprocate. One state may also reject the other's unilateral concession if it believes that the other state is militarily inferior and is simply trying to use an arms control agreement to reduce its vulnerability. Since military officials tend to engage in "worst case" thinking about the opponent's military capabilities, however, the likelihood that they will view an adversary's concession as a sign of weakness is reduced. Remarkably, according to former Secretary of State George Shultz, some CIA analysts continued to overestimate the military power of the Soviet Union despite Gorbachev's many unilateral concessions. In 1986, officials from the CIA and the Defense Department still stressed the Soviet military buildup and portrayed the Soviet Union as a "mighty nation" confronting the United States everywhere.[87]

The language that the initiator uses to frame conciliatory gestures can help shape the way the target explains and interprets them. That Gorbachev portrayed his unilateral concessions as an outgrowth of "new thinking" served to counteract the perception that his actions were born of desperation.

Because images of states as hostile and untrustworthy tend to endure, the target will probably not reciprocate at first. When the adversary fails to respond, the initiator should consider continuing to make concessions at least for a while until the target either makes a reciprocal move or takes actions that reveal its lack of interest in cooperation. The number of concessions that a state must make to elicit a cooperative response depends on the prior beliefs of the target. A policymaker such as John Foster Dulles or former Secretary of Defense Caspar Weinberger may have such a low opinion of the adversary's probity that there is virtually nothing the adversary can do to modify his beliefs significantly. Other policymakers, such as Eisenhower or Shultz, may be willing to concede a higher probability that the other is prepared to cooperate; these more cognitively flexible individuals will not require as many signals from the opponent to convince them that it is safe to trust the other side in a limited arrangement. If the target tries to take advantage of initial concessions, however, then the conciliatory state should retaliate. Otherwise, the state that is the object of conciliatory overtures may not feel any obligation or need to reciprocate: it may believe that the other side has no choice but to cooperate.[88]

If its estimate that the conciliatory state is trustworthy exceeds a critical threshold, then the target may enter into negotiations, reciprocate, or accept the proposed arrangement. I shall argue that some level of trust is a necessary but not a sufficient condition for states to enter into agreements on security issues. For example, they must also have a shared interest in controlling their competition, adequate domestic support, and the ability to verify an agreement.

Images of other states as hostile or aggressive tend to endure. As a result, time usually elapses between a state's peaceful or conciliatory actions and the development of trusting attitudes in the target. For example, in 1955 Dulles remained convinced that the Soviets were wolves in sheep's clothing even after Khrushchev withdrew from Eastern Austria, entered into formal diplomatic relations with West Germany, and accepted the West's demands in the Soviet disarmament proposal of 10 May. More recently, even after Gorbachev had freed political prisoners, withdrawn Soviet troops from Afghanistan, demobilized 500,000 men in arms, and ordered the withdrawal of 5,000 Soviet tanks from Eastern Europe, President Bush was skeptical about his commitment to reform.[89] There are several reasons for such time lags.

First of all, the other side may need time to see whether the state has carried out its promise. When a state announces its intent to destroy a weapon system or withdraw from territory, it can provide positive evidence that it has complied. Whether the state has faithfully fulfilled its commitment not to build a weapon system, develop nuclear weapons, or support terrorism, however, rests on a continuing absence of evidence to the contrary. "Not doing something" has indefinite timing. Thus, it is easier to build trust when the initiator chooses a conciliatory action that can be carried out promptly and that the other side can verify unambiguously.

Second, a few conciliatory actions or instances of compliance do not prove that a state is reliable. Even an expansionist state might feign an interest in cooperating by making a token concession as a propaganda gesture or as a way of gaining breathing space. Thus, leaders may fear that the other side is pursuing a strategy of deception and is planning to blackmail or attack at an opportune moment. That the enemy complies with an agreement might only mean that it is biding its time, waiting until the gains from cheating are greatest.[90]

More evidence is required to prove that an actor is trustworthy than one needs to show he is unreliable. People believe that a good person will never do anything bad, whereas a bad person can do occasional good as well as bad deeds. As a a result, just one misdeed indicates that an actor is immoral, whereas one good act does not demonstrate much. To illustrate: when George Bush violated his "read my lips, no new taxes" pledge, the American public concluded that he was untrustworthy. The public was angered not just because their taxes went up, but because the president had broken a sacred compact. Good traits, then, are hard to acquire and easy to lose, whereas bad traits are easy to acquire and hard to lose. A state widely regarded as unreliable, such as the former Soviet Union, will have to carry out *many* cooperative acts to convince the other side that it can be trusted to honor an agreement. Whereas trust takes a long time to create, it can be destroyed in an instant.[91]

In its earlier stages, trust between two states is fragile, because it is based on scant evidence. Differing interpretations of an agreement, therefore, may lead to charges of cheating and an increase of mistrust. One of the reasons why U.S.-Soviet détente collapsed in the late 1970s was the superpowers' failure to agree on a code of conduct, particularly with respect to intervention in the Third World. The United States and the Soviet Union tried to establish "rules of the game" in the Basic Principles Agreement (BPA) of 1972 and the 1973 Agreement on Prevention of Nuclear War, but those documents contained many ambiguities, contradictions, and loopholes. Brezhnev believed that he had adhered to the BPA when he warned the United States in general terms that the Egyptians were planning to go to war, but critics in Congress expected him to give a more specific, timely warning.[92]

Third, policymakers are usually conservative about changing their beliefs. It is not that people *ignore* contradictory information entirely, but that they subject it to more rigorous scrutiny than they do information that fits prior beliefs. When faced with evidence that violates well-established beliefs, we tend to discount its validity, to code ambiguous data so that they fit our beliefs, or to recall belief-consistent information.[93] The slowness with which governmental officials adjust their beliefs means that in the beginning, several concessions may be necessary to persuade them to cooperate on particular security issues.

In sum, the trust placed in a state may lag behind changes in its behavior for the following reasons: (a) difficulty in detecting compliance; (b) the need for repeated observation of cooperative behavior to rule out deception; and (c) observers' slow updating of beliefs. Thus, we may speak of a learning process, as each side becomes more confident in the other. Trust must be built up over time.[94]

From a psychological perspective, then, trust is more difficult to establish than it is in economic theory. Policymakers may completely miss the significance of concessions offered by the other side, or they may view such actions as part of a deceptive strategy. A tit-for-tat strategy will not be effective in eliciting cooperation between states in a deeply hostile relationship. Instead, one or both sides may have to take several dramatic actions to reassure the other so that an agreement can be signed. Beliefs about the other state are altered all at once, in a major jump, rather than changing gradually in response to each new piece of evidence.

METHOD

Structural conditions such as the strategic balance or the military-industrial complex may have rendered U.S.-Soviet cooperation highly unlikely on certain issues. We can derive some clues as to what was objectively possible by seeing what the same leaders did with respect to similar issues, or what other leaders did in comparable cases.[95]

Even if international or domestic conditions did not *preclude* an agreement on a particular issue, this is not to say that it could have been achieved with any certainty. The plausibility of particular missed opportunities varies greatly. Some possibilities for agreement may be be viewed as *virtually certain*—that is to say, extremely probable if a leader had chosen differently. In other cases, a better outcome may be viewed as *highly probable*. Finally, still other scenarios may be viewed as merely *possible*. The more numerous the intervening steps that would have had to happen for a contrary-to-fact event to be realized, the less probable it is. In general, we should not have to rewrite too much history to realize a missed possibility for cooperation.[96]

Case Selection

To see what was objectively possible, one must start with a good explanation of the historical case. Normally, we identify the factor or factors that *changed* in a given context as the cause or causes of an event.[97] During the Cold War, such conditions as Marxist-Leninist ideology, the bipolar distribution of power, and domestic structures were constant. What changed was the foreign policy strategy of individual leaders. Thus, I examine five cases in which there was a major policy shift: the 1953–55 period after Stalin's death, the post-*Sputnik* peace offensive, Kennedy's inauguration, the early Nixon presidency, and Gorbachev's initiation of reform in the Soviet Union.

Of course, there were other instances in which the U.S. government proposed arms control and other security agreements to the Soviets. In 1948, President Truman had Ambassador Walter Bedell Smith reassure the Soviet foreign minister Vyacheslav Molotov that the United States had no aggressive intentions toward Eastern Europe and was prepared to negotiate. In 1964, President Lyndon B. Johnson offered to "build bridges" toward Eastern Europe and three years later proposed strategic arms limitation negotiations. In 1977, President Jimmy Carter made a radical proposal for "deep cuts" in strategic weapons.[98] Yet these cases do not meet my criteria, because they did not represent major changes in foreign policy strategy. Truman did not have Smith make any concrete proposals to Molotov. Johnson and Carter were continuing the détente policies of their predecessors; they made no major theoretical or operational innovations. Johnson was too preoccupied with Vietnam to make a sustained effort to improve U.S.-Soviet relations. Even Carter's "deep cuts" proposal was less original than it seemed, for it tried to reduce Soviet heavy missiles while leaving unconstrained U.S. cruise missiles, issues that Soviet leaders believed had already been resolved with the 1974 Vladivostok agreement.[99]

The five cases I have chosen have the potential to be "branching points" where U.S.-Soviet relations could have taken a different path. To establish that these cases were indeed the origin of alternative feasible historical paths requires historical evidence and argumentation.[100]

These historical episodes also have intrinsic interest and importance. They include not only the most famous and dangerous Cold War confrontations over Berlin and Cuba but also prominent examples of U.S.-

Soviet cooperation, such as the Limited Test Ban Treaty and SALT I. The Cold War is a "least likely" case for U.S.-Soviet collaboration and, therefore, a good test of cooperation theory in international relations.

Necessary Conditions

I argue that mutual trust is a necessary but not sufficient condition for adversaries to cooperate on security issues. If my argument is correct, then we should find either that there was already sufficient trust or that at least one superpower made a successful attempt to establish greater mutual trust in cases where the superpowers were able to reach agreement.[101] Of course, the superpowers' greater willingness to trust each other could have been an epiphenomenon of other conditions, such as the emergence of the People's Republic of China as a common enemy, a shortage of economic resources, pressure from allies, or domestic public opinion. In the case studies, I shall consider these alternative, interest-based explanations for the signing of cooperative agreements between the United States and the Soviet Union.

If the historical cases suggest that increased trust was a necessary condition for U.S.-Soviet agreements on security questions, then this gives us grounds in addition to theory for asserting the counterfactual that U.S. and Soviet policymakers might have been able to cooperate in other cases where such confidence was lacking. Trust is not sufficient, however: even if the United States and the Soviet Union had believed the other would observe an agreement, they might still have been unable to converge on a common solution because of strategic considerations, domestic public opinion, Soviet political instability, opposition from allies, the cognitive rigidity of policymakers, and so on.[102] It is also possible that diplomatic failures could have reflected an assessment by one or both sides that the superpowers had no interest in cooperating on a particular issue, in which case it is difficult to make the case for missed opportunities.

Although I compare cases, I do not mean to suggest that these cases should be viewed as independent. Each leader's efforts to improve relations and achieve cooperative agreements drew on the experience of those who came before him. Further, as I have noted, trust can only be established over time, as each side tests the other's compliance with particular agreements. If we only assess a historical effect immediately before and after a policy change or other innovation, then we may miss an important cause and incorrectly infer a causal relationship where there is none. As David Collier points out, "Causal inferences about the impact of discrete events can be risky if one does not have an extended series of observations."[103]

Therefore, comparison of cases should be supplemented by the "process tracing" method of explaining things, whereby we examine each of the steps intervening between independent and dependent variables.[104] Process tracing is essential for uncovering the causal mechanism—in this case, cognitive processes of interpretation and inference. Did the two states distrust each other? Were there possible areas of agreement between the two sides? How did the state proposing cooperation attempt to signal its intentions? Did the target perceive the initiator's action as credible? Why or why not? Did the target respond favorably or unfavorably? Why? And so on, for the duration of the historical case.

Inference and Evidence

The concept of missed opportunities implies that there must have been at least one arrangement that both sides actually favored or would have favored over the status quo. To make such an inference, we need evidence concerning U.S. policymakers' preferences. We must also piece together Soviet preferences from various sources, including hints, diplomatic communications to the West, and what we know to be the policy priorities of particular Soviet leaders. Although I may refer to the preferences of the "United States" or the "Soviet Union," this is merely shorthand for the principal decisionmakers on each side: usually the U.S. president and the general secretary of the Soviet Communist Party.

When making such judgments, we must be careful not to take at face value statements that leaders may have made for the historical record, or to curry favor with subordinates, or for domestic political purposes. Political leaders are instrumental in their use of language. Archival evidence—diaries, letters, memorandums, minutes of meetings—can provide an "unobtrusive" measure of policymakers' perceptions and reactions to events at moments when they are not being observed by the public and have less reason to distort their language for domestic political reasons. I have used archival sources for the chapters on Eisenhower and Kennedy.

At the same time, however, we must be alert to the possibility that the thoughts that officials express in private or intragovernmental documents may be biased by a desire to win favor with superiors, by organizational interests, or by a concern for "history." Further, archival evidence for the United States is generally available only after a thirty-year lag. Although some archives are being opened up in the former

Soviet Union, the release of documents has been spotty, confined to less-sensitive and lower-level files, and often motivated by political goals.[105] When possible, I have used secondary works that make use of new Soviet sources; otherwise, I have reviewed the standard secondary works about Soviet foreign policy, public statements and actions by Soviet leaders, and relevant U.S. archival evidence, such as memorandums of conversations with Soviet officials, reports by the U.S. ambassador in Moscow, minutes of summit meetings, and the like.

Contemporary news sources can compensate for the absence or bias of archival evidence by providing a narrative of events and of domestic and foreign reactions that is untainted by hindsight. One difficulty with public sources as well as with private communications aimed at persuading others is that the subject may use instrumental language intended to serve purposes other than merely expressing his or her beliefs or intentions. To allow for bias, I have used an indirect method of inference. I first try to ascertain the subject's communication goal and its effect on verbal content before I make any judgments about beliefs or perceptions. By looking at *who* said *what* to *whom* under *what circumstances*, one can often infer more confidently *what goal* the communicator was trying to achieve in expressing a belief or judgment.[106]

AN OVERVIEW OF THIS BOOK

Chapter 2 makes the case that the United States lost an opportunity to obtain German reunification in 1953 in return for German neutralization. The United States also passed up a serious Soviet proposal on disarmament. Chapter 3 gives an account of the unsuccessful effort by Eisenhower and Khrushchev to negotiate a test ban and reach a modus vivendi concerning Berlin. Khrushchev experienced even greater difficulty in persuading Eisenhower to consider disengagement or a nuclear-free zone in Central Europe. Chapter 4 shows why Kennedy succeeded where Eisenhower failed, persuading Khrushchev to agree to a limited test ban treaty. Still, Kennedy could not come to terms with Khrushchev on a solution to German question or Berlin. In Chapter 5, I examine how President Richard Nixon and General Secretary Leonid Brezhnev agreed to limits on antiballistic missiles, but missed the opportunity to agree to a ban on MIRVs. In chapter 6, we see how the Soviet leader Mikhail Gorbachev tried without success to induce Ronald Reagan to cooperate: namely, to restrain the deployment of defensive weapons in space in return for deep reductions in strategic weapons. But the various unilateral actions that Gorbachev took to reduce the West's distrust of the Soviet Union ultimately contributed to the end of the Cold War.

[2]

German Reunification
and Disarmament

From 1953 to 1955, the United States and the Soviet Union had a brief opportunity to settle the German question and make progress on arms control. After Joseph Stalin died in March 1953, his successors made overtures to the Eisenhower administration for a summit meeting and a reduction in tensions. Faced with the nightmare of a rearmed Germany, the Soviets hinted that they might be willing to allow Germany to be reunified in return for its neutralization. In May 1952, after prolonged negotiations, the United States had signed a treaty for a European Defense Community (EDC) which would have integrated West German military forces into a multinational army, and that treaty now awaited ratification by the European parliaments. Soviet fears made West German rearmament a valuable bargaining chip. The United States had little to lose by testing Soviet offers, because the EDC Treaty faced major difficulties in the French National Assembly. On 10 May 1955, the Soviet Union made a disarmament proposal which moved toward the Western position on several important issues, including acceptance of on-site inspection. Both opportunities were lost, however, because the Eisenhower administration did not trust that the Soviets would give up East Germany or observe a disarmament agreement.

We cannot say that there was a missed opportunity for German reunification and an arms control agreement if neither side wanted an agreement. After all, Soviet leaders were only being prudent in making concessions to the West. The leaders of the Soviet Union feared an outbreak of panic among the population after the death of Stalin, who had been portrayed as the wise father figure who defeated Hitler and brought the Soviet people into the industrial age. The collective leadership was also concerned with finding a new formula to legitimize the regime after

Stalinist terror was relaxed and political prisoners were returned from the gulag. Among the Soviet people there was long pent-up demand for better and more consumer goods; to provide those goods would require a change of priorities in the war economy. Internationally, the regime was isolated. Stalin's enactment of harsh restrictions against foreign diplomats and journalists, together with the "hate America" campaign in the Soviet press, contributed to a belligerent image in the West. The Korean War armistice negotiations were deadlocked. Soviet officials needed to improve the image of the Soviet Union, reduce overseas commitments, and increase the supply of consumer goods for the Soviet people.[1] That the Soviets made accommodations to external and internal pressures did not necessarily indicate that they would go any further to obtain cooperative agreements with their capitalist adversary. They might have been content with a mere relaxation of tensions, a breathing spell.

Other conditions, however, suggested that the Soviets might have an interest in withdrawing from East Germany and achieving a disarmament agreement. Still not fully integrated into the Soviet bloc, East Germany was the only satellite country not to be termed a "people's democracy." Stalin had deflected East German Communist requests to socialize their country, perhaps because he wanted to keep the diplomatic option of offering to trade the Soviet zone of Germany. In his famous 10 March 1952 note, Stalin offered German unification and free elections on condition that the country remain neutral. It was not until July 1952, after the West had rejected his March 1952 note, that Stalin formally approved the East German Communist Party program of socialization. After Stalin did give his approval for the "construction of socialism," the East German Communist leader Walter Ulbricht's ill-considered policy of rapid industrialization and collectivization resulted in shortages of foodstuffs and consumer goods, strikes, and a mass exodus of refugees. Ulbricht visited Moscow for Stalin's funeral and requested Soviet subsidies, but the Kremlin informed him that he should not expect additional financial assistance. Thus, Soviet leaders may have had an interest in ridding themselves of a burdensome client—if they had guarantees against a recurrence of German aggression. For the Soviet war economy had suppressed the demands of the Soviet people for consumer goods, better housing, and more food.[2]

Quite possibly the United States was not willing to resolve any issues with the Soviet Union. Eisenhower and Dulles might have preferred a divided, manageable Germany over the risks of a neutral country, unanchored to the West, that could act like a loose cannon rolling between the Eastern and Western blocs. But Eisenhower and Dulles believed that the division of Germany was a dangerous anomaly—one that had to be resolved in order to achieve peace and stability in Europe. Besides, most

U.S. officials believed a united Germany would lean toward the West.[3] Perhaps the United States rejected the Soviet disarmament proposal of 10 May 1955 because American officials had no interest in curbing an arms race that placed a greater burden on the Soviet economy.[4] Yet Eisenhower believed that the cost of continuing the arms race indefinitely would drive the United States to war or to some form of dictatorship. Dulles worried that the Western democracies could not maintain their resolve to resist Soviet aggression unless there was some lessening of international tension.[5]

An agreement on German reunification and negotiated arms reductions, then, would have been in both sides' interests. Nevertheless, we should not engage in hindsight. The U.S. refusal to acknowledge Soviet overtures was reasonable if Eisenhower and Dulles used available information to infer that the Soviets had no interest in withdrawing from East Germany. The president and secretary of state might have believed, with some justification, that the risks of probing Soviet offers—ending any chances for ratification of the EDC Treaty and opening up rifts in the alliance—outweighed the small chance that the Soviets would give up East Germany. Scholars disagree even today over whether the Soviets would have withdrawn from East Germany in 1953.[6] By hinting at the possibility of German reunification, the Soviet government could have been pursuing the traditional Leninist strategy of offering concessions to divide its opponents and weaken the NATO alliance. Stalin had made a similar offer for German reunification in his famous note of 10 March 1952, an initiative that U.S. diplomats regarded as propaganda designed to block the EDC Treaty.[7] The evidence suggests, however, that Eisenhower and Dulles never seriously considered whether the Soviet offer might be genuine.

The Eisenhower administration might have judged that the Soviets had no intention of observing a disarmament agreement. On the other hand, the 10 May 1955 Soviet disarmament proposal called for on-site inspection; while the details of verification had not been worked out, the proposal showed that the Soviets at least acknowledged the possibility of cheating. Again, assuming that the Soviets would violate an agreement, the United States refused to engage the Soviet government in negotiations.

Ultimately, diplomatic talks might not have made a difference. Domestic political pressures and ideological disputes might have prevented the U.S. and Soviet leaders from realizing their shared interest in controlling arms spending and coming to terms on the German question. Perhaps Georgi Malenkov's consumer goods policy was destined to fail because it challenged the interests of the powerful Soviet military-industrial complex. Eisenhower as well confronted domestic political constraints on his ability to deal with Soviet leaders: notably, Senator Joe McCarthy and the anticommunist hysteria he had aroused.

Nevertheless, despite ideologically driven mistrust on both sides, if Premier Malenkov had made a significant concession, such as signing the Austrian State Treaty, Eisenhower would have tried to meet the Soviet leader halfway. An early summit meeting could have probed and reinforced emerging signs of flexibility in Soviet foreign policy. Just two years later, Eisenhower would agree to a summit meeting after Nikita Khrushchev made a series of costly concessions—signing the Austrian State Treaty, rapprochement with Marshal Tito, and recognizing West Germany—which helped make credible the Soviets' interest in controlling the arms race and reducing tensions. By then, however, it was too late, to trade German nonrearmament for reunification.

Stalin's death on 5 March 1953 opened up new possibilities for U.S.-Soviet détente and cooperation. Georgi Malenkov and Lavrenti Beria quickly grasped control of the government. Malenkov became chairman of the Council of Ministers while Beria took over the combined state security and police, now called the Ministry of Internal Affairs (MVD). There is some evidence that, as early as 1949, Malenkov had favored adopting a more conciliatory foreign policy than Stalin's. Beria had long been politically allied with Malenkov. His background as a Georgian and as chief of the secret police were formidable handicaps to his selection as supreme leader, so Beria chose to work through Malenkov. As Stalin's former police chief, responsible for sending thousands to their deaths, Beria was concerned with winning greater legitimacy and establishing a new, more favorable image as an elder statesman, as evidenced by his support for freeing 1 million political prisoners and his repudiation of Stalin's notorious "Doctors' Plot." Nikita S. Khrushchev was in charge of the Central Committee Secretariat, and Vyacheslav Molotov returned to head the Foreign Ministry.[8] On 15 March, Premier Malenkov announced that there was no dispute between the United States and the Soviet Union that "could not be settled by peaceful means, on the basis of mutual agreement."[9]

After the death of Stalin, Eisenhower had considered making a major speech to the Soviet Union in which he would offer new European security arrangements and propose foreign ministers' negotiations aimed at reunifying Germany and Austria. He was dissuaded by Dulles, who had argued that offering to negotiate with the Soviet Union would derail chances for the success of EDC, because no European government would take action on the treaty until it was known whether the Soviets would give up East Germany in return for German neutralization.[10]

Eisenhower acknowledged Dulles's concerns, but he pointed out that they needed to do "something dramatic to rally the peoples of the world around some idea, some hope of a better future." Eisenhower suggested he might say instead that "he would be ready and willing to meet with anyone anywhere from the Soviet Union provided the basis for the meeting was honest and practical."[11]

On 16 March, the day after Malenkov's statement, speechwriter Emmet J. Hughes went in to see Eisenhower at 3:45 P.M. with a draft of the speech.[12] The president spent about ten minutes reading it carefully. Then he rose from his desk and began pacing the room, his face serious, his words flowing easily and cogently. Eisenhower said that it was a good speech, but what did it mean? He complained that "I'm tired, and I think everyone is tired, of indictments of the Soviet regime." The president continued: "What matters is this—what have WE got to offer the world? What are WE ready to do? If we cannot say that—A, B, C, D, E, F, G, H—just like that—these are things we propose—then we really have nothing to say. Malenkov isn't going to be impressed by speeches."

Instead of trying to win propaganda points, Eisenhower wanted to make concrete proposals for cooperation between the superpowers. "Let us come out, straight, no double-talk, no slick sophisticated propaganda devices—and say: this is what we'll do—we'll withdraw our armies from there if you'll withdraw yours. . . . We want to talk to the Russian people—if their government will give us so much unjammed time, we would do our best to give them facilities to state their side of the case."

Eisenhower hoped to appeal to the Soviets by indicating the economic benefits that both states could gain from a disarmament agreement. He stressed that a jet plane "costs three quarters of a million dollars. . . . more money than a man earning $10,000 every year is going to make in his lifetime." What nation could afford this sort of thing? The United States and the Soviets, said Eisenhower, were in an arms race in which "everyone is wearing himself out to build up his defenses." Where was it going to lead? At worst to atomic war. But at the least, it meant that "every people, every nation on earth is being deprived of the fruits of its own toil."

The other choice before the two nations, the road to disarmament, meant "for everybody in the world—butter, bread, clothes, hospitals, schools, the good and necessary things of decent living." If they took this road, the United States could help the Soviets and the rest of the world produce more of these things.

Hughes replied, "I couldn't agree more with the spirit of this, Mr. President, but. . . . it was difficult in this draft even to refer to Soviet troop

[43]

withdrawal—because we don't according to [the] State [Department] dare withdraw our own troops." Eisenhower exploded: "If these very sophisticated gentlemen in the State Department, Mr. Dulles and all his advisers, really don't mean they can talk about peace seriously, then I'm in the wrong pew. I surely don't know why I'm wasting my time with them. Because if it's war we should be talking about—I know the people to discuss that with, and it's not the State Department. Now we either cut out all this fooling around and make a serious bid for peace—or we forget the whole thing."

President Eisenhower was in favor of accepting Malenkov's invitation if he could be sure that the offer was genuine. "If you only could trust that bastard Malenkov," Ike declared passionately at a meeting with State Department officials and the White House staff. He had not given up the idea of a foreign ministers' meeting, despite Dulles's objections. When Hughes asked the president whether he really wanted a meeting—because, if so, Moscow would take advantage of the speech—Eisenhower replied: "I have no objection to a meeting, provided only we have a plan of action before it."[13] At a 19 March press conference, Eisenhower stated that any Soviet effort to seek peace would be "just as welcome as it is sincere."[14]

In contrast, Secretary of State Dulles was confident that the softer line in Soviet foreign policy was merely a tactical shift, which should not tempt the United States to change course. He interpreted Soviet actions in line with his belief that the Soviets were innately hostile and aggressive. On 20 March 1953, Dulles told the press that "we have evaluated these speeches, but we do not receive any great comfort." In a 24 March speech before the Advertising Council, the secretary of state argued that the "softening" in Soviet language and behavior was a "tactical retreat" as prescribed in Stalin's *Problems of Leninism* and that the Soviets were engaged in a peace offensive because they feared "the forces of disintegration at work within the Soviet empire."[15] If the Soviets made concessions, it was because they were under extreme external duress.

President Eisenhower thought that the character of Soviet foreign policy could be affected by individual leaders. Against all available intelligence, Eisenhower believed that Stalin would have preferred an easing of the tension between the Soviet Union and the Western powers after World War II, but had been obliged to concede to the Politburo, which insisted on picking up the tempo of the Cold War. If the Soviet dictator had been able to do what he wanted, the president told the NSC in March 1953, Stalin would have sought more peaceful and normal relations with the rest of the world.[16]

Although Secretary Dulles did not contradict the president on this occasion, he did not agree. Dulles believed that Soviet foreign policy was motivated by Marxist-Leninist ideology, and that the death of one man could bring no major change in that policy. Before 1946, Dulles had regarded the Soviet Union as a typical great power. He then underwent an intellectual conversion and concluded that the Soviet Union was a fundamentally evil totalitarian system, a barbarian challenge such as the world had not seen since the Islamic invaders in the tenth century. Dulles began to read Marxist-Leninist writings, and he became convinced that they were an infallible guide to Soviet foreign policy.[17]

As if to answer Eisenhower's request for proof of its sincerity, the Soviet government made numerous conciliatory gestures. The Soviets eased restrictions on the diplomatic corps and on journalists and adopted a more restrained rhetoric. On 27 March 1953, the Soviet government apologized to the British government for a fatal air collision over East Germany; and shortly afterward the chairman of the Soviet Control Commission in Berlin, General Vasily Chuikov, invited the United States and France to join in British-Soviet talks on air-corridor safety. The Soviets also loosened traffic blocks around Berlin and admitted a group of American journalists to Moscow.[18]

In addition, the Soviet leadership tried to disengage the USSR from overseas conflicts in Korea and Indochina that risked war with the United States. Even such a committed Stalinist as Molotov believed that Stalin should never have approved the North Koreans' plan to reunify their country. Soviet leaders accepted the Chinese premier Zhou Enlai's request for help in ending the Korean War, and in a 19 March memorandum to the Chinese Communist leader Mao Zedong and the North Korean leader Kim Il Sung, the Soviet Council of Ministers drew up a series of steps to accomplish that end. On 28 March, Chinese Communist leaders accepted an American proposal to exchange sick and wounded Korean War prisoners, an act regarded by U.S. officials as an important gesture. The Chinese statement of 30 March went further by accepting the principle of voluntary repatriation of prisoners of war, a major step forward in the Korean armistice negotiations.[19]

Finally, the Soviets expressed interest in disarmament and détente with the United States. The Soviet representative at the United Nations, Andrei Vyshinsky adopted a milder tone in U.N. discussions on disarmament. On 8 April 1953, Vyshinsky urged the United States to respond to Soviet overtures in kind and to "begin to dig the tunnel of friendship from both ends." Through Norway's U.N. representative, the Soviets transmitted a proposal for a meeting between Eisenhower and Malenkov concerning atomic energy control and disarmament.[20]

The new trend in Soviet policy was marked. A *New York Times* editorial on 2 April 1953 observed that "since the death of Stalin an unmistakably softer wind has begun to blow out of Moscow and the various Communist moves are beginning to fall into a pattern which, if completed and validated, holds out the promise of at least a temporary easing of international tensions." Paul Nitze told Secretary of State Dulles that it was just "possible that the present Soviet actions are inspired by a desire to test—possibly once and for all—the feasibility of dealing with some of the outstanding issues without disastrous consequences to their objectives." Allen Dulles, head of the Central Intelligence Agency, reported to the National Security Council that they were witnessing "quite shattering departures," the most significant changes in Soviet domestic and foreign policy since 1939.[21]

These indications of increased Soviet flexibility following Stalin's death revealed disagreements between the president and his secretary of state over how to interpret and respond to Soviet conciliation. The two men had different images of the Soviet Union. Eisenhower, because he believed that a change in leadership could affect the substance of Soviet policy, was willing to give the Soviets the benefit of the doubt, to err on the side of hope. Thus, at a press conference, Eisenhower declared that we should take at face value every offer that was made to us until it was proved unworthy of confidence. When several officials tried to persuade the president that there was no evidence that the Soviets had changed their intentions, Eisenhower retorted: "Well, just as a matter of debate anyway, I'd say there also isn't the slightest evidence that they HAVEN'T."[22] Dulles, in contrast, viewed Soviet foreign policy as emanating from deeper, more enduring sources. If the Soviets changed their policy, Dulles inferred that they must have done so out of weakness. This meant that the United States should push the Soviets even harder: "It's obvious that what they're doing is because of outside pressure," he said, "and I don't know anything better we can do than keep up those pressures right now."[23]

DEEDS, NOT WORDS

Secretary Dulles feared that acknowledging changes in Soviet policy with a public statement might "fall in" with Soviet plans, implying that Soviet conciliation must have ulterior motives.[24] Eisenhower nonetheless decided to go ahead with a speech to impress the Soviets with the potential benefits of cooperation. Such a speech, Dulles feared, would get the president "trapped" into talks with Malenkov. Seeing the president's vehemence on the issue, Dulles said nothing but instead took steps to muddy the message that Eisenhower intended to convey.[25] (Hughes, of course, had to get the speech cleared with the Department of State.) Dulles agreed with Eisenhower that signing the Austrian State Treaty was, "next to Korea the clearest test of Soviet intentions which we should welcome" and suggested that Austria be mentioned twice.[26] Under Stalin, more than two hundred fifty sessions were held to negotiate such a treaty, albeit with Sisyphean progress.[27] In addition to Austria and the return of captured prisoners of war, though, Dulles inserted references to free elections in Eastern Europe and German reunification as preconditions for a summit meeting. Eisenhower, on the other hand, realized that "obviously we aren't going to liberate East Europe tomorrow, my God that's a job for ten years—but what we want . . . [is] simply this— some ACTS, ANY acts that show a desire to be nice boys."[28]

On 11 April 1953, Ike told Hughes to suggest several specific acts that the Soviets could carry out to show their good faith, but he did not want them to be viewed as preconditions. "All we want is sincerity, sincere acts, not talk, sincerity—whatever they want to do—the Austrian treaty— the POWs—they don't need any damn conferences to do these things— all they [have] got to do is DO them—and we'll welcome that and we'll meet them half way."[29] By making one or two costly concessions, then, the Soviets could prove their intent to negotiate seriously on the major issues at stake between the United States and the Soviet Union.

Whereas Eisenhower wanted to offer the Soviets concrete benefits for cooperating, Dulles had various suggestions for immediate U.S. concessions cut from the speech. For example, the president inserted a paragraph saying that the United States would meet "halfway" any tangible proposals in "any Congress or conference or meeting" with the Soviets; but after a quick phone call to Dulles, Hughes omitted this suggestion as a "needless" invitation to talks. Hughes also took out Eisenhower's suggestion that the United States and the Soviet Union swap unjammed radio time so that each side could present its own case. Ike's offer to travel to meet Malenkov was likewise cut. "State would kill them anyway," Hughes rationalized.[30]

On 16 April 1953, in the "Chance for Peace" speech, Eisenhower urged the Soviets to make some costly concession to prove their peaceful intent. "We care nothing for mere rhetoric," the president said. "We are only for sincerity of peaceful purpose attested by deeds." There were many opportunities for deeds that required only the simple will to carry them out. "Even a few such clear and specific acts, such as the Soviet Union's signature upon an Austrian treaty or its release of thousands of prisoners still held from World War II, would be impressive signs of sincere intent."[31]

As a result of Dulles's insertions and interference, however, Eisenhower's speech asked the Soviets to give up their security zone in Eastern Europe in order to "prove" their good faith but offered nothing more than the chance for negotiations. Adding further noise to Eisenhower's signal, the following day Dulles made a speech to the same audience of American Newspaper Editors in which he attributed the favorable changes in Soviet foreign policy to such U.S. policies as EDC, aid to the French in Indochina, and the Captive Nations Resolution in Congress. Recent Soviet moves amounted to a "peace defensive." Contradicting Eisenhower's benevolent offer, Secretary of State Dulles signaled that the U.S. policy of pressure against the Soviet Union would continue.[32]

On 25 April, the Soviet government published the full text of Eisenhower's speech, including its criticism of Soviet policies, in both *Pravda* and *Izvestia*, an event that the U.S. ambassador to Moscow Charles ("Chip") Bohlen called "unprecedented." A Soviet expert on the United States, Georgi Arbatov recalls that the reprinting of Eisenhower's speech in *Izvestia* was a signal to Americans that Moscow noticed it and to Soviet citizens that they should take the president's words seriously. But commentary in *Pravda* also complained that Dulles's speech, delivered only two days after the president had spoken, made it difficult to judge the political attitude of the United States.[33]

Why did Eisenhower fail to assert his will more forcefully over Dulles? Did Eisenhower hesitate to risk a summit meeting with the Soviets for fear of inciting attacks from right-wing Republicans? Senator Joseph McCarthy was at the height of his power, denouncing "communist sympathizers" within the State Department, vetoing appointments, having hundreds of government employees fired. In fact, the president's nominee for ambassador to the Soviet Union, Charles Bohlen, faced a confirmation fight because he had served as a translator at the Yalta Conference. In April 1953, McCarthy's assistants Roy M. Cohn and G. David Schine went on an overseas tour, investigating "subversive" books in U.S. embassies. But 78 percent of the American public favored a summit meeting, whereas only 15 percent were opposed. Eisenhower certainly could have weathered criticism from McCarthy and other right-wing Republicans. The president had contempt for McCarthy. Eisenhower had ignored McCarthy's warning that he would have to "waltz" with him through Wisconsin if he wanted to carry the state, and had won Wisconsin by 200,000 more votes than the senator.[34]

Why, then, did Eisenhower allow Dulles to distort the aim of his speech? Contemporary observers believed that Eisenhower delegated authority over foreign policy to John Foster Dulles, a formidable Cold Warrior who resisted any effort at relieving Cold War tensions. Drawing on a large volume of declassified documents, though, "Eisenhower revisionists" have challenged the conventional wisdom that Eisenhower abdicated his foreign policy powers to Dulles, giving him carte blanche in relations with other governments. The secretary of state consulted with the president daily and made no initiative without Eisenhower's approval. Eisenhower was well informed, articulate, and decisive on foreign policy issues.[35]

On the other hand, although Eisenhower made the decisions, he did not always follow through to see if his will had been done. The president set the broad lines of policy and delegated implementation to others. For example, Eisenhower said nothing when Hughes removed his proposals to share unjammed radio time and to travel to meet the Soviet leader. The file does not indicate that Dulles's 18 April speech had been cleared by the White House.[36]

Had Eisenhower benefited from more confidence in Malenkov's good intentions, he might have been more motivated to override the secretary of state. But Malenkov had done nothing out of the ordinary, nothing that could not have been explained away as a mere tactical shift in Soviet foreign policy. For example, as Philip Mosely pointed out, the Soviet recommendation that the Chinese agree to exchange sick and ill prisoners of war "could be regarded as an act of great generosity only by people who have unconsciously accepted the Soviet assumption that not only its own people but captured prisoners are the property of the captor." Moscow's intercession to secure the release of U.N. civilians illegally detained in Korea would have been a "routine action on the part of any Western Power." Finally, the decision to accept Dag Hammarskjöld as the successor to Trygve Lie as head of the United Nations meant merely the "scrapping of a profitless obstinacy."[37]

A Missed Opportunity for German Reunification?

The Soviets responded to Eisenhower's "Chance for Peace" speech with more "deeds." At the end of May 1953, the Soviet government renounced previous claims to territory and bases in Turkey. Most important, the Soviet government enacted a series of democratic reforms in East Germany that may have been designed to facilitate its reunification with the West.[38] As a prelude, General Vasily Chuikov, chairman of the Soviet Control Commission in Berlin, had announced on 31 March that "reunification of the country" would be "wholly and fully" in accord with Soviet wishes.[39]

Owing to Ulbricht's policies of rapid industrialization and forced construction of socialism, which had been launched in July 1952, East Germany was in a crisis verging on civil war. Farmers were given the choice of joining a collective farm or meeting onerous delivery quotas. In 1953 alone, 37,296 farmers left the country, further contributing to food shortages throughout the country. Owners of small businesses, denied ration cards, were forced to buy food at inflated prices. Despite peasant resistance and outbreaks of strikes, the East German Communist leadership stepped up efforts at ideological mobilization and repression. In mid-May, Ulbricht raised industrial work norms by 10 percent for several categories of workers, tantamount to a decrease in wages. More than 500,000 East Germans had fled the country since 1951.[40]

On 27 May, the Soviet Presidium (as the Politburo was called from 1952 to 1966) met to discuss the wording of the directive that would go to the East German Communist Party (Sozialistische Einheitspartei Deutschlands, SED) on how to handle the crisis and bring the refugee flow under control. The session, chaired by Malenkov, was lively. According to Molotov's recollection, the Ministry of Foreign Affairs had drafted an instruction to the SED not to implement a policy of "forced socialism" in the German Democratic Republic (GDR). Beria, however, wanted to eliminate the word "forced," so that the Presidium would have advised the East Germans against "building socialism in the GDR." At the Presidium meeting, Beria reportedly asked, "Why should socialism be built in the GDR? Let it just be a peaceful country. That is sufficient for our purposes. . . . The sort of country it will become is unimportant."[41]

Molotov objected that it mattered a great deal whether the GDR was socialist or capitalist. East Germany lay within the heart of Europe and was a highly developed capitalist country. Germany could never be peaceful unless it took the path of socialism. Did the Soviet people shed their blood in vain?[42] For Molotov, Germany's history of aggression derived from the nature of capitalism, an internal source, which could not be altered by changed international conditions.

Beria, an opportunist and schemer, had little interest in ideology. As secret police chief, he probably knew the dire economic conditions in East Germany better than anyone else. Further, Beria was the administrator of the Soviet atomic energy program; he understood well the power of nuclear weapons. Less worried about a conventional war in Europe, Beria may not have been concerned about maintaining strategic positions such as East Germany.[43]

According to Molotov, the Politburo was split on the issue. Khrushchev supported the foreign minister, while Malenkov did not take a clear position. Because the meeting could not come to a consensus, a committee—Malenkov, Beria, and Molotov—was set up afterward to resolve the dispute. In the end, Khrushchev persuaded Beria to accept an instruction that advised the SED against "forced construction" of socialism.[44]

After an ultimatum from Moscow, on 9 June 1953 the Politburo of the East German Communist Party adopted a program of liberalization for East Germany, the "New Course," which halted collectivization of agriculture and the war on private enterprise, offered to return lands to East German farmers who had left the country if they came back, promised better living standards, gave amnesty to East German refugees, and ended judicial repression and political regimentation.[45] The 9 June directive concerning the New Course, taken verbatim from the Soviet instruction, explained that the "grand goal of establishing German unity" required measures from both sides that would "concretely facilitate the rapprochement between both parts of Germany." Significantly, the statement referred to "both parts of Germany" rather than "two German states." By order of the SED Politburo, all banners referring to "construction of socialism" were removed from official materials.[46] Since the slogans were displayed in thousands of locations, including houses, bridges, and factories, their removal was not a minor or inconspicuous act.[47] According to a Berlin district secretary of the SED who defected, the head of the Soviet High Commission in Germany, Vladimir Semenov, told the SED leaders to prepare themselves for the loss of power that would follow reunification under democratic conditions.[48] On 16 June, the acting U.S. high commissioner for Germany, Samuel Reber, cabled that a "series of sensational moves in [the] Soviet zone have revitalized [the] unity theme in Germany." Reber believed that Moscow had reversed pressure for socialization in order to signal that it would permit creation of a unified and free, but neutral, Germany in order to prevent inclusion of Germany in the Western defense coalition.[49]

The New Course did not, however, repeal the increased work norms. Rising expectations and simmering discontent over the work norms prompted East Berlin construction workers to go out on strike on 16 June. The protest quickly took on political overtones as the workers demanded democracy and free elections. The following day, according to recent estimates, more than 500,000 people in 350 East German cities joined in protest marches and seized control of factories. East Berlin workers marched in massive demonstrations for improved living standards and free elections. The crowds demonstrated in front of GDR government buildings, and some protestors breached the security barriers. Soviet troops and tanks ultimately crushed the uprising, but isolated outbreaks occurred for several days.[50]

Alarmed by Beria's grasping for the levers of power and fearing that he was planning a coup, Khrushchev organized a daring plot to have the interior minister arrested at a 26 June Presidium meeting while MVD troops loyal to their chief guarded the Kremlin outside. Other members of the conspiracy included Molotov, Malenkov, and Nikolai Bulganin. Beria commanded two MVD divisions as well as the troops guarding the Kremlin, so Khrushchev could not have succeeded without assistance from elements of the Soviet military—notably, Marshal Georgi Zhukov.[51]

At the Central Committee Plenum held to discuss Beria's crimes (2–7 July 1953), Beria's colleagues charged that the former secret police chief and interior minister had tried to seize total power, attempted to bring capitalism to Russia, encouraged nationalism in the Soviet Republics, spied on other members of the Politburo, and advocated the creation of a unified Germany as a "bourgeois, peace-loving state."[52] Indeed, Beria's fall had repercussions in East Germany. At the end of June, before news of Beria's arrest became public, Wilhelm Zaisser, head of the East German secret police, and Rudolf Herrnstadt, editor of the Communist Party newspaper, tried to force Ulbricht to resign as general secretary and to eliminate the post entirely. Zaisser and Herrnstadt were reformers who had links to Beria. After he found out about Beria's arrest, Ulbricht had Zaisser and Herrnstadt expelled from the SED Politburo. Manipulating divisions within the Soviet Presidium, Ulbricht ended up in an even stronger position, despite his responsibility for the 17 June uprising. Why had the Soviet leadership not forced Ulbricht's removal? Perhaps they were concerned that removing Ulbricht from power in the context of the East German uprising would have given an impression of weakness and disarray within the GDR and the Soviet leadership.[53] The United States therefore had a very narrow window of opportunity, between Stalin's death and Beria's arrest on 26 June 1953, in which to press for German reunification.

Beria's fall greatly reduced but may not have eliminated the prospects for German unity. Malenkov was now the most powerful figure in the Soviet leadership, but Soviet participants have conflicting recollections concerning Malenkov's views on Germany. Andrei Gromyko remembers that Malenkov flatly opposed Beria's proposal to abandon socialism in East Germany, while Khrushchev recalled that Malenkov had joined with Beria in making it.[54] At the July 1953 Central Committee Plenum, Malenkov claimed that he had opposed Beria's plans for a bourgeois Germany. It is telling, however, that Malenkov emphasized the weakness of the East German regime and its unsuitability for constructing socialism. He noted that "we were obliged to soberly face the truth and admit that without the presence of Soviet troops the existing regime in the G.D.R. is unstable." He did not condemn Beria for handing over the GDR to the West or for abandoning socialism. Malenkov may have been reluctant to prop up a weak East German Communist regime with expensive subsidies because that would interfere with his domestic reform program.[55] Apart from Molotov, no one at the July 1953 plenum gave unconditional support to Ulbricht.

Molotov argued that bourgeois Germany had started two world wars. The idea that such a Germany could become a "peace-loving" or "neutral" state was not only an illusion but antithetical to communism.[56]

Khrushchev agreed with Molotov that a united, capitalist Germany could not be trusted to remain neutral. Beria's plan to reject the construction of socialism in the GDR meant "handing over 18 million Germans to the rule of the American imperialists." Beria had proposed that Germany should be neutralized by treaty, but "if a treaty is not reinforced by might," said Khrushchev, "then it is worth nothing, they'll be laughing at us, thinking us naive."[57]

That the July Central Committee Plenum condemned Beria for trying to make the GDR into a bourgeois state would have made it difficult for Malenkov to make such a proposal himself, but he might have been favorably disposed toward an exchange of reunification for neutralization if suggested by Eisenhower. Beria had proposed halting the construction of socialism unilaterally without first obtaining a quid pro quo from the United States in the form of limits on West German rearmament.

Even if the United States had expressed interest, though, Malenkov might not have been a strong enough leader to push a proposal for German reunification through the Presidium. Khrushchev and Molotov described Malenkov as weak and vacillating. Molotov criticized Malenkov for his silence on critical issues. Later Khrushchev would charge that Malenkov was "unstable to the point of being dangerous because he was so susceptible to the pressure and influence of others." We may discount Khrushchev's criticisms, for he had viewed Malenkov as a rival since their days under Stalin. Malenkov had been considered Stalin's heir apparent after the death of Andrei Zhdanov in 1948 and gave the leading address at the Nineteenth Party Congress in 1952. Nor was Malenkov afraid to take unpopular, controversial positions. As will be discussed below, Malenkov was the first Soviet leader to call for increased production of consumer goods and to question Stalinist dogma on the inevitability of war: these bold stands placed him outside the realm of ideological orthodoxy.[58]

Then, too, some members of the Presidium must have shared Malenkov's doubts about the advisability of imposing socialism on East Germany. The Soviet leadership did not repudiate Beria's policy toward East Germany, the New Course, even after Beria's arrest. In their 24 June report to Moscow, Vladimir Semenov, his deputy Pavel Yudin, and Deputy Defense Minister Marshal V. D. Sokolovsky blamed the 17 June uprising on Ulbricht's policy of "construction of socialism, regardless of any difficulties." The Soviet representatives in Berlin recommended that Ulbricht be removed from his position as deputy prime minister and that his position as general secretary be divided among several secretaries of the Central Committee. Semenov, who was deeply involved in efforts to push back the communization of East Germany, not only was not reprimanded but subsequently had a distinguished diplomatic career, including participation in the SALT I negotiations.[59]

As Director of the CIA Allen Dulles pointed out to his brother John Foster, the New Course was continued even after Beria's arrest not only in East Germany but in Hungary and Czechoslovakia. Ambassador Bohlen cabled from Moscow that the New Course should not be "dismissed as a 'tactical' maneuver designed to influence West German opinion," especially since the Soviets persisted in their reform policies even after the East German uprising, but should be regarded as an indication that the Soviet government was prepared for "serious discussions on German unification." The Soviets wanted to prevent German rearmament, to be sure, but now, in contrast to their previous propaganda and threats, Bohlen thought they were prepared to make a "serious political and diplomatic effort to achieve this objective."[60]

As Bohlen's observation suggests, there were important differences between Stalin's note of 10 March 1952 and Soviet policies toward the GDR in 1953 which suggest that one cannot dismiss the latter as a continuation of Stalin's propagandistic policy. In 1952, Stalin waited less than a month for the U.S. response before telling the East German Communists that they should build an army and reinforce border controls. The relaxed attitude of the GDR leaders, who appeared to be not the least concerned about the prospect of losing power, belied the sincerity of Stalin's offer. The timing of Stalin's initiative a few months before the signing of the EDC Treaty and his use of a public letter as the means of transmitting the proposal raises further doubts.[61] In 1953, in contrast, conservative East German Communists were alarmed by the New Course and resisted the reforms proposed by Moscow.[62] The East Germans had been instructed by the Kremlin to enact reforms that would facilitate reunification. Instead of making a public offer that they could use to prevent ratification of EDC, Moscow hinted at a deal.

Was this a missed opportunity for the United States and the Soviet Union to resolve the German question? Would Eisenhower and Dulles have favored a deal to trade German reunification and free elections in return for Germany's neutralization? Dulles later admitted that the Soviets would not give up East Germany without some form of international control in which the Soviet government would participate, and he noted that the United States would have to agree to this in order to meet German desires for reunification. Eisenhower on at least one occasion expressed support for German neutralization, so long as the Germans were allowed to maintain an army. At a 1955 press conference, when asked his opinion about a neutral belt of states in the middle of Europe, Eisenhower replied that the armed neutrality of a Switzerland or an Austria was not a military vacuum, a remark that in the context of public discussion about applying the Austrian precedent to Germany was interpreted as an implied acceptance of German neutrality.[63]

For the U.S. government to probe Soviet intentions in regard to Germany would have further delayed ratification of the EDC Treaty, perhaps beyond the point where it could be resurrected. On the other hand, Eisenhower and Dulles already knew that the chances for French approval of EDC were not good. Dulles admitted that there was no urgent need to rearm Germany, because the risk of a general war seemed less than at any previous time in history. If the Soviets proved unwilling to give up East Germany in return for guarantees of its demilitarization, then doubters within France and Germany would have been more receptive to German rearmament. There were alternatives to EDC, such as a German national army within NATO or a U.S. arming of West Germany.[64]

A neutral Germany would have deprived the United States of twelve West German divisions envisioned for NATO as well as the use of West German territory to station American troops. The U.S. policy statement on Germany, NSC 160/1, warned that a neutralized united Germany "would deny Germany [sic] strength to the West, wreck present and prospective plans for building augmented European strength through union, and open up the whole of Germany to Soviet intrigue and manipulation which would aim at the absorption of Germany into the Soviet bloc." On the other hand, the policy statement recognized that the United States could not resist West German demands for unification. If the Germans chose neutrality, the United States would have to adjust U.S. NATO-defense plans, taking into consideration U.S. atomic superiority.[65]

The inconvenience, expense, and difficulty of reformulating U.S. defense plans for Western Europe would have been balanced by political advantages, however. A neutral Germany would have been politically and economically aligned with the Western camp. Neutralization of Germany also might have allowed the United States and the Soviet Union to withdraw some of their troops from Europe, thus relieving the burden on the U.S. balance of payments and allowing Europe to return to its traditional role as an independent force rather than a pawn of the superpowers. Eisenhower never envisioned a permanent U.S. military presence in Europe, and he wanted Europeans to take more responsibility for their own defense.[66] German reunification would have put more pressure on the Soviets to allow greater domestic liberalization in the East European countries, where reformist regimes were already beginning to undo Stalinist policies.[67] Paul Nitze, the author of NSC 68, which made the case for larger U.S. conventional forces, stated: "I don't think we'd have any choice if the Soviets really put it up to us—and I'm not so sure it would be a bad exchange—the EDC for a free united Germany with Russian armies pulled back."[68]

The Soviets would have gained strategically from pushing Western military forces farther away from their borders and from guarantees that the Germans would not be allowed to have nuclear weapons. At the same time, the Soviet government would have been released from the economic burden of propping up its weak, unstable client East Germany, a task that was hampered by the presence of a rival national regime with a healthier, more vibrant economy, and by an alien entity within its borders, West Berlin.

Finally, both sides would have benefited from an international relaxation of tensions and European stability. If the German question had been resolved early in the Cold War, the United States and the Soviet Union could have avoided dangerous crises over Berlin, confrontations that escalated to nuclear threats and contributed to an arms buildup on both sides.

Dulles believed that the Soviet hints of a willingness to negotiate and the reforms in East Germany were designed to divide the Western powers, to block ratification of EDC with the false hope of German unification.[69] Undoubtedly, in some sense Dulles was partly right. German unity was not something that the Soviets desired as an end in itself: it was a *price* that they might have been willing to pay to achieve other objectives.

Before responding to Soviet overtures, the foreign ministers of France, Great Britain, and the United States met in Washington from 10 to 14 July 1953 to formulate a position for negotiations with the Soviets concerning Germany and Austria. The French foreign minister insisted that the French National Assembly would not ratify the EDC Treaty unless some attempt had been made to negotiate with the Soviets on the German question. The British favored negotiations at the summit level, but they preferred a meeting of foreign ministers to no negotiations at all. Dulles then changed his mind about inviting the Soviets to a foreign ministers' conference, but *not* because the Soviets had proved their sincerity or because the EDC Treaty had been ratified; rather, East-West negotiations appeared to be a prerequisite for ratification of EDC. In their communiqué, the allies invited the Soviets to a four-power foreign ministers' conference to discuss establishing a unified German government (through free elections) that would be free to join NATO.[70] The Soviets, however, declined to negotiate on such a one-sided agenda, and proposed a conference on relaxation of tensions in Europe and Asia that would also include the People's Republic of China (PRC).[71]

It is true that the Politburo was divided over giving up East Germany, but Soviet policy was in a state of flux after Stalin's death. Some reciprocal moves by the United States to reduce tensions would have supported Malenkov's argument that negotiations with the West could be fruitful and would have reinforced his political position. That there was additional support in the Politburo for improved relations with the West is evidenced by the continuation of the Soviet policy of relaxing tensions even after Beria's arrest. In June and July, the Soviets granted exit visas to several Soviet wives of U.S. citizens. On 27 July, the Korean armistice was signed.[72]

In an important speech on 8 August 1953, Malenkov reaffirmed his goal of negotiating a reduction in tensions. The Soviet premier announced plans to increase the supply of food and consumer goods, a radical reversal of the Stalinist privileging of heavy industry. Malenkov pointed out that the Soviet Union had renounced its territorial claims in Turkey, made overtures to both Turkey and Iran, reestablished diplomatic relations with Israel, and exchanged ambassadors with Yugoslavia and Greece. The Soviet leader said defensively that some U.S. officials saw the Soviet Union's concern for easing international tension as an indication of weakness, then pointed out casually that the United States no longer had a monopoly on the hydrogen bomb—an important revelation. He repeated that there were no issues that could not be solved peacefully on the basis of mutual agreement. The Soviet Union still stood for "peaceful coexistence" and was confident that the security interests of both countries could be safeguarded. Malenkov welcomed President Eisenhower's 16 April statement that there was no problem so controversial that it could not be solved if the rights of other countries were respected. Unfortunately, added the premier, the actual policy of the United States was in contradiction to Eisenhower's statements.[73]

Bohlen reported that Malenkov's speech represented a "continuance and emphasis [of the] main line of Soviet policy since Stalin's death which tend to bear out [the] view that these changes stem from sources deeper than simple maneuver."[74]

A POWER STRUGGLE IN THE SOVIET UNION

One month later, however, Malenkov's rival Nikita Khrushchev was elected first secretary and delivered the leading speech on agriculture at the Central Committee Plenum. Like Malenkov, Khrushchev maintained that the regime must greatly increase food supplies and raise the living standards of the peasants. Unlike the Soviet premier, Khrushchev proposed to do so not by increasing material incentives to farmers, which would be expensive, but by expanding the amount of land under cultivation and by managing collective farms more efficiently through

[57]

the Communist Party instead of through the Ministry of Agriculture. Khrushchev's program promised faster results at lower cost than Malenkov's plan, which called for increased investment in agricultural machinery and fertilizers.[75]

Khrushchev's challenge to Malenkov's authority made it impossible for the premier to make any major foreign policy initiatives. Given the domestic political infighting between Khrushchev and Malenkov, the desperate agricultural situation, and the shock of the East German uprisings, it is not surprising that the Soviets temporized in order to avoid negotiations on Germany. In addition, Molotov was in charge of the Foreign Ministry, which had responsibility for implementing foreign policy, and was thus strategically placed to veto any innovative proposals for concessions.[76]

In response to a U.S. proposal for a meeting of foreign ministers in Switzerland, the Soviets proposed a five-power conference, including the PRC, to discuss elimination of foreign bases and tension reduction, followed by a four-power conference to discuss Germany. On 26 November, the Soviets unexpectedly accepted without preconditions the West's proposal for a foreign ministers' meeting.[77]

Both Eisenhower and Dulles doubted that the four-power negotiations would solve the German question. "The question," Secretary of State Dulles said, "is how do you get it over with with as little damage as possible." The secretary of state believed that the meeting "might represent the last major Soviet effort to disrupt the Western alliance and to destroy the security of Western Europe."[78]

In September 1953, Dulles had considered capitalizing on the U.S. position of strength (as indicated by Konrad Adenauer's victory in the West German elections and the Korean armistice) by making a "spectacular effort" at global relaxation of tensions. He suggested to Eisenhower that the United States join with the Soviets in a mutual withdrawal of forces from Europe and in major arms limitation agreements. As part of this arrangement, the Soviets would have to allow domestic autonomy in Eastern Europe and give up trying to promote world communism. Dulles was concerned that the NATO allies' growing vulnerability to a Soviet attack would cause them to expel U.S. military bases and turn to neutralism. Eisenhower emphatically agreed that it was important to make renewed efforts to relax world tensions and that mutual withdrawal of Soviet and American forces could be suggested as a first step. But the president expressed fears that the Europeans might panic if word leaked out that the United States was considering withdrawing its troops.[79] In the end, nothing came of Dulles's idea.

Malenkov's offer to negotiate on subjects of East-West tension was not credible because Soviet concessions did not entail significant costs or risks to the new regime. The official statement of the "New Look" defense policy, NSC 162/2, observed that "the various 'peace gestures' so far have cost the Soviets very little in actual concessions and could be merely designed to divide the West by raising false hopes and seeking to make the United States appear unyielding." As the annual review of the Council on Foreign Relations pointed out, "many of the Soviet 'concessions' represented no more than the correction of gross breaches of normal international usage."[80] Thus, the Soviet 1953 peace offensive was not fully credible to the West and led Eisenhower to call for "deeds not words" as evidence that the Soviets would negotiate in good faith.

As predicted, the foreign ministers met from 25 January to 18 February 1954, but achieved nothing. Presenting the West's position, Foreign Minister Anthony Eden of Britain called for free elections throughout Germany to elect a provisional government, which could draw up a constitution and conduct further elections for a unified German government. The new German state would be free to join NATO. Reflecting his unwillingness to withdraw Soviet troops from any place occupied at the end of World War II, Molotov refused to sign the Austrian State Treaty unless they first reached agreement on Germany. Foreign Minister Molotov proposed that the ministers appoint a provisional government including representatives of East and West Germany which would then conduct elections for a unified German government. Since East Germany would have a veto over the electoral machinery as well as over the groups allowed to participate, Molotov's plan made it unlikely that any elections would be held.[81]

During the rest of 1954, Malenkov made no further conciliatory initiatives. The Kremlin was now immobilized by a power struggle. From March until December, the Soviet political and military leadership debated the impact of nuclear weapons on strategy and defense, partly in response to Dulles's "massive retaliation" speech and partly as a result of the Soviet acquisition of hydrogen weapons. On 12 January 1954, Dulles had announced that the United States must reinforce local defenses with the "further deterrent of massive retaliatory power." The free world must "be willing and able to respond vigorously at places and with means of its own choosing."[82]

In his 12 March election speech before the Supreme Soviet, Premier Malenkov warned that continuation of "cold war policies" could lead to a "new world war" which would mean the "destruction of world civilization." This was the first time any Soviet leader had admitted that a nuclear war would not just destroy capitalists. Because Soviet nuclear weapons would deter the capitalists from launching an attack, argued Malenkov, Soviet military expenditures could be reduced, releasing funds for increased production of consumer goods. The premier implied that the Soviets should be content with a minimum number of nuclear weapons, for deterrence, and that they should try to relax tensions with the West.[83]

Malenkov believed that the Soviet Union could influence Western leaders through concessions and diplomacy. At a diplomatic reception in Moscow in November 1954, according to Bohlen, Khrushchev threw up his hands emotionally when talking with the French ambassador about NATO and declared, "There is nothing to be done." Malenkov then quietly observed, "There is always something to be done." Bohlen regarded Malenkov as more educated, intelligent, and Western than other Soviet leaders. Moreover, as head of the Soviet state, Malenkov understood the power of the hydrogen bomb and how its enormous power would give second thoughts to any leader contemplating aggression. The United States had recently tested a hydrogen bomb with a yield of fifteen megatons in the Bikini Islands.[84]

Malenkov's statements that a nuclear war would destroy civilization and that the Soviet government could safely reduce defense expenditures got him into political trouble. He could count on support only from P. N. Pospelov, Maxim Saburov, and Mikhail Pervukhin; a majority of the Presidium, including Defense Minister Bulganin, Khrushchev, Molotov, Lazar Kaganovich, and Klement Voroshilov, vigorously objected. Bulganin, for example, protested that imperialists did not expend enormous material and financial resources on armaments merely to frighten the Soviets. The imperialists would not be restrained by humanitarianism from using nuclear weapons, he contended.[85] In a fiery speech in Prague, Khrushchev maintained in June 1954 that a nuclear war would mean the end of capitalism. He charged that reactionary capitalist circles were seeking a way out of their difficulties by preparing a new war.[86]

Dulles's announcement of "massive retaliation" and his hints that the United States might intervene in Indochina to save the French at Dien Bien Phu both undermined Malenkov's arguments that the capitalists would be deterred from resorting to nuclear weapons by Soviet retaliatory capabilities and strengthened the position of conservatives and the military who objected to reduced defense expenditures.[87] By late April, Malenkov was forced to retreat from his earlier rejection of Soviet Cold War policies. Malenkov now claimed that nuclear war would only destroy the "capitalist system," and he promised that the armed forces would get everything they needed.[88]

This speedy retraction did not save Malenkov politically. From April 1954 through February 1955, Malenkov gradually lost his authority while Khrushchev assumed a more prominent role among the collective leadership. In August 1954, Khrushchev plotted with Bulganin, Anastas Mikoyan, and regional party leaders to overthrow Malenkov. A month later, Khrushchev made a state visit to Beijing, a role that would normally go to Malenkov as head of the Soviet government. By November, Khrushchev was chairing meetings of the Presidium instead of Malenkov.[89]

German membership in NATO further weakened Malenkov, for it contradicted his line that a conciliatory Soviet foreign policy would separate the West European states from the United States and lead to agreements with the West on security issues. The French parliament had turned down the EDC Treaty on 30 August, 1954, but Great Britain quickly developed an alternative plan—even worse from the Soviet perspective—for integrating a national German army into NATO, and the Western countries approved the new plan in Paris in late October. Germany's impending remilitarization made it difficult for Malenkov to maintain that the Soviets could safely cut defense expenditures. In November 1954, the party newspaper *Pravda* used the Paris agreements as an excuse to write a series of editorials attacking Molotov.[90]

Malenkov had failed to get a summit meeting, which would have supported his assertion that United States was willing to pursue a policy of cooperation with the Soviet Union. Had Eisenhower accepted Malenkov's call for a summit, the Soviet leader would have received the added prestige accruing from negotiations with Western leaders, and that would have assisted him in his struggle for preeminence. The Soviet public's approval of his success in negotiating with the capitalists would have been a political asset. Overtures from Eisenhower would have supported more peaceful tendencies in the Soviet leadership. That Malenkov hung on for so long suggests that there was considerable governmental support for his policies of reducing defense expenditures and improving popular living standards, and the large turnover of personnel after his resignation provides additional evidence.[91]

Ambassador Bohlen would regret that he did not recommend that Eisenhower meet with Malenkov at a summit. "After the death of Stalin," Bohlen wrote, "there might have been opportunities for an adjustment of some of the outstanding questions, particularly regarding Germany." In his memoirs, Khrushchev claimed that the Soviet leadership favored a summit meeting because they believed that the Soviet Union and the West could come to terms and agree on rational principles of peaceful coexistence.[92]

At a Central Committee Plenum on 25 January 1955, Khrushchev attacked Malenkov for his attempt to buy "cheap popularity" through his consumer goods campaign. He charged that Malenkov's argument that world war would mean the end of civilization was not only mistaken but politically harmful, for it would lead to feelings of hopelessness about the Soviet ability to frustrate aggressors. On 8 February, Malenkov resigned as chairman of the Council of Ministers in favor of Bulganin, who was rewarded for his vigorous support of Khrushchev. Khrushchev remained first secretary of the Communist Party. Malenkov continued to be a member of the Presidium and became minister of electric power stations.[93]

Having defeated Malenkov, however, Khrushchev then co-opted his rival's foreign policy. Khrushchev's opposition to Malenkov was primarily political and tactical, not substantive. Despite his earlier bluster about the need for increased defense expenditures, Khrushchev agreed with Malenkov on the need to boost production of consumer goods and reduce international tensions. Khrushchev had used the issue of heavy industry priorities to gain the support of conservatives on the Presidium against Malenkov. After Malenkov's resignation, though, even some conservatives claimed to see a relaxation of tensions.[94]

Khrushchev decided to sign the Austrian State Treaty and, against Molotov's determined opposition, persuaded the rest of the Presidium to go along with him. The Soviet foreign minister maintained Stalin's view that war might break out at any minute, and he therefore opposed giving up Eastern Austria, a strategic area in the center of Europe. Molotov thus suffered a humiliating defeat on the Austrian State Treaty issue, and although he remained in the position of foreign minister for another year, he had no influence on foreign policy.[95]

On 8 February 1955, the same day that Malenkov resigned, Molotov announced that a withdrawal of occupation forces from Austria need not wait until a German peace treaty was signed, thereby decoupling the Austrian State Treaty from the German question. On 24 March, Molotov invited the Austrian chancellor Julius Raab to Moscow for negotiations on a treaty, and the Soviet and Austrian representatives reached an agreement in principle within just four days (11–15 April). Although the Austrian-Soviet negotiations had produced an agreement that exceeded his expectations, Dulles insisted on a preliminary conference of ambassadors to close any remaining loopholes before the foreign ministers signed the treaty on 15 May 1955.[96]

The Austrian State Treaty did not come about through a tit-for-tat exchange of concessions: it was a unilateral Soviet initiative, not contingent on a reciprocal action from the West and irrevocable. The West did not offer attractive new terms; indeed, the final treaty was much less favorable to the Soviets than the draft they had refused to sign a year earlier. As the *Nation* pointed out, the treaty terms were "more generous at almost every point than Austria and the West expected and were ready to accept—even including the demand for Austrian neutrality." Alexander Kendrick, writing in the *New Republic*, found the Soviet gesture peculiar in that "the Western Three and Austria have been perfectly will-ing to sign a treaty without concessions."[97]

Could Khrushchev have intended to make neutral Austria a model for Germany? Certainly the Soviets, when they initialed the bilateral Vienna-Moscow agreement in April, could not have hoped that the Austrian formula of reunification through neutralization might be used as a bait to prevent ratification of the Paris agreements and West German entry into NATO. The process had already gathered irreversible momentum. Final ratification of the Paris agreements on 5 May 1955 had no effect on the four-power negotiations on Austria then under way. After Germany was admitted to NATO, the Soviets shifted to a "two Germanys" policy, as evidenced by their June decision to establish diplomatic relations with Bonn and to invite Adenauer to visit the Soviet Union.[98]

Khrushchev decided to withdraw from Austria as a way of undermin-ing the U.S. image of the Soviet Union as aggressive. If the Soviets were merely trying to lull the West into a sense of complacency, then they would not voluntarily have decreased their military power. In May 1955, Khrushchev cited the Austrian State Treaty as evidence that the Soviets did not intend to conquer Europe. "Is there any stronger proof necessary to show that the Soviet Union does not want to seize Europe to carry on any sort of war?" Khrushchev asked. "Who would evacuate troops if he wanted to attack?" In retrospect, Khrushchev explained that the Soviets needed "to create the kind of relations with other countries that would strengthen peace and the peaceful coexistence of nations with differing social and political systems." The Austrian State Treaty was a "first step," a "demonstration that we could conduct negotiations and conduct them well."[99]

INVITATION TO A SUMMIT

Because the Austrian State Treaty entailed real costs and risks to the Soviets, Eisenhower reversed his opposition to a summit meeting. Ac-cording to the *New York Times*, "By making concessions to Vienna, the Russians have hopes to meet the test of 'deeds not words' posed by President Eisenhower two years ago as a token of Soviet good faith." On 10 May 1955, the Western countries invited the Soviet Union to a summit, and the Soviet government formally accepted on 13 June. When re-minded by reporters that he had said he would require deeds rather than words from the Communists before agreeing to sit down with them, Eisenhower pointed out that the Soviet willingness to conclude an Aus-trian settlement was one of the deeds he had mentioned. Eisenhower recalled that the Soviet signature of the Austrian State Treaty "gave at least a glimmer of hope that [the Soviets], under their new leadership, might be genuinely seeking mutually acceptable answers."[100]

Had the Soviets not given Austria its freedom, it is doubtful that Eisenhower would have acceded to Prime Minister Eden's pleas for a summit. As recently as December 1954, Eisenhower had written to Winston Churchill that a social or exploratory meeting "would merely give a false impression of accord which, in our free countries, would probably make it more difficult to get parliamentary support for needed defense appropriations."[101]

On 10 May, the Soviet government made a disarmament proposal that accepted important elements of the Anglo-French position. The Soviets agreed that conventional forces should be cut to the levels proposed by the British and French, instead of by a proportional amount that would perpetuate Soviet conventional superiority; that conventional troops should be reduced before nuclear weapons were eliminated; and that a single international disarmament agency, with expanding powers and a permanent staff of inspectors, would be allowed to go behind the Iron Curtain to carry out on-site inspections. In addition, the Soviets proposed that ground control posts should be established at large ports, railway junctions, highways, and airports to detect dangerous concentrations of troops; that the international organization could exercise control "to the extent [deemed] necessary," including stationing on-site inspectors who would have "unimpeded access at all times to all objects of control"; and that the great powers should agree to a ban on nuclear testing.[102]

Granted, the 10 May disarmament proposal repackaged many old objectionable Soviet positions, such as the elimination of foreign bases, a world disarmament conference, and a ban on the use of nuclear weapons. The Soviets had an unrealistic timetable of two years for carrying out a vast, unprecedented program of comprehensive disarmament. Nevertheless, the initiative was a remarkable improvement over previous Soviet disarmament positions. New Russian evidence suggests that the Soviets were making a sincere effort to achieve agreements that would reduce arms spending. One of the authors of the proposal, A. A. Roschin, has written that "in essence they represented acceptance by the USSR of the proposals of the Western states."[103]

Secretary Dulles told the NSC that the Soviets were seeking "some limitation on the arms race, some easing of the armaments burden. . . . not merely as a trick but because they could ill afford to sustain this burden." The Soviets, continued Dulles, believe they must do something in order to raise consumption levels for the populations of the USSR and its satellites.[104] But instead of responding to the Soviet proposal, President Eisenhower would present his "Open Skies" proposal at Geneva (July

1955), and in September the U.S. disarmament representative Harold Stassen would put a "reservation" on all previous U.S. disarmament positions.[105]

Eisenhower did not refuse to cooperate with the Soviets on arms control out of any desire to maintain U.S. military superiority. In 1955, Eisenhower rejected the Air Force's doctrine of nuclear superiority and settled on a policy of "adequacy," which he unveiled the following year. At an NSC meeting on 30 June, confronted with the Joint Chiefs' opposition to U.S. disarmament proposals, Eisenhower replied heatedly that the current arms race was a "mounting spiral towards war." Our real problem, he said, was how to achieve a stalemate vis-à-vis the Soviets in the nonmilitary realm in order to complement what had already been achieved in the military field.[106]

Nor was Eisenhower inhibited by the Joint Chiefs' and Defense Secretary Charles Wilson's opposition to any sort of arms control agreement. No president was less in awe or wielded such firm control over the military as Eisenhower, a former general. He canceled various weapon systems and maintained tight control over defense spending.[107]

Eisenhower and Dulles simply did not trust the Soviets. In January 1955, Dulles expressed doubt whether the "U.S. could work out any disarmament plan with a powerful nation which we did not trust and which we believed had most ambitious goals." If every "detail was not buttoned up," he predicted, "the Soviets would take advantage of any loopholes." Six months later, despite the Austrian State Treaty and other Soviet concessions, Dulles warned that "Soviet creed and conduct" imposed "grave risks" for U.S. participation in an arms limitation plan. Plans to stabilize or reduce arms should be "tentative and exploratory" until the Soviets had demonstrated "good faith and good will."[108]

Eisenhower's caution, no matter how understandable, led to a missed opportunity to probe Soviet intentions on arms control. The United States backed away from its previous disarmament position just as the Soviets had agreed to it. Roschin recalls that "for us who had worked out the proposals of May all this was incomprehensible." By the November foreign ministers' meeting, the Soviets had gone back to advocating disarmament without inspection.[109]

The Soviets then made a series of moderately costly concessions to improve the atmosphere for negotiations at the upcoming Geneva summit. In May, Khrushchev, Bulganin, and Mikoyan visited Marshal Josef Tito in Yugoslavia to apologize for past Soviet foreign policy mistakes. On 7 June, the Soviets offered to establish diplomatic relations with West Germany and invited Adenauer to Moscow, thus accepting the legitimacy of the West German state and enhancing the chancellor's status.[110]

The president and his secretary of state regarded these actions as significant. Secretary Dulles characterized the Soviets' actions as "not superficial but involv[ing] very important risks to themselves (the Austrian Treaty, trip to Belgrade, wooing of Adenauer, etc.)." Dulles declared that the Soviet rapprochement with Tito was "without precedent in history" and was bound to have "tremendous" repercussions because it risked splintering the unity of the Soviet bloc in Eastern Europe. In a letter to his friend Swede Hazlett, Eisenhower related that the "Soviet agreement to the Austrian Treaty, their invitation to Adenauer to come to Moscow ... and finally the general attitude of the new Kremlin masters ... encouraged the belief that possibly a new attitude might be developed in the conduct of foreign relations."[111]

When the Soviets shot down a U.S. plane over the Bering Strait in June 1955, they not only apologized for the first time in that type of incident, but offered to pay 50 percent of the damages. Moscow also relaxed restrictions on the entry of foreign correspondents into the Soviet Union. As the Council on Foreign Relations annual survey pointed out, "None of these by itself was necessarily significant, but their confluence was taken as an indication that Stalin was indeed dead and his cantankerousness with him."[112]

Nevertheless, U.S. perceptions lagged behind the changes in Soviet foreign policy. Dulles attributed the change in Soviet policy to external pressures, rather than to internal goals. He believed that the Soviets had made a tactical shift for economic reasons but were still committed to a hostile strategy. When asked to explain the changes in Soviet policy, Dulles speculated to the NSC that "they had not changed their ideology, but ... the Russians were in some respects overextended and overcommitted." Part of the explanation of their changed policy was internal—the need to raise consumption levels for the people of the Soviet Union and its satellites. In addition, "the Soviets had come to recognize their external policy was a failure and was bankrupt." The secretary of state thus warned a bipartisan group of legislators that Soviet "conduct may be a trap to give them a breathing spell, and we must conduct ourselves so as to be in good position to meet any outcome."[113]

DEADLOCK AT GENEVA

At the Geneva conference, which lasted from 18 to 23 July 1955, Bulganin was the formal head of the Soviet delegation (although everyone knew that Khrushchev was in charge). Eisenhower represented the United States; Prime Minister Anthony Eden led the British delegation; and France was represented by Premier Edgar Faure. The issues on the agenda were disarmament, East-West exchanges, European security, and German unification.

Eden again proposed that Germany both be unified by free elections and be allowed to join NATO. Now that West German rearmament had been approved, however, the Soviet government would allow reunification only if NATO were dismantled and U.S. forces left the continent.[114] For that matter, Dulles and Eisenhower knew that the Soviets would never allow a unified Germany to contribute its military power to NATO. Both sides made propagandistic proposals concerning Germany, knowing that the other would not accept.

As noted above, instead of responding to the 10 May Soviet disarmament initiative, Eisenhower made a surprise proposal on 21 July for "Open Skies." The idea was that the United States and the Soviet Union would trade blueprints of their military establishments and provide facilities within their own countries for aerial photography. Eisenhower argued that Open Skies would reduce the reciprocal fear of surprise attack, relax tensions, reduce mutual distrust, and lead to the establishment of a more comprehensive disarmament inspection system.[115]

The Soviets rejected the Open Skies proposal because it would have allowed a potential aggressor to gather information on Soviet force dispositions, installations, and soft strategic deployments. Khrushchev told Eisenhower politely but frankly that Open Skies was little more than an easy means of acquiring intelligence information and that the right way to lessen international tension was to reduce armaments, which would be unaffected by the president's proposal and could even increase. A year later, General Zhukov informed the U.S. Air Force chief of staff, General Nathan F. Twining, that "the creation of a system of aerial control in fact means the creation of a reliable system of reconnaissance." The result of Eisenhower's Open Skies proposal would not be the "strengthening [of] good faith and removal of fear, but on the contrary . . . of mistrust and fear."[116]

Some historians have charged that Open Skies was pure public relations, because American officials knew the Soviets would not accept it. Eisenhower had admitted privately that the Soviets already knew the location of virtually all U.S. military installations, and that mutual agreement to overflights would undoubtedly benefit the United States more than it would the Soviets.[117] The president, however, regarded Open Skies as a first step toward arms control, a means of reassuring his Soviet counterpart and building greater trust. Eisenhower told Dulles that the idea "might open a tiny gate in the disarmament fence."[118] He thought that the great value of an inspection system would be to enable states to develop confidence in just what military forces and installations existed in other countries.[119] If states could check on the means of delivery, such as four-engine bombers, atomic cannons, warships, and so on, a potential aggressor's capability for surprise attack would be severely limited.[120] In a 25 July letter to his friend General Alfred Gruenther, Eisenhower argued that Open Skies would reduce the danger of devastating surprise attack and would thus result in an "immense gain in mutual confidence and trust" which would establish a "truly realistic basis" for disarmament.[121]

To the Soviets the president explained that Open Skies was "a beginning—a beginning which would reduce mutual distrust—and that it was designed to promote rather than replace a comprehensive system of inspection and disarmament." When Khrushchev attacked the proposal on the grounds that it would merely improve intelligence, Eisenhower replied that he was trying to outline "one first concrete step" in order to "dispel fear and suspicion and thus lighten international tension by reassuring people against the dangers of surprise attack."[122] The Soviets, however, were not willing to accept inspection without disarmament.

After the summit conference in Geneva, the Soviet Union continued making concessions. The Soviets unilaterally cut conventional forces by 640,000, returned the Porkkala naval base to Finland, established diplomatic relations with West Germany, and released German prisoners of war. According to the annual Council on Foreign Relations survey, though, these concessions "cost the Soviet Government little and could be essentially meaningless."[123]

Western observers questioned whether a reduction of Soviet soldiers meant a proportionate decrease in the combat effectiveness of Soviet troops. Moscow could have been imitating the U.S. "New Look" policy of relying more on nuclear weapons than on massive field armies. In addition, Soviet soldiers were released partly in order to meet labor shortages in industry and agriculture. The State Department commented that the security of the United States would have been better served by keeping the men in uniform than by diverting them to production of the means of war.[124]

Khrushchev's 1955 troop cuts were the first of several from 1955–58 that gradually reduced Soviet conventional forces from about 5.7 million in 1955 to about 3.6 million in January 1960. In May 1956, Khrushchev announced a more substantial reduction in Soviet ground forces by over 1.2 million. Again, these troop cuts did help the Soviet government meet pressing economic needs for workers in industry and agriculture by reallocating the released troops to civilian labor. Khrushchev may also have diverted the savings to his program to build ICBMs and tactical nuclear weapons. The Soviet Union could not afford to maintain its traditionally massive and economically parasitic ground forces while competing with the United States in increasingly costly nuclear weapon systems. Given

[68]

these constraints, Khrushchev believed that nuclear firepower reduced the need for conventional troops. General Zhukov agreed with Khrushchev on the need to prune the overgrown military establishment and reduce some salaries. Through unilateral reductions, Khrushchev explained, "we could demonstrate our own peaceful intentions and at the same time free some of our resources for the development of our industry, the production of consumer goods, and the improvement of living standards."[125]

But if Khrushchev's troop cuts were economically and strategically rational, they were insufficiently persuasive to the United States as evidence of Soviet peaceful intentions. Although the Soviet government insisted that the troop cuts were intended to reduce tensions as well as to improve the Soviet economy, the Eisenhower administration did not view them as sound evidence of peaceful intent because paring down oversized ground forces would not decrease Soviet military power. President Eisenhower commented that the Soviets were only doing what his own government had done earlier as part of its New Look strategy of relying more on nuclear weapons. Secretary Dulles stressed the Soviet need to put more manpower into industry and agriculture.[126]

At the Twentieth Party Congress, Khrushchev not only denounced Stalin's crimes but modified Marxism-Leninism to allow for better relations with the West. Contrary to Lenin's doctrine that war was the midwife of revolution, the Soviet leader said that war was not inevitable, and he therefore called for peaceful coexistence with the capitalist world. Indeed, Khrushchev said that the two systems could do more than coexist: "It is necessary to proceed further, to improve relations, to strengthen confidence among countries and cooperate."[127]

In Hungary and Poland, however, de-Stalinization raised expectations, leading to demands for democratic reform and, in Hungary, an uprising beginning on 23 October 1956. Mikoyan, who had recently returned from Budapest, warned Khrushchev that Soviet military intervention would "undermine the reputation of our government and party" and reportedly threatened to commit suicide. Briefing the Yugoslav ambassador, Khrushchev portrayed his decision to intervene as necessary in order to demonstrate Soviet resolve to the West: "If we let things take their course the West would say we are either stupid or weak, and that's one and the same thing." The bloody Soviet military intervention in November 1956 greatly damaged Khrushchev's image abroad and frightened him into putting the brakes on domestic reform and de-Stalinization.[128]

Stalin's death created new opportunities for East-West cooperation on arms control and the German question. Soviet Premier Malenkov had strong incentives to settle sources of tension in East-West relations. Not only did the Soviet leader realize that East-West tensions had risen to a dangerous level, but he wanted to bring more consumer goods to the Soviet people, and that meant that he had to reverse the traditional Stalinist emphasis on heavy industry and defense production. To gain domestic political backing for this reordering of priorities, Malenkov needed a more benign international environment. Malenkov was also moved to act by a fear of German rearmament and by the hope that a more conciliatory Soviet policy would lessen support for the EDC in the parliaments of France and Germany.

There is no evidence that Dulles or Eisenhower weighed the Soviet interest in a lasting reduction of tensions or in solving the German question. Eisenhower suspected that Malenkov's overtures were merely a tactical shift aimed at disrupting Western attempts to build a defense coalition, and so he refused to negotiate a relaxation of tensions at a summit until the Soviet leader had proved his good intentions through "deeds not words." He did not try to use the valuable Western bargaining chip of possible German rearmament.

Ideology was a source of mistrust. Molotov and Dulles were mirror images of each other—ideologues who were convinced that there was no hope of accommodation with the enemy, whose behavior reflected ideological imperatives.

Like many chief executives, President Eisenhower was undecided. If Eisenhower had accepted Malenkov's invitation to a summit, they might have discussed how to deal with the German question in such a way as to preserve stability in Europe. Beria and Malenkov were willing to allow Germany to be reunified in return for guarantees of German neutrality. Both regarded East Germany as a weak, unstable, and potentially explosive ally. Yet Malenkov made only minor concessions, which did not meet Eisenhower's test of "deeds not words."

The president's unwillingness to reciprocate Malenkov's overtures and Dulles's rhetoric about "massive retaliation" contributed to the Soviet politician's loss of power, although he may have been irreparably handicapped by his reliance on the bureaucracy as a power base. Nevertheless, the influence of the Soviet military and heavy-industrial complex did not rule out the pursuit of détente with the West. After taking control in February 1955, Khrushchev pursued policies of détente and negotiation with the West that were virtually identical to those proposed by his defeated rival Malenkov. Moreover, he pursued them more effectively.

When Khrushchev sacrificed the Soviet position in Eastern Austria, Eisenhower regarded Soviet professions of their desire for peace as more credible and agreed for the first time to a summit meeting. The Austrian State Treaty was the first in a series of Soviet concessions, including the apology to Tito, the opening up of relations with Adenauer, and the Soviet acceptance of Western positions on disarmament.

The Soviet disarmament proposal of 10 May 1955 adopted Western force totals and the principle that nuclear disarmament should come last. As the failure of Eisenhower's Open Skies proposal demonstrated, the main obstacle to a disarmament agreement between the United States and the Soviet Union was not really verification, but mistrust. Dulles believed that Soviet intentions were fundamentally malevolent: even if they observed the letter of a treaty, they might chisel or seek aggrandizement elsewhere. Eisenhower's and Dulles's beliefs were not influenced by Khrushchev's May 1956 signal of good intentions (cutting his troops unilaterally by more than 1.2 million) because the troop reductions could have served economic objectives. Eisenhower was so wary of Soviet cheating that he proposed inspection without disarmament in the Open Skies plan. The Soviets, on the other hand, feared that the United States could use aerial surveillance to identify targets for attack—not an unreasonable apprehension at a time when the U.S. held a first-strike advantage. United States verification demands and Soviet fears of espionage, both reflecting a lack of trust, were the main obstacles to arms reduction agreements in the 1950s.

[3]

Disengagement, German Nuclear Weapons, and the Test Ban

Eisenhower's arms control legacy includes several lost possibilities for cooperation with Khrushchev on controlling the arms race: disengagement, a Central European nuclear-free zone, and a comprehensive test ban. The most striking waste of diplomatic opportunity occurred during Eisenhower's second term, when he and Khrushchev came agonizingly close to agreement on a comprehensive test ban. Khrushchev and Eisenhower moved from giving lip service to disarmament to searching for enforceable arms control agreements. Rather than reading prepared speeches at each other, the Soviets and the Americans actually reacted to each other's proposals and engaged in a problem-solving effort to accommodate their differences over verification. After having rejected all inspection as espionage, Khrushchev now accepted the idea of a quota for inspections. The meeting of Khrushchev and Eisenhower at Camp David in September 1959 was the climax of steady if uneven progress in U.S.-Soviet efforts to cooperate on nuclear testing and Germany. Had it not been for the U-2 incident, the two leaders might have made substantial progress toward a test ban. Without the diplomatic foundation laid by Dulles and Eisenhower, John F. Kennedy could not have achieved a détente and test ban treaty during his short term in office. Why did Eisenhower and Khrushchev fail to achieve any arms control agreement?

Their diplomatic failure would be understandable if Eisenhower or Khrushchev did not *want* to achieve an agreement. Eisenhower's private anticommunist rhetoric as well as his use of covert action and psychological warfare lends support to the idea that he had little desire to cooperate with the Soviets. Some historians have portrayed Eisenhower, the public peacemaker with the benign grin, as a ruthless Cold Warrior in private, a man whose anticommunism inhibited him from taking up

Khrushchev's offers to negotiate arms control agreements.[1] Certainly Eisenhower found it difficult to trust the Soviets.[2] On the other hand, Eisenhower's drive for a balanced budget along with his desire to go down in history as a peacemaker led him to place a high priority on achieving verifiable arms control agreements with the Soviet Union during his second term. In 1957, Eisenhower declared that in view of the severe financial and budgetary problems facing the United States, halting the arms race was an "absolute necessity." A year later, Eisenhower wrote Dulles that the task of reaching "reliable agreements" on arms reduction "transcends all other objectives we can have."[3] Eisenhower certainly wanted to prohibit nuclear testing as a first step toward more significant disarmament agreements.

It may be that Khrushchev was trying to drive the United States out of Europe and undermine the unity of NATO, that his rhetoric about détente was an attempt to lull the West into neglecting necessary defensive measures.[4] Other scholars have argued that Khrushchev wanted to stabilize the division of Europe and dampen East-West military competition so that he could cut defense spending and produce more consumer goods.[5]

If the United States and the Soviet Union shared an interest in cooperating on arms control, then it would have been reasonable for Eisenhower and Khrushchev to give consideration to their reputation for reliability and to shape their own actions to convey a good impression to the other side. Khrushchev's unpredictable shifts between conciliation and confrontation caused Eisenhower to question his sincerity about cooperating to control the arms race. As a result of his ambivalence over Soviet intentions, the president did not follow a consistent strategy in negotiations for the test ban, and American wavering intensified Khrushchev's suspicions that the United States was not really interested in an arms control agreement. That Eisenhower sent the U-2 over the Soviet Union not two weeks before the summit hardly assuaged the Soviet leader's concerns.

Khrushchev's and Eisenhower's failure to reach an agreement cannot really be blamed on domestic political constraints. The American public favored a summit meeting and disarmament negotiations; as for the test ban, the public followed the president's lead. Khrushchev achieved his strongest position of authority after defeating the anti-Party group in July 1957, and he no longer bothered to consult with the Communist Party Central Committee which was the vehicle of his triumph.[6]

Mutual mistrust led to a series of missed opportunities for cooperation on both arms control and the German question. Eisenhower did not understand how Khrushchev might feel threatened by German nuclear weapons or the collapse of the East German economy. If the president was concerned that the Soviets were making proposals for a nuclear-free zone or for disengagement of foreign troops from Europe in order to divide the United States from its allies, then he should have tried to determine whether Soviet actions and statements suggested an interest in arms control or in propaganda. Instead, Eisenhower did not critically evaluate his presuppositions about Soviet motives; he simply dismissed Khrushchev's initiatives as misleading and deceptive. It would have been sensible for Eisenhower to moderate his belief that Khrushchev had no desire to cooperate with the United States when the Soviet leader made major unilateral troop reductions, but the president deferred to Dulles's warnings that a summit meeting would allow the Soviets to lull the free world into relaxing its guard. Khrushchev, on the other hand, did not understand how his bluff and bluster increased Eisenhower's mistrust of his motives. Desperate to attain a summit and negotiations on Germany, Khrushchev provoked a crisis over Berlin.

Near the end of Eisenhower's term, after Secretary Dulles's death, the president agreed to summits with Khrushchev at Camp David and Paris. The United States and the Soviet Union made major progress toward a threshold test ban agreement. Mutual suspicions, however, culminated in Eisenhower's sending a U-2 spy plane over Soviet territory a few weeks before the Paris summit. Khrushchev demanded a personal apology, and an opportunity for arms control was squandered. Each state missed the other's signals and conveyed misleading impressions to the other.

KHRUSHCHEV'S PEACE OFFENSIVE

After the Soviets launched *Sputnik*, the first artificial satellite, on 4 October 1957, Khrushchev went on the diplomatic offensive. At a meeting with Dulles on 5 October, Foreign Minister Andrei Gromyko argued that because the problem of disarmament was exceedingly difficult, the United States and the Soviet Union should work for partial agreements. For example, there were no objective obstacles to a test ban if the United States and the Soviet Union wanted to reach an understanding. Gromyko reminded Dulles that the Soviet Union had recently proposed (in the U.N. disarmament talks) that control instruments be installed on the territory of the Soviet Union, the United States, Great Britain, and France, as well as in the Pacific Ocean, to monitor a test ban. The Soviet foreign minister maintained that a test ban would facilitate agreement on more complicated questions—not to mention removing a threat to human health and preventing the development of more nuclear weapons with greater explosive force. An agreement on test suspension could be a real turning point, he said, leading to a better atmosphere in which other aspects of disarmament could be settled.[7]

Sputnik, however, increased the reluctance of most Americans to consider arms control negotiations with the Soviets. That the Soviets had rockets powerful enough to launch a satellite into space suggested that they had the capability to build intercontinental ballistic missiles able to reach American territory. Politicians and the news media in the United States hysterically claimed that the Soviets would have a three-to-one or four-to-one advantage in ICBMs by 1962. Eisenhower tried to alleviate the hysteria by pointing out that an overwhelming U.S. advantage—America's nuclear stockpile, bomber forces, and overseas bases—would preserve the U.S. deterrent.[8]

Khrushchev made a series of ambiguous statements in interviews with Western journalists suggesting that the Soviet Union "possessed" ICBMs, but he did not actually claim that the Soviets had deployed an operational system. In an interview with James Reston of the *New York Times* three days after the launch of *Sputnik*, Khrushchev boasted that "we now have all the rockets we need: long-range rockets, intermediate-range rockets and short-range rockets."[9] Moscow argued that Soviet advances in science and technology were changing the "correlation of forces" (an ideological concept including social, economic, and political as well as military factors) rather than the strategic balance. Instead of claiming to have military superiority, Soviet publicists maintained that strategic rockets canceled out former U.S. advantages by eradicating the invulnerability of U.S. territory, reducing the value of strategic bombers, and diminishing the value of U.S. overseas bases. Soviet leaders frequently used the claim for a favorable correlation of forces as an ideological justification for détente with the West, implying that Soviet strength would deter the imperialist aggressors.[10]

At a 6 November session of the Supreme Soviet, Khrushchev proposed a high-level meeting to discuss "ruling war out as a means of dealing with international tensions."[11] On 10 December 1957, Premier Nikolai Bulganin sent a public letter to President Eisenhower appealing for bilateral talks to end the Cold War and the arms race. The Soviet premier suggested that Great Britain, the United States, and the Soviet Union suspend nuclear tests for two or three years. He also recommended— only days before a NATO Council meeting at which the Western allies were supposed to decide whether to place intermediate-range ballistic missiles (IRBMs) in Europe as a countermeasure to *Sputnik* and Soviet ICBMs—the establishment of a nuclear-free zone in both Germanys, Poland, and Czechoslovakia. The proposal for a nuclear-free zone in Central Europe was known as the Rapacki Plan, after its author, Foreign Minister Adam Rapacki of Poland. Bulganin and Eisenhower could solve these matters at a summit conference, suggested the Soviet premier, who expressed his desire for a personal meeting with the president.[12]

Bulganin's letter to Eisenhower marked the beginning of a new Soviet campaign for a summit, using public letters and speeches. Over the next nine months, the Soviets sent Eisenhower about thirty letters proposing, in addition to a summit meeting, a variety of disarmament measures including nuclear-free zones, neutralization, prevention of nuclear proliferation, a test ban, and disengagement of U.S. and Soviet forces.[13]

Eisenhower delayed answering Bulganin's letter, ostensibly because he had suffered a slight stroke two weeks earlier which had left him temporarily unable to speak anything but gibberish. Nevertheless, the president vowed that he would resign if his infirmity kept him from attending the NATO heads-of-government meeting in Paris. Eisenhower did not regard the IRBMs as militarily necessary to counter the alleged Soviet ICBM capability, because he believed that manned bombers would be the preferred method of delivering nuclear weapons for at least five years, when the United States would have solid-fueled Minuteman and Polaris missiles. But he did consider them psychologically necessary, to reassure Europeans that the United States would defend them even after Soviet nuclear weapons could reach American territory.[14]

Much to Dulles's surprise, West European leaders were reluctant to emplace the liquid-fueled, slow-firing IRBMs, which were highly vulnerable to attack from Soviet medium-range missiles in Central Europe. Chancellor Adenauer did not want to accept the IRBMs for fear of provoking the Soviets and blocking a chance for German reunification.[15]

Before accepting U.S. missiles, European leaders wanted to try to reach an agreement with the Soviets on disarmament and inspection. The European representatives viewed Bulganin's letter less skeptically than Dulles. Adenauer judged Bulganin's recent letter to be "moderate," and he suggested that the allies "should probe [the] Soviets' vague words to get their meaning."[16] Foreign Minister Christian Pineau of France suggested that, along with their decision to strengthen the alliance, they invite the Soviets to a foreign ministers' conference to discuss disarmament; the representatives from Norway, Canada, Britain, Denmark, and Belgium immediately agreed.[17] Although Dulles objected to proposing talks without evidence that the Soviets were willing to negotiate solutions to major international problems, the Europeans had substantial bargaining leverage: with American ICBMs still under development, the United States needed its overseas bases to launch missiles against Soviet territory. Thus, to persuade the European countries to agree "in principle" to accept the American missiles, Dulles had to approve an invitation to the Soviets to attend a foreign ministers' conference on disarmament.[18]

But Khrushchev did not want to waste time on foreign ministers' meetings, where Dulles could block any agreement. At a Supreme Soviet session immediately following the meeting of the NATO Council, Khrushchev again proposed a meeting of heads of government, preferably preceded by a conference between the "two strongest" powers. Pending an agreement on disarmament, said Khrushchev, the Soviet Union would continue to develop modern weapons, although within "reasonable limits" in order not to burden the Soviet economy—an unprecedented statement by a Soviet leader.[19]

On New Year's Eve, Khrushchev hosted a cordial party for the diplomatic corps, in marked contrast to previous gloomy gatherings. He made a special toast to President Eisenhower and declared that "if the Soviet Union and the United States can get together and reach an agreement, most of the world's problems will be solved."[20] Khrushchev backed up his words with an announcement on 6 January 1958 that the Kremlin would reduce Soviet troops by 300,000, including 41,000 to be withdrawn from East Germany and 17,000 from Hungary. The Soviet statement described this military cutback as a "new serious contribution to the cause of easing tension and creating an atmosphere of confidence in the relations between states" and called on NATO powers to take similar actions to bring an end to the arms race.[21]

The Eisenhower administration, however, dismissed Khrushchev's unilateral reductions as propaganda. State Department officials believed that if in fact Khrushchev's statement foreshadowed actual reductions, that it was because developments in science and technology had made it possible to maintain Soviet military effectiveness with smaller expenditure of resources. U.S. officials also doubted whether the troop cuts reflected actual additional reductions. Khrushchev could merely be completing reductions announced in 1955–56 (although Soviet officials claimed that the new reductions were in addition to earlier ones). Paradoxically, State Department officials interpreted Khrushchev's cuts as an indication that he was uninterested in serious negotiations on disarmament, not that he had given up hopes of getting an agreement.[22]

Before Eisenhower could answer Bulganin's first letter, the Soviet premier addressed another message (8 January 1958) to various heads of government in which he called for a summit conference to discuss a two- or three-year nuclear test moratorium, the Polish plan for a nuclear-free zone in Central Europe, an East-West nonaggression pact, a reduction of foreign troops in Europe, measures to guard against surprise attack, an expansion of East-West trade, and renunciation of the use of force in the Middle East. Bulganin rejected the notion of a foreign ministers' conference because the "prejudiced position of certain possible participants" (John Foster Dulles) would raise additional obstacles to a summit meeting.[23]

Denuclearization and Disengagement Rejected

Dulles was under substantial domestic public pressure to agree to a summit. A January 1958 poll in twelve major cities showed that 62 percent were in favor of an Eisenhower-Khrushchev meeting, against only 17 percent opposed. Washington and Chicago combined showed 54 percent in favor, 29 percent opposed.[24]

Dulles informed Foreign Minister Selwyn Lord of Britain that he and Eisenhower were opposed to a summit meeting unless there was some evidence that it would be productive. It would be dangerous to raise public hopes which were destined to be dashed to the ground. For the summit meeting to break down would be a disaster. Even if a communiqué resulted, little would be gained if it contained nothing but platitudes, and it might even undermine the vigilance of public opinion in the free world.[25]

On 12 January, Eisenhower finally answered Bulganin. He would attend a summit conference if the issues had been previously discussed and refined at lower levels in a way that promised "good hope" for success. The president then proposed an agenda to which the Soviets were unlikely to agree: German reunification through free elections; self-determination for Eastern Europe; restricted use of the veto in the U.N. Security Council; measures to guarantee against surprise attack; and a proposal to use outer space only for peaceful purposes, an item aimed at restraining the Soviet rocket-and-missile program.[26]

Khrushchev, however, wanted a summit to recognize the status quo in Europe. In a fiery speech at Minsk before a group of peasants, Khrushchev said that reunification of Germany was a matter for the Germans themselves and that negotiations over the status of East European countries would constitute interference in other nation's affairs. He insisted that the Soviet Union was not intimidated by U.S. overseas bases. He boasted that whereas it would take the West two or three years to arm its bases with nuclear missiles, the Soviet Union now had a rocket "tested and perfected" that could wipe out the bases and points beyond. He declared that the Soviet Union could send a missile with a hydrogen warhead to any spot on the globe. The Soviet government, therefore, could not be intimidated and would not accept agreements that did not recognize the legitimacy of all the world's communist governments. Khrushchev seemed not to understand how his threats interfered with his attempts to convey a peaceful image. When the Yugoslav ambassador cautioned him afterward that circles in the West who were opposed to talks would use his speech to spoil the atmosphere, Khrushchev assured him that the sharp words on both sides would soon be forgotten, and that they would see what each side stood for and what sort of an understanding was possible between East and West.[27]

Khrushchev told the press that he objected to a foreign ministers' meeting because "some foreign ministers are like midwives who are not interested in insuring the birth of the child." In a letter on 3 February, Bulganin maintained that any preliminary negotiations should only address procedural questions involved in preparing for a summit meeting, not substantive issues.[28] President Eisenhower curtly replied on 17 February that Secretary of State Dulles's participation was mandatory. The president commented publicly that there was no use going to a summit conference where "you would just be glaring at each other across the table and go home."[29]

The two sides fired off increasingly acerbic and curt public letters over whether preliminary negotiations could deal with substantive issues and the proposed agenda for a summit. Eisenhower and Dulles found this public correspondence increasingly annoying, because it forced them repeatedly to give negative answers to attractive Soviet proposals for disarmament and détente. At one point, Dulles complained that the Soviets were "prostituting" normal diplomatic channels.[30]

In May, the United States formally rejected the Rapacki Plan because a nuclear-free zone could not be controlled by inspection, would depend on the good intentions of powers outside the area, and would leave Germany vulnerable to superior Soviet conventional forces and nuclear missiles. A nuclear-free area would not protect Germany from Soviet IRBMs fired from outside the zone. Without tactical nuclear weapons, the West German army could not defend itself against the large Soviet conventional army.[31] On the other hand, by Eisenhower's own logic a nuclear-free zone would not have seriously interfered with NATO's ability to protect West Germany because nuclear weapons in France and the Low Countries could have substituted for those in Germany.[32]

Adam Ulam views refusal of the Rapacki Plan as "one of the most fundamental errors of Western policy in the postwar period." The plan would have had advantages for the United States. The version that Rapacki proposed in 1958 included phased reductions of conventional forces, thus meeting Western objections that eliminating tactical nuclear weapons would create a strategic imbalance in favor of the Soviet Union. The plan provided for international control and inspection, which would have given the West information on Soviet military facilities and capabilities in Poland, Czechoslovakia, and East Germany.[33]

Adenauer opposed the Rapacki Plan on the grounds that it meant the continued partition of Germany and indefinite Soviet superiority in the field of conventional forces. The West German chancellor merely reinforced Dulles's position, though, and his opposition was not the critical factor behind U.S. objections to a nuclear-free zone. Some conservative West German politicians expressed support for the Polish plan, and the West German president Theodor Heuss made a speech suggesting that the Eisenhower administration was too inclined to rely on propaganda and military muscle-flexing over serious diplomacy.[34]

The Rapacki Plan was originally a Polish idea intended to reduce tensions in Europe. Khrushchev's initial reluctance to approve the plan suggests that it was not merely a propaganda ploy. Only after months of persuasion and after the success of *Sputnik* reduced his concerns about security implications did Khrushchev give his permission for Rapacki to propose the plan. In February 1958, Rapacki had visited Moscow to persuade the Soviets to accept modifications in the plan, and the Polish and Soviet foreign ministries engaged in much hard bargaining before Moscow agreed to negotiate on methods of control, without an agreement in principle on a zone of partial disarmament, and to include conventional weapons. If the Soviets made the proposal purely as a propaganda gesture, knowing that it would be rejected by the West, then they should not have been concerned about specific features of the plan.[35]

Eisenhower also refused to negotiate on mutual reductions of U.S. and Soviet forces in Europe, or "disengagement." Disengagement had become a popular issue in response to George F. Kennan's "Reith lectures" for the British Broadcasting Corporation in October 1957. Kennan maintained that a mutual thinning out of allied and Soviet forces along both sides of the Iron Curtain would lead to greater independence in Eastern Europe, more contacts between East and West, and eventual German reunification. The West European public and many prominent political figures enthusiastically supported various forms of disengagement involving either mutual withdrawal of American and Soviet forces from the continent or a restricted armaments zone. Former Prime Minister Anthony Eden, the British Labour Party leader Hugh Gaitskell, Marshal of the Royal Air Force Sir John Slessor, the noted strategist Liddell Hart, and the German Social Democratic Party leader Eric Ollenhauer advanced other disengagement proposals, varying in the amount of territory covered and the number of troops withdrawn.[36]

Disengagement could have served the strategic interests of the United States. Removal of foreign forces from Germany would have increased the stability of Europe by making offensive action more difficult. Mutual troop withdrawals from Germany would have reduced the likelihood of a catalytic or accidental conflict arising from the close juxtaposition of U.S. and Soviet military forces. As the numerically inferior power, the United States would have improved its position through an agreement establishing parity in East-West conventional forces. The United States could have more easily matched Soviet strength through negotiated restrictions on conventional forces in Germany than by trying to build NATO forces up to thirty divisions, which if achieved, might have provoked the Soviets to engage in their own buildup. Instead of mobilizing additional U.S. and West German forces to counter Soviet divisions in Eastern Europe, it would have made more sense, as George Kennan argued, to persuade the Soviets to withdraw those troops. U.S. troops would not have been necessary if the Federal Republic of Germany achieved its rearmament goal of twelve divisions by 1961. West German troops would have been sufficient to prevent the Soviets from grabbing territory quickly, delaying a Soviet invasion long enough for NATO to mobilize.[37]

The president had long regarded U.S. troops in Europe as a temporary measure, intended only to tide the Europeans over until they had rebuilt their economies, and he was irritated by what he perceived as their continued free-riding on American efforts. He had expressed support for a mutual reduction of foreign troops in Europe as a disarmament measure.[38] Why, then, did Eisenhower refuse to discuss reciprocal troop withdrawals?

The State Department objected to a disengagement of forces from Central Europe because the United States would have to withdraw its troops across the Atlantic, while Soviet troops would only have to retreat a few hundred miles to the east and could easily return.[39] What Dulles ignored was that once Soviet troops were withdrawn from Eastern Europe, their return would require the communist regimes' approval, not to be taken for granted, or else would be an act of war. If the Soviets were willing to withdraw their troops from Central Europe, that would mean they were interested in a relaxation of tensions or in other political advantages that would be sacrificed if they reinvaded the countries. The Soviets, it should be noted, did not invade Yugoslavia, Austria, Finland, or Sweden—even without a specific Western deterrence guarantee.[40]

COSTLY SIGNAL AND LAGGING RESPONSE

On 31 March 1958, Foreign Minister Gromyko announced that the Soviet Union was suspending all nuclear tests and invited Great Britain and the United States to do the same. This bold initiative had all the marks of Khrushchev's leadership. Just four days previously, Bulganin had resigned and Khrushchev became premier as well as first secretary of the Communist Party, the first Soviet leader to hold both positions since Stalin.[41]

By acting to halt tests, Khrushchev made credible his desire for a negotiated test ban, making it difficult for Eisenhower to explain why he would not go along with the idea. "Moscow acted," the columnist James Reston pointed out, while "Washington reacted with words, and found itself once more on the defensive." Khrushchev's unilateral moratorium was costly because the United States was ahead of the Soviets in numbers of tests and in nuclear weapons design. The Soviet leader pointed out that the United States had set off more nuclear explosions than the Soviet Union. According to the *New York Times*, the United States had conducted a hundred tests while the Soviets had carried out fifty. Just one month earlier, Khrushchev told the Yugoslav ambassador that he was opposed to a unilateral Soviet renunciation of tests because it would give the Americans an advantage.[42]

The Eisenhower administration lagged behind the Soviet initiatives. At first, Eisenhower and Dulles tried to minimize the significance of the Soviet action by pointing out that it could be easily revoked, was contingent on U.S. restraint, and would not affect Soviet weapons programs. On 1 April, in a State Department auditorium jammed with reporters and government officials, Dulles explained slowly and with immense weariness that the Soviet announcement was a trick, timed to coincide with the Soviets' completion of their nuclear tests and with the beginning of a new series by the United States. By beginning the test suspension just after intensive Soviet testing, Khrushchev could exploit a normal hiatus to bring world public pressure to bear on the United States to stop its planned nuclear tests. If the United States nonetheless went ahead with its testing program, the Soviets would have an excuse to resume testing, thereby avoiding any damage to their weapons programs. Gromyko had stated that if Great Britain and the United States refused to go along, the Soviet Union would consider itself free to test. At his 2 April press conference, Eisenhower dismissed the Soviet nuclear test suspension as a "gimmick" that was "not to be taken seriously."[43]

The liberal news media and antinuclear protesters did not care, however, if the timing of the moratorium was strategic. The *Nation* objected that "if all this is a 'gimmick,' one can only wish to God that our statesmen could concoct such gimmicks once in a while." According to *Newsweek*, the Soviet test suspension won worldwide approval as a "major move toward peace." The *New Republic* called the test suspension a "brilliant political move, even in an area when almost anything reasonably astute looks brilliant by comparison with the sleepwalking that passes for American diplomacy." In London, five thousand people gathered in Trafalgar Square to begin a protest march to the British atomic research establishment at Aldermaston, fifty miles away. Demonstrators also conducted protests in West Germany, India, and Japan.[44]

Conservative commentators, on the other hand, viewed Khrushchev's unilateral moratorium as a propaganda gesture, a trick. In *U.S. News & World Report*, David Lawrence wrote that "to the gullible and the craven, to the weak-kneed and the 'practical'—who used to advocate doing business with Hitler and who now want to do business with Khrushchev— the Moscow proposal is a 'stroke of genius.' " In the view of *Time*, the test halt would "serve the double purpose for Russia of making peace propaganda for the credulous and avoiding the bothersome problem of the inspection system needed to make any test suspension worth more than a tinker's curse."[45]

Making the administration's embarrassment worse, Dulles admitted that Eisenhower had considered announcing a test suspension himself, before the Soviets did. The idea was rejected, Dulles said, because the administration decided that it must go ahead with the program to develop smaller, "cleaner" tactical nuclear weapons. James Reston complained about "opportunities squandered" by U.S. officials.[46] American intelligence had received warning of the Soviet unilateral moratorium. At an NSC meeting, on 24 March 1958, Secretary of State Dulles pleaded with Eisenhower to announce his own unilateral moratorium in order to "beat the Soviets to the punch." Dulles warned that a Soviet unilateral test ban would place the United States "in an extremely difficult position throughout the world." During the planned U.S. test series from April to September, he predicted, the United States "will be under heavy attack worldwide. The Soviets will cite their test suspension and their call for a summit meeting while we continue to test." The United States would then lose the "confidence of the Free World as the champion of peace."[47] Defense Department and Atomic Energy Commission (AEC) representatives objected that additional tests were needed to develop advanced weapon systems such as Polaris, tactical weapons, and defenses against nuclear attack.[48]

At the meeting, Eisenhower conceded that a test ban would probably hurt the United States militarily relative to the Soviets. "On the other hand, we need some basis of hope for our own people and for world opinion," he said. "It is simply intolerable to remain in a position wherein the United States, seeking peace, and giving loyal partnership to our allies, is unable to achieve an advantageous impact on world opinion." But Ike did not want to come out in favor of a test ban until Congress had amended the McMahon Act so that the United States could share nuclear weapons information with the British, eliminating their need to test. The president told the NSC that if they got the new law and if the Soviets accepted an inspection system, the United States would have to suspend testing.[49]

Had the Eisenhower administration followed its self-interest, the United States would have immediately matched Khrushchev's gesture or, even better, made use of available information and preempted the Soviet move by making an announcement first. The United States had conducted many more tests than the Soviets, and even Deputy Defense Secretary Donald Quarles conceded that the United States was ahead in nuclear weapons design. Instead, Eisenhower waited several months, and lost all the propaganda value of the gesture.

At first, Eisenhower was willing to go no further than to propose to Khrushchev that technical experts from East and West meet to discuss a control system for international disarmament. Such willingness was no concession, for the president continued to link U.S. acceptance of a test ban with an agreement to end the production of fissionable material for nuclear weapons (as he had done in his 12 January letter to Bulganin), a condition that made Soviet acceptance very unlikely, because the Soviets would not allow the intrusive on-site inspection required to monitor a halt in the manufacture of nuclear weapons material. The Eisenhower administration justified the "production cutoff link," as it was called, by arguing that a test ban was not really a disarmament measure since it would not reduce the number of weapons, but it might nonetheless give the Western democracies the illusion that they could relax their defense efforts.[50]

In response to Eisenhower's proposal to set up technical groups to study methods of disarmament control, Khrushchev said that it would be impossible for technicians to contribute to a solution of the disarmament problem unless an agreement had already been reached by their governments.[51] Dulles drafted another letter for Eisenhower which repeated the president's earlier offer to hold technical talks on test ban verification, but with one significant addition: "Studies of this kind are the necessary preliminaries to putting political decisions into effect." This statement implied that the United States would negotiate a separate test ban if the Soviets agreed to an inspection system. Eisenhower approved the letter, which was sent on 28 April.[52]

Dulles took the initiative in delinking the test ban from an end to the production of nuclear weapons material because he was concerned that continued testing was giving the United States the image of a "militaristic nation," and such an image could result in America's "moral isolation."[53] But it was Khrushchev's unilateral moratorium which made the United States appear intransigent. If Khruschhev had not stopped testing without waiting for a U.S. response, Eisenhower probably would have continued to drift along, even though he was personally opposed to nuclear testing. The Joint Chiefs, Deputy Secretary of Defense Quarles, and the AEC head Admiral Lewis Strauss strongly opposed a halt to U.S. nuclear testing, and it was easier for Eisenhower to defer to their wishes.[54]

Khrushchev picked up Eisenhower's signal and, on 9 May 1958, proposed that the United States and the Soviet Union designate experts who would begin a study of methods for detecting violations of a test ban, thus marking the first time that the Soviets had agreed to study an inspection system without prior agreement on disarmament. After a further exchange of letters, expert talks on verification opened in Geneva in early July 1958. When the Geneva experts' conference began, Khrushchev unexpectedly agreed also to technical talks concerning methods of preventing surprise attack. The Soviet leader told President Eisenhower that he hoped joint efforts by the two countries would lead to greater trust among the great powers.[55]

On 27 May, at a Warsaw Pact conference, the Soviet premier had announced that the Soviet Union would withdraw all troops from Romania and remove an additional division from Hungary; further, the East European countries would reduce their forces by 119,000 men.[56] As with Khrushchev's previous troop reductions, the United States viewed his actions as meaningless. The *New York Times* derided the announced troop cuts as empty gestures, because the withdrawals could not be independently verified and even if the Soviets did take out some troops, they could easily send them back in.[57]

The scientists who were meeting at Geneva to discuss methods of verification concluded on 21 August that a ban on tests over five kilotons could be verified by a network of from 160 to 170 land-based control posts supplemented by ten ships, air patrols, and mobile inspection teams.[58] This was the first time that negotiators from the East and West were able to agree on a control system to limit nuclear weapons. The following day, President Eisenhower proposed that the nuclear powers begin test ban negotiations in New York on 31 October and that they suspend nuclear testing for one year from that date. He offered to extend the moratorium, one year at a time, if an inspection system were established and there were satisfactory progress toward other arms control measures. Khrushchev quickly agreed to negotiations, if held in Geneva.[59]

Eisenhower's suspension of nuclear testing was contingent on Soviet reciprocity, and could be revoked if the Soviets resumed testing or if U.S. scientists insisted on the need for further tests. On the other hand, the initiative did increase U.S. vulnerability to Soviet cheating, since the Soviets could conduct small underground tests without being detected by U.S. seismographs. As *Time* magazine pointed out, the Eisenhower administration had done what it had always said it would never do, "stopped its own tests primarily on good faith, without any provision for inspection."[60] His agreement to an informal moratorium was risky because it reduced Soviet incentives to agree to a negotiated test ban with on-site inspection. The Soviets could delay the talks; meanwhile, world public opinion might make it impossible for the United States to resume testing.

Eisenhower had taken the initiative in proposing an uninspected test ban because he felt a need to take some action to prove his sincerity about controlling the arms race. When Prime Minister Macmillan of Britain warned against agreeing to suspend tests until an inspection system was at least partially in place, the president replied in an "unusually excited" telegram that "we are up against one of those moments that we regard as psychologically correct." The new head of the AEC, John McCone, recalled the president telling him that he had to "take some risk" in order to "do away with atmospheric testing, thus eliminating the health hazard, and at the same time . . . slow down the arms race."[61]

DEADLOCK ON SURPRISE ATTACK

In contrast to the Geneva experts on verification, the scientists who met from 10 November to 18 December 1958 to discuss methods of preventing surprise attack could not even agree on an agenda. In part, the deadlock reflected differing beliefs about the causes of surprise attack and, hence, about the proper remedies. The United States envisioned a massive, bolt-from-the-blue attack involving long-range missiles or manned aircraft carrying nuclear weapons, whereas the Soviets argued that a surprise attack would arise out of low-level skirmishes between large concentrations of troops in close proximity to each other. On the other hand, these diagnoses gave the two states a pretext to put forward their standard arms control proposals: the United States recommended aerial inspection, and the Soviets suggested mutual force reductions in Eastern Europe and a ban on nuclear weapons in Germany.[62]

Neither side trusted the other's motives in making such proposals. The Soviets feared that the United States would use aerial inspection for military intelligence,[63] while the Americans believed the Soviets were trying to lure the United States out of Europe, so that they could gain control of Germany through conventional forces or, at the least, split the NATO alliance. Soviet proposals for a nuclear-free zone showed their heightened anxiety about the prospect that the Germans would acquire nuclear weapons.

On 10 November, the same day that the surprise attack conference opened, Khrushchev claimed at a Soviet-Polish friendship meeting that Western militarization of the Federal Republic of Germany had invalidated the Potsdam agreements on occupation arrangements for Berlin, and that he planned to turn the Soviet sector of Berlin over to the East

[86]

Germans.[64] This speech was a trial balloon for a formal note on 27 November 1958 in which the Soviet government demanded that the West agree to make West Berlin a "free city" in six months. If not, the Soviet Union would unilaterally end four-power occupation rights and the West would have to make arrangements with the East German regime for access to West Berlin.[65]

His efforts to persuade Eisenhower to agree to a summit meeting having been stymied by Dulles, Khrushchev created a crisis to force the president to negotiate on the German question. As recently as August, Khrushchev had again requested a summit meeting, but the Eisenhower administration repeated the refrain that a meeting would have to be prepared in lower-level conferences. After a private Kremlin conference with the Soviet leader in December, Senator Hubert Humphrey reported that Khrushchev "very badly wants a summit conference and wants to be invited to the U.S."[66]

Almost immediately, Khrushchev began backing away from the six-month deadline and emphasizing his desire for negotiations. On 28 November, a Soviet embassy spokesman in East Berlin said that the six-month limit for negotiations was not rigid, that the Soviet Union would delay transfer of its Berlin responsibilities if the talks showed any hope of success. At an Albanian embassy reception on the following day, Khrushchev said that the Soviet government might not act unilaterally if the Western governments agreed to *begin* negotiations within six months.[67]

What Khrushchev hoped to achieve at a meeting with Eisenhower was at least tacit recognition of the division of Germany and a ban on West German nuclear weapons.[68] When asked why he had chosen to propose a solution to Berlin at that time, Khrushchev told the press that the Western powers had too long resisted recognizing the "reality" of two Germanys.[69] Khrushchev viewed West Berlin primarily as a lever with which to achieve other objectives rather than as an intrinsic prize.[70] True, the East German leader Walter Ulbricht had long pressured the Soviets to recognize GDR sovereignty over West Berlin. But the available archival evidence suggests that the ultimatum was Khrushchev's idea and that he failed even to consult with the East German Communists about his intentions. Certainly Khrushchev had to consider the international reaction to any seizure of West Berlin, and he was not about to risk war with the United States to save Ulbricht.[71]

Fear of German nuclear weapons, of course, strongly motivated Khrushchev to issue his Berlin ultimatum. In early November 1958, Khrushchev told Polish leader Władysław Gomułka that "the West will have to be forced to solve the German problem, to neutralize Germany's military potential. Berlin is our lever." Since December 1957, Khrushchev had repeatedly proposed the Rapacki Plan for a nuclear-free zone, but Eisenhower had refused to negotiate on German nuclear weapons. At his 27 November press conference, Khrushchev implied that he had sent the note because Eisenhower had refused to negotiate on a nuclear-free zone. As Kennan later commented, "We might well have foreseen that Moscow would be likely to reactivate [the Berlin] question following the North Atlantic Treaty Organization decision to introduce nuclear weapons and missiles into the continental NATO defenses, and particularly into the armed forces establishment of Western Germany."[72]

The Eisenhower administration regarded Soviet concerns as exaggerated because the United States had only promised to provide the Germans with nuclear-capable weapons. The December 1957 NATO agreement to establish stockpiles of tactical nuclear weapons gave custody of the warheads to the Americans, while the allies maintained the delivery systems. The Soviets had reason to believe, however, that the NATO decision was a first step toward sharing nuclear weapons with the West Germans. Beginning in 1956, Chancellor Adenauer had repeatedly requested that the United States provide the Bundeswehr with tactical nuclear weapons, arguing that West German military forces must be equipped with the most modern weapons and that the Germans should not have armaments inferior to those of the Americans. The West German government did not distinguish between delivery systems and warheads as it pressured the United States for tactical nuclear weapons. In November 1957, Secretary of Defense Neil McElroy stated publicly that the United States would seek IRBM bases in Europe and might give the allies control over the warheads as well as the missiles. A few days later, Secretary of State Dulles told a press conference that the United States planned to create nuclear stockpiles in Europe and wanted "a very considerable measure of allied participation" in handling the weapons.[73]

The Soviets expressed concern over Germany's nuclear armament in private as well as in public statements. In October 1958, the Soviet ambassador to West Germany, Andrei Smirnov, told Ulbricht that "since April of this year, the situation in West Germany has become much more complicated for us. . . . In West Germany they are continuing the arming of the Bundeswehr with nuclear weapons, which are now legal." Smirnov reported that "our general goal is to continue to exert a braking influence on the arming of the Bundeswehr."[74]

Yet U.S. officials did not understand how the Soviets might have felt threatened by nuclear armament of the Bundeswehr, thus showing the general psychological tendency to attribute the other side's actions to internal goals while failing to see how the other side could be responding to one's own moves. Apart from Ambassador to Moscow Llewellyn Thompson, Ambassador to Bonn David Bruce, and George Kennan, almost no one in the U.S. government or news media connected Khrushchev's November 1958 ultimatum with the Soviet fear of German nuclear weapons.[75]

Other analysts have suggested that Khrushchev's objectives were more far-reaching, that he believed Soviet progress in developing ICBMs had shifted the balance of power, justifying further changes in the status quo to the disadvantage of the West, including withdrawal of the United States from Europe. By threatening West Berlin, Khrushchev hoped to increase West German insecurity, undermine European confidence in U.S. commitments, and create the impression that communism was the wave of the future.[76] Shortly after his 10 November speech, Khrushchev announced for the first time that "production of the intercontinental ballistic rocket has been successfully set up."[77]

But it is difficult to reconcile this offensive interpretation of Khrushchev's motives with his ambitious goals for economic development, which required détente and cooperation with the West. To achieve his Seven-Year Plan objective of overtaking U.S. living standards in twelve years, outlined at the Twenty-first Party Congress in January 1959, Khrushchev needed a détente in order to justify directing investment away from the unproductive military sector and heavy industry to consumer goods. At the party congress, the Soviet leader argued that production of steel and guns could be reduced because the danger of war with the capitalist powers was receding. Khrushchev's declaration that the Soviet Union was no longer encircled by capitalism opened the way to accommodation with the West and relaxation of repression at home. After Zhukov's removal from power in the autumn of 1957, the military lost much of its influence over policy, and the new defense minister, Rodion Malinovsky, was not a member of the Presidium.[78]

Khrushchev's erratic behavior is difficult to place within a rational-decision calculus. Had Khrushchev been skillfully pursuing his objectives of détente and cooperation with the United States, one would have expected him to behave politely and firmly, not resort to emotional outbursts and threats. Khrushchev may have intended to use "missile diplomacy" to expand Soviet influence while permitting a reduction in defense spending and a diversion of resources from heavy industry to consumer goods.[79] If this was his objective, however, then it is hard to see why he so persistently pursued a summit meeting with Eisenhower, or why he swung from conciliation to confrontation.

Eisenhower was willing to consider making Berlin a "free city" so long as the access routes were under U.N. control and the arrangement applied to all of Berlin rather than just the Western sectors. But the Soviet proposal called for a withdrawal of Western occupation forces and for East German control over access. Deprived of its means of communication and defenses, dependent on the sufferance of the Soviet Union for access to the rest of the world, West Berlin could hardly be an "independent political unit," as the Soviets claimed.[80] Dulles advised Eisenhower that "paper agreements" were "no good," and that only American troops kept West Berlin free. Past Soviet harassment of traffic into the city did not leave the West much confidence that Moscow would resist the temptation to blackmail West Berlin. As E. W. Kenworthy of the *New York Times* put it, "What Moscow now asks is that West Berlin be left to the mercies of a regime that ten years ago was willing to use starvation as a means of breaking its hold to the West."[81]

Adding to the difficulty of devising a response, in early December 1958 Dulles had to be hospitalized for an inflammation of his intestine, and there were indications that his cancer had returned. Against his doctors' advice, Secretary of State Dulles flew to Paris for the annual meeting of the NATO Council.[82] There Dulles proposed that the allies negotiate their way out of the crisis, adding that the agenda should include the issues of German unity and free elections, where the West had a much stronger strategic and political position, in addition to the question of West Berlin. On 31 December the three Western powers sent separate communications stating that they were willing to negotiate—but only if Berlin were considered within the larger context of the German problem and only if there were no ultimatum.[83]

On 10 January, the Soviets proposed a conference to sign a peace treaty with the two German governments. Moreover, during his visit to the United States, Deputy Premier Anastas Mikoyan assured the American public that the Soviets were given to asking for more than they expected to get and that they had not intended any ultimatum.[84]

Dulles was surprisingly accommodative to this evidence of Soviet flexibility. At a 13 January press conference, Dulles conceded that "free elections" might not be the only method of reuniting Germany. A few weeks later, Dulles clarified the point and went even further, saying: "You can have a confederation which is, in fact, of very considerable progress toward reunification." The implication was that the United States might accept the Soviet proposal.[85]

How serious Dulles was about these concessions is another matter, because he and Eisenhower decided to use negotiations as a strategy for buying time until Khrushchev's deadline expired. At first, Khrushchev insisted on a summit meeting. He accused the West of trying to inveigle the Soviets in endless diplomatic talk, a "labyrinth of which the Soviet Union has had many years of experience." Then, on 2 March 1959, Khrushchev abruptly relieved the tension when he grudgingly accepted a foreign ministers' conference, tacitly withdrawing his deadline.[86]

Eisenhower regarded an invitation to Khrushchev to visit the United

States as America's "ace in the hole" for dealing with the Berlin crisis. The president doubted whether anything could be settled with Gromyko, who was "incapable of negotiating; he merely sits and glowers until he receives his orders from Moscow." For Dulles, though, the idea of a summit meeting was still anathema. Hospitalized for abdominal cancer, Dulles lamented to a State Department official on 13 March that a summit conference was probably inevitable even though he had been fighting one off for a year and a half and thought it would be nothing but disastrous. On another occasion, Dulles asked: "How do you justify going to another Summit when all the former pledges have been violated—how can we rely any more surely on these?" From Walter Reed Hospital on 20 March, an emaciated Dulles vigorously admonished Eisenhower and Macmillan against a summit meeting unless the Soviets paid a reasonable price in "deeds not words," as in 1955 when they had signed the Austrian State Treaty.[87]

Dulles advised against agreeing to the Rapacki Plan or any "thinning out" of foreign troops in Europe because the principal strength of the Western allies lay in the forward position of German, British, and U.S. forces, and there was no very good alternative position in Europe where these could be shifted, especially given General Charles de Gaulle's attitude. The Soviets could put their troops anywhere in the area they dominated. President Eisenhower expressed agreement, but pointed out that "there might possibly be some advantages in the thinning-out program which involved inspections and controls of the kind we had been trying to get in various aspects of our disarmament talks."[88]

A U.S. Reversal and an Inadvertent Invitation

The United States had reneged on its earlier agreements in the Geneva test ban negotiations, resulting in a new deadlock. On 5 January 1959, the U.S. representative at the test ban talks, James Wadsworth, had informed the Soviet negotiator Semen Tsarapkin that the most recent U.S. test series showed that it would be more difficult to discriminate between earthquakes and underground explosions than the Geneva experts had realized and, consequently, that the United States would require ten times as many on-site inspections, between 200 and 1,000 a year, or at least 500 control stations in order to maintain the ability to verify an explosion down to five kilotons.[89]

This must have appeared to the Soviets as only the most recent U.S. reversal. In May 1955, when the Soviets accepted a long-standing U.S. request for on-site inspection, the United States had refused to negotiate on their proposal, but substituted Open Skies, an even more intrusive scheme. In 1957, when the Soviets again accepted the principle of on-site inspection to control a test ban, Eisenhower recalled his overeager disarmament representative Harold Stassen. Mikoyan told Dulles that the Soviets were "generally not too suspicious" but did draw doubts from certain facts. Moscow had been apprehensive about the earlier test ban talks, but scientists had been able to reach agreement. Now, after they had been talking for several months, suddenly American scientists came up with a new discovery that underground tests could not be detected. Mikoyan said that the Soviets had the "impression that if this difficulty were overcome, a new one would be put up."[90]

Their suspicions aroused, Soviet negotiators refused even to consider the new scientific data. Khrushchev later complained to W. Averell Harriman that "we do not believe that the U.S. is taking a serious attitude toward the control of nuclear weapons."[91] For his part, Eisenhower was troubled by the Soviets' continuing insistence on having a veto over all phases of the inspections. If the president had been mainly concerned to alleviate popular concern over fallout, he could have done so merely by testing underground. But, of course, Eisenhower did not just want to suspend atmospheric testing, although he could have done so without having to deal with the Soviets: he wanted an agreement with the Soviets which both sides could verify that the other was observing, as a way of building trust.[92] President Eisenhower said that "anything we and the Soviet can do to build confidence in each other's word is a step forward."[93]

Ike searched for ways to accommodate U.S. as well as Soviet preferences. On 25 February, the president commented to his scientific adviser, James R. Killian, that because Soviet tests in the air and large underground tests could be monitored with control posts, the idea of mobile inspection teams was rendered "rather secondary in importance." The president therefore considered excluding tests below ten kilotons from the test ban agreement.[94] Had Eisenhower proposed a threshold test ban, as he did one year later, the United States and the Soviet Union might have reached an agreement.

New evidence about the risk of Soviet cheating, however, caused Eisenhower to put aside the idea of a threshold ban. In mid-March, a scientific advisory panel reported to Eisenhower that the Soviets could "decouple" a nuclear explosion by testing within a large cavity so that the signal was reduced tenfold. Thus, for example, the United States might believe that the Soviets had exploded only a five-kiloton device when in reality they had tested a fifty-kiloton bomb. Killian advised Eisenhower that this "loophole" invalidated the concept of a threshold test ban and that they should retreat to an agreement suspending atmospheric testing only.[95]

[92]

On 13 April, Eisenhower proposed to Khrushchev that they prohibit nuclear tests in the atmosphere as a first step while negotiators continued to work out the details of a treaty banning underground and space tests.[96] Khrushchev objected that a partial test ban would not "prevent the creation of new and more destructive types of nuclear weapons." He wanted to continue to try for a comprehensive test ban, and he suggested that they adopt Prime Minister Macmillan's idea of an annual quota on the number of inspections. The Soviet representative at the Geneva negotiations, Semen Tsarapkin, implied that the Soviets would drop their demand for a veto over on-site inspections if Eisenhower accepted the quota proposal.[97]

In a letter to Khrushchev on 5 May 1959, Eisenhower offered to have U.S. representatives in Geneva explore the plan for a predetermined number of inspections. The president told representatives from AEC, State, and Defense that if the Soviets gave up the veto and the United States was able to install a control system on Soviet territory, "we would then be at something that had to be accepted."[98]

The foreign ministers of France, Britain, the United States, and the Soviet Union met in Geneva from 11 May to 5 August to discuss Berlin and the German question. Christian Herter, who had replaced Dulles as secretary of state, proposed the old formula of German reunification through free elections and alignment with NATO. The only novel feature of the Herter Plan was that a "mixed German committee" would draft an election law, a gesture toward the Soviet position that the Germans should be in charge of their reunification.[99] On 16 May, speaking from Moscow, Khrushchev summarily rejected the Herter Plan. Eisenhower "racked his head" to think of something he could offer Khrushchev that would not appear to be a concession but that could lead to progress justifying a summit.[100]

On 7 July, Khrushchev signaled the president that he was still interested in a summit meeting. The Soviet leader told a visiting group of American governors that he would very much like to visit the United States and that he thought a visit by Eisenhower to the Soviet Union would be very beneficial for relations between both countries. Eisenhower was caught off guard when questioned about Khrushchev's statement at a press conference, but he later spoke with Secretary Herter and commented that the Soviet leader's suggestion might be just what was needed to break the "logjam" at Geneva. Eisenhower thought he might invite Khrushchev for a day's talks after the Soviet leader visited the Soviet exhibition in New York; the president could then visit the U.S. exhibit in Moscow. Instead of the president's plan for a quick and informal meeting not tied to results at Geneva, the State Department advised Eisenhower to invite Khrushchev to bilateral talks at Camp David, followed by a four-power summit meeting at Quebec if there were progress in the Berlin negotiations.[101] Eisenhower asked Undersecretary of State Robert Murphy to give the note of invitation to Soviet Deputy Premier Frol R. Kozlov, who was visiting New York. Murphy reported that it had "quite an impact."[102]

The impact of the invitation was enhanced because it was unconditional. Murphy had not understood that a Khrushchev-Eisenhower meeting should be contingent on results in the Berlin negotiations, and he extended to Khrushchev an unqualified invitation to visit the United States. Eisenhower was "staggered" by the prospect of Khrushchev's visit. He just did not see how he could entertain Khrushchev for ten days in the United States if the Geneva negotiations had broken down.[103]

"I must say, I couldn't believe my eyes," Khrushchev recalled. "We had no reason to expect such an invitation—not then, or ever for that matter. Our relations had been extremely strained." Khrushchev viewed the invitation as a symbol that the United States recognized the USSR as an equal with whom solutions to international problems must be sought. The Soviet leader made an unusually conciliatory speech in which he omitted his threat of a separate peace treaty with the GDR and expressed optimism about finding solutions at the Geneva foreign ministers' conference that would preserve the prestige of the participant states. Khrushchev gave special praise to Eisenhower, saying that as a former general the president knew firsthand what war was really like, and that he had "honorably fulfilled all conditions of agreement with us" as commander of Allied forces during World War II.[104]

On 11 August 1959, Khrushchev pledged that the USSR would not be the first nation to resume testing nuclear weapons. Because of Khrushchev's promise, Eisenhower felt he could not break the moratorium without incurring world condemnation. Against the "wild" opposition of the Defense Department and the AEC, both of which wanted to resume underground testing, the State Department announced on 26 August that President Eisenhower had decided to extend the moratorium until the end of the calendar year, rather than until 31 October.[105]

The president's invitation to Khrushchev was a political gamble. For Eisenhower had done what he had previously said he would never do— negotiate under threat of an ultimatum, without "progress" at lower levels of negotiation that held promise for a successful summit. Even Americans who favored Khrushchev's visit as a tension-reducing measure worried that the Soviet leader had gotten what he wanted out of the Berlin crisis without paying any price. If the visit failed or if Khrushchev became more belligerent, the president and his party would be charged with being "soft on communism" or with having perpetrated "another Munich."[106] Senator Stuart Symington (D–Mo.) observed that

Congress would have impeached Harry Truman if he had dared invite Khrushchev to a white-tie dinner at the White House. Senator Homer E. Capehart (R–Ind.) observed that "it looks like we're again being taken in by the Russians." Representative Walter H. Judd (R–Minn.) charged that a visit by Khrushchev would be "a major advance for him in his relentless political offensive to soften up the West preparatory to the kill."[107]

Businessmen, labor leaders, and clergy objected that a visit from Khrushchev would be dangerous. Richard Cardinal Cushing, the Roman Catholic archbishop of Boston, warned that "inviting Khrushchev here is like opening our frontiers to the enemy in a military war." Without mentioning Khrushchev by name, Archbishop Francis Cardinal Spellman of New York warned that some Americans were "deaf to all save the husky voice of the sorcerer, as glibly he speaks of 'peaceful coexistence,' and 'competition in consumer goods.' " During Khrushchev's visit, more than two thousand anticommunists led by William F. Buckley Jr. held a protest rally at Carnegie Hall at which they wore black armbands as symbols of mourning for the victims of communism.[108]

During their first of two days of talks in Washington, 15–16 September, Khrushchev and Eisenhower agreed that the main thing was to establish trust. The question was, Eisenhower said, how could they start to clear away the underbrush of confusion and mutual mistrust and begin to solve some of the problems between them?[109]

Khrushchev explained that the Soviets were not interested in Berlin as such, but rather in the conclusion of a peace treaty that would also settle the status of West Berlin. The Soviet leader explained that if they "could work out common language recognizing the fact of the existence of two German states and confirming that neither side would try to bring about a socialist or a capitalist solution by force," they could remove the danger from the situation. American sympathies lay with West Germany and the system there, Soviet sympathies with East Germany and the system prevailing on that side. They might as well recognize that fact. That did not mean that the United States would accord juridical recognition to the GDR, he continued, but merely accept the state of fact.[110]

Neither entirely believed the other. "Those sweet words—but he won't change his mind about anything," Eisenhower later complained to his secretary, Ann Whitman. Khrushchev, for his part, accused Eisenhower of being able with a "wink" to determine what kind of reception he would receive from the American people. Eisenhower tried to explain to the Soviet leader how impossible that was.[111]

During his tour around the country, Khrushchev learned for himself that the United States was not monolithic and that the president did not control public opinion. The Soviet leader became progressively disappointed and aggrieved by the heckling and hostility he received during his trip around the country. The nadir was Los Angeles, where the Mayor Norris Poulson gave Khrushchev a one-line greeting at the airport; crowds along Khrushchev's route through the city, which had not been announced in advance, were disappointingly sparse; Khrushchev was subjected to a "tasteless" display of the cancan dance at a Hollywood movie lot; the Soviet premier was not allowed to visit Disneyland because local police could not guarantee his security; and Mayor Poulson deliberately baited Khrushchev by taking his famous "We will bury you" remark out of context at a dinner in the Soviet leader's honor. Khrushchev even threatened to pull out of the tour and never return to the United States.[112]

Khrushchev inferred that the consistently hostile reaction he was receiving from the American people was no coincidence. Gromyko complained to Ambassador Henry Cabot Lodge, who accompanied Khrushchev on his visit, that "in almost every place questions are being raised which . . . should not be raised if you are guided by good intentions" and these questions did not seem "fortuitous." Lodge explained that the cause of the trouble was an ambitious local politician who wanted to use Khrushchev's visit to get into the limelight.[113]

The following day, Khrushchev told Lodge that now he was beginning to understand the problems the president had in trying to improve relations with the Soviet Union. He was "surrounded by certain elements who wanted to prevent a normalization of relations with the Soviet Union." When he returned home, the Soviet premier announced that Eisenhower "sincerely wanted to liquidate the 'cold war' and to improve relations between our two great countries." Khrushchev described American ruling circles as divided between "madmen and realists," and claimed that the "realists" were now gaining the upper hand.[114]

In the concluding round of talks at Camp David, the two men tried to resolve the Berlin crisis. Eisenhower refused to negotiate under the gun of an ultimatum, whereas Khrushchev suspected that Adenauer would prolong negotiations for years unless there were some deadline. The two men crafted a compromise whereby Eisenhower would make a public statement that the Berlin negotiations should not be prolonged indefinitely, but "there would be no fixed time limit on them," and then Khrushchev would confirm the statement.[115]

The removal of Khrushchev's ultimatum met Eisenhower's earlier requirement for "progress" as a condition for a summit meeting, and so the president announced that he would be willing to attend a meeting at the "highest level." In late 1959, the United States, Britain, France, and the Soviet Union agreed to hold a heads-of-government conference at Paris in mid-May 1960, the first of a series of meetings.[116]

FROM TROOP REDUCTIONS TO THRESHOLD TEST BAN

In his speech to the Supreme Soviet on 14 January 1960, Khrushchev announced that Soviet troops would be cut by 1.2 million, or about one-third, including the demobilization of 250,000 officers. Even worse from the standpoint of the military, Khrushchev proclaimed a new strategic doctrine which consigned Soviet conventional forces to obsolescence, upset institutional empires, ended careers, and confined the military to a rigid doctrine formulated by political outsiders.[117]

But these troop reductions did not undermine Western suspicions because U.S. officials did not believe that the demobilization decreased Soviet military power. The troop cuts could have been part of a program of military modernization, for example. Indeed, Khrushchev had minimized the significance of his own concession when he said that large conventional forces were no longer necessary in the nuclear era. In his speech to the Supreme Soviet, Khrushchev declared that because the power of a country was determined not by the number of men in arms but by its total firepower and the quality of its delivery systems, the Soviet Union could afford to reduce its army, surface navy, and bomber fleets.[118] In order to justify the unilateral troop cuts, Khrushchev claimed that the Soviet Union had enough nuclear weapons and rockets to "literally wipe from the face of the earth the country or countries that attacked us." This statement was deceptive, because the Soviets probably did not have more than a handful of ICBMs.[119]

Although Eisenhower did not reciprocate Khrushchev's bold troop reductions, he did try to accommodate the Soviet leader's desire for a comprehensive test ban while satisfying American concerns about Soviet cheating. On 11 February 1960, Eisenhower proposed that they halt tests in the atmosphere, the oceans, and outer space as well as all underground tests registering above 4.75 on the Richter scale. At the Geneva test ban negotiations, the U.S. representative said that the United States was prepared to accept a fixed quota of on-site inspections for seismic signals under the threshold, about twenty inspections a year in the Soviet Union.[120]

Ambassador Thompson had advised Eisenhower that Khrushchev would take it pretty hard if the president retreated to an atmospheric ban, because the Soviet leader's main objective was to prevent China and West Germany from acquiring nuclear weapons, and a resumption of underground testing would enable those two countries to develop a nuclear capability. In early November 1959, Eisenhower had decided to continue pursuing a comprehensive test ban, despite the difficulty of developing a monitoring system for small underground tests, a decision that his science adviser George Kistiakowsky called a "tremendous change from the attitude which prevailed recently that really all we can do is to seek disengagement from the comprehensive treaty concept and try for an atmospheric ban." The president had received no new scientific evidence justifying an effort to limit underground testing. Indeed, if the decoupling theory was valid, no verification system would have been adequate to prevent the Soviets from cheating on a comprehensive test ban.[121]

On 19 March 1960, the Soviets accepted Eisenhower's proposal for a threshold ban and proposed that the superpowers enter into a voluntary moratorium on small tests below the threshold of 4.75, a moratorium that would be based solely on good faith. The Soviet negotiator (Tsarapkin) promised that if the United States accepted their offer, a test ban treaty could be signed within a month. These were considerable concessions for the Soviets. They had agreed to a supervised ban on tests in the atmosphere and on larger underground tests, and that meant having American inspectors on their territory. The Soviets also had accepted the concept of a threshold, tacitly admitting for the first time that some underground explosions could not be readily detected and identified by national means.[122]

Anxious to make some small agreement on the arms race, Eisenhower decided at a 24 March meeting with his principal test ban advisers to accept the Soviet proposal, including the uninspected moratorium, "as otherwise all hope of relaxing the cold war would be gone." He sharply rejected McCone's arguments that the Soviets would cheat, and he became angry when the AEC head intimated that the moratorium was a surrender of U.S. policy. The president conceded that the United States would be accepting disarmament without inspection, but he pointed out that the two countries—by pronouncement alone—had already stopped testing for a year and a half.[123]

Khrushchev's initiatives on the test ban had paid off. Just a year before, Eisenhower had rejected the idea of a comprehensive test ban, because the Soviets might be able to conceal tests within large underground caverns. Khrushchev's acceptance of on-site inspection as well as his observance of the voluntary moratorium had convinced Eisenhower that the Soviets were serious about reaching a test ban. Kistiakowsky noted with wonder in his diary that since late July 1959 "a tremendous change" had taken place in the administration's attitude toward a test ban.[124] At a press conference, Eisenhower insisted that "all the signs are that the Soviets do want a degree of disarmament, and they want to stop testing. That looks to me to be more or less proved." He wrote to de Gaulle and Macmillan that the Soviets wanted to reduce their military burdens and also to prevent the Chinese from acquiring their own bomb.[125]

Indeed, as Eisenhower speculated, the Soviet leader did want an agreement that would lower tensions and allow him to divert resources from defense to consumer goods. In addition, he needed some foreign policy achievement to justify his drive for a summit conference and his plans to improve Soviet living standards. Accordingly, Khrushchev began a campaign at home to build domestic support for a test ban. At a March 1960 press conference in Paris, Khrushchev assigned a priority to disarmament even higher than that of resolving the Berlin question. Remaining differences on the test ban, said Khrushchev, had to do with an "insignificant range of problems." Back in the Soviet Union, Khrushchev predicted that a test ban agreement would be signed "in the nearest future."[126]

The president had also decided to give higher priority to a test ban. Eisenhower agreed with Ambassador Thompson that Berlin was "too hard a nut to crack" and urged that "our real effort should go into making some meaningful move toward disarmament." The president believed that progress in disarmament, trade, and exchanges would help in solving harder problems such as Berlin. The best that Eisenhower hoped to achieve on Berlin was an interim arrangement, whereby the Soviets would promise not to take unilateral action against West Berlin for a period of, say, two years while negotiations on Germany's status were conducted.[127]

On the threshold test ban, two major issues remained to be settled: the length of time for the moratorium, and the number of on-site inspections to investigate suspicious seismic events above 4.75 on the Richter scale.[128] Eisenhower and Khrushchev might have been able to make major progress toward deciding these at the Paris summit. The president told Secretary of State Herter that he would probably settle the issue of the quota with Khrushchev at Paris, tacitly admitting that the number of inspections was a political issue, not a technical one. After his conversations with Eisenhower at Camp David, Prime Minister Macmillan wrote in his diary on 29 March that the president was "really keen" on a nuclear test ban "and—although he has not said much about it yet—would accept further concessions in the course of negotiation to get it." During his visit with de Gaulle, Eisenhower constantly returned to the subject of the forthcoming summit conference. "What a splendid exit it would be for me to end up, without any sacrifice of principle, with an agreement between East and West!" the president declared.[129]

Both Eisenhower and Khrushchev were personally committed to achieving an enduring respite in the Cold War, small agreements that could build trust, and a lessening of the pace of the arms race. Both wanted to stabilize Europe and divert unproductive arms expenditures into improving domestic well-being.[130]

Eisenhower's ambivalence about Khrushchev's intentions resurfaced, however, when the president approved a U-2 espionage flight over Russia just two weeks before the Paris summit. Since the inception of the U-2 program in 1956, Eisenhower had authorized each flight, trying to balance the intelligence gained against the provocation it caused the Soviet Union.[131] In February 1960, Eisenhower told his advisers that he had one "tremendous asset" in a summit meeting—his "reputation for honesty." He warned that "if one of these aircraft were lost when we are engaged in apparently sincere deliberations, it could be put on display in Moscow and ruin [his] effectiveness."[132]

Still, Eisenhower went against his own instincts. The "missile gap" controversy was in full swing. Unwilling to reveal the secret U-2 flights to the American people, Eisenhower was under attack from newspaper columnists and Democrats in Congress for neglecting the country's defenses and for allowing the U.S. deterrent to be jeopardized by Soviet missiles. In the face of Khrushchev's boasts about Soviet missile capabilities, the CIA had not been able to discover a single ICBM site. Moreover, owing to cloud cover, limited pilot endurance, and the risks of penetrating too far into Soviet airspace, the U-2s had not been able to cover all Soviet territory.[133]

In late March, Allen Dulles and Richard Bissell, deputy director of the CIA, requested a U-2 flight, with the aim of checking new evidence from human agents and from signal intelligence that the Soviets might be building ICBMs. With Eisenhower's approval, the U-2 flew into Soviet airspace on 9 April.[134] Early in April, Dulles and Bissell asked Eisenhower to authorize another flight, focusing on a suspected ICBM site at Plesetsk. The CIA argued that the angle of light in the northern latitudes was critical for aerial photography, and that the months from April to July offered the best light for photographing Plesetsk. If the CIA waited until July to conduct the flight, and there was cloud cover, they might not be able to take clear pictures of the suspected site until April 1961, when it might be camouflaged.[135]

Eisenhower approved the CIA's request for another U-2 flight, provided it was carried out before 1 May, to avoid provoking the Soviets just before the summit. Bad weather and clouds over Russia, however, made it impossible to conduct the U-2 flight until 1 May.[136]

Why did Eisenhower approve the CIA request for another U-2 flight so close to the summit, particularly given his earlier restraint during the Berlin crises and the Camp David meeting? For more than two years, the Soviets had not complained about the U-2 intrusions. The president and his advisers interpreted Khrushchev's failure to protest the 9 April flight as tacit acquiescence, "virtually inviting us to repeat the sortie."[137] Instead, the fact was, the Soviets did not want to admit that they were unable to shoot down the U-2, which flew at an altitude of 70,000 feet.[138]

Then, too, if Khrushchev had not made exaggerated claims about Soviet missile capabilities, Eisenhower might not have felt pressured to acquire additional intelligence information on the eve of a summit. The U-2 flights enabled Eisenhower to resist demands within his administration and in Congress for increased defense spending. Khrushchev's alternation of belligerent threats with offers of a U.S.-Soviet condominium may have concealed Soviet weakness and forced the United States to negotiate, but it did not inspire trust among Western audiences, and trust was essential for negotiations to prove fruitful.

When he announced on 5 May that the plane had been shot down, Khrushchev did not blame the president: the Soviet leader wanted to rescue his détente policy. "I do not doubt President Eisenhower's sincere desire for peace," Khrushchev declared. On 7 May, Khrushchev continued in this vein: "I am quite willing to assume that the President did not know that a plane had been sent over Soviet territory and had not returned." Two days later, he attributed the incident to an "aggressive military clique." Several months later, the Soviet leader told Ambassador Thompson that he "had tried to leave [a] way out for [the] President to disavow [the] U-2 flight but he did not do so." Khrushchev explained that "it was in our interests to say that undisciplined people in the American intelligence organization, rather than the president, were responsible . . . [because] as long as President Eisenhower was dissociated from the U-2 affair, we could continue our policy of strengthening Soviet-US relations."[139]

Khrushchev did not understand that Eisenhower could not claim the U-2 flights took place without his knowledge, because that would suggest that the president was not in control of his intelligence services. On 11 May, Eisenhower took personal responsibility for the overflights. Khrushchev made Eisenhower's embarrassment worse, however, by deliberately concealing that the Soviets had captured the pilot so that he might catch the president in a lie. Different agencies of the U.S. government issued clumsy cover stories about a weather plane straying over Turkey, stories that Khrushchev gleefully exposed.[140]

The president's acknowledgment of his role in the U-2 incident not only cast a blow against Khrushchev's credibility, but undermined the Soviet premier's policy of seeking a détente with the United States. Khrushchev had praised Eisenhower extravagantly as a "sincere lover of peace." The U-2 incident gave Khrushchev's political opponents at home and in China a pretext for attacking the Soviet leader's policy of détente as naive and misguided. At the end of May, Marshal Malinovsky warned that "one should not trust the words of the imperialists, sweet as they may be. The latest lesson of Camp David is too clear to allow us to forget history."[141]

At the first plenary meeting in Paris on 16 May, Khrushchev demanded that Eisenhower publicly denounce the U-2 flights, renounce similar actions in the future, and punish those responsible. He argued that the summit conference should be postponed six months, until after the U.S. presidential elections. President Eisenhower would no longer be welcome in the Soviet Union. Anatoly Dobrynin recalls that while Khrushchev had advance authorization from the Presidium to criticize Eisenhower for the flights, he did not have permission to demand a personal apology.[142] Eisenhower said that he would not conduct further espionage flights, but he refused to apologize.[143]

According to Dobrynin, who was counselor to the Soviet delegation, Khrushchev held a conference with the other Soviet members that night to discuss whether or not to continue the summit. Khrushchev excitedly claimed that the president's close associates, if not the president himself, had intended to humiliate him, personally and as the head of the Soviet government, by sending planes across Soviet territory to show the world that he could not protect his country's borders. Khrushchev did not recognize that his rhetoric about rockets combined with Soviet secrecy placed Eisenhower in a position where it was necessary for him to take extraordinary measures to find out what the Soviets had in the way of ICBMs. Marshal Malinovsky supported Khrushchev. Gromyko, on the other hand, took a surprisingly moderate position, in view of his subsequent reputation in the United States as a conservative. The Soviet foreign minister agreed with Khrushchev that "Eisenhower has to be taught a good lesson," but he wanted to find some way to save the summit conference.[144] On 17 May, Khrushchev stayed away from the plenary sessions, hoping that Eisenhower would apologize. The following day, Khrushchev delivered an emotional tirade against the president at a press conference.[145]

Some scholars have argued that Khrushchev used the U-2 incident as a pretext to disrupt the summit because he knew that an agreement on Berlin was unlikely. Others have argued that he was under pressure from Soviet hard-liners, or that he succumbed to Chinese criticism.[146]

According to press reports of the December 1959 summit between Eisenhower, Macmillan, de Gaulle, and Adenauer, the allied leaders had decided to reintroduce their June 1959 plan for German reunification at the Paris conference in May 1960. Adenauer had supposedly persuaded Eisenhower to withdraw previous concessions made by the West at the Geneva negotiations on Berlin. Khrushchev, then, may have received some intelligence from the KGB indicating that Eisenhower had nothing new to offer the Soviets on Germany and planned to support Adenauer's position.[147] Even if they did not reach agreement on Berlin, though, Khrushchev and Eisenhower could have cleared away remaining obstacles to a threshold test ban treaty. Khrushchev had vigorously pursued a test ban despite having lukewarm support, at best, from nuclear scientists and the military.[148]

The argument that Khrushchev was experiencing severe domestic political troubles is based on changes in personnel that occurred in May 1960. A 4 May plenum reduced the size of the Central Committee Secretariat (which Khrushchev had packed with supporters) by half and demoted several who were closely identified with Khrushchev. The hard-liner Frol Kozlov replaced Khrushchev's protégé A. I. Kirichenko as the second most influential man in the Secretariat after Khrushchev.[149]

More recent evidence, however, suggests that Khrushchev was still in charge, although he was weakened by the U-2 incident. The May 1960 changes had been planned in advance, and involved the replacement of some of Khrushchev's loyal clients with more competent officials, a sign of the Soviet leader's greater confidence. Khrushchev enjoyed good relations with Kozlov, despite the latter's more conservative orientation. Also, Khrushchev was the only leader who had positions on all three major executive bodies below the Presidium: the Council of Ministers, the Secretariat, and the Central Committee Bureau for the Russian Federation.[150] Another indication of Khrushchev's power is that at the 5 May Supreme Soviet session at which he announced the downing of the U-2, the Soviet leader maintained his policies of détente, defense cuts, and more consumer goods. Nor did the U-2 incident have an immediate effect on U.S.-Soviet relations. On 4 May, for example, *Pravda* reported that Marshal Konstantin Vershinin, commander of the Soviet air force, would arrive in Washington in ten days. At the Geneva test ban talks, moreover, the Soviets cordially agreed on 11 May to participate in a joint research program on ways to monitor small underground tests.[151]

It is also doubtful that Khrushchev reverted to Cold War policies in order to accommodate the more militant Chinese. After the U-2 incident, Khrushchev circulated a lengthy attack against the Chinese Communists at the Bucharest Conference of Communist Parties, recalled Soviet specialists from China, cut Soviet trade with China, and tried to overthrow the Chinese-backed Albanian leadership. Khrushchev had an interest in preventing any Sino-Soviet rapprochement, because the hard-line Chinese would certainly try to block his efforts at détente and economic reform.[152]

According to Dobrynin, who was part of the delegation, Khrushchev did not come to Paris with the intention of breaking up the summit. The Soviet delegation brought with it detailed proposals for every item on the agenda, which had already been approved by the Presidium. In short, the last Big Four summit in history, Dobrynin writes, was "a summit of lost opportunities." Khrushchev's former speechwriter Fedor Burlatsky, who also participated in drafting the Soviet negotiating positions, confirms that the Soviet delegation brought a "whole package of important proposals." Burlatsky describes the Paris summit as a "graveyard of lost opportunities."[153]

Available evidence suggests that Khrushchev blundered badly in insisting on an apology from Eisenhower at the Paris summit. The Soviet leader had placed himself in an untenable position where he could not back down without appearing weak to hard-liners in the Soviet Union. Then, too, Khrushchev felt personally betrayed by Eisenhower, and had decided to wait for the next president. The shift was immediately apparent in the test ban negotiations as the Soviets retracted provisions that they had previously accepted, such as a program for cooperative seismic research in order to devise improved methods of verification.[154]

Eisenhower's depression after the collapse of the Paris summit should lay to rest any suspicion that the president had approved the U-2 flight because he anticipated that the meeting would fail. The president emotionally confided to Kistiakowsky that he had concentrated his efforts over the past few years on ending the Cold War and that he had been making big progress until the "stupid U-2 mess" ruined all his efforts. Very sadly Eisenhower remarked that he "saw nothing worthwhile left for him to do now until the end of his presidency."[155]

Despite their shared interest in stabilizing Europe and halting the arms race, Eisenhower and Khrushchev failed to reach a modus vivendi concerning either Germany or a test ban. Mutual mistrust had been exacerbated by inept signaling. Eisenhower did not understand how the Soviets felt threatened by impending German nuclear rearmament and by the refugee crisis in the GDR. The president refused even to consider partial arms control measures such as a nuclear-free zone in Central Europe and disengagement, and Khrushchev did nothing that would convince the United States that his offers were genuine. That the Soviet leader oscillated between heart-felt expressions of his desire for peace and boasts about Soviet nuclear capabilities increased Western distrust of his motives and confirmed suspicions that his peace offensive was a devious strategy to undermine the safety and cohesion of the United States and its allies.

If Eisenhower had agreed to a summit meeting in 1958 to discuss the Rapacki Plan for a nuclear-free zone, Khrushchev might not have provoked the Berlin crisis, which led to spiraling tensions. The East German refugee crisis was made more acute by Khrushchev's ultimatum.[156] A summit meeting would have supported Khrushchev's argument that the relaxation of tensions justified further Soviet defense cuts and more production of consumer goods. Confronted with Dulles's diplomatic casuistry and stalling, Khrushchev resorted to threats to bring Eisenhower to a summit, ultimately succeeding.

The failure of Eisenhower and Khrushchev to conclude a threshold test ban cannot be blamed on superpower competition for military superiority. The president maintained a policy of what would later be called "sufficiency," the idea that having more weapons than the other side served no purpose once each had enough survivable weapons to retaliate after a first strike.[157] Further, Khrushchev enacted and observed a testing moratorium with the United States even though the Soviets were behind in nuclear weapons technology.

Would a more consistent Soviet conciliatory line, backed up with "deeds," have elicited a more forthcoming response from the United States with respect to German nuclear weapons and disengagement? In contrast to his erratic behavior vis-à-vis Germany, Khrushchev steadily pursued a test ban (although the Soviets did waffle on the question of having a veto over on-site inspection) and here the Soviet leader enjoyed much greater success. It is important to note, however, that the level of trust required for agreement on a test ban was lower than that needed for an agreement on Germany. That a test ban could be monitored with relative ease by each side and would not alter the strategic balance meant that the risks associated with a test ban agreement were much less than those associated with arms control measures relating to Germany, the center of Europe. Perhaps it is unrealistic to expect Eisenhower to have persuaded Adenauer to accept U.S. recognition of a divided Germany in return for guaranteed Western access to Berlin.

In the last year of his presidency, Eisenhower became more confident about Khrushchev's sincerity, partly because of his conversations with the Soviet leader but also because of the Soviet leader's initiatives concerning the test ban. In turn, Khrushchev's experience with hard-liners and hecklers during his visit to the United States persuaded him that Eisenhower was pursuing cooperation with the Soviet Union against strong anticommunist sentiment. If they had met in Paris under different circumstances, the two leaders might have surmounted the remaining obstacles to a threshold test ban. Such a test ban would not have ended the nuclear arms race, of course, because small underground testing would have been permitted. And it is doubtful that the Soviets would have agreed to strategic arms limitations while they were in a position of nuclear inferiority and vulnerability. As the first major U.S.-Soviet agreement, however, a threshold test ban would have given both sides an opportunity to prove that they were serious about arms control and would comply with an agreement. A threshold test ban would have built greater mutual trust and could have led to more significant agreements, such as a comprehensive test ban, disengagement, or a nuclear-free zone. Khrushchev's deliberate campaign of deception about Soviet ICBM capabilities put pressure on Eisenhower to increase defense spending and, ultimately, led the president to act against his better judgment by approving a U-2 flight on the eve of the Paris summit.

[4]

JFK, Khrushchev, and
the German Question

Despite lengthy negotiations, John F. Kennedy and Nikita S. Khrushchev failed to reach an agreement either on Berlin or on a comprehensive test ban. The Berlin Wall stabilized the division of Europe, but at the price of brutally separating German families and isolating East Germany from any contact with the West. Both Kennedy and Khrushchev would have preferred to recognize the division of Germany. Although they reached an agreement banning atmospheric testing, the exclusion of underground testing from the test ban allowed a continuation of the race to develop more-sophisticated, deadlier weapons.

Historians have offered contrasting explanations for these diplomatic failures. According to orthodox historians, Khrushchev initially underestimated Kennedy's determination, partly because of the president's youth and his indecisiveness at the Bay of Pigs. Kennedy masterfully combined force and diplomacy, demonstrating his resolve through such measures as increasing U.S. conventional forces, calling up the reserves, and carrying out military force demonstrations while at the same time holding out his hand to Khrushchev with the offer of constructive negotiations. When the United States and Soviet Union finally learned to cooperate in 1963, after undergoing trial by fire in the Cuban missile crisis, the détente process was prematurely and tragically cut short by Kennedy's death. Still, there were limits to how far the U.S.-Soviet détente could extend, given Khrushchev's commitment to promoting communism and his unwillingness to tolerate a pluralism of ideas.[1] New evidence from the former Soviet Union, however, suggests that while Khrushchev did indeed initially underestimate Kennedy's will and intelligence, the Soviet leader was trying desperately to bolster the faltering East German regime and win recognition of the Soviet Union's status as a superpower.[2] If so, if Khrushchev did not intend to drive the United States out of West Berlin or Europe, then Kennedy's refusal to negotiate before carrying out military preparations was an ineffective strategy, because it provoked Khrushchev to take reciprocal action, leading to a spiral of conflict.

Revisionist historians blame Kennedy for missed diplomatic opportunities, charging him with increasing the defense budget to eliminate a nonexistent missile gap, stimulating fallout shelter panic in the United States, using martial rhetoric, and gratuitously bringing the superpowers to the brink of nuclear war in Berlin and Cuba. If not for Kennedy's gratuitous military buildup, they argue, the superpowers might have signed a comprehensive test ban. Kennedy thus chose to turn the Vienna summit meeting into a confrontation over Berlin, whereas Khrushchev merely wanted recognition of the division of Germany.[3] This argument is one-sided because it overlooks Khrushchev's terrifying boasts about Soviet rockets and his threats against U.S. allies. Kennedy's defense increases helped to ignite the U.S.-Soviet arms race and made it difficult, if not impossible, for Khrushchev to pursue his policy of domestic reform and détente with the United States. Nevertheless, Kennedy did not intend to provoke the Soviets: he was trying as best he could to negotiate from strength, to prevent Khrushchev from underestimating his will and give him an incentive to agree to a truce in the Cold War. In the process of labeling Kennedy a Cold Warrior, the revisionists have lifted the president's statements out of historical context. Kennedy was only slightly to the right of such prominent "soft-liners" as Walter Lippmann and Averell Harriman.

In retrospect, Kennedy's and Khrushchev's failure to reach agreement is difficult to interpret from a rational perspective, because the two leaders' goals were complementary. Khrushchev was a domestic reformer who wished to stabilize the international situation so that he could divert resources from the military to the production of consumer goods. He wanted the United States to give tacit recognition to East Germany and was prepared to acknowledge the U.S. interest in preserving West Berlin's independence. Khrushchev was also obsessed with winning acceptance of the Soviet Union's status as an equal superpower. Although he was a committed communist, Khrushchev believed that Marxist-Leninist ideology could win the support of the working class in Western countries and that socialism could triumph without war or revolution. In 1961, he needed a diplomatic success to justify his campaign for summit meetings and détente with the United States.[4]

Kennedy's objectives were to preserve the balance of power in Europe, reduce international tensions and sign a test ban as the basis for more far-reaching disarmament agreements. Kennedy understood and accepted Khrushchev's desire to obtain Western recognition for the East German state. Just as the U.S. ties to West Germany were a vital interest of the United States, so were Soviet relations with East Germany. In 1959, Kennedy had referred to "the necessity for the East German government to have increased status—the importance of East Germany to the Soviet economy and its political system." He had criticized Secretary Dulles's Berlin policy as "a little too rigid and unyielding to changing currents in European policies." Before becoming president, he favored Averell Harriman's suggestion that the United States acknowledge East German authority but not give formal recognition. Kennedy had supported a test ban since 1956. Privately, Kennedy believed that the United States could have obtained a test ban in 1960 if its negotiating position had been better prepared and more reasonable.[5]

It should have been relatively easy for two reasonable leaders to communicate their preferences to each other, to signal their desire to reach an agreement on Germany and the test ban. One would certainly not expect Khrushchev to renew his six-month ultimatum, from which he had been forced to back down. In fact, though, neither leader clearly signaled his intentions, in part because Khrushchev and Kennedy were uncertain about each other's motives and about how best to convey their own objectives without appearing weak. Neither understood how his actions might be viewed by the other. Kennedy's mixing of hard and soft options, his attempts to negotiate from strength, sent ambivalent messages to the Soviets.[6]

If Kennedy had continued Eisenhower's strategic programs and resumed negotiations on Berlin at the point where they were broken off in Geneva at the end of July 1959, if his relations with Khrushchev had not gotten off to such a turbulent start, the two men might possibly, if not certainly, have agreed on a test ban treaty with on-site inspection. It is also possible that Khrushchev and Kennedy might have agreed to recognize implicitly the division of Germany, through East German membership in the United Nations or separate peace treaties, in return for Soviet guarantees of Western access to West Berlin. Instead, psychological, ideological, and bureaucratic factors inhibited the two leaders from seizing these opportunities.

Step by Step

After the fiasco at Paris, Khrushchev was eager to begin again with Eisenhower's successor, to achieve an agreement on Germany that would repair his image after he had been forced to back down on the threat to sign a separate peace treaty. At the traditional midnight New Year's Eve party in the Kremlin, Premier Khrushchev announced that he was dropping the Soviet complaint to the United Nations with respect to the U-2 incident in order to improve relations with the Kennedy administration. Soviet diplomats spread the word that Khrushchev was eager for a summit meeting with Kennedy.[7]

Undermining the credibility of Khrushchev's overtures to the United States, however, was Soviet aid to the antigovernment guerrillas fighting the U.S.-supported government in Laos and Khrushchev's rhetoric about supporting national liberation movements. The *New York Times* noted that "like Janus, the Soviet leader has two faces and two policies." On 6 January 1961 Khrushchev gave a speech before a closed Kremlin meeting of party theoreticians and propagandists. He bragged that there was "no force on earth now able to prevent the peoples of more and more countries from advancing to socialism." Explaining that the problem of war arose out of the division of society into classes, he classified conflicts into world wars, local wars, and wars of national liberation. Khrushchev asserted that the power of the socialist camp would deter the imperialists from starting a world war. Local wars might still recur as long as imperialism existed, but were becoming less probable. National liberation wars began as "uprisings of colonial peoples against their oppressors, [then] developed into guerilla wars." The Soviet Union would support wholeheartedly and without reservation wars of national liberation, such as the conflicts in Algeria, Cuba, and Vietnam. Khrushchev maintained that the policy of peaceful coexistence "promotes the development of the forces of progress, the forces fighting for socialism; and in the capitalist countries it facilitates the work of the Communist parties."[8]

The West did not learn about Khrushchev's speech until 18 January, when the address was published in both English and Russian, indicating its importance as an authoritative expression of Communist Party doctrine. Commentators in the U.S. press viewed the speech as an unusually blunt statement of the Soviet aim to establish communism throughout the world and of their use of disarmament and peaceful coexistence as a mere tactic in the struggle for world dominance.[9]

Kennedy regarded Khrushchev's 6 January speech as a clue to Soviet intentions; he directed his staff to study it, and read extracts aloud at the National Security Council. He was more disturbed by this belligerent speech, with its self-confident predictions about the world victory of communism, than he was impressed by the Soviet leader's conciliatory signals.[10] Not only was the national liberation speech at odds with the cooperative actions of Khrushchev, but it supported Cold War beliefs that one could not deal with the Soviets because they would resort to any means necessary to ensure the victory of communism.

In his inaugural address, Kennedy called on American citizens to pay any price, bear any burden, and meet any hardship to defend liberty. At the same time, he asked that the United States and the Soviet Union "begin anew the quest for peace." Kennedy observed that the two alliances could not take comfort from their present course—"both sides overburdened by the cost of modern weapons, both rightly alarmed by the steady spread of the deadly atom, yet both racing to alter that uncertain balance of terror." So, he said, "Let us never negotiate out of fear. But let us never fear to negotiate." As an indication of the importance he attached to arms control, Kennedy increased the disarmament staff in the State Department from forty-three to a hundred or more. He also appointed John J. McCloy, a prominent Republican adviser to presidents, as his special disarmament adviser. The president's scientific adviser, Jerome B. Wiesner, was a pioneer in arms control theory. In his State of the Union address, the president announced that he intended "to make arms control a central goal of our national policy under my personal direction."[11] Later, following in the best tradition of John Foster Dulles, Kennedy informally turned aside Khrushchev's invitation to a summit with the statement that he would consider meeting with the Soviet leader only after agreements had been properly prepared at lower levels.[12]

On inauguration day, Premier Khrushchev and President Brezhnev cabled President Kennedy that they hoped for a "radical improvement" in relations and called for "step by step" efforts "to remove the existing suspicion and mistrust, to grow the seeds of friendship and businesslike cooperation" between their two countries.[13] As a first step, on 25 January, Khrushchev released the two United States RB-47 pilots who had been shot down near the Soviet Union in July 1960. During the campaign, representatives from both Richard Nixon and JFK had approached Khrushchev and asked him to free the pilots as a sign of good faith, but the Soviet leader had waited, not wanting to do anything that might strengthen Nixon's political position in the elections.[14]

Some periodicals scoffed at Khrushchev's cheap political gesture. For example, *Time* called the release "a blatant Khrushchev move in the continuing cold war, a Soviet gesture toward the new U.S. Administration that cost Russia nothing." Nevertheless, in the prevailing context, Khrushchev's relatively inexpensive signal was symbolically important. The Soviet concession was the first diplomatic move since the U-2 incident disrupted U.S.-Soviet cooperation, and it improved the atmosphere for negotiations.[15]

To reciprocate Khrushchev's release of the RB-47 pilots, Kennedy announced at a press conference that he had discontinued military flights over the Soviet Union. Kennedy made other small concessions to demonstrate his desire for cooperation with the Soviet Union. The White House instructed generals and military leaders to refrain from making

[111]

"tough" anti-Soviet speeches, invited the Soviet Union to resume civil aviation talks, lifted a ten-year-old ban on imports of Soviet crabmeat, relaxed the requirement that Soviet journalists be fingerprinted, stopped censoring incoming Soviet publications, and proposed an increase in the number of consulates.[16]

But Kennedy muddied the meaning of these gestures by greatly augmenting the conventional as well as the nuclear capabilities of the United States. In his 30 January State of the Union address, President Kennedy warned that "each day, we draw nearer the hour of maximum danger, as weapons spread and hostile forces grow stronger." The expression "maximum danger" was a phrase used by those who charged that there was a missile gap in order to refer to the period in which the Soviets might use their superiority for blackmail or attack. Kennedy issued orders to speed up Polaris submarine construction, increase the number of transport planes for limited-war situations, and accelerate the missile program.[17] In the same speech, Kennedy asked Congress for greater flexibility in the use of trade and aid to Eastern Europe in order to decrease East European dependence on the Soviet Union, an action bound to arouse Soviet ire. Kennedy had long advocated using U.S. economic leverage to pry the East European countries from the Soviet grip.[18]

Despite his rhetoric about the urgency of the international situation, Kennedy's initial increments to the defense budget were mostly modest and symbolic. The president had called for no new appropriations or missiles. What Kennedy did was to take five Polaris submarines, which Eisenhower had included in the FY 1962 budget, and program them in the budget for FY 1961, using $128 million in unallocated funds already held by the Navy. Wiesner and McCloy had recommended the Polaris to Kennedy because it could not be located by Soviet missiles and would therefore reduce Soviet incentives to carry out a surprise attack.[19]

But the Soviets may not have perceived the president's increases as modest. Before Kennedy assumed office, Vasily V. Kuznetsov of the Soviet Foreign Office had warned Walt Rostow, deputy assistant for national security affairs, and Wiesner that the Soviets would not sit still if Kennedy followed up his "missile gap" campaign rhetoric with massive rearmament. Rostow replied that any Kennedy rearmament would be "designed to improve the stability of the deterrent and that the Soviet Union should recognize this as in the interests of peace." Kuznetsov, however, was not persuaded. The Soviets did not understand the concept of "stability" in U.S. deterrence theory or the notion that one side might launch an attack, without provocation or warning, simply because the other's nuclear forces could in theory be taken out in a first strike. After Kennedy's State of the Union address, *Izvestia* complained about the reappearance of Cold War policies. The Soviet newspaper contended that

[112]

the president's actions to strengthen American armed forces were obviously incompatible with his stated desire to proceed toward agreement on disarmament.[20]

In mid-February 1961, Kennedy held a meeting with the leading experts on the Soviet Union—George Kennan, Charles ("Chip") Bohlen, Averell Harriman, and Ambassador Llewellyn Thompson. Thompson believed that Khrushchev was eager to achieve some concrete diplomatic successes during 1961, especially in disarmament. Soviet interest in disarmament appeared real: "We do have one common enemy—war." Thompson predicted that Khrushchev would not try to bring the Berlin situation to a boil unless there was a breakdown of negotiations on disarmament. The experts believed that Khrushchev was eager for an early meeting with the president, and they felt strongly that such a meeting might provide a useful opportunity to exchange courtesies and become personally acquainted. On 22 February, Kennedy sent a letter inviting Khrushchev to an informal meeting.[21]

Kennedy's timing was off, though, because the Soviet leader had already lost patience with the president and returned to a hostile policy. When Thompson tried to deliver Kennedy's letter, he had to wait for a fortnight and then travel to Siberia to see Khrushchev on 9 March. In mid-February, there were other signs that Khrushchev was becoming cool to the idea of U.S.-Soviet cooperation. After the assassination of the Congolese leader Patrice Lumumba, the Soviets bitterly attacked Western "imperialists" and refused to cooperate with U.N. Secretary-General Dag Hammarskjöld. The Soviets continued to support communist forces in the civil war in Laos, ignoring Western appeals for help in bringing about a cease-fire. On 17 February, the Soviet ambassador to Bonn, Andrei Smirnov, delivered an aide-mémoire stating that the Soviet Union could not wait until after the fall 1961 West German elections to solve the German problem. The Soviets offered to negotiate with the Federal Republic of Germany (FRG) for a peace treaty. If the West German government refused, however, the Soviet Union would sign a separate peace with the German Democratic Republic (GDR) which would end the occupation regime in West Berlin.[22]

On 8 March, the administration's roving ambassador Averell Harriman announced that "all discussions on Berlin must begin from the start," meaning that Kennedy was not committed to the concessions Eisenhower had made in the July 1959 Geneva negotiations.[23] At their 9 March meeting in Novosibirsk, Khrushchev assured Thompson that the Soviets "were not striving for West Berlin." The Soviet premier was ready to accept the capitalist island of West Berlin within the GDR because in 1965 the USSR would "surpass West Germany in per capita production." President Eisenhower had understood the Soviet position,

Khrushchev said, but the "Pentagon and others had deliberately exploded relations between us and sent [the] U-2." Khrushchev declared that he would like very much for President Kennedy to understand Soviet views on the German question. The Soviet leader promised that a peace treaty with Germany "would mark great progress in American-Sov[iet] relations." The treaty could be implemented in installments, including the gradual withdrawal of American and Soviet troops from Germany, and an "atmosphere of trust would be established to help disarmament negotiations."[24]

Khrushchev showed little interest in a test ban. The main question was disarmament, he said. Khrushchev now insisted that a test ban could not be an isolated agreement, just as Eisenhower had maintained until April 1958, a stance that could only have been intended to block a test ban treaty.[25]

Ironically, just as Khrushchev had abandoned support for a test ban, the president was trying to come up with new concessions that might win Soviet acquiescence. Kennedy favored a test ban because it would prevent leukemia and other health problems stemming from radioactive fallout, inhibit other nations from acquiring nuclear weapons, and enable the United States and the Soviet Union to develop greater confidence in each other's intentions. A test ban would be a first step and could lay the basis for more significant agreements. In a December 1959 speech, Kennedy had observed that "disarmament talks historically fail when nations refuse to trust each other's intentions enough to take the first step." Not only did an agreement require adequate inspection and enforcement, "but this, too, requires a minimum of trust." In short, "trust we must—in each other's rational recognition of self-interest—in our mutual self-interest in survival." Kennedy asked McCloy to supervise a study of the test ban negotiations in order to determine if there were any basis for Soviet complaints against the West and to identify concessions that the United States could offer the Soviets.[26]

McCloy concluded that underground testing posed the major obstacle to a treaty, because the Soviets could secretly test unless the United States had the right to make a sufficient number of on-site inspections. The Soviets had accepted the idea of a quota for inspections, but they would accede to no more than three per year. The United States, however, had settled on twenty as a minimum, and this had become a sacred number in Congress even though the figure had no scientific justification or logic. McCloy had an ingenious plan to preserve the number twenty for domestic political reasons while offering the Soviets the possibility of fewer inspections in any given year. He suggested that the United States propose a minimum of ten on-site inspections per year, plus one inspection for every five unidentified seismic events above fifty to a maximum of twenty. Because there was an average of a hundred unidentifiable seismic events each year in the Soviet Union, this formula would give the United States an average of twenty on-site inspections per year, although the annual total could vary. Although representatives from both the AEC and the Joint Chiefs opposed putting any upper limit on U.S. inspections, Kennedy quickly accepted McCloy's proposal. At a meeting with congressional leaders on 7 March, President Kennedy emphasized that it was important to make a strong effort at Geneva, since much more was at stake than just a test ban. If the United States and the Soviet Union could gain agreement on a test ban, he said, that success might enable us to move toward agreement on other East-West issues, such as Berlin and Laos.[27]

Based on the recommendations of an elite group of scientists, Kennedy approved several other concessions, including a three-year voluntary moratorium on underground tests below 4.75 on the Richter scale, fewer control posts, and parity for East and West in staffing the control commission.[28] But on 21 March 1961, without even waiting to hear the new U.S. position which had been previewed in the newspapers, the Soviet diplomat Semen Tsarapkin demanded that the control commission be headed by a three-man secretariat, or "troika," representing communists, Western powers, and neutrals, each of whom would have a veto.[29] The Soviet veto would amount to self-inspection—which the United States could not accept, given the risk that the Soviets would cheat.

KENNEDY'S MILITARY BUILDUP

Still, Kennedy's defense buildup continued. On 28 March Kennedy delivered a budget message in which he requested an additional $1,194.1 million in defense appropriations. Kennedy recommended expanding and accelerating the Polaris program, placing more strategic bombers on alert, improving continental defense and warning systems, and strengthening command-and-control systems. He called for doubling production of Minuteman missiles, the maximum possible. Together with the 30 January acceleration, this meant that the United States planned to produce 600 Minuteman missiles in FY 1962, beginning in July 1961. Kennedy requested that 29 submarines and 464 Polaris missiles be operational by June 1965, instead of 19 submarines and 304 Polaris missiles under Eisenhower.[30]

Why did Kennedy proceed with his military buildup at a time when Soviet behavior was relatively benign? Revisionists charge that Kennedy wanted to win a victory in the Cold War, to force the Soviets to accept a Pax Americana.[31]

[115]

When Kennedy submitted his first three requests to the Congress for supplemental defense appropriations, intelligence information on Soviet military capabilities was insufficient to rule out a missile gap. Kennedy had continued Eisenhower's suspension of the U-2 flights. A July 1960 CIA report on those portions of the Soviet Union covered by U.S. intelligence sources between January 1959 and June 1960 estimated that the U-2s had provided usable photographs of less than 15 percent of the areas suitable for ICBM deployment and of only 5 percent of the areas considered high priority for observation. The report concluded that "in view of the large areas still uncovered and the limited number of ICBMs that are likely to be deployed so early in the Soviet program, it is not surprising that none of these sites has been positively identified." In August 1960, film from the first photographic reconnaissance satellite, *Discoverer 14*, had been recovered by air. While the film was of lower resolution than that used in the U-2s, the photographs from this one satellite mission covered a much greater area of the Soviet Union than the total produced by all the U-2 missions. By August 1961, more than seventeen camera-carrying satellite missions (Corona program) had been attempted, but usable photographs had been recovered from just four.[32]

In a background briefing on 6 February 1961, Robert McNamara had slipped and according to some journalists said, "There is no missile gap." The defense secretary later claimed that he had been misinterpreted, that what he meant to say was that there was no evidence of a Soviet "crash effort" but that he was still looking for information concerning Soviet missiles. McNamara's explanation is probably accurate, because the intelligence community did not have enough information at that point to exclude the possibility of a missile gap. At a news conference the following day, President Kennedy stated that studies had not been completed and that it would therefore be "premature" to reach a judgment as to whether there was a missile gap.[33]

When he made his decisions in January and March 1961 to increase U.S. nuclear capabilities, Kennedy was probably acting under the assumption that he had to redress the missile gap. The intelligence community was soon divided. Even as late as the 7 June 1961 National Intelligence Estimate 11-8-61, which used some satellite intelligence as well as microfilm delivered by the Soviet defector Oleg Penkovsky, the CIA together with the State Department's Bureau of Intelligence Research and the U.S. Army predicted that the Soviets would have from 50 to 100 ICBMs by mid-1961, while the Air Force projected more than 300 Soviet ICBMs. The Office of Naval Intelligence, on the other hand, estimated the Soviet operational ICBM capability at 10 or perhaps fewer. The United States had about 27 liquid-fueled Atlas DICBMs and 32 Polaris SLBMs (submarine-launched ballistic missiles).[34]

On 21 September, 1961, a revised National Intelligence Estimate (NIE) 11–8/1–61 which made full use of the available satellite photography reported that "new information, providing a much firmer base for estimates on Soviet long range ballistic missiles, has caused a sharp downward revision in our estimate of present Soviet ICBM strength." The satellite photographs showed that many previously suspected areas of the Soviet Union did not have ICBM complexes. The intelligence community now estimated that the Soviets had from 10 to 25 launchers from which missiles could be fired against the United States, and that this force level would not increase markedly until the last half of 1962. The Soviets had probably decided to deploy only a small number of their cumbersome, first-generation ICBMs and to press for the development of a smaller, second-generation system. This second-generation missile would probably not be ready for operational use until the latter half of 1962. At this point, NIE 11-8/1-61 predicted that the Soviets would greatly increase the number of ICBM launchers, reaching 75–125 by mid-1963.[35]

Members of the intelligence community, however, had such bitter disagreements that they did not even try to project Soviet missile totals for 1965–1967. Defense Secretary McNamara, says Raymond Garthoff, formulated his own optimistic–median–pessimistic assessments of future Soviet missile capabilities to arrive at his 23 September decision to increase the U.S. Minuteman force to about 1,200 missiles.[36]

Without hard intelligence data, Kennedy had to take into consideration Khrushchev's previous boasts about Soviet rockets during the Eisenhower presidency, but he also had some reason to regard those claims with skepticism. In his introduction to a compilation of Soviet remarks about their ICBM capabilities, which Kennedy received in March 1961, Director of the CIA Allen Dulles concluded that "where hard evidence is available it generally shows that these statements have some basis in fact, but [it] often [also] reveals the calculated use of ambiguity and innuendo to magnify the Soviet capability or to present an anticipated development as if it were a current capability."[37]

If there had been greater "transparency," would the United States have overreacted to the alleged missile gap? Even if he had known the extent of U.S superiority before September 1961, Kennedy probably would have increased production of Minuteman and Polaris missiles, although perhaps not to the level of 1,000 land-based ICBMs. If the "intelligence gap" had been his main consideration, Kennedy could have waited a few months, until more satellite photographs had been processed, before deciding on the outlines of his military buildup. Up to three months later, for example, revisions could have been made to the FY 1962 budget. Most of the major decisions concerning the size and character of the U.S. nuclear buildup were made after the missile gap was revealed to be a myth in the fall of 1961. Kennedy declined several opportunities to reduce U.S. missile programs even after he had received more realistic assessments about future Soviet forces. In November 1961, after learning of McNamara's inflated numbers, the CIA issued a supplemental intelligence report which projected much lower Soviet missile forces for 1965–1967. Carl Kaysen, a member of Special Assistant for National Security Affairs McGeorge Bundy's staff, twice alerted Kennedy that the forces programmed by McNamara did not take into consideration the revised estimates of Soviet missile forces. In August 1962, Kennedy asked a special high-level group of intelligence, defense, and foreign policy officials whether the United States should alter its defense and foreign policies in light of the reevaluation of Soviet military capabilities; they concluded that there was no reason to do so. As Raymond Garthoff (who drafted the study) recalled, the question was whether U.S. defense capabilities were *sufficient*, not whether they were *excessive*.[38]

There are several reasons why Kennedy would have increased U.S. nuclear capabilities even if he had better intelligence on Soviet deployments. First of all, the "missile gap" hysteria was based as much on what the Soviets *might* do as it was on their actual deployments. As former Defense Secretary Neil McElroy pointed out, the U.S. government estimated how many missiles the Soviets could produce, and compared that figure to the number of missiles the United States planned to produce. No matter how few Soviet missiles were shown by U-2 or satellite photographs, U.S. defense planners had to take into consideration projected Soviet deployment rates.[39]

Second, Kennedy would have put more U.S. missiles out at sea and reduced the U.S. reliance on bombers because what he feared was not a missile gap but a deterrent gap—that the vulnerability of U.S. bombers and medium-range missiles deployed at overseas bases might tempt the Soviets into launching a first strike or allow them to make low-level gains with impunity. For Kennedy and his advisers had been influenced by Albert Wohlstetter and his group at the Rand Corporation. Wohlstetter argued that deterrence rested on the U.S. ability to retaliate against a Soviet first strike; thus, U.S. nuclear forces had to be well protected. Kennedy's famous August 1958 "missile gap" speech was based on a draft of Wohlstetter's then forthcoming delicate balance article in *Foreign Affairs*. In that speech, delivered to the Senate, Kennedy emphasized that the danger to U.S. security was not so much that the Soviets had greater numbers of intercontinental and intermediate-range ballistic missiles, but that the United States had an inadequate supply of missiles with which to retaliate. America's manned bombers, therefore, would have to be dispersed and placed on a higher alert status to avoid decimation. During the period of the "gap," JFK warned, the Soviets could use their missile power to achieve their political objectives in ways other than direct attack—through "Sputnik diplomacy, limited brush-fire wars, indirect non-overt aggression, intimidation and subversion, internal revolution, increased prestige or influence, and the vicious blackmail of our allies."[40]

Third, most U.S. officials believed that the United States needed nuclear superiority to deter Soviet aggression and to serve as a hedge against Soviet secrecy. Within the Kennedy administration, the goal of maintaining military superiority was virtually sacrosanct. Officials within the executive branch believed that the United States needed to maintain a substantial edge in nuclear weapons in order to deter Soviet aggression and provide a margin of safety in light of Soviet secrecy, to offset the Soviet advantage in conventional forces, and to enhance the credibility of the U.S. commitment to defend Europe against a Soviet attack.[41]

The president did not recognize that increasing the already enormous U.S. margin of superiority would both alarm and infuriate Khrushchev. Believing in negotiation from strength, Kennedy quoted with favor Churchill's statement that "we should arm to parley." The commanding U.S. strategic position gave Kennedy ample leeway to propose to the Soviets an equitable limitation of the numbers and types of nuclear weapons deployed, but he did not take advantage of this genuine opportunity to negotiate from strength.[42]

In sum, Kennedy greatly augmented and accelerated U.S. strategic missile programs because of incomplete intelligence information, an overestimation of Soviet deployment rates, a desire to decrease the vulnerability of U.S. nuclear weapons, and a belief that the United States needed a sufficient margin of superiority to deter Soviet aggression. In hindsight, Kennedy's military buildup was clearly excessive, unnecessary, and provocative, given token Soviet deployments. The force originally programmed by Eisenhower—450 Minuteman missiles and 19 Polaris submarines—would have been a powerful deterrent.[43] While Kennedy was no doubt prudent to reduce the U.S. reliance on bombers, he did not have to increase American missile strength to such an extent and so precipitously. He could have waited until the United States had better intelligence about Soviet ICBM capabilities. Soon after he took office, President Kennedy must have been informed about the results of the *Discoverer 14* mission; he must have been aware of the high-quality photographs that satellites could provide.

But would it have been politically feasible for Kennedy to avoid major defense increases, given the domestic debate over the missile gap and his own promises during the 1960 presidential campaign? According to the recollection of White House and Pentagon staff members, Kennedy and Defense Secretary McNamara would probably have preferred a total missile count lower than 1,000, but feared a revolt of the Air Force and of the conservatives in Congress. On the other hand, at the beginning of his administration, Kennedy announced that he had ordered studies on U.S. and Soviet nuclear capabilities, and he could have used the need for further information as an excuse for delaying major decisions on U.S. strategic forces. From March through October 1961, the administration was silent about the missile gap and the issue simply evaporated. Journalists did not question Kennedy about Soviet nuclear forces at press conferences, and the president made no public statements. One of the reasons no questions were raised was that no congressional hearings were held on the subject. Congress was controlled by the president's own party, and the Democrats had no desire to embarrass Kennedy on this issue.[44]

If Kennedy had delayed making important decisions on the size of the U.S. missile force, he might have given Khrushchev an incentive not to provoke the United States. If the summit at Vienna proved to be unproductive or incited Khrushchev to new heights of belligerence, then Kennedy would have been justified in embarking on a measured military buildup, with an emphasis on improving U.S. conventional capabilities.

Kennedy's military buildup had wide-ranging repercussions, virtually all unintended: a delay in Khrushchev's domestic reforms; the Soviet ICBM buildup; Khrushchev's abrogation of the nuclear test moratorium; and missiles in Cuba. Kennedy had introduced his program just as the Soviet leader was beginning a campaign against the military-industrial complex, the "steel-eaters." But Khrushchev could not justify diverting Soviet resources from defense to the production of consumer goods when the United States had sharply accelerated its arms spending.[45]

Kennedy's program to increase the production of Minuteman missiles at a time when the Soviets had deployed only a handful of ICBMs appeared to the Soviet military as an attempt to ensure a first-strike capability. Dispersal of the U.S. missiles and the hardening of silos meant, paradoxically, that the Soviets needed greater numbers of more accurate missiles in order to have some assurance of destroying their targets. The Soviet military buildup in the late 1960s and early 1970s, then, stems from the early Kennedy defense policies, not from the Cuban missile crisis as is popularly assumed.[46] Granted, the Soviets probably would not have tolerated for long their position of gross nuclear inferiority to the United States, but the level of missiles on both sides might not have reached such heights if Kennedy had not accelerated the pace of the arms race.

To meet the immediate deterrent gap, the Soviets decided to deploy large-yield weapons, which could destroy cities, air bases, and so on, despite their low accuracy, through "area devastation." The need to test such weapons was the major consideration behind Khrushchev's violation of the moratorium in August 1961.[47]

Because the Soviets' first-generation ICBMs had technical problems, Khrushchev decided to deploy medium-range missiles in Cuba, which provoked the most dangerous confrontation of the Cold War.[48] According to one defector, Arkady Shevchenko, the Soviet military opposed "quick fixes" to the problem of Soviet nuclear inferiority and would have preferred a measured long-range program designed to achieve genuine parity with the United States, both in quality and quantity of strategic weaponry, and then to achieve superiority. Khrushchev's bungling in the Cuban missile crisis discredited such quick-fix strategems and strengthened the military's claims for increased resources to pay for improved strategic forces.[49]

Kennedy's missile buildup increased Khrushchev's sense of urgency with respect to achieving a Berlin solution before the Soviet military position grew weaker. Then Kennedy's sponsorship of the Bay of Pigs invasion in mid-April 1961 persuaded Soviet hard-liners that the president was simultaneously belligerent and indecisive. Sensing an opportunity to bully the young and inexperienced president, Khrushchev accepted Kennedy's invitation to a summit on 12 May. According to Dobrynin, who was counselor to the Soviet delegation, Khrushchev previewed his summit strategy before a special session of the Presidium, ten days before the meeting in Vienna. Khrushchev apparently believed, owing to the failure of the American-backed invasion of Cuba, that Kennedy would yield to his pressure on Berlin and Germany. Although the other members, with the exception of Mikoyan, voiced their approval of the plan, the decision to bully Kennedy at Vienna was Khrushchev's own idea.[50]

Shortly before the meeting with Kennedy, Khrushchev warned Ambassador Thompson that if no agreement were reached on Berlin, the Soviets would sign a separate peace treaty in fall or winter after the German elections, which would end U.S. occupation rights as well as access to West Berlin. When Thompson had suggested that Berlin might be left as it was, Khrushchev declared heatedly that the United States apparently wished to damage his prestige; the matter could not go beyond fall or winter.[51]

Before he left for Europe, Kennedy continued his planned modernization and restructuring of U.S. defenses. On 25 May, President Kennedy delivered a second State of the Union address in which he requested from Congress more than $1.8 billion in supplemental appropriations for defense and foreign affairs. Kennedy's program included increased foreign economic and military assistance, additional funds for conventional weapons for the Army, reorganization of the Army and a bolstering of the Marine Corps, a tripling of expenditures for fallout shelters, and a commitment to beat the Russians to the moon.[52]

Kennedy later wondered what went wrong in his relationship with Khrushchev, and surmised that his March and May messages to Congress calling for an increased defense budget might have threatened the Soviets.[53] In a very real sense, the "missile gap" was a self-fulfilling prophecy stimulated by Kennedy's military buildup.

DEADLOCK

At their meeting in Vienna (3–4 June 1961), Khrushchev and Kennedy clashed over the test ban and Berlin. Concerning the test ban, the Soviet leader said that there were two main issues: the control organization and the number of on-site inspections. Khrushchev complained that after his experience with the United Nations in the Congo, he could not accept a neutral chairman to head the control commission. Events in the Congo had taught the Soviet Union that the United Nations could act against the interests of individual states. Consequently, the Soviet Union wanted three men to chair the control organization. As for monitoring a test ban, he said, three on-site inspections a year should be sufficient. Any larger number would be tantamount to gathering intelligence.[54]

When Kennedy objected that a test ban along those lines would not deter violations and that he could not send it to the Senate, Khrushchev retorted that a test ban itself had little value because the production of nuclear energy, rockets, and bombs would continue full blast. The Soviet Union, he said, could not accept controls tantamount to espionage if the weapons themselves were not eliminated. This was what the Pentagon had wanted all long. Eisenhower's Open Skies proposal was part of that scheme.[55]

Turning to the question of Germany, Khrushchev noted that sixteen years had passed since World War II; no further delay in signing a peace treaty could be justified. Khrushchev said that he would like to reach an agreement with the president—he wanted to emphasize the words "with you"—on this question. On the other hand, if the United States failed to understand this desire, then the Soviet Union would sign a peace treaty alone, which would end the state of war and invalidate all commitments stemming from Germany's surrender, including "all institutions, occupation rights, and access to Berlin, including the corridors." A free city of West Berlin would be established, and there would be no blockade or interference in the internal affairs of the city. If the United States wished, there could be guarantees of the city's links with the outside world. If the United States wanted to retain its troops in West Berlin, that would be acceptable under certain conditions; however, Soviet troops should be there too.[56]

Kennedy informed Khrushchev that the United States was in Berlin not by agreement with the East Germans but by contractual right. Berlin was an area to which every president of the United States since World War II had been committed by treaty, and every president had reaffirmed his faithfulness to those treaty obligations. If the United States were expelled from that area and accepted the loss of its rights, its commitments would be regarded as a "mere scrap of paper."[57]

The president said that he recognized the situation in Berlin was not satisfactory, and that in the conversations Khrushchev had with President Eisenhower the word "abnormal" had been used. However, because conditions in many parts of the world were not satisfactory, it was not the right time to change the situation in Berlin and the balance in general. The United States was not asking the USSR to change its position, but was simply saying that the USSR should not seek to change the U.S. position and thus disturb the balance of power. If the balance changed, the situation in Western Europe would change, and that would be a serious blow to the United States. Khrushchev would not accept such a loss and the United States could not accept it either. The issue was not a German peace treaty, continued the president, but other aspects of Khrushchev's proposal which would affect U.S. access to Berlin and U.S. rights there.[58]

Kennedy wanted to negotiate a standstill in the Cold War, based on recognition of the balance of power and neither side's ability to achieve major gains without war. But Khrushchev interpreted Kennedy's support for the status quo as a repudiation of the implicit deal that he thought he had worked out with Eisenhower at Camp David: namely, that there would be an interim agreement on Berlin, the two Germanys would negotiate between themselves, and the Soviets would then sign a separate treaty with the GDR.[59]

Khrushchev said that he was "sorry that he had met with no understanding of the Soviet position." The United States was "unwilling to normalize the situation in the most dangerous spot in the world," whereas the Soviet Union wanted to "eliminate this thorn, this ulcer." He reiterated that he was "very sorry" but he had to assure the president that "no force in the world would prevent the USSR from signing a peace treaty."[60] Kennedy asked whether a peace treaty would block access to Berlin. Khrushchev replied that it would.[61]

Khrushchev recalled that President Eisenhower had agreed that the situation in Berlin was abnormal. They had discussed an interim agreement, an arrangement that would not compromise the prestige of their two countries. The Soviet Union was prepared to accept such an agreement even now. He proposed that they set a six-month time limit for the Germans to solve the question of reunification, after which the United States and the USSR would be free to conclude a peace treaty.[62]

For their part, the Soviet Union could no longer delay and would probably sign a peace treaty by the end of the year. The status of West Berlin as a free city would be guaranteed and complete noninterference would be ensured. However, access would be subject to the GDR's control, since the communication lines went through its territory. "If the US wants to start a war over Germany, let it be so," he said.[63]

Kennedy emphasized that signing a peace treaty would not be a belligerent act, but any denial of U.S. contractual rights would be grounds for war.[64] At a private afternoon session, Khrushchev reiterated that "it is up to the US to decide whether there will be war or peace." In any case, the "decision to sign a peace treaty is firm and irrevocable and the Soviet Union will sign it in December if the US refuses an interim agreement." Kennedy observed that "it will be a cold winter."[65] Khrushchev then handed Kennedy an aide-mémoire stating his six-month deadline for the two Germanys to agree on reunification, after which both sides would be free to sign a separate peace treaty and West Berlin would become a demilitarized "free city."[66]

Could this confrontation between Khrushchev and Kennedy have been avoided? Actually, the two leaders' positions were not so far apart as they appeared at the time. Khrushchev did not expect the United States to give formal recognition to the GDR; he would have been content with negotiations between the GDR and the FRG which would amount to tacit recognition of the East German regime. In November 1960, Khrushchev had met with the East German leader Walter Ulbricht to map out a strategy after the collapse of the Paris summit. Khrushchev had told Ulbricht that a peace treaty with the two German states was not likely. However, the Soviet peace treaty proposal also included the possibility of an interim agreement for West Berlin, that is, an agreement between the four powers on a temporary status for West Berlin for an established time. While the agreement was in effect, both Germanys would negotiate on the issues between them. "This was our concession to Eisenhower so as to save his prestige and not create the impression that we would expel them from West Berlin." Khrushchev predicted: "You Germans probably will not agree amongst yourselves and then we will sign a peace treaty with you, and the Western powers will not conclude any peace treaty at all. But this does not worry us."[67]

Kennedy was prepared to be flexible about dealing with the GDR in return for guarantees of Western access to Berlin. As his later statements suggest, Kennedy might very well have agreed to de facto recognition of East Germany, through such mechanisms as negotiations between the two Germanys. The president, however, did not communicate his willingness to make concessions to Khrushchev because he feared that the Soviet leader would take initial indications of accommodation as a sign of weakness and press further. Kennedy was pursuing a two-stage strategy in which he would first demonstrate his resolve to defend U.S. interests in West Berlin, even at the risk of war, before offering Khrushchev a modus vivendi on Germany. Bundy had advised the president to be firm at Vienna on the issue of allied access to Berlin, while avoiding substantive negotiations. "What we might later be willing to consider with respect to such items as the Oder-Neisse line and a de facto acceptance of a divided Germany is matter for further discussion, and we ourselves might indeed have new proposals at a later time," Bundy wrote.[68]

Kennedy believed that the only reason the Soviets had not absorbed West Berlin was because they feared U.S military power. Accordingly, Kennedy believed that he had to demonstrate U.S. resolve to stay in Berlin before offering Khrushchev any concessions. Before the Vienna meeting, during his trip to Paris in May 1961, the president had asked Charles de Gaulle whether there was "something which would go beyond mere words which we should do in order to convince Mr. Khrushchev of our firmness." Kennedy expressed concern that Khrushchev might doubt the United States would resort to war and, as a result, try to undertake the strangulation of Berlin step by step.[69]

Was Kennedy's assessment correct? Would Khrushchev have interpreted the president's acknowledgment of Soviet interests in East Germany as an invitation to ask for further gains? Eisenhower had admitted to Khrushchev that the Berlin situation was "abnormal" during their Camp David talks, and the Soviet leader had not taken advantage of that concession but instead reciprocated by withdrawing his threat to change Berlin's status. According to his adviser and speechwriter Fedor Burlatsky, Khrushchev could not understand, and was greatly frustrated by, Kennedy's apparent unwillingness to recognize the GDR's existence and to consolidate postwar boundaries. Khrushchev attributed Kennedy's stubbornness to an arrogance conferred by the U.S. numerical superiority in missiles.[70]

The Soviet leader did not believe that the United States would be so irrational as to use nuclear weapons because of a dispute over Berlin. "Of course, in signing a peace treaty," he told Ulbricht, "we will have to put our rockets on military alert. But luckily, our adversaries still haven't gone crazy; they still think and their nerves still aren't bad."[71]

In fact, what deterred the Soviets was probably not U.S. nuclear weapons but fear of an economic blockade directed against East Germany. The East Germans were dependent on West Germany for imports of such critical raw materials as rolled iron, pipes, chemicals, forgings, and cast iron, and the Soviets could not make up the difference. In November 1960, Khrushchev had chastised Ulbricht for allowing the East German economy to rely so heavily on West German imports: "You got used to thinking that Germany was one." In the meantime, Khrushchev supported a continuation of trade relations between the two Germanys "since we don't want to kill the goose that lays the golden eggs." The East Germans asked the Soviets for additional aid to make up the difference should the West Germans carry out their threat to cancel the FRG-GDR trade agreement. Alexei Kosygin, chairman of Gosplan (the State Planning Committee of the Council of Ministers), complained that "several of their requests create difficulties for us also, since they request about 50 million dollars of hard currency, and also those goods which we buy for ourselves on the external market." Khrushchev admonished Ulbricht not to "encroach on our gold." Ulbricht himself was ambivalent about the prospect of a separate peace treaty in 1961—again, because of the disastrous effects of a blockade on the staggering East German economy.[72]

If Khrushchev had signed a separate peace treaty, it is unlikely that he would have allowed the East German regime to cut off Western access to West Berlin. To do so would have risked an economic embargo not only against the GDR, but against the Soviet Union as well. In 1961–62, the Soviets restrained Ulbricht from harassing traffic to and from West Berlin.[73]

SPIRALING CONFLICT

It is evident that Khrushchev tried to intimidate Kennedy into negotiations on Germany. Moreover, the Soviet leader's threats undermined the credibility of his peaceful overtures. In his 15 June televised report to Soviet people concerning Vienna, Khrushchev pointed his finger for emphasis and declared that a peace settlement in Europe "must be accomplished this year." If any country crosses the borders of another country, he warned, it "will receive a proper rebuff." For his 21 June speech, commemorating the anniversary of Hitler's invasion of the Soviet Union, Khrushchev donned his lieutenant general's uniform and appeared on a platform surrounded by Soviet generals. He warned that the Soviet armed forces and military budget might have to be increased if the United States pushed ahead with its military buildup.[74]

Kennedy did not reply to Khrushchev's aide-mémoire for more than seven weeks. His administration was deeply divided over how to respond to Khrushchev's challenge. The president waited for former Secretary of State Dean Acheson, who was brought in as a special consultant, to draft a report on Berlin and for the State Department to coordinate its replies with Britain, France, and West Germany.

Adding to Kennedy's frustration, the Joint Chiefs' military contingency plans, which the president had not even seen, were published in the 3 July issue of *Newsweek*, which appeared on the newstands on 26 June. Perhaps in reaction to the *Newsweek* story, on 28 June 1961 the Soviet premier delivered a stirring speech in which he claimed that Western mobilization would not catch the Soviets "unaware."[75] On 2 July, Khrushchev sought out the British ambassador Sir Frank Roberts to warn him that any additions to Western ground forces in Germany could be contained by massive increases in Soviet forces. The Soviet leader bluntly reminded the British ambassador that "six . . . H-bombs would be quite enough to annihilate the British Isles, and nine would take care of France."[76]

Kennedy's advisers were divided into two groups with respect to how to meet Khrushchev's challenge. The "hard-liners," led by Acheson, believed that the Soviet Union continued to pursue expansionist objectives. Supporters of Acheson included Assistant Secretary of State for European Affairs Foy Kohler, Deputy Special Assistant for National Security Affairs Walt Rostow, Assistant Secretary of Defense for International Security Affairs Paul Nitze, General Maxwell Taylor, the Joint Chiefs of Staff, Vice-President Lyndon B. Johnson, and the German desk in the State Department.[77] The hard-liners fundamentally distrusted Soviet intentions as malevolent and inimical to Western interests.

The hard-liners interpreted Khrushchev's ultimatum as *offensive*, and capable of being contained only through deterrence and/or defense. If the United States offered negotiations, Khrushchev might push to the limit, miscalculate U.S. resolve to stay in West Berlin, and provoke a major war. The hard-liners believed that the United States had to establish its commitment to remain in West Berlin and acquire credible military capabilities in order to minimize the chances of war.[78]

In his 28 June report to the president, Acheson characterized the Berlin issue as involving much more than a city, or even the German question. The very position of the United States in the world was in the balance. Until the "conflict of wills" between the United States and the USSR was resolved, Khrushchev would view any concession by the West as a sign of weakness. Acheson argued that Soviet fear of nuclear war with the United States had protected West Berlin and access to it. That Khrushchev now considered interfering with access to Berlin meant that he no longer believed the United States was willing to go to war over Berlin.

Accordingly, Kennedy must improve the credibility of the U.S. deterrent by increasing the preparedness of U.S. conventional and strategic forces.[79]

Acheson opposed any offer of negotiations until U.S. military preparations had convinced Khrushchev that the West was firm. Then, to help Khrushchev save face, the United States might agree to renounce espionage and subversive activities in West Berlin, freeze the number of Western troops, and perhaps even recognize the Oder-Neisse boundary.[80]

If Khrushchev went ahead with his threat to sign a separate treaty, Acheson contended, the United States should take no action unless the East Germans cut off access to Berlin. Then the United States should undertake an airlift and economic sanctions against the Soviet bloc. If the Soviets interfered with the airlift, the United States should use ground forces to restore access, beginning with a battalion and then one division with another held in reserve. The purpose of the ground force operation would be to persuade the Soviets to negotiate for a resumption of access by demonstrating that the Western allies would not submit to Soviet demands but would use whatever force was necessary to resist them. Acheson conceded that nuclear war could result either from a premature and unauthorized local use of nuclear weapons in Europe or a miscalculation of the other side's response.[81]

Acheson argued strongly that Kennedy must issue an immediate declaration of national emergency, which entailed calling up 1 million reserves and bringing back U.S. dependents from Europe, in order to convince Khrushchev of his resolve. The purpose of the declaration of emergency would be psychological—to deter Khrushchev and convince the American people of the gravity of the crisis.[82]

In contrast, the "soft-liners" believed that the expansionist dynamic of Soviet foreign policy had moderated, that the Soviets were pursuing nationalistic and consolidationist goals. Soft-liners included Llewellyn Thompson, Averell Harriman, George McGhee of the State Department Policy Planning Council, Henry Kissinger, Ambassador to the United Nations Adlai Stevenson, and the White House advisers Arthur Schlesinger and Carl Kaysen.[83]

The soft-liners believed that Khrushchev had delivered his ultimatum because he was desperate to prop up the East German regime, which was being steadily weakened by an accelerating outflow of refugees. Accordingly, while the soft-liners favored some strengthening of U.S. conventional forces, they urged active negotiations without delay. Only by offering Khrushchev negotiations promptly could they convince him that the United States would respect legitimate Soviet security interests. On 14 July 1961, Kissinger wrote Bundy that "firmness should be related to the substance of our negotiating position," not proved by seeming to shy away from a diplomatic confrontation. Kissinger recommended that Kennedy accompany an improvement in military readiness with a statement of a range of diplomatic options relating to a general European settlement, not just to the Berlin issue. "Should we not develop a 'Kennedy Plan' for Central Europe?" he asked.[84]

The soft-liners opposed a declaration of national emergency because it would be provocative, back Khrushchev into a corner, and should be held in reserve for use against a more serious Soviet provocation. In a 17 July memorandum, Theodore Sorensen argued that a declaration of emergency might "engage Khrushchev's prestige to a point where he felt he could not back down from a showdown, and provoke further or faster action on his part in stepping up the arms race."[85]

As Kennedy struggled to find a solution, Khrushchev began to wonder about the president's silence. On 5 July, Georgi Kornienko, who was a counselor at the Soviet embassy, told Arthur Schlesinger that he was puzzled about U.S. policy. "The real trouble," Kornienko said, "is that you don't believe that we are sincere when we say that we honestly wish to keep things as they are in West Berlin within the new context." Schlesinger admitted this was true: the so-called guarantees that the Soviets offered guaranteed nothing. Kornienko replied: "Well, if you do not consider these guarantees adequate, why don't you propose your own guarantees? All we want to do is to have a chance to discuss these things."[86]

Troubled by the emphasis on military measures in Acheson's Berlin report, Schlesinger wrote a memorandum in which he pointed out that Acheson had presented no political objectives "other than present access procedures for which we are prepared to incinerate the world." Schlesinger urged that Kennedy seriously consider alternatives to the U.S. policy toward Germany, such as confederation, living indefinitely with a divided Germany, or a comprehensive European solution.[87] Kennedy agreed that Berlin planning was too narrowly focused, and asked Dean Rusk to prepare a negotiating position for a Central European settlement.[88]

On 8 July 1961, in a speech to graduates of Soviet military academies, the Soviet leader combined military measures with peaceful overtures. Khrushchev said that it would be a good thing to reconsider some of the disarmament proposals made in recent years—the Rapacki Plan for a nuclear-free zone, disengagement of foreign troops, an agreement on the prevention of surprise atttacks, and a reciprocal inspection zone in Europe. Acceptance of these proposals would ease international tension, speed the end of the Cold War and promote better mutual understanding. Although the West had not reacted formally to Soviet proposals for a German peace treaty, there were reports in the Western press that Western governments would stand firm and would resort to force in order to break through to West Berlin. Chancellor Adenauer was "shouting himself hoarse" asking for nuclear weapons, which the Bundeswehr needed for starting a third world war. Khrushchev pointed out that Kennedy had stepped up America's development of missiles, increased U.S. military preparedness, and boosted military expenditures by more than $3.5 billion. "This is how the Western powers are replying to the Soviet Union's unilateral reduction of armed forces and military expenditures," the Soviet leader complained. Consequently, Khrushchev announced that he had been "compelled" to suspend the one-third reduction in Soviet armed forces planned for 1961 and had to increase the Soviet defense budget by more than 3 billion rubles. "These are forced measures, comrades," he added with some embarrassment. He ended by calling for a four-power summit meeting on Germany.[89]

The defense budget increases forced Khrushchev to give up plans to redirect Soviet priorities from defense and heavy industry to agriculture and consumer goods production. The draft party program issued on 19 June announced that the heavy-industrial sector must ensure the expansion of industries producing consumer goods, but the version published on 30 July avoided the issue of the relative priority of light versus heavy industry. In addition, the program had a clause that made achievement of welfare goals contingent on a stable global atmosphere, thus allowing opponents of a change in investment priorities to use U.S.-Soviet tensions over Berlin as a pretext for insisting on the traditional policy.[90]

Typically, Kennedy took elements from hard-line as well as soft-line positions. He announced his decisions to the Berlin Steering Group and the full NSC on 19 July. The president had decided to request a $3.2 billion rather than a $4.3 billion increase in the defense budget and to ask Congress for standby authority to call up the reserves instead of an immediate mobilization. He planned to have six American divisions ready for transfer to Europe by the end of the year. At the same time, he also adopted the advice of White House staff members that he convey a "forward-leaning position" in his negotiations with Khrushchev. Kennedy also accepted Sorensen's suggestion that he make a nationally televised speech to clarify U.S. interests in Berlin while offering negotiations to the Soviets.[91]

In his 25 July speech, Kennedy declared that the threat posed by Khrushchev's policies did not apply just to Berlin: "The threat is world wide. Our effort must be equally wide and strong and not be obsessed by any single manufactured crisis."[92] Kennedy defined U.S. interests as an American presence in West Berlin, access to West Berlin across East German territory, and the right of the West Berliners to determine their own future and choose their own way of life. Throughout the speech, Kennedy referred only to *West* Berlin, implying that what the Soviets did with their half of the city was not a U.S. concern.[93] He warned the Soviets of the U.S. determination to stay in West Berlin. "We do not want to fight," the president said, "but we have fought before." Kennedy called for an increase in Army strength from 875,000 to 1 million and for smaller increases in the Air Force and Navy. To meet these manpower needs, draft calls would be doubled and tripled and certain reserve units would be called up to active duty. Kennedy also proposed a new civil defense effort, including a national survey of fallout-shelter space.[94]

To convey his interest in negotiations, Kennedy said that the United States recognized the historical Russian concern about Central and Eastern Europe and was willing to consider any arrangement for a treaty in Germany "consistent with the maintenance of peace and freedom and with the legitimate security interests of all nations." In his conclusion, Kennedy said: "I must tell you that there is no quick and easy solution. The Communists control over a billion people, and they recognize that if we should falter, their success would be imminent."[95]

Sorensen, who drafted the speech, conceded that "the necessarily generalized passages dealing with diplomatic approaches were thus the weakest part" of the president's speech. "What is still missing," James Reston noted in the *New York Times*, "is any evidence of a new basis for a political accommodation."[96]

"The President's words about his readiness to conduct negotiations are drowned out by his militaristic program," commented Tass.[97]

TIT FOR TAT

Kennedy's attempt to demonstrate resolve through costly military measures provoked countermeasures from Khrushchev to show that he could not be intimidated. According to John McCloy, who happened to be with Khrushchev in Sochi conferring about disarmament, the Soviet leader (who had previously been a cordial host) flew into a rage over Kennedy's speech. Khrushchev exclaimed emotionally that Kennedy had in effect declared preliminary war on the Soviets: he had presented them with an ultimatum and said that if the Soviets did not accept it, that would mean war. Khrushchev claimed that such a war would be decided by whoever had the biggest rockets—and that was the USSR, he said. Khrushchev kept repeating that the Soviets would sign a peace treaty no matter what; occupation rights would thereupon cease, access would be cut off, and the West would have to make a deal with the GDR. If the United States attempted to force its way through, that would mean war, and war was bound to be "thermonuclear." Although the United States and the Soviet Union might survive, all of America's European allies would be destroyed. He viewed the president as a reasonable young man full of energy. However, if war occurred, JFK would be the last American president.[98]

For the first time, the Soviet premier boasted of having rockets capable of lifting a 100-megaton superbomb. But such a bomb would require testing, he said. Khrushchev may have been hinting at his intent to break the nuclear moratorium. The Soviet leader also claimed that war would be decided by the *biggest* rockets, not the side with numerical superiority, as if to deflate later American claims to a strategic advantage.[99]

Khrushchev's official response came on 7 August 1961, in a televised speech that was a mirror image of Kennedy's 25 July address. After hearing their president's speech, Khrushchev complained, the American people might get the idea that the Soviets were out to start a third world war, rather than to eliminate the remnants of the last war. If anyone had resorted to threats, it was the U.S. president, Khrushchev said.[100]

"War hysteria is now being whipped up in the United States," the premier charged. At the same time, certain quarters were trying to accustom the American people to the idea that nothing particularly terrible would happen if war broke out. If a clash did occur between the two giants, he warned that neither would admit defeat without having used all its weapons, including "the most destructive ones."[101]

Khrushchev repeated his threats to sign a separate peace treaty and thereby force the West to negotiate with the GDR. He promised that the Soviet Union would not block access to West Berlin or blockade the city after signing a peace treaty with the GDR. But he warned that the USSR might have to reinforce its army on the western borders and call up the reserves as retaliatory measures against U.S. mobilization.[102]

Speaking emotionally and at times departing from his text, Khrushchev declared that "the Soviet Union does not want to go to war with anyone." He asked the Western powers to meet in a "roundtable conference," "not create war hysteria," and to "rely on reason and not on the power of thermonuclear weapons."[103] A *New York Times* editorial noted that Premier Khrushchev "has now delivered a double-barreled reply to President Kennedy, in which he mingles peaceful professions with threats even more dire than heretofore."[104]

At a reception on 9 August to honor the Soviet cosmonaut Major Gherman S. Titov, Khrushchev again boasted that the Soviet Union had the capability of constructing a rocket with a 100-megaton warhead. He repeated his determination to sign a peace treaty with the GDR. Khrushchev said with feeling that the Soviet Union did not want war and that he was not making any threats. Nevertheless, he warned that if Adenauer tried to reunify the German nation by force, "Germany will be reduced to dust."[105]

Two days later, in a speech delivered before a Soviet-Romanian friendship meeting, Khrushchev predicted that if there were war between the United States and the Soviet Union, "not only the orange groves of Italy may perish then, but also the people who cultivated them." Khrushchev warned the Greek ambassador that although he would not "issue orders that bombs be dropped specifically on the Acropolis," nor would he spare NATO bases located in Greece. The Soviet leader ridiculed the Western threat to fight for Berlin, a city of 2.2 million inhabitants, as a "fairy tale." If war were unleashed, "hundreds of millions might die." Khrushchev accompanied these bloodcurdling threats with pleas for reason, for an adjustment of differences. He proposed to sit down at the conference table and discuss calmly, in a businesslike way and without inflaming emotions, what should be done so that the seeds of new conflicts did not sprout in the soil left over from the last war.[106] At a reception afterward, Khrushchev mingled affably with Western diplomats and assured them that there would soon be negotiations over Berlin and that there would be no war. The premier claimed that the Soviet Union was not threatening anyone. "It would be madness to unleash an atomic war," he declared.[107]

A few minutes after midnight on 13 August 1961, East German soldiers and police began stringing barbed wire and establishing roadblocks along the border between East and West Berlin.[108]

In March, at a Warsaw Pact conference, the East German leader Ulbricht had proposed building a wall, but the other East Europeans voted against the idea on the grounds that it would be provocative and a propaganda embarrassment for the Soviet bloc. By early August, Khrushchev had apparently changed his mind. He informed Ulbricht that the Soviets would not sign a separate peace treaty, and he gave the East German leader permission to close the border with West Berlin, "but not [to go] one millimeter further."[109]

What had changed in the interim was that the flood of refugees had accelerated to the point that the East German authorities were in danger of losing control of the situation. In addition, Kennedy signaled to Khrushchev that he would not challenge an East German decision to close their borders. The flow of refugees from East Germany through West Berlin was approaching a runaway state. During the first six months of 1961, more than 100,000 persons had fled East Germany. In June alone, some 20,000 East Germans had crossed over into West Berlin. About 30,000 fled in July. The East German economy could not accommodate the loss of so many young professionals and technicians.[110]

Various U.S. statements may have encouraged Khrushchev to solve his problems by building a wall. In a television interview on 30 July, Senator J. William Fulbright commented: "I don't understand why the

East Germans don't close their border because I think they have a right to close it." Kennedy had considered appointing Fulbright as secretary of state, and the two men kept in close contact by telephone and letters. While there is no evidence that Kennedy asked Fulbright to make the statement, apparently the Arkansas senator had expressed publicly what Kennedy administration officials were thinking privately. Premier Amintore Fanfani of Italy, who had just spent several days with Khrushchev, reported that the Soviet leader had referred several times to statements made by Senators Mansfield and Fulbright, commenting that he thought the U.S. president agreed with their remarks "about 80%." Fanfani's warning alerted Kennedy to the need to disavow Fulbright's comments if he did not want Khrushchev to interpret them as a deliberate signal from his administration. He chose not to do so. When asked about Fulbright's statement, at a 10 August press conference, Kennedy said only that the United States would neither encourage nor discourage the movement of refugees.[111]

Kennedy, who was in Hyannis Port on 13 August, when the wall went up, ascertained from Secretary of State Dean Rusk that the East Germans had made no attempt to interfere with access to West Berlin. He asked Rusk to make a public statement but to pass the word along to his subordinates that they should do nothing to aggravate the situation. Kennedy also advised Rusk to attend a baseball game as he had planned. The president intended to go sailing.[112]

Secretary Rusk thus announced that the East German government had denied its people access to West Berlin. He reassured the American people that the allied position and Western access to West Berlin was unaffected.[113]

State Department and White House officials believed that the Soviet leader had been mainly concerned with the hemorrhaging of East Germany; now that the refugee problem had been solved, negotiations would follow. Bundy told the president that the White House staff unanimously recommended that the United States arrange negotiations with the Soviets within the next week or so. The border closing was "one reason more for calling talks" because of the "dangerous and explosive weakness it reveals in the GDR." Rusk commented that "while the border closing was a most serious matter, the probability was that in realistic terms it would make a Berlin settlement easier." The immediate problem was the "sense of outrage in Berlin and Germany which carries with it a feeling that we should do more than merely protest."[114]

Kennedy's passive response to the Soviet abrogation of four-power rights in Berlin disturbed West Berlin's mayor, Willy Brandt, who delivered a rousing address to more than a quarter-million West Germans milling in front of the West Berlin town hall. Brandt released to the press the text of a letter to Kennedy complaining about this weak U.S. response.[115] To boost the West Berliners' morale, Kennedy sent his reply to Brandt through Vice-President Johnson and General Lucius B. Clay, commander of the 1948 Berlin airlift. Kennedy also ordered a 1,500-man battle group to proceed down the autobahn from West Germany to West Berlin. The president later appointed General Clay as his personal representative to Berlin, even though the military commander had a reputation for taking independent action without approval from Washington.[116]

After reassuring the West Berliners, Kennedy made a serious effort to engage Khrushchev in negotiations. "I want to take a stronger lead in Berlin negotiations," Kennedy wrote Rusk on 21 August. The president firmly maintained that "We cannot accept a veto from any other power." Washington should make it plain to its allies, Kennedy wrote, that the administration planned to invite the Soviets to negotiations before 1 September, and they must either come along or stay behind.[117]

Kennedy urged that our proposals be as "fresh as possible—they should *not* look like warmed-over stuff from 1959." The president told Rusk to "examine all of Khrushchev's statements for pegs on which to hang our position. He has thrown out quite a few assurances and hints here and there, and I believe they should be exploited." Bundy advised Kennedy that the United States "can and should shift substantially toward acceptance of the GDR, the Oder-Neisse line, a non-aggression pact, and even the idea of two peace treaties."[118]

Solving the refugee problem did not meet Khrushchev's objective of obtaining some international recognition for the GDR, and the Berlin Wall did not end the crisis. On 23 August, the Soviet government sent notes to the allied powers accusing them of "abusing" their air rights by using their assigned air corridors to transport West German "revanchists, extremists, saboteurs and spies" to West Berlin. Although the Western powers warned that any interference with their access to Berlin, particularly by air, would have serious consequences, the Soviets escalated their interference to a new threshold by harassing allied aircraft flying into West Berlin. Soviet planes buzzed Western aircraft while Soviet and East German forces from the ground shone bright searchlights into the pilot's compartment. On 29 August, the Kremlin raised tensions by announcing dramatically that Soviet military personnel whose terms expired in 1961 would remain in uniform until a German peace treaty had been signed. If Khrushchev had been solely concerned with halting the refugee flood, he need not have stepped up military pressure because the United States had already shown through its pro forma protests that it did not intend to challenge the Berlin Wall.[119]

On 30 August 1961, the Soviets announced that they were forced by the threatening attitude of the United States and its allies to resume nuclear tests. Over the next sixty days, the Soviets conducted fifty such tests, the most intensive sustained test series in history. Khrushchev told two leftist members of the British Parliament visiting his retreat at the Black Sea that he intended to shock the West into negotiations on Berlin and disarmament.[120]

Using the Berlin crisis as a pretext to resume nuclear explosions, Khrushchev was probably trying to cover up the Soviets' nuclear inferiority which made it necessary to end the moratorium. Unable to match the sheer numbers of U.S. missiles in the short term, the Soviets had chosen to deploy larger-yield weapons ("more bang for the buck"), and that required additional testing.[121]

Kennedy decided to order the Atomic Energy Commission to make plans for a resumption of U.S. testing, but to refrain from any announcement until after Labor Day in order to derive maximum propaganda benefit from the Soviet tests. On 2 September, Kennedy telephoned Rusk from Hyannis Port with the suggestion that the United States propose to Khrushchev an agreement that there be no testing in the atmosphere. After some discussion among Kennedy's advisers and in coordination with the British, a press release announced on 3 September that Kennedy and Macmillan proposed an immediate ban on atmospheric tests, without any on-site inspection, and that Khrushchev had one week to agree. According to Glenn Seaborg, head of the AEC, Kennedy made the offer in order to embarrass Khrushchev and sway world public opinion to the U.S. side; no one believed he would accept it. Nevertheless, the atmospheric ban was significant as the first U.S. arms control proposal that did not include international control machinery.[122]

After three Soviet tests, on 5 September, Kennedy lost patience and ordered resumption of underground testing. Khrushchev contemptuously rejected the proposal for an atmospheric test ban, saying that the way to halt tests was to work on disarmament and a German peace treaty. An additional consideration, which Khrushchev did not mention, was that a limited test ban would be relatively advantageous to the United States, because the Soviets had not yet tested underground. Khrushchev later said that only "capitalist countries could engage in the expensive practice of underground testing."[123]

RECIPROCAL SIGNALS FOR DE-ESCALATION

Both Kennedy and Khrushchev used unofficial channels to signal their desire to end the Berlin crisis through negotiation. In a 5 September interview with James Reston of the *New York Times*, Kennedy confided that he was "puzzled" as to why he had been unable to "get down to rational discussion" with the Soviet leader about the situation in Berlin and Germany.[124] Similarly, Khrushchev used a long interview with the *New York Times* journalist C. L. Sulzberger to convey a desire for negotiations. The Soviet leader invited President Kennedy to visit the Soviet Union, offering assurances that he would be met warmly. Afterward, Khrushchev gave Sulzberger a private message for Kennedy, offering to establish informal contact to formulate a German settlement that would not damage U.S. prestige—but again on the basis of a German peace treaty and a free city of West Berlin. When Kennedy did not respond, the premier had Foreign Ministry Press Chief Mikhail Kharlamov inform Kennedy's press secretary, Pierre Salinger, that Khrushchev was willing to consider American proposals for a rapprochement on Berlin.[125]

Foreign Minister Gromyko and Secretary of State Rusk held three meetings in New York, on 21, 27, and 30 September, to prepare for substantive negotiations on Berlin. On 12 September, President Kennedy had sent a memorandum to the secretary of state instructing him not to put forward the 1959 Western peace plan for "early reunification of Germany or Berlin on the basis of free elections" because "these are not negotiable proposals; their emptiness in this sense is generally recognized; and we should have to fall back from them promptly." Kennedy wrote that he was "talking about a real reconstruction of our negotiating proposals, and not about a modest add-on."[126]

Throughout the negotiations, however, State Department officials dragged their feet with respect to meeting President Kennedy's request for new ideas, and suggested only minor cosmetic changes in Berlin's status. State Department officials saw no basis for cooperation with the USSR. They believed that the Soviets were trying to destroy NATO, that any willingness to negotiate would be regarded by the Soviets as a sign of weakness, and that any changes in Berlin's status could only damage the West's position. Rusk believed that Khrushchev's goal was not to improve the status of the GDR but to attack the U.S. right to access. Ambassador to Yugoslavia George Kennan was frustrated and alarmed by the State Department's pessimistic attitude toward the negotiations and by its failure to advance real negotiating proposals of its own. In a letter to Undersecretary of State Chester Bowles, Kennan wrote: "I am at a loss to know how anyone could form any judgment of what the Soviets are or are not willing to do in the absence of any negotiations, either private or public, and in the absence of any proposals or suggestions or ideas from our side." Despite Kennedy's admonitions, Rusk gave no indication in his talks with Gromyko of U.S. goals for a Berlin solution other than guarantees for Western access.[127]

During the Gromyko-Rusk discussions, President Kennedy hinted publicly that the United States might grant de facto recognition to East Germany in return for guaranteed access to Berlin. General Clay told journalists that West Germany would have to accept the "reality" of two German states. Then, in his 25 September speech to the United Nations on disarmament, Kennedy himself stated that "we recognize that troops and tanks can, for a time, keep a nation divided against its will, however unwise that policy may be." The journalist C. L. Sulzberger interpreted Kennedy's speech to mean that the United States would grant some provisional form of de facto recognition of East Germany in return for a new deal on West Berlin.[128]

Khrushchev reciprocated by initiating a private informal correspondence with President Kennedy. In the first letter, delivered on 29 September, Khrushchev said that he had planned to write the president earlier, but Kennedy's 25 July speech was so "belligerent" that his letter might have been misunderstood. Thereafter, continued the Soviet leader, both of them had not only made speeches but had taken actions that could not yield moral satisfaction for either party. Khrushchev added that it would be most unwise from the standpoint of peace to enter into such a "vicious circle" of measures and countermeasures.[129]

Khrushchev commented also that he was gratified by General Clay's statement about the need to recognize that two Germanys existed, and the Soviet leader offered to sign an agreement guaranteeing West Berlin's independence and freedom. In order not to prejudice the sovereign rights of the GDR, Khrushchev contended that token contingents of the troops of Britain, the United States, France, and the Soviet Union should be left in West Berlin.[130]

The Soviet premier reminded Kennedy that the Soviet Union was a rich country, that its expanse was boundless, its economy on the upgrade, its culture and science in their efflorescence. "And yet it is said that we want to seize West Berlin!" It was ridiculous even to think of it. What would that give the Soviet Union? "What would that change in the ratio of forces in the world arena? It gives nothing to anyone."[131]

On 2 October, Foreign Minister Gromyko elaborated on Khrushchev's letter, by proposing that the Soviet Union guarantee West Berlin's freedom and access routes so that the United States would not have to negotiate with the GDR. In return, the Soviets wanted the following: (1) legal formalization of existing German borders; (2) respect for GDR sovereignty; (3) agreement that nuclear weapons would not be transferred to either German state; and (4) the status of a free city for West Berlin. Gromyko explained that "respect for the sovereignty" of the GDR did not necessarily imply formal diplomatic relations.[132]

At his meeting with Kennedy on 6 October, the Soviet foreign minister withdrew Khrushchev's six-month ultimatum, noting that there was no "fatal date" for signing a German peace treaty. Even so, as Kennedy pointed out to Gromyko, the Soviet proposal would give the Soviets more than it would give the United States. Soviet troops would remain in East Berlin, while the United States would be forced to share its responsibilities with the Soviets in West Berlin. Further, these troops could only be stationed for a specific period of time, and their status would have to be renegotiated at some point. In return for a worsening of the U.S. position in Berlin, then, the United States would have to accept the boundaries of the two Germanys, including the line between East and West; induce the West German government to abandon its claims to East Germany; and agree not to provide nuclear weapons to West Germany. President Kennedy stressed that "this was not a compromise" but amounted to "trading an apple for an orchard." The United States would end up having to make concessions in return for less than its current rights in West Berlin. As Kennedy later wrote in a letter to Khrushchev, the United States would be "buying the same horse twice." That is to say, the United States would be conceding Soviet objectives to retain what it already possessed: namely, the freedom of West Berlin and Western access. Khrushchev and Kennedy did agree that Thompson and Gromyko would hold future talks in Moscow.[133]

It is difficult to determine whether the Soviet Union was presenting an initial bargaining position from which they were prepared to make concessions, for the United States offered no counterproposals of its own. Nor was the Soviet proposal as one-sided as Kennedy suggested, because the Soviets were not asking for formal U.S. recognition of the GDR, and the concessions that they did request—recognition of the Oder-Neisse boundary and agreement not to transfer nuclear weapons—were proposals that the White House had already considered making. In return, the Soviets were for the first time offering to guarantee West Berlin's political and social system as well as Western access to the city; they were not demanding that the Western allies negotiate with the GDR. Both sides could have gained from an agreement that would stabilize East Germany and permit more contacts between East and West, regardless any token Soviet military presence in West Berlin. As Khrushchev wrote in a letter to Kennedy, "it can be said that by the conclusion of a German peace treaty we would have planted an orchard the fruits of which would be enjoyed by all the states, all the peoples."[134]

At the Twenty-second Party Congress on 17 October, Khrushchev announced that since the "Western powers were displaying a certain understanding of the situation" and "were inclined to seek a solution for the German problem and for the West Berlin issue," he would not "insist on the signing of the peace treaty before December 31, 1961."[135] Khrushchev could withdraw the six-month deadline because the Berlin Wall had helped prop up the East German regime, and Kennedy had offered bilateral negotiations on the German question.

Despite Khrushchev's retreat, the president undertook a series of measures to impress the Soviet leader with his determination to stay in Berlin. The U.S. government began sending military reinforcements to Europe. In Berlin, General Clay led the military garrison through battle maneuvers.[136]

Most important, to prevent Khrushchev from miscalculating, Kennedy asked Deputy Secretary of Defense Roswell L. Gilpatric to reveal that there was no missile gap. In a speech on 21 October 1961, Gilpatric asserted that U.S. nuclear forces could survive a surprise Soviet attack and still retaliate against the Soviet Union with greater destructive force than the Soviets could deliver in their first strike. Subsequent statements by Secretary of Defense McNamara and other high officials repeated the theme that the United States had strategic superiority over the Soviet Union.[137] Gilpatric's statement took the wind out of Khrushchev's sails, and deprived him of any remaining leverage for negotiations on recognition of the GDR.

COLLAPSE OF THE TEST BAN NEGOTIATIONS

On 30 October 1961, the Soviets climaxed their test series with a 50-megaton bomb. Facetiously, Khrushchev commented that his scientists had made a mistake: "Instead of fifty megatons it proved to be more, but we will not punish them for that." According to AEC calculations, if the weapon been encased in uranium instead of lead, the yield of the explosion might have been 100 megatons. This gigantic explosion prompted Kennedy to announce three days later that he had ordered contingency preparations for atmospheric tests. Kennedy did not, however, decide to renew atmospheric testing just yet.[138]

When the Geneva test ban talks resumed on 28 November, the Soviet Union introduced a draft treaty for (a) an atmospheric test ban monitored by national detection systems and (b) an uninspected moratorium on underground testing. But Kennedy believed he could not accept another moratorium after the Soviets had violated the previous one.[139]

Because the Soviets had been making secret preparations for testing while negotiating on the test ban, Kennedy could not trust the Soviets to observe a ban on underground testing. In December, the president observed that Soviet behavior over the preceding nine months suggested that they did not want an agreement. Had they not been preparing since February 1961 the tests they initiated in September? What assurances could the United States have? Kennedy stated that he favored testing unless there were major progress on either Germany or disarmament. He agreed that the Soviet edge, if any, was not decisive now, but the problem was what would happen in 1964 if the United States did not continue testing and the Soviets did. "We could not get taken twice," he remarked. This had to be his view, said Kennedy, even though he was a "great anti-tester."[140]

At a news conference on 15 January 1962, Kennedy said that the most disappointing event of his first year in office was his failure to get an agreement with the Soviets on a nuclear test ban. On 29 January, the United States and Britain broke off the Geneva test ban negotiations in protest against the Soviet refusal to discuss international controls. The talks adjourned after 353 sessions, and the delegates had been unable to agree even on a communiqué for the end of the conference.[141]

From 2 January through 6 March, Ambassador Thompson held talks with Gromyko on the question of Berlin. Thompson's negotiating latitude was strictly limited, though, out of consideration for the French, who refused to negotiate with the Soviets on this issue. The ambassador was authorized to conduct a "probe" to see if substantive negotiations might be warranted. Prime Minister Macmillan had objected fiercely to these "long drawn out preliminary stages." The question was, "Do we want to reach an agreement with the Russians or don't we?" As Kennan had complained in a letter to Thompson, "It is now well over three years since Khrushchev began his efforts to get us to the negotiating table. I should have thought *their* interest in negotiation had been far more liberally documented than our own."[142]

Rather than address the German question, Thompson was instructed to negotiate on only two issues: access to West Berlin and an international access authority. Not surprisingly, Gromyko was not very forthcoming. He argued that the problem of access could not be separated from other relevant issues. For the Soviets to guarantee Western communications with Berlin, without obtaining any quid pro quo such as greater recognition of East Germany, would have meant giving up their leverage.

His patience severely tried by JFK's reluctance to advance concrete negotiating proposals, Khrushchev initiated a new form of pressure on Berlin. On 7 February, the Soviet representative on the Control Commission, General Ivan Konev, announced that allied flight corridors would be reserved for Soviet military flights. The Soviets began a program of harassment: they reserved airspace for Soviet military aircraft in Western air corridors at times and altitudes designated for commercial flights, flew Soviet fighter planes dangerously close to allied commercial and military aircraft, and dropped pieces of aluminum foil in the corridors in order to interfere with Western radar. Soviet interference continued sporadically until 29 March.[143]

On other issues, the Soviets were conciliatory, combining their pressures on Berlin with positive inducements. On 10 February, the Soviets released Francis Gary Powers, the U-2 pilot, in exchange for Colonel Rudolf I. Abel, a convicted Soviet spy. On 21 February, after Colonel John Glenn's orbit of the earth, Khrushchev proposed U.S.-Soviet cooperation in space, something Kennedy had suggested thirteen months earlier and to which he now readily agreed. A few days later, the U.S. and Soviet governments signed another agreement for exchanges in science, education, and culture.[144]

By early March 1962, Kennedy had decided to go ahead without the French, but Soviet harassment of civilian air traffic made it difficult for him to advance any constructive negotiating proposals. Rusk met with Gromyko at the eighteen-nation disarmament conference from 10 to 27 March. On the 19th of March, Gromyko retracted Khrushchev's previous offer to allow the three Western states to maintain token troops in West Berlin. The question of whether U.S. troops would have to be withdrawn proved to be the sticking point in U.S.-Soviet negotiations concerning Berlin and Germany. On 22 March, Rusk informally outlined some principles for a modus vivendi. These included the following: noninterference with West Berlin's status; an exchange of nonaggression declarations between NATO and the Warsaw Pact; the establishment of several mixed technical commissions of East and West Germans to increase cultural and technical contacts and to promote economic exchanges; the nondiffusion of nuclear weapons to countries not already possessing them; agreement not to use force to change existing borders; and a permanent forum of deputy foreign ministers to negotiate on unresolved issues. Rusk emphasized that he had presented an informal working paper, for discussion only. The secretary of state also proposed an international access authority, on which four Western states, four communist states, the two Germanys, and three neutrals would be represented.[145]

On 3 April, the State Department revised the proposed modus vivendi slightly to make it more acceptable to the Soviets. State sent a copy to Bonn on 13 April, and gave the West German government only forty-eight hours to approve the document so that Rusk could formally present it to Ambassador Dobrynin by 16 April, before the United States resumed nuclear testing in the atmosphere. To say that Adenauer objected strongly is to put it mildly. Adenauer said that he was "shocked" by the American proposals, which amounted to recognition of the Soviet zone regime (the GDR). The following day, the American proposal appeared in West German newspapers. Kennedy and Rusk complained to Foreign Minister Gerhard Schroeder that they were "shocked" by this serious breach of confidence on the part of the FRG.[146]

In deference to Adenauer, Rusk did not present the revised proposal to Dobrynin when they met on 16 April. Nevertheless, in an exclusive interview with Gardner Cowles, the editor of *Look*, Khrushchev said he detected some "glimmers of hope" for a solution to the Berlin question. Similarly, in his 24 April report to the Supreme Soviet, Gromyko said that the talks on Berlin had yielded "some glimpses of hope" that an agreement could be attained.[147]

Worried that the Soviets might accept the U.S. proposal on Berlin, Chancellor Adenauer predicted at a 7 May press conference that U.S.-Soviet talks on Berlin and Germany would fail. Conceding that the U.S. proposal for an international access authority did not entail formal U.S. recognition of the GDR, the chancellor charged that the East Germans would interpret their membership in the authority as a form of diplomatic recognition; therefore, he would prefer that the FRG not participate. Adenauer's intervention effectively stymied further progress in the U.S.-Soviet negotiations on Berlin.[148]

On 12 May, Khrushchev told Kennedy's press secretary Pierre Salinger that the Soviet Union could not recognize the right of the Western powers to keep their troops in Berlin.[149] Khrushchev's obduracy is not hard to understand: the United States first offered him nothing concrete, then allowed Adenauer to block presentation of the United States' 3 April proposals, which did contain points of interest to the Soviet Union. The major obstacle to agreement was Soviet insistence on the withdrawal of U.S. troops. On the other hand, Khrushchev had previously agreed that U.S. troops could stay in West Berlin, and he might have been persuaded to withdraw this condition in return for signs of a greater U.S. acceptance of the GDR.

Another reason for Khrushchev's unwillingness to concede with respect to the presence of U.S. troops may have been that he expected a radical improvement in his bargaining position. In late April or early May 1962, while vacationing in Bulgaria, Khrushchev conceived of the idea of installing missiles in Cuba. When Khrushchev learned from Marshal Malinovsky that the United States could strike Soviet cities with missiles fired from Turkey, the Soviet leader became outraged and asked the Soviet defense minister whether it might be possible to deploy missiles secretly in Cuba. After discussing the idea with a few Presidium members, Foreign Minister Gromyko, Marshal Sergei Biryuzov, the commander of the Soviet Rocket Forces, and Malinovsky, Khrushchev called in the newly appointed Soviet ambassador to Cuba Aleksandr Alekseyev and instructed him to seek Castro's permission.[150] Although Khrushchev's principal motivation for putting medium-range missiles in Cuba was probably to improve the Soviet strategic position quickly, without having to build so many of the technologically more complex and expensive ICBMs, he must have anticipated also that he could use increased Soviet strategic power to win concessions from the West vis-à-vis Berlin, just as he had done with his boasts about Soviet rockets.[151] At the end of July, the Soviets harassed civilian and military air traffic into Berlin. Soviet MiG-17 fighters buzzed and made passes at U.S. military transports and civilian airliners.[152]

The Soviets were also inflexible in the test ban talks, despite Kennedy's efforts to break the stalemate. On 27 August 1962, Kennedy and Macmillan offered the Soviets the choice between a comprehensive treaty with reduced on-site inspection or an atmospheric test ban monitored by national means.[153] The Soviets rejected both—the comprehensive treaty because of the obligatory on-site inspections, the limited version because it permitted underground testing which would stimulate the arms race. The Soviet negotiator Vasily Kuznetsov said that the Soviets would accept a limited test ban only if it were accompanied by an unpoliced moratorium on underground tests until control measures could be worked out.[154]

Because of the Soviets' violation of the last moratorium, however, Kennedy did not trust them to observe another. "Gentlemen's agreements and moratoria do not provide the types of guarantees that are necessary," the president said. "This is the lesson of the Soviet Government's decision just a year ago."[155]

Khrushchev had evidently put all U.S.-Soviet negotiations on hold until he could unveil the missiles in Cuba. At the end of September, Khrushchev wrote Kennedy that the only issue standing between them and a Berlin agreement was the presence of Western troops in West Berlin. Khrushchev said that he understood how candidates could get carried away in U.S. election campaigns, how they could say absurd things that might increase the risk of war. The Soviet leader promised to put the German problem "on ice" and not to take on action on West Berlin until after the November congressional elections. A few weeks later, in an interview with the new ambassador to the Soviet Union, Foy Kohler, Khrushchev offered to meet with Kennedy when he visited the United Nations at the end of November, so that they could discuss a test ban, disarmament, and West Berlin. Kennedy accepted Khrushchev's invitation, although he did not see what Khrushchev hoped to accomplish, since the Soviets would not budge on the issue of U.S. troops in West Berlin. But, then, Kennedy did not know about the missiles in Cuba. New evidence from the Soviet side indicates that Khrushchev evidently intended to travel to Cuba in early November, sign an agreement with

Fidel Castro and announce the missiles as a fait accompli, then meet with Kennedy at a summit.[156]

DECEPTION, DISTRUST, AND MISUNDERSTOOD SIGNALS

Placing missiles in Cuba was perhaps the most egregious contradiction in Khrushchev's policy. How could he have hoped to pursue domestic reform and lower defense spending while threatening Kennedy with nuclear missiles?

According to the conventional wisdom, Kennedy and Khrushchev agreed to a détente after their harrowing experience at the brink of nuclear war sobered both men and encouraged them to adopt more realistic objectives. It is apparent that the experience of having jointly resolved the missile crisis, of having avoided a cataclysmic nuclear war, gave each leader a new understanding of the other's perspective, a greater empathy, and a sense of shared responsibility for preserving world peace. Immediately after the Cuban missile crisis, both sides made some minor concessions to signal their desire to reduce tensions. The Soviets agreed to the election of U Thant as U.N. secretary-general, abandoning Khrushchev's "troika" plan. The United States refrained from bringing up the issue of Hungary's Soviet-imposed government in the U.N. General Assembly, thus discontinuing what had been an annual tradition since 1956. The Cuban missile crisis also demonstrated the vital need for the United States and the Soviet Union to have an efficient means of communication during a crisis: it had taken up to four hours to code, decode, and translate messages. In fact, in order to make sure that his final message came through—agreeing to withdraw the missiles—Khrushchev had it broadcast over the radio as well as transmitted through normal diplomatic channels. Consequently, on 20 June 1963, the United States and the Soviet Union signed a memorandum of understanding with respect to establishing the "hot line" as well as a teletype communications link between Moscow and Washington.[157]

But these examples of cooperation were minor. Kennedy did not consider making major initiatives; now, after the Soviet attempt to deploy missiles in Cuba surreptitiously, JFK trusted Khrushchev less. In his 22 October speech announcing the presence of the Soviet missiles in Cuba, Kennedy had recounted the various times the Soviets assured him that they had no desire or need to place offensive weapons in Cuba. The following night, Robert F. Kennedy visited Ambassador Dobrynin at the Soviet embassy. In an agitated state, RFK complained that President Kennedy had relied on the declarations of Khrushchev, whom he had "always trusted on a personal level." The president had been greatly impressed by Khrushchev's statement that the Soviets would not do any-thing to complicate the international situation and worsen relations dur-ing the U.S. election campaign. Accordingly, the president had staked "his own political fate" on Khrushchev's assurances when he stated to the American people that the Soviets had delivered only defensive weap-ons to Cuba. RFK reported that the president "felt himself deceived and deceived intentionally," which was a "a heavy blow to everything in which he had believed and which he had strived to preserve in personal relations with the head of the Soviet government: mutual trust in each other's personal assurances." In both a letter to Khrushchev and a No-vember interview with Mikoyan, President Kennedy reminded the Soviet leader that the Cuban missile crisis had originated in a high-level cal-culated effort by the Soviets to deceive him. He told Mikoyan that the prospects for improving U.S.-Soviet relations had suffered a severe blow from this deception. As the Council on Foreign Relations survey ob-served, "Even the Soviet Government depended for the success of its international dealings on the maintenance of at least some reputation for credibility, and it was difficult to see how any other nation could be expected to trust its word after so glaring an exhibition of the way it handled the truth in practice." Referring to Khrushchev's assurances to President Kennedy that the Soviet Union would never put weapons in Cuba that could reach the United States, the columnist Joseph Alsop noted that "for a chief of state to take great pains to cause a grossly and demonstrably false personal message to be transmitted to another chief of state is something altogether novel in post-war political history."[158]

The Soviet leader knew that he had violated norms of communication between leaders. In his memoirs, Khrushchev tries to excuse his decep-tion of Kennedy by arguing that the president had rebuffed his efforts to establish greater trust between them. For years, Khrushchev con-tended, "I made many honest attempts to come to an agreement about trust and establish good, friendly relations. Yet all efforts were rejected and ignored." Because of this, he rationalized, the Soviets had "both a legal and a moral right to make an agreement with Cuba [concerning the missiles]."[159]

Khrushchev miscalculated the U.S. reaction to his use of secrecy and deception. If the Soviets had openly reached an agreement with Cuba to place the missiles, as the United States had done with Turkey, it would have been much more difficult for the Kennedy administration to object. That the USSR not only installed the missiles in secret but gave false assurances to Kennedy only caused Americans to infer that the Soviets had offensive intentions and could not be trusted.[160]

The Cuban missile crisis did not cause Kennedy to abandon his sup-port for a test ban. But, because of the Soviet deception in Cuba, he regarded it as even more important that the Soviets agree to on-site inspection. Khrushchev would not do this at first.

Initially, mutual suspicions, bureaucratic stagnation, and miscommunication blocked cooperation between the superpowers even after their close encounter with nuclear war. On 19 December 1962, Khrushchev sent Kennedy a long letter in which he offered to accept two or three on-site inspections per year if that would help Kennedy persuade the Senate to ratify a test ban treaty. The Soviet leader noted that Ambassador Arthur Dean had informed Deputy Foreign Minister Kuznetsov that two to four on-site inspections a year in the territory of the Soviet Union would be sufficient. Later, Khrushchev asserted that Kennedy's science adviser Jerome Wiesner had mentioned a "few" inspections to the Soviet scientist Yevgeni K. Federov.[161]

After fifteen months during which the Soviets had refused to consider any inspections at all, White House officials regarded Khrushchev's initiative as a "major breakthrough." Kennedy replied that he was encouraged by Khrushchev's acceptance of the principle of on-site inspection, and he hoped that the Soviets would move toward the U.S. position, just as the United States had reduced its requirements from twenty to eight to ten inspections.[162]

But Khrushchev was suspicious of what appeared to be yet another U.S. retraction. Soviet diplomats walked out of the three-power test ban negotiations on 31 January 1963, bitterly accusing Kennedy of trying to embarrass Khrushchev in front of his critics. Khrushchev had been ambivalent and had grave doubts about allowing foreign inspectors on Soviet soil. When the Soviet leader accepted three inspections, he did so without support from other members of the Presidium. The Kennedy administration, however, did not appreciate how difficult it had been for Khrushchev to accept on-site inspection.[163]

If Kennedy had accepted Khrushchev's offer, the two states could have signed a comprehensive test ban. A team of British and American scientists concluded that the Soviets could only make improvements in low-yield tactical nuclear weapons through secret underground testing, and that the need to conceal the tests would substantially increase the time scale and cost of the program.[164] The problem, though, would have been to obtain Senate ratification with so few on-site inspections. A comprehensive test ban would have constrained technological advances in weaponry. Without testing, ballistic missiles with multiple independently targeted reentry vehicles (MIRVs) and nuclear-tipped cruise missiles could not have been developed.[165]

On 8 February, President Kennedy authorized the U.S. negotiator (William C. Foster) to go as low as six inspections, but left it up to him when and how to present it. One week after the eighteen-nation disarmament committee discussions had resumed in Geneva (12 February), Foster offered to accept seven inspections.[166]

Khrushchev's feelings of betrayal and his distrust of the United States erupted in an interview with the journalist Norman Cousins of the *Saturday Review*. President Kennedy had asked Cousins to reassure the Soviet leader that the United States wanted a test ban, despite the disagreement over inspections. Khrushchev professed skepticism: "If the United States really wanted a treaty, it could have had one." The Soviet leader claimed that he had persuaded the Council of Ministers to accept three inspections because of assurances that this concession would secure a test ban and that otherwise Kennedy could not get the treaty through the Senate. "Back came the American rejection. They now wanted neither three inspections nor even six. They wanted eight. And so once again I was made to look foolish. But I can tell you this: it won't happen again." Finally, said Khrushchev, he accepted Kennedy's explanation that it was an honest misunderstanding. "But the next move is up to him," the Soviet premier warned.[167]

On 11 April 1963, Kennedy sent a letter to Khrushchev explaining that there was an honest misunderstanding over the number of inspections. The president offered to send a "senior personal representative" to discuss the test ban and other issues with the Soviet leader. On 24 April, the British and U.S. ambassadors delivered to Khrushchev a letter from Kennedy and Macmillan offering to send "very senior representatives" to Moscow for direct discussions with the Soviet premier. Khrushchev asked whether the letters accepted the Soviet proposal for three inspections. When Gromyko said no, Khrushchev launched into a lengthy diatribe on how a test ban was really of no importance.[168]

In his reply to the Kennedy-Macmillan letter, on 8 May, Khrushchev contended that underground explosions could be detected by national means, as evidenced by the fact that Soviet seismic stations had detected the vibrations in the earth's crust produced by recent French tests in the Sahara. Since no inspection was needed for detection of underground tests, Western demands for international inspection could only be intended to introduce NATO's intelligence men into Soviet territory. He had agreed to on-site inspection not because he thought it was necessary for verification, but because President Kennedy had said that without a certain minimum of on-site inspections he would not be able to persuade the U.S. Senate to ratify a test ban. Instead of responding positively to his initiative, however, the Western powers began to "haggle" over the number of inspections and the conditions for conducting them. The Soviet leader complained that the sense and significance of his concession on on-site inspection had not been fully appreciated. So be it. He was now ready to try discussions in Moscow with high-level representatives of the United States and Britain.[169]

The president therefore decided to make a dramatic gesture that would reassure Khrushchev about America's sincerity and break the deadlock in U.S.-Soviet negotiations. Kennedy asked Sorensen to draft a speech about peace, with additional inputs coming from Norman Cousins, McGeorge Bundy, Carl Kaysen, Walt Rostow, Schlesinger, and Tom Sorensen (Theodore's brother). The bureaucracy was not consulted. Kennedy wanted to emphasize the peaceful and the positive in U.S. relations with the Soviets, undiluted by threats, boasts, or lectures. On his own, the president decided that the United States would not be the first to resume nuclear tests in the atmosphere, and that he would put that announcement in the speech.[170]

KENNEDY'S SIGNAL

In his commencement address at American University on 10 June 1963, Kennedy warned against the tendency to view "conflict as inevitable, accommodation as impossible, and communication as nothing more than an exchange of threats." He asked Americans to reexamine their attitudes toward the Soviet Union: "No government or social system is so evil that its people must be considered as lacking in virtue." Americans might find communism repugnant as a negation of human freedom, "but we can still hail the Russian people for their many achievements—in science and space, in economic and industrial growth, in culture and in acts of courage." He reminded Americans how the Soviets had suffered in World War II: at least 20 million lost their lives; homes and farms were burned or sacked; a third of its territory was turned into a wasteland.[171]

The president lamented that both sides were "caught up in a vicious and dangerous cycle in which suspicion on one side breeds suspicion on the other, and new weapons beget counterweapons." Both sides, he pointed out, were devoting massive sums of money to weapons that could be better spent fighting ignorance, poverty, and disease. Kennedy stressed the two countries shared an interest in avoiding a hot war and in halting the arms race. Agreements to that end, therefore, were in both sides' interest, "and even the most hostile nations can be relied upon to accept and keep those treaty obligations, and only those treaty obligations, which are in their own interest."[172]

To demonstrate his good faith, Kennedy pledged that the United States would refrain from atmospheric nuclear testing as long as others did the same. The president was pledging the sort of informal, "gentleman's agreement" moratorium, without inspections, that he had said he would never again accept![173] This offer, of course, was politically risky. Senator Everett Dirksen complained: "And do we now accept another self-imposed moratorium on atmospheric testing, particularly after experiencing a Soviet doublecross, only a short two years ago when a previous moratorium existed?" Congressional Republicans charged that the speech was a triumph for "accommodators" in the administration.[174]

The Soviets signaled by their actions that they were impressed by the speech. The following day, the Soviet representative at the U.N. Security Council surprised the delegates by abstaining on a vote to send a peace-keeping mission to Yemen. A few days later, the Soviets stopped jamming Western broadcasts, after fifteen years of almost continuous interference. The president's speech was reprinted in both *Izvestia* and *Pravda*. The Soviets also reversed themselves and agreed to allow inspection of nuclear reactors by the International Atomic Energy Agency.[175]

Most important, on 2 July, Khrushchev offered a ban on nuclear testing in the atmosphere, in outer space, and underwater that would require no inspections.[176] This was the first time the Soviets had accepted a limited ban.

The timing of Khrushchev's shift suggests that he must have been impressed by Kennedy's bold and politically risky American University speech. Khrushchev warmly praised the speech to Harriman, saying with deep feeling that it was the best speech made by any president since Franklin Roosevelt and that it took courage on Kennedy's part to make it.[177]

Kennedy had selected Averell Harriman, undersecretary for political affairs, as his diplomatic representative in Moscow. The president instructed Harriman to try for a comprehensive test ban, but if the Soviets did not agree, to propose a ban on testing in the atmosphere, outer space, and underwater. Kennedy sent a personal letter to Khrushchev through Harriman, stating that a comprehensive agreement would be best. He assured the Soviet leader that the United States had no interest in using inspections for espionage.[178] If Khrushchev had agreed to a comprehensive test ban, the president was prepared to submit it for ratification, despite anticipated opposition from the Joint Chiefs. Kennedy had told the National Security Council that "if the Russians accept our treaty, we will have to fight for it in the Senate, win, lose or draw."[179]

It was not domestic political constraints or the Joint Chiefs' opposition which prevented Kennedy and Khrushchev from agreeing to a comprehensive test ban, however, but the Soviet leader's deep distrust of U.S. intentions. Khrushchev insisted to Harriman that inspection *was* espionage: you could not let the cat in the kitchen only to hunt the mice and expect that it would not also drink the milk. Seeing that Khrushchev could not be reassured, Harriman settled for a limited ban.[180] The Soviets would not allow on-site inspections because the United States might use them for espionage; the United States would not agree to a test ban without on-site inspection because the Soviets might clandestinely test underground.

Harriman, Gromyko, and Lord Hailsham (Quintin Hogg), British minister for science and technology, initialed the treaty to prohibit nuclear testing in the atmosphere and underwater on 25 July 1963. It was the first major East-West accord since the 1955 Austrian State Treaty.[181]

The test ban allowed the two sides to test each other's trustworthiness without much risk. In his televised address to the nation on 26 July, Kennedy described the treaty as "an important first step—a step toward peace—a step toward reason—a step away from war." When the foreign ministers of Britain, the United States, and the Soviet Union formally signed the treaty on 5 August, each described the limited test ban as a "first step." Secretary of State Rusk explained that "if on this particular point there is compliance over time, and if it is possible to find another point on which some agreement and compliance is found, it may be that, little by little, some degree of confidence will be built up." Defense Secretary Robert McNamara testified before the Senate that "probably more important than purely military implications, the treaty should provide us with an opportunity to test the sincerity of Soviet protestations about their desire to explore more sweeping arrangements for preserving the peace."[182]

In the American University speech, Kennedy had referred to the Moscow test ban negotiations as the first step in a "strategy of peace" (in other words, making small agreements in which each side could demonstrate its good faith). In summer 1963, the United States and the Soviet Union signed new bilateral agreements on atomic energy and cooperation in space. The two governments began negotiations for a new consular convention, and they made progress toward a civil aviation agreement. In October the two superpowers agreed to support a U.N. resolution to keep weapons of mass destruction out of outer space.[183]

On 9 October, Kennedy announced his decision to grant export licenses so that the Soviets could purchase several million tons of wheat worth $250 million, a controversial decision that Vice-President Johnson called "the worst political mistake we have made in foreign policy in this administration" because of the furor it aroused in Congress. Kennedy was trying to be consistent in word and deed. In his response to Kennedy's American University speech, Khrushchev had noted that the U.S. refusal to trade with the Soviet Union contradicted the president's call for better relations. "Trade is an indicator of good relations between states," Khrushchev declared. In light of the importance that the Soviets attached to trade, Kennedy concluded that a failure to respond favorably to Soviet requests for grain could lead to a "renewal of the Cold War."[184]

On 13 December 1963, Khrushchev announced a 4.3 percent cut in military spending, and suggested that he might undertake the previously postponed unilateral reductions in conventional forces. In return, Lyndon Johnson, now president, announced that the U.S. defense budget would be cut by $500 million. Khrushchev replied that they might make progress in disarmament through a policy of "mutual example."[185]

That Khrushchev attempted to make cuts in defense even after the Cuban missile crisis suggested that he favored a minimal deterrent. He believed that superior Soviet living standards would ensure the worldwide victory of socialism. The Soviet premier did not have adequate domestic political support, however, to continue making unilateral reductions. Thus Khrushchev's troop cuts once again aroused the opposition of military leaders, who publicly attacked him for his overemphasis on rockets and his neglect of conventional capabilities, and the cuts were never fully implemented.[186]

Nevertheless, the Soviet military did not play a role in Khrushchev's overthrow by a palace coup in October 1964. Although memoirs by members of the party elite conflict on the details of who initiated plans for Khrushchev's overthrow, they agree that the leading figures in the plot were not the conservatives who criticized his policies openly, such as Mikhail Suslov, but Khrushchev's own protégés: Leonid Brezhnev, Nikolai Podgorny, and Aleksandr Shelepin. Moreover, foreign policy issues were not emphasized in the indictment against Khrushchev's leadership. Khrushchev's successors charged that he had become too arbitrary and dictatorial in his leadership practices.[187]

Why were the United States and the Soviet Union able to cooperate on a limited test ban but not a comprehensive one? Why did Kennedy and Khrushchev fail to reach agreement on the Berlin and German questions? Kennedy and Khrushchev's preferences overlapped; they both wanted a test ban and the stabilization of Central Europe. As reasonable men, they *should* have been able to communicate their goals to each other and reach some kind of agreement. Their shared interests outweighed ideological differences, which mainly concerned the Third World. Kennedy's objective was to maintain the balance of power; Khrushchev's was to obtain Western recognition that the Soviet Union was a superpower and that there were two Germanys in Europe.

A series of linked events flowing from Kennedy's decision to build up U.S. strategic and conventional capabilities led to escalating tension, confrontation, deception, and intimidation. Had Kennedy acted differently in the early months of his administration—by delaying his military buildup until after U.S. satellites had produced adequate intelligence on Soviet missile capabilities, meanwhile engaging in serious negotiations on Germany and Berlin—history might have played out differently. The early months of his administration would have been an opportune time to reach an accommodation on the issue of Germany and Berlin. Believing that the great powers had a special responsibility for world order, Kennedy was willing to go a long way, and over Adenauer's opposition, toward meeting Soviet interests in stabilizing their security sphere in Eastern Europe. An agreement on Berlin would have averted the most dangerous superpower confrontation, in Cuba, and would have improved the climate for arms control agreements. With the Berlin issue settled, Khrushchev could have focused on his domestic reform programs and on improving the living standards of the Soviet people.

But Kennedy decided to augment U.S. military power and demonstrate his resolve before offering any indication of a willingness to compromise with Khrushchev, which led the Soviet leader to lose interest in a test ban and renew his threats against West Berlin. Khrushchev interpreted Kennedy's abandonment of the 28 July 1959 Western position at Geneva as a sign that the president had reneged on the implicit agreement Khrushchev had worked out with Eisenhower. Even after the Soviet leader issued his six-month ultimatum against Berlin, Kennedy could have tried to engage the Soviets in negotiations. Instead, the president increased the defense budget again and threatened to go to war over Berlin, prompting Khrushchev to do likewise. After the Berlin Wall was erected, Kennedy was finally willing to enter into negotiations, but he failed to press the State Department to formulate a proposal for a political solution. When Kennedy finally had Rusk present the U.S. proposal for a modus vivendi, it was only an informal working paper; the president allowed Adenauer to block its presentation as a formal offer.

Both Kennedy and Khrushchev allowed their allies to obstruct U.S.-Soviet cooperation. Kennedy should not have allowed the U.S. interest in obtaining a Central European settlement to be held hostage to Adenauer's whims. There were other officials within the West German government with whom the United States could have worked to achieve a Berlin agreement. Even if Kennedy had pursued a more independent policy, it is very unlikely that the West Germans would have tilted toward the Soviet Union. As Kennedy pointed out to Adenauer in May 1962, the United States was bearing the major financial and military burden of defending West Berlin, and had the onerous task of trying to negotiate with Khrushchev as well.[188] Similarly, Ulbricht was dependent on the Soviet Union for economic assistance and internal order. The East German leader ultimately had to swallow Khrushchev's refusal to sign a separate peace treaty.

Domestic politics, whether in the Soviet Union or in the United States, probably was not the chief obstacle to agreement on a comprehensive test ban. While little has been revealed on decisionmaking within the Presidium, what little evidence is available does not suggest that Khrushchev faced any serious opposition to his policies toward the United States. He was careful to associate other members of the Presidium with his decisions concerning Berlin and Cuba.[189] Kennedy, in contrast, had to obtain Senate ratification of any treaty that would limit nuclear tests. Even so, the main impediment was a fundamental American mistrust of Soviet intentions, and that mistrust was only exacerbated when the Soviets broke off the moratorium and attempted to install missiles secretly in Cuba. Because of the widespread belief that the Soviets could not be trusted, Kennedy believed that he needed some on-site inspection within the Soviet Union in order to monitor a test ban. But from Khrushchev's perspective, one could not trust foreign inspectors not to make use of whatever intelligence information they acquired.

Movement toward détente after the Cuban missile crisis was almost interrupted by a spiral of misunderstanding, missed signals, and recrimination. Kennedy's speech at American University was politically controversial because it asked Americans to reexamine their attitudes about the Soviet Union and stated that the Cold War was not entirely the Soviets' fault. Kennedy's initiation of an uninspected moratorium on atmospheric nuclear tests made the United States vulnerable to the possibility that the Soviets would secretly prepare to resume testing. Khrushchev concluded that Kennedy must be serious about cooperation on arms control, and he accepted an atmospheric test ban after having rejected a similar agreement four times previously.

The two countries finally signed the Limited Test Ban Treaty and entered into small cooperative agreements, such as the pledge not to orbit nuclear weapons in outer space, as a means of testing each other's trustworthiness. But one could not expect U.S. and Soviet attitudes toward each other to be transformed overnight. Belief systems lagged; progress was incremental and halting. The two states remained deeply distrustful of each other, and after Kennedy's death and Khrushchev's overthrow, U.S.-Soviet relations stagnated.

[5]

Success and Failure in SALT

Richard M. Nixon and Leonid I. Brezhnev achieved cooperative agreements unprecedented in both number and significance—concerning accidental war, trade, scientific cooperation, medicine, strategic arms limitation, and prohibition of nuclear defenses. On the other hand, the two leaders failed to limit multiple independently targetable reentry vehicles (MIRVs), which endangered deterrence by making it theoretically possible for one side to destroy the other's missiles in hardened silos and thus escalated the arms race.[1]

Strategic and domestic political conditions favored U.S.-Soviet cooperation. The United States was desperate to get out of Vietnam, while the Soviet leadership had no desire to allow the Vietnam conflict to interfere with their efforts to improve relations with the United States. The Soviet Union and the United States had achieved rough equality in their nuclear forces. The postwar blocs were breaking down. West European countries, particularly France and West Germany, were pursuing a more independent policy of building bridges between East and West. The Soviet rift with China had become dangerously tense and had even erupted into armed conflict. An emerging multipolarity created more complexity for the United States but also opened up an opportunity for more creative diplomacy. Moreover, the American public was weary of foreign involvements and high levels of defense spending, and the Soviet economy was stagnating, with defense spending consuming a large portion of the budget.[2]

The Nixon administration wanted Soviet help in ending the war in Vietnam, joint restraint on arms spending in order to alleviate domestic political pressure for unilateral reductions, normalization of relations with the Soviet Union to restore America's freedom of diplomatic maneuver, and greater cooperation with the Soviet Union in managing regional conflicts in order to prevent nuclear crises. Brezhnev wanted to decrease the burden of arms spending, to reduce the risk of nuclear war, to prevent the United States from blocking Soviet efforts at rapprochement with West Germany, and to consolidate his own leadership within the Soviet Union.[3]

Despite their shared interests, Nixon and Brezhnev had to work through a heavy layer of mistrust with respect to each other's intention to achieve a summit and a SALT agreement. Nixon and Kissinger were concerned about Soviet intervention in Middle East conflicts and their effort to establish a naval facility in Cuba. Kissinger used military force demonstrations and ultimatums to induce the Soviets to play a constructive role in Jordan and to halt possible construction of a naval base in Cuba. The Soviets regarded U.S. coercive diplomacy as inconsistent with the president's expressed desire to open an era of negotiation, not confrontation. The deadlock in U.S.-Soviet relations did not begin to break until spring 1971, when Brezhnev made a consistent series of concessions relating to European security. Yet Nixon was still undecided as late as 1972, when Brezhnev showed himself willing to subordinate Soviet credibility and alliance commitments to U.S.-Soviet cooperation.

The U.S.-Soviet détente established in May 1972 did not endure, though. Domestic political factors prevented the United States from meeting its commitments to improve U.S.-Soviet trade. Ideological aspirations tempted the Soviets into intervening in the Third World. Thus both sides, largely for domestic political reasons, undermined the trust on which U.S.-Soviet cooperation rested.

A SOVIET PROPOSAL

Despite his fundamental mistrust of the Soviet Union, Nixon came into office with several ideas about improving relations with the Soviet Union through negotiation. A realist, Nixon rationally assessed the Soviet interest in cooperating with the United States. He believed that the Soviets' attainment of nuclear parity with the United States might give them an incentive to control the arms race. He thought that their fear of China might motivate Soviet leaders to stabilize their relationship with Western Europe. And he expected that the Soviets would be willing to abstain from competing for influence in South Asia, the Middle East, Africa, and Latin America so as not to jeopardize chances for progress on more important issues.[4]

In his inaugural address, President Nixon declared that "after a period of confrontation, we are entering an era of negotiation. Let all nations know that during this administration our lines of communication will be open. . . . With those who are willing to join, let us cooperate to reduce the burden of arms, to strengthen the structure of peace."⁵ A few hours after Nixon's speech, Soviet Foreign Ministry officials called a rare press conference to announce that they were ready to "start a serious exchange of views" concerning the control of nuclear missiles. Since they had attained rough parity with the United States in numbers of ICBMs, the Soviets believed that they could cooperate in stabilizing the arms balance without fear that the United States would try to negotiate from a "position of strength." The immense effort to catch up with the United States had imposed a heavy economic burden, and the Soviets also were interested in limiting a U.S. antiballistic missile (ABM) system, which might prevent Soviet nuclear weapons from reaching their targets after the United States had launched a first strike. The Strategic Arms Limitation Talks (SALT) had been scheduled to begin in 1968 but were canceled by the Johnson administration after the Soviet invasion of Czechoslovakia.⁶

At his first meeting with President Nixon, on 17 February 1969, Ambassador Anatoly Dobrynin said that his government wanted to move toward the era of negotiation that Nixon had mentioned in his inaugural speech. The Soviet ambassador offered to negotiate on a broad range of issues. He reported that the Soviets' main goals were to enforce the Nuclear Nonproliferation Treaty, resolve the conflict in Vietnam, open bilateral negotiations to settle the conflict in the Middle East, recognize the status quo in Europe, and continue Soviet-American exchanges on strategic weapons in order to curb the arms race. He asked when the United States would be ready to engage in talks about limiting strategic arms.⁷

Nixon, though, was noncommittal. The president said that arms talks required careful preparation. Further, freezing arms would not ensure peace unless both sides exercised political restraint. Nixon also asked Dobrynin to take up important matters with the national security adviser, Henry Kissinger, thus bypassing the secretary of state.⁸

Four days later, Dobrynin met privately with Kissinger, who stressed that Nixon wanted to promote better relations between their two governments, and that included the issues of interest to the Soviets. Dobrynin, however, noticed that Kissinger did not mention the Soviet offer to resume negotiations on the limitation of strategic weapons.⁹

Nixon and Kissinger were wary about being "stampeded" into strategic weapons talks until they could study the problem and form some opinion about Soviet attitudes. They wanted to have a clearer idea of Soviet motives before undertaking talks that could serve those objectives. In December 1968, Kissinger had told the newly selected Nixon cabinet that the apparent Soviet eagerness to pursue SALT could be a tactical device to regain respectability after the invasion of Czechoslovakia, a maneuver to split the NATO alliance, or an effort to stabilize the strategic balance.[10]

Nixon wanted the Soviets to prove their good faith by making concessions and by cooperating in different areas before he would enter into negotiations to control strategic weapons. At a 27 January press conference, Nixon declared that he wanted to have "strategic arms talks in a way and at a time that will promote, if possible, progress on outstanding political problems at the same time." He mentioned the Middle East, although he really wanted the Soviets to help the United States disengage from Vietnam.[11]

This was "linkage." Linkage meant that the Soviets should cooperate consistently across issue areas. In his memoirs, Kissinger recalled that the administration attached two meanings to linkage. What might be called "tactical" linkage referred to a diplomat's use of an issue in negotiation as leverage on another issue. "Inherent" linkage, on the other hand, meant that a great power's actions in one part of the world had consequences beyond the issue or region directly involved; in other words, "linkage was a reality, not a decision."[12]

Nixon was criticized for using tactical linkage—in other words, for making arms control negotiations with the Soviets contingent on political settlements of unrelated issues. In practice, however, the Nixon administration defined linkage more loosely as consistent cooperation across issue areas. Thus, instead of asking for a quid pro quo on issue B in return for a U.S. concession on issue A, Nixon expected the Soviets to show a cooperative attitude on the major issues at stake in the U.S.-Soviet relationship.

Linkage, then, was not merely a bargaining strategy but, more important, a test of Soviet credibility. The Nixon administration could not trust the Soviets if they cooperated in areas of interest to them, but tried to achieve unilateral advantage at the expense of the United States in other parts of the world. At a briefing for reporters on 6 February, Kissinger explained that "linkage" meant there should be "some demonstration of something other than words that together with reducing the competition on arms there will be an attempt to reduce the conflict in the political fields." During his March 1969 European trip, Nixon called for "signs of good faith" across the board, so that progress in one area would not be undermined by crisis in another. Nixon pointed out that he could not "be expected to develop trust for the Russians in one area if he is given cause for suspicion and hostility in another." Nixon's approach to linkage was reminiscent of Eisenhower's insistence that the Soviets would have to prove their good faith by "deeds not words" before he would agree to a summit meeting.[13]

Nixon's efforts at tactical linkage failed, for the Soviets refused to submit to what they perceived as blackmail. In mid-April 1969, Kissinger informed Dobrynin that U.S.-Soviet relations were "at a crossroads" and that "a settlement in Vietnam was the key to everything." The national security adviser proposed sending Cyrus R. Vance to Moscow to negotiate principles of strategic arms limitation. Vance could also meet with a North Vietnamese representative to discuss a political and military settlement in Vietnam. The Soviets, not wanting to reject Kissinger's suggestion, never formally replied. In his memoirs, Kissinger reports that during 1969 he mentioned settling the war in Vietnam to Dobrynin ten times, but that the Soviet ambassador was "evasive."[14]

Vietnam was a difficult issue on which to test Soviet credibility. Aid to the North Vietnamese was tied in with the Soviet self-image as the leader of "proletarian internationalism." The Soviets themselves had only recently delinked SALT from their demand that the United States withdraw from Vietnam. The Soviets may nevertheless have been willing to act as interlocutors with the North Vietnamese if not as formal mediators.[15]

While not complying with Nixon's demands for linkage, the Soviets did make conciliatory gestures in several issue areas in order to signal their desire to improve relations with the United States. In mid-March, the Soviet government agreed to a new rapid-communications link between the U.S. embassy in Moscow and the State Department which they had previously held up for months. The Soviets also proposed reviving the U.S. consular office in Leningrad and establishing a new Soviet consulate in San Francisco. For the first time since World War II, the Soviet celebration of May Day did not feature a parade of the latest tanks and military equipment rumbling across Red Square. Instead of the usual address by the Soviet defense minister, General Secretary of the Communist Party Brezhnev made a speech from atop Lenin's tomb in Red Square in which he called for peaceful coexistence with the West. In a major speech to the Supreme Soviet on 10 July, Foreign Minister Gromyko called for closer Soviet-American relations. As for President Nixon's call for an era of negotiations, Gromyko said that if the United States was prepared to move in that direction, "we for our part are ready."[16]

In retrospect, the Soviets' actions in 1969 suggest that they really did want to cooperate with the United States to control the arms race, although there was some disagreement within the leadership.[17] Perhaps because Brezhnev did not have adequate political backing within the Politburo to make bold moves, the Soviet government made no concessions significant enough to prove its sincerity to a suspicious Nixon administration and they were unable to persuade the United States to cooperate until 1971.

By 1969, the Soviets wished to avoid a costly race in ABMs, which would put further pressure on their meager economic resources. Many Soviet scientists also doubted that it was feasible to build a system that could defend a population against nuclear attacks.[18]

President Nixon also had an interest in negotiated limits on ABMs, largely because of domestic political considerations. In September 1967, President Johnson had decided to deploy the Sentinel ABM system to defend fifteen sites against a Chinese nuclear attack. In January 1969, the outgoing secretary of defense Clark Clifford had submitted a defense budget request for the Sentinel program that included $335 million for research and development, $736 million for procurement, $647 million for construction, and $70 million for operations; but many congressmen and newspaper columnists were urging that Nixon delay further deployment of ABMs pending the outcome of arms control negotiations with the Soviet Union.[19]

By 1968, strong opposition to ABMs had developed in Congress, in the academic-scientific community, and among the residents of cities where ABMs were scheduled to be deployed. Many senators believed that the Vietnam War had diverted economic resources that were needed to attack urban problems, and the ABM system would cost additional billions that could be spent on domestic needs. Arms control supporters pointed out that the Soviets might justifiably interpret the ABM system as intended to protect American cities from retaliation against a first strike. For the United States to deploy ABMs would stimulate the arms race by prompting the Soviets to deploy more delivery vehicles in order to penetrate U.S. defenses. Scientists questioned whether a defensive system could reliably intercept Soviet missiles, and argued that the Soviets could defeat the system with relatively inexpensive countermeasures. Urban residents close to potential ABM sites feared that a nearby interceptor missile might accidentally explode and that the presence of a defensive system would make their community a target for Soviet missiles.[20]

Nixon did not want to give up any weapon system unilaterally, thereby making the United States appear weak to the Soviets at a time when he was seeking their help to end the war in Vietnam. Explaining his ABM decision to the cabinet, Nixon contended that the United States had to have real military superiority as a basis for negotiations. "The war will be over by next year," he said flatly, but until then they would have to take the public position that the outlook was tough while negotiating in private. Military strength was necessary as a basis for successful negotiation, Nixon contended. The intellectuals were all opposed to this approach. "It's only us nonintellectuals who understand what the game is all about," he said.[21]

Once he had decided to deploy an ABM system, Nixon used political criteria to determine its mission, configuration, and hardware. On 14 March, Nixon announced that his program for an ABM system, called Safeguard, would shift the emphasis away from defending city populations against a Chinese attack to protecting U.S. missile sites, but would retain the option of defending cities as well. Nixon moved ABM defenses away from major cities to remote missile bases in order to quell protests from angry residents and arms control advocates. Initially, the ABM system would be deployed at two Minuteman missile bases, but it would be extended to twelve sites for area defense by 1973. A phased deployment would reassure those who were worried about the impact of the ABM system on the budget.[22] Even with these changes, in August 1969 a congressional amendment to prohibit the Safeguard system while permitting research and development on other antiballistic missile programs was defeated by the narrowest possible margin (50–51), with Vice-President Spiro Agnew casting the tiebreaking vote.[23]

The issue of MIRVs was even more urgent, for the United States was rapidly approaching deployment. The military had begun testing MIRVs in August 1968, but a new and final round of tests was scheduled to begin in May 1969. In contrast to the vigorous congressional debate and organized grass-roots lobbying with respect to ABMs, the issue of MIRVs received little attention from the public. Yet most strategists believed that it was even more urgent to come to an agreement with the Soviets on a ban against MIRVs than it was to restrict ABMs.[24] A MIRV was a Hydra-headed weapon, a launcher with multiple warheads, each of which could be launched separately and targeted individually.

Both superpowers had an interest in limiting MIRVs, because increases in yield and accuracy of the warheads could in theory provide MIRVed missiles with the ability to destroy several of the opponent's missiles in their silos. The United States may have had a temporary advantage in MIRV technology because the Soviets had only tested multiple reentry vehicles (MRVs), which could not be aimed at widely dispersed targets, but the considerations for banning MIRVs were also compelling. In the long run, MIRVs would damage the U.S. strategic position relative to the Soviet Union because larger Soviet launchers equipped with MIRVs would have more "throw-weight" (i.e., could lift more and heavier missiles and reentry vehicles). In a June 1969 memo, George W. Rathjens and Jack P. Ruina, professors at the Massachusetts Institute of Technology, warned Kissinger that "a decision to go ahead with MIRV tests probably also implies eventual abandonment of Minuteman missiles by the United States."[25]

The spring of 1969 offered a narrow window of opportunity to ban MIRVs. Most scientists believed that a ban on MIRV testing could be monitored by satellite surveillance or radar tracking, whereas an agreement not to deploy MIRVs could be verified only by intrusive on-site inspection to determine how many warheads were deployed on a launcher. MIRVs, therefore, could be limited only if the two states agreed before either side had carried out enough testing to develop an operational capability. Navy and Air Force testing of MIRVs was scheduled to resume late in May and to continue through July 1969.[26]

Accordingly, congressional proponents of a MIRV ban focused their efforts on obtaining a moratorium on MIRV testing while SALT negotiations were under way. In early June, Senator Edward W. Brooke (R–Mass.) sponsored a sense-of-the-Senate resolution calling on the president to propose to Moscow an immediate and mutual moratorium on flight testing of MIRVs while SALT negotiations took place. On 5 June, Senators William B. Saxbe (R–Ohio) and J. W. Fulbright (D–Ark.) joined with forty-three other members of Congress in a statement warning that "once large-scale ABM deployment begins and MIRV testing has been completed, the nuclear genie will be out of the bottle." The Brooke resolution for a ban on MIRV testing was endorsed on 17 June by thirty-nine senators, only twelve short of a majority.[27]

The Joint Chiefs and the Department of Defense strongly opposed any limits on MIRVs. They regarded MIRVs as a cheap, cost-efficient means of meeting U.S. targeting requirements, at a time when Congress was cutting the defense budget. Instead of trying to cooperate with the Soviets in eliminating both sides' multiple-warhead systems, the Department of Defense tried to get the SALT agreement to include reductions in Soviet heavy missiles and throw-weight, in order to limit future Soviet MIRV potential.[28]

On 11 June, Nixon disarmed his critics by authorizing Secretary of State William P. Rogers to propose SALT negotiations to the Soviets, even though the Kremlin had not assisted the United States in Vietnam or the Middle East. At a press conference on 19 June, Nixon even stated that "we are considering the possibility of a moratorium on tests as part of any arms control agreement." On the same day that Nixon professed his willingness to consider a MIRV ban, however, the Air Force quietly awarded an $88 million contract to General Electric to produce sixty-eight MIRV missiles. The Air Force and the Navy continued their tests of multiple warheads for Minuteman 3 and Poseidon missiles throughout the summer.[29]

In congressional hearings held on the MIRV issue in the summer of 1969, opponents of a ban argued that the Soviets could clandestinely test in violation of a moratorium. The deputy director of the Arms Control and Disarmament Agency, Philip J. Farley, testified before a House sub-committee that the Soviets might already have sufficient knowledge to deploy MIRVs without additional testing. Farley doubted that a moratorium on MIRV testing could be monitored by satellite surveillance or other national technical means. The Pentagon's top scientist, John S. Foster, director of Defense Department Research and Engineering, testified that the Soviets could get around a test moratorium with shots in outer space, tests on the vast Soviet landmass beyond the reach of American radar and satellites, or piecemeal testing of MIRV components. As a *New York Times* editorial pointed out, this argument was reminiscent of opposition to the 1963 Nuclear Test Ban Treaty, when "it was said that the Soviet Union would evade the ban by testing behind the moon or in far outer space." Foster appointed an advisory panel under Daniel Fink, a former Defense Department official employed by General Electric, which was a major MIRV contractor. The Fink panel agreed that the Soviets could acquire an operational MIRV capability through secret testing. The panel unanimously recommended that the United States continue MIRV testing and make no move in strategic arms talks to ban MIRVs.[30]

The Soviets, however, did not accept the U.S. proposal to begin SALT negotiations until October. Why, after the Soviets professed to be so eager for negotiations, did they delay? Soviet leaders, despite the congressional proposals for a moratorium while SALT negotiations were under way, may have been wary about Nixon's intentions because of his decision to proceed with both an ABM deployment program and MIRV testing. Just a few weeks after his offer of strategic weapons talks, moreover, the president announced that he would visit Romania, and this must have heightened Soviet anxieties about maintaining their sphere of influence in Eastern Europe. The domestic affairs of Czechoslovakia—only one year had passed since the Soviet invasion—were still unsettled and potentially unstable. Finally, since March, the Soviet Union had been engaged in a series of border clashes with China, and Soviet leaders may not have wished to enter into major talks with the United States until they had controlled the potential for escalation by beginning negotiations with the Chinese. On 20 October 1969, Dobrynin called on President Nixon and informed him that the Soviet government was prepared to open official discussions about limiting strategic arms. At the same time, the Soviet ambassador warned Nixon against making any attempt to exploit differences between the Soviet Union and China.[31]

Exploratory negotiations began on 17 November, at Helsinki. Both sides were probing; neither presented formal proposals. Soviet negotiators agreed on the need to reinforce mutual deterrence by restricting arms. The Soviets were willing to limit ABMs to low levels. But Soviet negotiators also insisted on limiting U.S. forward-based systems—that is to say, nuclear-delivery-capable aircraft based in Europe or on aircraft carriers near the Soviet Union. Soviet diplomats argued that the United States could strike Soviet territory with these weapons, and that they should therefore be included even if they did not meet American criteria for "strategic" weapons.[32]

MISSED OPPORTUNITY FOR A MIRV BAN

At the second round of SALT, beginning on 16 April 1970, the U.S. negotiator Gerard C. Smith was authorized to present two package proposals. The first called for limiting ABMs to Moscow and Washington (called NCAs, or national command authorities) or, alternatively, for a complete ban. It limited offensive weapons to the number then possessed by the United States (1,710 ICBMs and SLBMs) and included a ban on MIRVs which would be monitored by on-site inspection.[33]

Nixon and Kissinger knew that, because of its intrusive nature and the danger that the United States might obtain targeting information, the Soviets would never accept on-site inspection. Another objectionable feature of the MIRV proposal from the Soviet standpoint was that it banned testing and deployment of MIRVs, but not production. A ban on flight testing would prevent the Soviets from acquiring the capability to produce MIRVs, freezing the USSR in a position of inferiority. The United States, on the other hand, could produce and maintain a stockpile of MIRVs, so long as it did not deploy them.[34]

Why did the Nixon administration propose a MIRV ban certain to be rejected by the Soviets? Kissinger did not try for a workable MIRV ban because he calculated that the Pentagon and the Joint Chiefs would not tolerate limits on multiple-warhead missiles and that an agreement limiting ABMs was "all that the traffic would bear." When congressional leaders, even those sympathetic to the ABM system, were unwilling to support deployment of Safeguard beyond the initial two sites, Nixon decided in April 1970 to offer the Soviets limits on ABMs. Nixon had to heed congressional sentiment with respect to ABMs because the lengthy process of deployment would provide Congress with numerous opportunities to cut off funding, whereas MIRVs were rapidly approaching operational status in 1969–70. In addition, Nixon and Kissinger agreed with the Pentagon that a ban on MIRV testing could not be verified with confidence by national means and that the Soviets might already have sufficient knowledge to deploy MIRVs without further testing.[35]

At the same time, Nixon and Kissinger were under substantial pressure from Congress and opinion leaders to delay MIRV testing. On 9 April, the Senate passed the Brooke resolution, which called on President

Nixon to propose that both sides immediately suspend deployment of offensive and defensive nuclear-strategic weapons. The president's own General Advisory Committee on Arms Control and Disarmament (GAC) recommended to Nixon that the United States halt MIRV testing. The GAC included such well-known conservatives as John J. McCloy, Dean Rusk, and William J. Casey.[36]

By including the requirement for on-site inspection, Nixon and Kissinger had designed a proposal for a MIRV ban that would satisfy Congress yet be unacceptable to the Soviets. Kissinger himself added the requirement for on-site inspection, after an NSC meeting in which alternative negotiating options were discussed, much to the disappointment and frustration of officials who had written the proposal for a MIRV ban. Neither the NSC nor the verification panel had discussed the details of on-site inspection or whether it could detect a clandestine Soviet deployment of MIRVs. There was no interagency study of the verification requirements of a MIRV ban until *after* the United States had demanded on-site inspection. Indeed, Kissinger and his staff doubted that on-site inspection would detect determined Soviet efforts at cheating, because the Soviets could easily conceal their multiple-warhead missiles.[37]

U.S. actions cast doubt on the seriousness of the American offer to ban MIRVs. In March, one month before SALT negotiations were to begin, Secretary of the Air Force Robert C. Seamans said at a congressional hearing that the United States would begin deployment of MIRVs by early summer, ahead of schedule. In June, the first MIRVed Minuteman 3s were deployed.[38]

The Soviet negotiator Vladimir Semenov rejected the MIRV proposal immediately. On-site inspection, he said, was tantamount to intelligence activity. In a private conversation with Smith later in June, Semenov charged that the MIRV proposal had been designed to be rejected. At the beginning of the Vienna negotiations, the United States had announced its intent to deploy Minuteman 3s equipped with MIRVS, he said, which made the U.S. proposal "propagandistic." In November 1970, the Soviets told Smith that they had never considered the U.S. MIRV proposal as genuine; it was just a "cheap sop" to appease congressional opinion.[39]

Moscow might have accepted a MIRV ban on testing and production monitored by national means. To be sure, some Soviets might have objected to a ban on MIRVs when only the United States had tested the weapons, for that would place the Soviet Union in an inferior position and allow the Americans to break out of the treaty unexpectedly. On the other hand, Soviet embassy officials, through informal contacts with legislators or their aides, had indicated some interest in a MIRV ban. The Soviet Defense Ministry's newspaper *Krasnaya zvezda* hinted at support for such an agreement. The *New York Times* reported that the Soviet leadership was divided over the wisdom of halting MIRVs, with the military opposed and some civilians in favor, but would be receptive to a proposal if the Americans raised it. At a private meeting of the Council on Foreign Relations in March, Dobrynin suggested that the Soviets would be responsive to a U.S. offer of a moratorium or limitation on the testing of multiple warheads. Yuli Vorontsov, minister at the Soviet embassy, said much the same thing to a congressional staffer at a cocktail party. Privately, Soviet negotiators expressed surprise that the United States had not mentioned a ban on MIRV testing at the exploratory talks in Helsinki; they considered the problem of controlling multiple warheads an "American" issue, perhaps because only the United States was close to deployment.[40]

Was this a missed opportunity to ban MIRVs? Although neither Kissinger nor Nixon favored a MIRV ban, an agreement would have been consistent with their underlying preferences and, under different circumstances, they might have accepted it. In retrospect, Kissinger said that he wished he had thought through more carefully the implications of a MIRVed world. Nixon saw little use in having more nuclear weapons than the Soviet Union. In his memoirs, Nixon recalled that once each side had the ability to destroy the other, the most important consideration was maintaining the strategic equilibrium, not acquiring more weapons than the other. When Nixon came into office, he changed U.S. military doctrine to one of "sufficiency"—that is, having adequate military forces to defend U.S. interests around the world. Thus Nixon's acceptance of parity with the Soviets underlay his decision to enter into SALT negotiations. According to Kissinger, the president was primarily concerned about preventing Soviet geopolitical challenges, not a Soviet nuclear attack; he feared an upset in the global balance of power, not a change in the strategic balance.[41]

Although it would have been difficult to secure an arms control agreement without the support of the Joint Chiefs, Nixon might have been able to buy off the military by granting them concessions on other issues, such as a new submarine. In 1969–70, the president probably could have obtained congressional ratification of an agreement banning MIRVs.[42]

The second negotiating package presented to the Soviets had the same ABM provisions but also entailed major reductions in intercontinental ballistic missiles and submarine-launched missiles, from the U.S. level of 1,710 to 1,000 over a seven-year period. The proposal singled out land-based missiles for cuts, while freezing the U.S. advantage in bombers. It included Soviet medium-range missiles capable of striking Europe, but not U.S. forward-based aircraft that could reach Soviet territory. It contained a special sublimit on Soviet modern large ballistic missiles (MLBMs), such as the SS-9, but allowed the United States to install multiple warheads freely.[43] The Soviets objected that the reductions option would diminish their greatest strength, land-based ICBMs, while leaving aside weapons where the United States enjoyed an advantage: namely, submarine-launched missiles, bombers, and forward-based systems.[44]

The one proposal the Soviets did accept was the Nixon administration's suggestion that ABMs be confined to the national capitals. The problem was that this limitation would give the Soviets a unilateral advantage, because they could keep their Galosh system around Moscow, whereas Congress would never support an ABM system around Washington, not wanting to convey the impression that they were interested only in protecting "politicians and generals."[45] On 23 June, Dobrynin suggested privately to Kissinger that they settle for an agreement limiting ABMs, but the national security adviser rejected this option as a thinly veiled Soviet attempt to deprive the United States of its advantage in defensive systems without any reciprocity in the form of restraints on Soviet programs.[46]

On 4 August 1970, at Nixon's instruction and approval, Smith introduced a new SALT proposal which maintained a limit of 1,710 on ballistic missiles launchers but did not include a MIRV ban or on-site inspection. The offer contained sublimits on Soviet heavy missiles such as the SS-9, but no restrictions on warheads, thus allowing the United States to increase its superiority. As for defensive weapons, the United States offered the Soviets a choice between two alternatives: a ban on ABMs or capital defense.[47]

The Soviets were baffled. They had already accepted the U.S. proposal for ABMs to be limited to the national capitals. Now the United States had proposed still another option. From the Soviet perspective, the 4 August proposal was an improvement, because it did not include Soviet medium-range missiles or submarine-launched tactical cruise missiles that could not strike U.S. territory. Nevertheless, the Soviets insisted on some form of compensation for U.S. forward-based systems. Such a trade-off was difficult for the United States to accomplish, however, because of the potential impact on the interests of its allies.[48]

COMPETITION AND CONFRONTATION IN PERIPHERAL AREAS

In 1970 a series of crises in the Middle East and Cuba exacerbated mutual superpower distrust. American passivity in the face of Soviet probes encouraged the Soviets to test the unspoken rules. Then, interpreting unfolding events as part of a deliberate Soviet challenge, Kissinger responded with threats and force demonstrations, raising Soviet suspicions with respect to U.S. trustworthiness and reliability.

In the Middle East, a few days after the 7 August cease-fire (sponsored by the United States to end the Egyptian-Israeli war of attrition) went into effect, the Soviets helped the Egyptians violate the standstill agreement by moving antiaircraft missiles near the Suez Canal. The United States was handicapped in its ability to protest the cease-fire violations by poor intelligence and sloppy negotiations. The State Department had neglected to secure aerial surveillance of the area until several days after the cease-fire went into effect. In addition, State had not obtained a firm commitment from the Soviets to participate in the cease-fire, so the Soviet government was not a formal party to the agreement. Moreover, the text of the agreement was vague, and the United States did not provide the Egyptians with its unilateral interpretation until thirty-six hours after the cease-fire went into effect. In any case, Kissinger argued that the United States must protest Egyptian violations immediately and forcefully, including a description of the remedial action that the Soviets must take. President Nixon, however, did not want any confrontation over the Middle East so near the congressional elections; he therefore tried to buy off the Israelis by approving their request for additional missiles and F-4 Phantom jet fighters. Finally, in early September, Nixon directed the State Department to lodge a very strong protest in both Cairo and Moscow. Yet the Egyptians continued to move missiles into the region of the Suez Canal.[49]

On 17 September, fighting broke out in northern Jordan near Syria, in reaction to King Hussein's efforts to restore order in Amman and expel any resisting Palestinian *fedayeen*. Syria then moved tanks to its border. At a meeting of the special crisis-decisionmaking body known as the Washington Special Action Group (WSAG), Kissinger recommended a significant increase in American forces in the region. The national security adviser suggested that the aircraft carrier *Saratoga* join the *Independence* near the Lebanese coast, and that the carrier *John F. Kennedy* be dispatched to the area from Puerto Rico. When Kissinger telephoned Nixon, who was in Chicago, the president approved the military force movements enthusiastically. Nixon startled Kissinger with the comment, "There's nothing better than a little confrontation now and then, a little excitement."[50]

The following day, Kissinger learned from the CIA director Richard Helms that a recent U-2 flight had photographed construction of a major Soviet naval facility on an island near the Cuban bay of Cienfuegos. Kissinger had ordered daily U-2 flights after a flotilla of Soviet ships—including a submarine tender and an amphibious landing ship pulling two barges commonly used for servicing nuclear submarines—was seen pulling into Cienfuegos on 9 September. Intelligence experts in the State Department, the CIA, and the Pentagon had concluded that Cienfuegos

[168]

was a rest-and-recreation facility for Soviet submariners. Kissinger went even further, concluding that the Soviets were constructing a permanent submarine base at Cienfuegos, in violation of the Kennedy-Khrushchev agreement not to station offensive weapons in Cuba. The Soviets were undoubtedly probing at the margins, trying to loosen the restraints imposed by the 1962 Kennedy-Khrushchev agreement so that they too, like the United States, could station weapons on the territory of an ally.[51]

At a meeting of the WSAG on 19 September, Kissinger argued that these naval activities were part of a consistent pattern of Soviet testing of American resolve around the world, in the Middle East as well as in Cuba. The national security adviser argued strongly that unless the United States reacted strongly to the challenge, the Soviets might misinterpret U.S. permissiveness and escalate their involvement until it would take a major crisis to remove the base. When Kissinger informed Nixon of the results of the meeting, however, the president decided not to take a strong stand before completing his trip to Europe and getting past the November congressional elections. Nixon said that he did not want some "clown senator" asking for a Cuban blockade in the middle of an election.[52]

On 20 September, Kissinger received intelligence that a column of Syrian tanks had invaded Jordan. Kissinger drafted a stiff note to the Soviets, issued in Secretary Rogers's name, calling on the Soviets to urge the Syrians to withdraw their forces and desist from any further intervention. The note warned of the serious consequences of any broadening of the conflict. At a WSAG meeting, the national security adviser also recommended various military movements in order to signal U.S. resolve to the Soviets, and Nixon later approved them: (1) improving the alert status of an American brigade in West Germany; (2) putting the Eighty-second Airborne Division on full alert; and (3) sending a reconnaissance plane from a U.S. carrier to Tel Aviv to pick up targeting information.[53]

The Soviets replied the following day. They shared U.S. concerns about the situation in Jordan and also considered outside intervention into the affairs of Jordan to be unacceptable.[54]

Tensions eased when Hussein launched an all-out attack against the Syrians on 22 September, and Syrian tanks began to withdraw the following day. To keep up the pressure for Syria's withdrawal, Kissinger ordered four more destroyers to proceed to the Mediterranean and two attack submarines to go through the Strait of Gibraltar.[55]

Kissinger congratulated himself on his use of diplomacy and military signals to contain Soviet expansion. As he saw it, Soviet officials had interceded with the Syrians to persuade them to withdraw their troops. No doubt the Syrians had been impressed as well by U.S. military power and the threat of Israeli intervention. But Kissinger probably exaggerated both the extent to which the Soviets were behind the Syrian invasion as well as their role in securing the withdrawal of Syrian tanks from Jordan. The fact is, the Soviets had difficulty controlling the Syrians, a weak, faction-ridden, and unstable client. That the Syrians retreated probably had more to do with internal Syrian politics than with Soviet pressure. General Hafez al-Assad refused to use the Syrian air force to support an adventure planned by one of his political rivals, and so Jordanian air power was able to be utilized.[56] Yet because the Syrians had behaved as he wished, Kissinger concluded that they must have been responding to outside pressure.

Only a few days after the Jordanian crisis was resolved, Kissinger delivered another ultimatum to the Soviets with respect to Cienfuegos. A Pentagon official had inadvertently informed journalists about the visit of the Soviet naval flotilla and the construction of a naval facility, and Kissinger used the leak as an excuse to go against Nixon's expressed wishes. In a background briefing on 25 September, Kissinger informed the press that they were watching the development of Soviet naval activity in Cuba and possible base construction there.[57] He warned that "the Soviet Union can be under no doubt that we would view the establishment of a strategic base in the Caribbean with the utmost seriousness."[58] Two hours later, Kissinger told Dobrynin privately that the United States would view continued construction with the "utmost gravity"; the submarine base could not remain.[59]

When Kissinger and Nixon returned from their overseas trip in early October, Dobrynin reported that the Soviets were not constructing a naval base in Cuba. The Soviet ambassador then reaffirmed that the Soviets were committed to the Kennedy-Khrushchev understanding on Cuba.[60]

After the crises were over, the United States and the Soviet Union exchanged public accusations and recriminations. The White House expressed concern that the Soviets seemed willing to seize narrow tactical advantages along the Suez Canal, in Jordan, or in Cuba at the risk of jeopardizing their larger interest in pursuing broader settlements with the United States.[61] In a television appearance on 11 October, Secretary of Defense Melvin Laird and Secretary of State Rogers listed examples of Soviet bad faith in areas ranging from the Soviet missile buildup to the Middle East and Vietnam. Deputy Defense Secretary David Packard noted that Soviet complicity in Egyptian cease-fire violations had disturbing implications for how much one could believe Soviet promises in the SALT negotiations.[62] In his address to the United Nations on 20 October, President Nixon called on the Soviets to "transcend the old patterns of power politics in which nations sought to exploit every volatile situation for their own advantage or to squeeze the maximum advantage for themselves out of every negotiation," because in the nuclear era such policies could lead to a confrontation that would spell disaster for all. He called for Soviet "actions," not "atmospherics." Despite U.S.-Soviet differences, the president pointed out, there were four "great factors" that provided a basis for working together: a common interest in avoiding a nuclear confrontation; the enormous cost of arms; economic self-interest in increasing trade and contacts; and the global challenge of economic and social development.[63]

Foreign Minister Gromyko publicly denied that the Soviets had ever been a party to the 7 August cease-fire. In the Soviet view, the related crisis was the work of the "old" Nixon, stirring up anticommunist sentiment in time for the November congressional elections. To protest what they regarded as an officially inspired anti-Soviet campaign, the Soviet Union decided not to send Premier Kosygin to the United Nations for the twenty-fifth anniversary session. Analysts in the Soviet Foreign Ministry, academic institutes, and official newspapers reiterated that Nixon "is not a reliable man." The president talked about wanting an "era of negotiation," they said, but his actions in North Vietnam, Cambodia, the Middle East, and Cuba made serious negotiation difficult.[64]

Nixon and Kissinger went from underreacting to Soviet probes to over-reacting to the misbehavior their own passivity had encouraged. The Soviets, for their part, did not understand how Moscow's scrambling for marginal gains in Third World areas, at the expense of the hoped-for relationship with the United States, fed Nixon's mistrust. The superpowers had calculated that they both had an interest in cooperating to reduce the risk of war and to control the arms race; yet they seemed unable to do so, owing to mistrust and a striving for petty advantage.

Because the U.S. SALT proposals were so one-sided, the Soviets began to wonder whether Nixon was serious about reaching an agreement on arms limitation. At the same time, the Soviets were anxious to limit ABMs before momentum developed for their deployment. In December 1970 the Soviets formally proposed that the United States and the USSR first enter into an agreement limiting ABMs, then sign a separate one having to do with offensive limitations.[65]

The Soviets emphasized that they did not intend for an ABM treaty to preclude an agreement limiting offensive arms. They maintained that negotiations on offensive weapons should proceed in parallel. An ABM treaty, for example, could be accompanied by an informal understanding on offensive forces. The Soviet argument was not persuasive, though, because once both sides had agreed to limit ABMs, the United States would have no leverage with which to persuade Moscow to restrain its ongoing weapons programs.[66]

In early 1971, the Soviet leadership was dissatisfied with the state of its relations with the United States. Nixon's intentions toward the Soviet Union were still unclear. Foreign Minister Gromyko and the head of the KGB Yuri Andropov submitted a memorandum to the Politburo arguing for continued efforts to deal with Nixon. The memo complained that the first two years of Nixon's presidency had produced only idiosyncracies and tactical delays in foreign policy, and no major changes from the policies pursued by Nixon's Democratic predecessors. Nevertheless, Gromyko and Andropov urged that the Soviet Union press for peaceful coexistence and emphasized the need to reach agreements with the United States that served Soviet interests.[67]

The Politburo approved the policy memorandum, calculating that Nixon wanted a summit in 1971 to boost his popularity in the presidential elections the following year. The Politburo, too, wanted a summit because, as the Gromyko-Andropov memo stated, it was "in our long-term interest to demonstrate the possibility of a further development of Soviet-American relations in spite of their inherent fluctuations."[68]

The assessment of Nixon's electoral concerns was accurate. When Kissinger met with Dobrynin in January 1971, he indicated that Nixon was interested in bringing a summit to fruition in 1971, and that they should make greater use of their secret channels to handle the issues of Berlin and strategic arms limitation.[69]

In spring 1971, the United States and the Soviet Union achieved breakthroughs in negotiating cooperative agreements on Europe and SALT. At the Twenty-fourth Party Congress in March 1971, Leonid Brezhnev consolidated his authority, achieving preeminence over Kosygin, and announced a Peace Program signifying the beginning of a "peace offensive" toward the United States. The Communist Party leader stressed his desire to improve relations with the capitalist world in order to boost the Soviet consumer's standard of living. For the first time, the general secretary's summary report gave priority to the production of consumer goods in the five-year plan.[70]

Brezhnev was not much of an ideologist, and he could not conceptualize abstractly about foreign policy. On the other hand, he had lived through one war, and knew that peace was popular among the Soviet people. His instincts inclined him toward détente and cooperation with the United States. By the beginning of the Nixon administration, Brezhnev had developed strong convictions about the need to improve relations with the West, particularly with the United States. Until 1971, however, Brezhnev had been battling with Kosygin for supreme leadership.[71]

In his speech to the Twenty-fourth Party Congress, Brezhnev signaled that he was prepared for cooperation with the United States on a range of political issues of interest to both sides. Besides the standard Communist peace proposals, such as liquidation of foreign bases and dissolution of NATO and the Warsaw Pact, Brezhnev proposed more feasible agreements with the West, such as settling the West Berlin question, holding a European security conference, coming to an agreement on SALT, making mutual force reductions in Central Europe, devising measures to prevent accidental war and bacteriological warfare, banning nuclear tests, and restraining nuclear proliferation.[72] At the same time, Brezhnev complained about "frequent zig zags in United States foreign policy," which he attributed to short-term political considerations. Foreign Minister Gromyko agreed that Nixon's stated desire to move from confrontation to an era of negotiations "should be supported by practical deeds."[73]

Before Dobrynin left the United States to attend the Twenty-fourth Party Congress, Kissinger had conveyed an informal message from Nixon to the Soviet leadership. The president was sure that a summit meeting in 1971 would be useful so long as both sides could reach agreement on Berlin by July and so long as an ABM agreement had been completed by about the same time for signature at the summit. After the party congress, the Politburo met to discuss a reply to Nixon's message. Dobrynin argued that Nixon's conditions could form a good basis for a summit meeting, and Kosygin supported him. Gromyko, on the other hand, insisted that Moscow should take advantage of Nixon's eagerness for a summit meeting by first solving the problem of West Berlin which "is passed from one American administration to another." Most other Politburo members then followed Brezhnev, who agreed with Gromyko that "a meeting with Nixon can wait."[74] Remembering past failures to achieve a Berlin agreement with Eisenhower and Kennedy, Gromyko perhaps had reason to mistrust the Nixon administration's intent to conclude such an agreement. But the Soviets' suspicions ultimately redounded to their disadvantage, for when the meeting with Nixon did take place, Brezhnev's bargaining position was weakened by the Nixon administration's opening to China.

According to Dobrynin, Brezhnev did not have as much flexibility or negotiating freedom as was enjoyed by American presidents. Brezhnev had to submit all major decisions, including his instructions for negotiations with foreign leaders, to the Politburo for approval. Major foreign policy positions were drafted by Gromyko, after consultation with the general secretary and a few other members. A formal vote was almost never taken. Instead, the Politburo made decisions by consensus. If the members of the Politburo could not resolve their differences, Brezhnev would postpone a decision and consult with individual members afterward to work out a compromise.[75]

The Soviets backed up their conciliatory rhetoric with several concessions. At the U.N. disarmament conference in Geneva, the Soviet Union agreed to the West's position that a separate ban on bacteriological weapons should be negotiated first, leaving aside the more difficult problem of limiting chemical weapons.[76]

On 14 May 1971, Brezhnev proposed negotiations for mutual force reductions in Central Europe, and the timing of Brezhnev's proposal cost him the opportunity to win unilateral U.S. troop reductions. For Brezhnev's unexpected offer cut the ground from under Senator Mike Mansfield's resolution to withdraw 150,000 American troops from Western Europe, predicted to pass the Senate on 19 May. Now the administration could, and did, argue before Congress that the United States should not unilaterally reduce its forces when there was a chance for reciprocal reductions.[77]

Since 1966, Mansfield had annually proposed the withdrawal of American troops. If the Mansfield amendment had passed, the Soviet Union could have reciprocated by withdrawing part of its troops. This was precisely the kind of informal reciprocal cooperation that Khrushchev had hoped to achieve through his unilateral reductions. That the Brezhnev government not only did not endorse, but undercut possible U.S. unilateral action suggested that Soviet interests had changed since Khrushchev's day. Mansfield had asked for Soviet support during the Johnson administration, but the Soviet government declined to offer the senator any encouragement. The Politburo feared that withdrawal of Soviet troops could destabilize Eastern Europe. Besides, the Soviets figured, the U.S. government would never accept the resolution.[78] Rather than trying to get the United States out of Europe, the Soviet leadership now apparently favored U.S.-Soviet collaboration in preserving both European stability and the bipolar division of the continent.

Next the two superpowers reached the 20 May agreement to work for an ABM treaty "together with" measures limiting offensive strategic weapons. In other words, Washington gave up its quest for a comprehensive treaty limiting offensive as well as defensive weapons, and Moscow softened its demand for an initial agreement limited to ABMs. Dobrynin and Kissinger had privately agreed to an interim freeze or moratorium on offensive weapons while negotiations for permanent limitations continued.[79]

In May, too, the Soviets persuaded the Stalinist East German party leader Walter Ulbricht to resign, removing a major obstacle to normalization of relations between East and West Germany. Brezhnev had thus sacrificed an ally to obtain an agreement with the West on Berlin.[80]

On 28 May, the Berlin negotiations reached a turning point when the Soviet government agreed to assume responsibility for guaranteeing access through the GDR to West Berlin. West German chancellor Willy Brandt's *Ostpolitik* gave the Soviets an incentive to sign a Berlin agreement. In August 1970, the FRG and the Soviet Union had signed a non-use-of-force treaty recognizing existing boundaries in Europe as "inviolable" but not unalterable. Bonn had also agreed to de facto recognition of East Germany. Brandt then told the Soviets that he could not submit the Soviet–West German Treaty to the Bundestag for ratification unless there were an agreement ensuring Western access to West Berlin.[81]

The spring thaw in U.S.-Soviet relations preceded President Nixon's July 1971 announcement of his visit to China. While U.S.-Chinese relations had been improving, as symbolized by "Ping-Pong" diplomacy, no one, including the Soviets, expected such a dramatic departure. When Nixon made public his plans to visit China, the Soviets were genuinely stunned and alarmed. Thus, while the Sino-American rapprochement may have stimulated and prodded the developing U.S.-Soviet détente, it was not the cause. According to Georgi Arbatov of the Institute for the Study of the USA and Canada, Soviet conflicts with China and fear of a Sino-American pact were not the principal motives for pursuing cooperation with the United States.[82]

On 19 July, at a private dinner with Dobrynin, Kissinger reassured him that the Sino-American agreement to hold a summit, which Nixon had announced on television just four days previously, was not directed against the Soviet Union. Kissinger complained that there had been serious "psychological difficulties" in establishing a personal understanding between President Nixon and Soviet leaders and in making unbiased assessments of motive. The national security adviser said that relations between the two states had been characterized by an "exaggerated mistrust" of each other's assurances, and that both sides should overcome this "psychological barrier." The president's attitude toward a summit, Kissinger said, remained unchanged. Nixon expected a meeting to take place in April or May 1972.[83]

On 27 July, Nixon made a goodwill gesture by authorizing a separate agreement on prevention of accidental war, an agreement that the Soviets had been proposing for ten years. The SALT delegation completed the negotiations, and agreements on averting accidental war and upgrading the hot line were signed by Rogers and Gromyko on 30 September 1971.[84]

On 5 August 1971, Nixon had made an important symbolic gesture. He had Kissinger inform Dobrynin that the president wished to send a message directly to General Secretary Brezhnev, in order to establish personal contact. Until then, Nixon and Kissinger had addressed all letters to Premier Kosygin, who was the formal head of government, because under diplomatic protocol he outranked any Communist Party official. Brezhnev had been trying to gain control over foreign policy, and Foreign Minister Gromyko helped him by instructing Ambassador Dobrynin to advise Kissinger that it was "more appropriate" to address the president's letters to Brezhnev. Kissinger also told Dobrynin that it would be a good idea to announce a date and agenda for a Soviet-American summit before Nixon went to China the following year.[85]

The 5 August message from Nixon to Brezhnev—the first letter from an American president to Brezhnev personally—had the desired effect. On 10 August, Dobrynin informed Kissinger that Nixon's visit to Moscow could take place in May or June 1972, and the president promptly accepted.[86]

On 3 September, 1971, the four powers concluded the Quadripartite Agreement on Berlin. The Berlin accord committed the Soviet Union to guarantee access for the Western powers and the West Germans to West Berlin, an arrangement that Khrushchev had offered Kennedy. This time, however, the Soviet Union acknowledged that the four powers would continue to be responsible for the entire city of Berlin, thus confirming the "occupation rights" that Khrushchev had so wanted to be eliminated. In return, the West German government agreed not to hold any more presidential elections or parliamentary meetings in West Berlin.[87]

In late November, Secretary of Commerce Maurice Stans visited Moscow to discuss normalization of economic relations with the Soviet Union, and was treated quite warmly.[88]

CONFRONTATION OVER THE INDO-PAKISTANI WAR

Nixon and Kissinger still suspected the Soviets of having expansionist intentions and were accordingly ambivalent about U.S.-Soviet cooperation. In December 1971, Kissinger turned a regional confrontation over East Pakistan's desire to secede from West Pakistan into a U.S.-Soviet crisis. In March 1971, West Pakistan's president General Yahya Khan had launched a brutal repression against supporters of a popular movement to form an independent Bangladesh, producing an influx of 10 million refugees into India. On 3 December, the Pakistani air force attacked eight Indian airfields, and Pakistani army units made limited strikes across the West Pakistan–India border in retaliation for Indian incursions in behalf of the Bengali separatists. India retaliated by launching a full-scale invasion of East Pakistan.[89]

Kissinger saw the Indo-Pakistani War as a proxy conflict between the United States and the Soviet Union. In his view, India, encouraged by the Soviets, was exploiting the Bangladesh crisis as a pretense to dis-member West Pakistan.[90]

On 6 December, Nixon sent a letter to General Secretary Brezhnev warning that an Indian "accomplished fact" would have "adverse con-sequences" on a range of issues to be discussed at the summit. According to Kissinger, he and the president had decided that the only way to keep India from destroying West Pakistan was to convey to Moscow that events on the subcontinent might endanger Soviet plans for the summit.[91]

In his reply, on 9 December, Brezhnev proposed a cease-fire and a resumption of negotiations between the parties in Pakistan. Kissinger, however, was suspicious that the Soviet message "might be a device to play for time" while India destroyed West Pakistan.[92]

Kissinger and Nixon took further action to persuade the Soviets to use their influence to restrain India. The following day, Nixon sent another letter to Brezhnev calling for an immediate cease-fire. Kissinger read to Yuli Vorontsov, the Soviet chargé d'affaires, a secret American aide-mémoire dated 5 November 1962 promising to assist Pakistan against Indian aggression. Kissinger warned that the United States would fulfill that pledge.[93] To signal resolve to the Soviets, Kissinger ordered an air-craft carrier and nine warships to head for the Bay of Bengal.[94]

Then Kissinger delivered an ultimatum. On 11 December, Kissinger told Vorontsov that the Soviet Union must provide assurances concern-ing West Pakistan by noon the next day or the United States would "proceed unilaterally." In the meantime, Vorontsov assured Kissinger that Deputy Foreign Minister Kuznetsov had been sent to New Delhi to urge Indian restraint and arrange for a satisfactory outcome.[95]

On 12 December, a few hours before the deadline, Vorontsov phoned with the message that "India had no aggressive designs in the West." Suspicious, Kissinger immediately noticed that the Soviets had made no reference to Kashmir. He worried that the Soviets could be trying to gain time for an Indian fait accompli. Nixon, Kissinger, and Alexander Haig were meeting in the Oval Office when they received Vorontsov's mes-sage.[96]

The president and his national security adviser decided to use the hot line to signal the seriousness of the crisis to Moscow. Nixon complained to Brezhnev that the Indian assurance lacked "concreteness," and ad-monished that "time is of the essence." To back up these words, Nixon ordered the carrier task force to proceed to the Bay of Bengal from its current location near the Strait of Malacca.[97]

On 14 December, Vorontsov delivered a formal note stating that the Soviet government had "firm assurances" from the Indian leadership that India did not plan to seize West Pakistani territory. Kissinger and Nixon agreed that this note was no improvement over the previous Soviet position since it did not clarify whether India regarded Pakistani-held Kashmir as West Pakistani territory. Kissinger informed Vorontsov that the Soviet assurances were insufficient.[98] Kissinger, however, must have been less worried about Soviet intentions than he conveyed in his memoirs. At a 15 December staff meeting, Kissinger was ecstatic. He reported that a deal had been made with the Soviets and that it was his maneuvering that had caused them to back down.[99]

Finally, the crisis ended on 16 December, when the Indian prime minister Indira Gandhi announced an unconditional cease-fire in West Pakistan. Vorontsov informed Nixon that the Soviets were prepared unconditionally to guarantee that there would be no Indian attack on West Pakistan or on Kashmir.[100]

When the war ended, Kissinger concluded that the Indian initiation of a cease-fire "was a reluctant decision resulting from Soviet pressure, which in turn grew out of American insistence, including the fleet movement and the willingness to risk the summit."[101] Because the Soviets had taken action consistent with American interests in controlling the conflict, Kissinger inferred that Soviet restraint must have been owing to U.S. pressure.

Whether India had entertained any ambitions for West Pakistani territory is not clear. Certainly India did not have an interest in dismembering West Pakistan into several states, for that might stir up ethnic conflicts within India's own borders. At the time of the cease-fire, India was occupying about twenty-five hundred square miles of West Pakistani territory and small parts of Pakistani-occupied Kashmir. But India was politically isolated. The Soviet Union had exercised two vetoes of a U.N. Security Council resolution calling for Indian withdrawal from East Pakistan. The General Assembly, though, had passed the resolution by a margin of 104 to 11. No Third World country supported India's military intervention.[102]

Clearly India was not acting as a proxy for Soviet interests. The political and economic cost of maintaining nearly 10 million refugees within its borders was a sufficient reason for India to intervene militarily to establish an independent Bangladesh.[103]

Nor were the Soviets persuaded by U.S. signals to exert pressure on India not to attack West Pakistan or Kashmir. The available evidence suggests that the Soviets had urged restraint on India throughout the crisis, beginning in March. The Soviet government wanted to maintain good relations with both Pakistan and India, to balance off China. Kosygin, in fact, had helped mediate the 1965 war between India and Pakistan. In line with that objective, the Soviets delayed in recognizing an independent Bangladesh, much to India's displeasure. Moscow also provided economic aid to Pakistan through July 1971. Finally, the Soviet

Union was anxious to bring an end to the war, because its support for India had antagonized Muslims in the Middle East.[104]

It is also doubtful that the U.S. naval force demonstration persuaded India and the Soviet Union to agree to a cease-fire. Since the carrier task force was off the coast of East Pakistan, the Indians thought that the United States was trying to evacuate Pakistani forces from the area. According to a CIA intelligence source, moreover, the Soviet ambassador to India told the Indian government that the U.S. deployment was a bluff and that the Soviets would match the Seventh Fleet. Indeed, the Soviet government sent twenty-six ships into the area to prove that they could not be intimidated by the United States. A more likely explanation of the cease-fire declaration is that the Indian cabinet decided that the political costs of acquiring additional territorial objectives—namely, international isolation—would exceed any military benefits, particularly since India could not count on the Soviets to support objectives other than an independent Bangladesh.[105]

For Nixon and Kissinger, Soviet behavior during the Indo-Pakistani War once again showed that the Soviets would pursue unilateral advantage at the expense of U.S. interests. Referring to the war, Nixon told Gerard Smith that world events clearly were linked and that he doubted whether one could have confidence in the USSR in SALT if the USSR tried to outmaneuver us in other areas. The president told the British prime minister Edward Heath that if India had forced Pakistan to surrender in the west, there would have been "serious repercussions in the world scene. It could be a lesson for other parts of the world. The Soviets have tested us to see if they could control events."[106]

In his February 1972 foreign policy report, Nixon complained that the Soviets' arms buildup, Middle East policy, behavior during the Indo-Pakistani War, and expansionist naval activities had caused him to wonder whether the Soviets had made a permanent change in their foreign policy to achieve a more stable international system or had merely engaged a temporary shift in tactics. The president pointed out that the Soviets seemed to regard international tension as "normal," hostility as "inevitable," détente as a "transitory opportunity to seek narrow tactical advantages," and negotiation as harsh competition for unilateral gain.[107]

VIETNAM AND THE MOSCOW SUMMIT

When the North Vietnamese launched a major offensive on 30 March 1972, Nixon was convinced that the Soviets were in collusion with Hanoi to keep him from prosecuting the war. In a 3 April meeting with Dobrynin, Kissinger accused the Soviets of complicity in North Vietnam's attack and refused the Soviet request that the United States urge West German ratification of the Soviet–West German Treaty.[108]

Dobrynin conveyed an invitation for Kissinger to visit Moscow, not only to discuss preparations for the Moscow summit but also to talk about the situation in Vietnam, thereby tacitly acknowledging linkage. Realizing that Kissinger was determined to go, Nixon reluctantly approved the visit—with the proviso that the national security adviser should warn Brezhnev that the summit was off unless the Soviets pressured Hanoi to end the Vietnam War. The president instructed Kissinger to stick to the subject of Vietnam until he had reached an understanding with Brezhnev.[109]

In Moscow, Kissinger informed Brezhnev that the United States might have to cancel the summit because of North Vietnam's offensive. Brezhnev suggested a cease-fire in place, a proposal that the United States had put forth earlier but that was now unacceptable to Kissinger because of the influx of North Vietnamese troops since 29 March. On the other hand, as Kissinger admitted, no negotiator ever accomplished at the table what could not be achieved on the battlefield. If the national security adviser had been more receptive to Brezhnev's suggestion, the Soviets might have involved themselves in the negotiations with the North Vietnamese. Brezhnev offered to transmit U.S. proposals to Hanoi, thus associating the Soviet Union with them. The head of the Soviet Central Committee section for dealing with foreign communist parties, Konstantin Katushev, did go to Hanoi, but the North Vietnamese made no concessions.[110]

Nixon ordered Kissinger to cut his visit short and wait for a Soviet decision on Vietnam. Kissinger sent back an ill-tempered cable arguing that Brezhnev wanted a summit "at almost any cost" and that they might be able to get Soviet help in de-escalating or ending the war, or at the very least acquiescence in pushing North Vietnam to the limit. Although the president relented, he said that Kissinger's stay was conditional on "progress on the Vietnam question." Kissinger cabled his assistant Al Haig that "I am reading your messages with mounting astonishment. . . . I do not believe that Moscow is in direct collusion with Hanoi." Contrary to Nixon's instructions, Kissinger moved to discuss SALT. Brezhnev made significant concessions that eliminated important obstacles to signing a SALT agreement at the summit. He proposed that each side be allowed two ABM sites, one to protect the capital and the other near a missile site. He agreed to limit submarine-launched ballistic missiles (which was important to the Joint Chiefs because only the Soviets were building new submarines) in return for being permitted to have more submarines and launchers than the United States. He also agreed that the interim freeze on offensive weapons could last five years, rather than three years as the Soviets had been proposing in the formal SALT negotiations. Kissinger insisted on the long interval because the United States would not be ready to deploy any new weapons for at least five years.[111]

Kissinger and Brezhnev also made substantial progress toward negotiating an agreement on basic principles to guide U.S.-Soviet relations in an era of détente. In March, at Dobrynin's request, Kissinger had presented the Soviets with a statement of general principles such as mutual restraint, noninterference in the affairs of other states, and renunciation of pressures for unilateral advantage. Brezhnev presented his own draft, heavily peppered with phrases that could have been taken from *Pravda*, but he asked Kissinger to "improve it." Kissinger and Gromyko developed a draft of "Basic Principles of U.S.-Soviet Relations" which emphasized the need for restraint in the world's trouble spots and which included a renunciation of any claim for special advantages in any part of the world—a renunciation that "we, at least, interpreted as a repudiation of the Brezhnev Doctrine for Eastern Europe," wrote Kissinger. The national security adviser did not carry out Nixon's instructions "to emphasize the need for a single standard; we could not accept the proposition that the Soviet Union had the right to support liberation movements all over the world while insisting on the Brezhnev Doctrine inside the satellite orbit."[112] The Soviets had always argued that peaceful coexistence did not imply any lessening of Soviet support for national liberation movements.

At their last session, Brezhnev denied that the Soviets were behind the North Vietnamese offensive. Hanoi had been hoarding weapons for two years. The United States was being challenged not by Moscow, but by the Chinese and the North Vietnamese, who were opposed to the summit. Brezhnev insisted that he was committed to an improvement in U.S.-Soviet relations and was going ahead with the summit in the face of a formal request by Hanoi to cancel it.[113]

Outraged, Nixon accused Kissinger of being "taken in" by the Soviets. In a long memo dictated at Camp David, Nixon admonished Kissinger that the Soviets' "primary purpose in getting you to Moscow to discuss the summit has now been served while our purpose of getting some progress on Vietnam has not been served." A SALT agreement, he said, was of concern only to "a few sophisticates." The main issue was Vietnam, and there Kissinger had failed.[114]

On 1 May 1972, Brezhnev sent a letter to Nixon asking him to refrain from aerial bombardment in Vietnam because it could hurt the chances for a successful summit. After the North Vietnamese representative taunted Kissinger at their 2 May meeting in Paris, Nixon considered various military options for escalating the war against North Vietnam. On 3 May, Nixon replied to Brezhnev by complaining about Kissinger's fruitless meeting with the North Vietnamese. It seemed as if Hanoi was demanding that the United States accept terms tantamount to surrender. Nixon's letter referred to U.S. "decisions" about to be made; it asked for Brezhnev's "assessment of the situation" as soon as possible.[115]

Nixon and Kissinger viewed escalation as necessary to restore the president's credibility, rather than to achieve any specifically military objectives. The North Vietnamese had behaved arrogantly at their private meeting with Kissinger in Paris. Since Nixon had told both the North Vietnamese and the Soviets that he would take a hard line if there was no action in Paris, Kissinger said, the president had no choice but to bomb North Vietnam, and that would mean canceling the summit. Kissinger did not see how Nixon could drink toasts to Brezhnev while Soviet-made tanks were rolling through South Vietnamese streets.[116]

In a meeting on 4 May, Nixon told his chief of staff H. R. Haldeman and Kissinger that he had been thinking it over and had decided that they could not lose the war in Vietnam. "The summit isn't worth a damn if the price for it is losing in Vietnam. My instinct tells me that the country can take losing the summit, but it can't take losing the war."[117]

President Nixon apparently expected opposition from his national security adviser, because he told Kissinger that he had made up his mind and did not want to be talked out of it. But Kissinger recommended mining the port of Haiphong, an action no previous president had been willing to take because of the risk that a Soviet ship might be hit. The national security adviser also advocated a continuous (not a symbolic) bombing of North Vietnam, carried out by fighter-bombers rather than B-52s. Nixon accepted Kissinger's recommendations to bomb North Vietnam and mine the harbors.[118]

Nixon also considered calling off the summit himself because he believed that this would be less humiliating than having the Soviets do so in an election year. In the end, however, Nixon allowed himself to be persuaded by Treasury Secretary John Connally and by Haldeman that he should bomb the North and leave the decision to cancel up to the Soviets. The Soviets might not call off the summit, and the United States would then end up with the best of both worlds.[119]

On 6 May Brezhnev sent a letter to Nixon assuring him, on the basis of Katushev's visit to Hanoi, that North Vietnam was ready to seek a political settlement. Brezhnev mentioned the "Pentagon Papers" as among the reasons why Hanoi mistrusted the actions and intentions of the United States. Again Brezhnev asked Nixon for restraint in North Vietnam, hinting that military escalation could "entail serious consequences" for peace and for U.S.-Soviet relations. The Soviet leader made it clear that the United States was responsible for negotiating an end to the war in Vietnam; the Soviet Union would not involve itself.[120]

On 8 May 1972, Nixon announced on television that he had ordered the mining of North Vietnamese ports and continued bombing of North Vietnamese targets, particularly rail lines. He also said that progress had been made in U.S.-Soviet negotiations in recent months. Nixon declared that the United States and the Soviet Union were on "the threshold of a new relationship" that could serve not only the interests of their two countries but the cause of world peace. The United States was prepared to continue to build this relationship. Responsibility would lie with the Soviets if they failed to do so. Ambassador Dobrynin recalls that he was very worried about the summit.[121]

Brezhnev's decision to go ahead with the summit was quite controversial. Soviet opponents of the summit argued that it would humiliate the Soviet Union politically, cast doubt on Soviet support for national liberation movements, and encourage American imperialists to engage in further adventures. The Politburo held several meetings to discuss whether to receive Nixon in Moscow while the United States was bombing a Soviet ally. Both the military, represented by Marshal Andrei Grechko, and President Nikolai Podgorny opposed the meeting. Kosygin and Gromyko, on the other hand, wanted to go ahead with the summit. Brezhnev was undecided, although for personal and political reasons he was eager for a meeting with the American president. The Soviet leadership finally decided that they could not allow Hanoi to exercise a veto over Soviet foreign policy. Despite the vast amounts of economic and military aid that the Soviets had provided to the North Vietnamese, Hanoi did not keep the Soviet government informed about North Vietnam's plans for Southeast Asia or its negotiations with the United States, a matter of some irritation to the Politburo. North Vietnamese actions, too, frequently put the Soviets in a difficult position.[122]

Other factors that weighed in the Soviet decision were the desire to ensure the ratification of the Soviet–West German Treaty and reduce the burden of arms spending. The Soviets had long aspired to stabilize the division of Europe, and to do so they needed to consolidate their détente with West Germany. Brezhnev was reluctant to aggravate international tensions when ratification of the Soviet–West German Treaty was still pending in the West German parliament. In addition, cancellation of the summit would endanger the SALT agreements and lead to another round in the arms race.[123]

Still unsure of himself, Brezhnev convened a special meeting of the Central Committee Plenum on 19 May so that others would share in the responsibility for his decision. At the meeting, Brezhnev conceded that the United States was the "main force of imperialism"; for that very reason, though, peaceful coexistence required efforts to regulate U.S.-Soviet relations. The more stable and normal Soviet relations were with the United States, Brezhnev maintained, the lower the threat of nuclear war. In addition, a worsening of relations with the United States would mean increased defense spending, whereas normalization of U.S.-Soviet relations would enable the Soviets to hold down such expenditures. This Central Committee Plenum was extremely important because it approved not only the summit meeting but the policy of peaceful coexistence with the West.[124]

The U.S. negotiator Gerard Smith remembered that he was "astonished" by the Soviets' "business as usual" attitude at a time when the United States was bombing the capital of their socialist ally and mining its port. "We went back to work confident that the Soviets really wanted SALT agreements," he recalled.[125]

If the Soviets had canceled the summit, the Soviet–West German Treaty might not have been ratified, thus unraveling a provisional solution to the German question. The SALT agreements would have been delayed, and it might have been difficult to develop sufficient negotiating momentum to bring them to a conclusion. The Soviets might then have escalated the arms race by building more ICBM launchers.

DÉTENTE AND ITS DECLINE

At the May 1972 summit in Moscow, U.S. and Soviet officials signed a impressive number of agreements on a variety of issues, the most important of which were the agreements concerning strategic arms limitation and basic principles. The SALT agreements consisted of a treaty confining each side to two ABM systems and an interim agreement providing for a missile freeze. These agreements were a first step toward strategic arms reduction. The SALT agreements allowed each side to test the other's good faith without significant risk, since each state would continue its nuclear modernization programs.[126]

In a special briefing to members of Congress after the summit, Kissinger stated that the SALT agreements did not stand alone but were "linked organically to a chain of agreements and to a broad understanding about international conduct appropriate to the dangers of the nuclear age." The Basic Principles Agreement enjoined the superpowers to conduct their relations on the basis of peaceful coexistence, avoid military confrontations, refrain from competing for unilateral advantage, exercise restraint, and try to prevent situations from arising that would increase international tension. The text was negotiated almost entirely by Kissinger and the Soviet leaders. According to Dobrynin, Kissinger was extremely conciliatory and went out of his way to accept Soviet language on many important points. Kissinger may have done so because he was grateful for the Soviet decision to allow the summit to go ahead despite the mining of Haiphong harbor and wanted to reciprocate. Moreover, since Kissinger regarded the BPA as largely rhetoric, he probably did not believe he had conceded anything of great value. The Soviet leaders, however, gratified that they had finally persuaded the Americans to accept the concept of peaceful coexistence, touted this concession before the Soviet public as a great triumph in order to legitimize détente.[127]

The document was a pseudoagreement because the parties did not agree on how to conduct their relations. The BPA simply tacked Nixon's notions of "forgoing efforts to obtain unilateral advantage" and "exercising self-restraint" onto the Soviet idea of "peaceful coexistence," which implied continuing ideological competition for influence.[128] This ambiguity later contributed to the unraveling of détente, as each side accused the other of violating its conception of the Basic Principles Agreement. The breakdown of vague agreements under differing interpretations, of course, contributes to further mistrust.

The Nixon administration had also reached agreement with Soviet officials on various functional agreements. In the first stage of détente, as Nixon later wrote, Washington sought "to involve Soviet interests in ways that would increase their stake in international stability and the status quo." Nixon explained: no one believed that "commercial, technical, and scientific relationships could by themselves prevent confrontations or wars, but at least they would have to be counted in a balance sheet of gains and losses whenever the Soviets were tempted to indulge in international adventures." Thus the United States and the Soviet Union established a joint commercial commission and signed cooperative agreements in science and technology, medicine, public health, environmental protection, and collaboration in the exploration of space. The Incidents at Sea Agreement, the first cooperative arrangement between the military establishments of the two powers since the wartime alliance against Hitler, provided "rules of the road" to prevent dangerous accidents at sea resulting from U.S. and Soviet naval activities.[129] Nixon's and Kissinger's strategy conforms to a rational model of building trust through step-by-step agreements that provide incentives for continuing good behavior.

According to Dobrynin, the Moscow summit "allowed both sides to overcome strong mutual suspicions and become engaged in more constructive relationships, though they continued to pursue their own goals in the international arena." At a special meeting of the Politburo held after the summit, Brezhnev declared: "You can do business with Nixon." The Soviet leader argued that it was time to prepare for a return visit to the United States.[130]

In July 1972, at the president's vacation home in San Clemente, California, Nixon told Ambassador Dobrynin that the success of the Moscow summit had convinced him that a series of summits would be feasible. The president invited Brezhnev to visit the United States in 1973. If re-elected, Nixon said, he would like to hold summit meetings on an annual basis.[131]

Brezhnev's June 1973 visit to the United States marked the halcyon days of U.S.-Soviet détente. U.S. and Soviet officials signed agreements for cooperation on transportation, oceanography, agriculture, and peaceful uses of atomic energy. They also agreed to scientific, technical, educational, and cultural exchanges; the expansion of passenger air service; and a tax treaty.[132]

The centerpiece of the Washington summit, though, was the Agreement on Prevention of Nuclear War (APNW), in which the two leaders elaborated and strengthened their resolve to cooperate in preventing crises. The agreement called on each state to refrain from the threat or use of force against the other state or its allies. The United States and the Soviet Union promised to consult each other immediately in situations that could lead to nuclear war, not only between the superpowers but between either of the superpowers and a third country.[133] Brezhnev had originally tried to induce Nixon to sign an agreement on "no first use of nuclear weapons," but the U.S. government insisted on retaining the deterrent option of using nuclear weapons against a Soviet conventional invasion of Western Europe. In the end, Kissinger persuaded the Soviets to revise the agreement so that it referred to the nonuse of force or the threat of force.[134]

As Dobrynin later reflected, it would become apparent during the Arab-Israeli war six months later that the idea of working together to prevent crises "did not operate too well without mutual trust and firm commitments." Each side's leadership had a different understanding of the meaning of the rules entailed in the BPA and APNW, and those different understandings were never hammered out or revealed in detailed negotiations. Nixon sought to constrain Soviet competition for advantage in the Third World; the Soviets sought to make such competition safer by an agreement to avoid the risks of military confrontation that could escalate to nuclear war.[135]

Détente and cooperation between the superpowers gradually grew cold, largely because of domestic political factors within each country. In the United States, Senator Henry ("Scoop") Jackson linked ratification of the 1972 trade agreement to Soviet assurances about Jewish emigration, thus arousing Soviet resentment at interference in their internal affairs and removing economic interests as an incentive for the Soviets to exercise restraint in the Third World. Liberal human rights advocates and conservatives who distrusted the Soviet Union on ideological grounds used the issue of Jewish emigration to apply the brakes to U.S.-Soviet collaboration.[136]

In the Soviet Union, the military-industrial complex escaped civilian control. Since the turbulent Khrushchev era, the oligarchs in the Politburo had tried to maintain close relations with the military by granting them autonomy, but by doing so they had abdicated oversight of military programs and doctrine. The military insisted on building at least as many high-technology weapons as the United States possessed. By the end of the 1970s, the Soviet economy was experiencing resource shortages and Brezhnev tried to reassert control, but it was too late. Brezhnev's illness and mental decline after 1974 contributed to the military's dominance, because the general secretary no longer played an important role in developing Soviet arms control positions.[137]

Ideological considerations drove Soviet intervention in Africa. Each Soviet official competed to be more "revolutionary" than the other; each touted his "internationalism." In 1975, the Soviet Union provided military aid, airlift assistance for Cuban troops, and military advisers to a faction in the Angolan civil war. The Soviets then provided aid and advisers to Ethiopia, Somalia, and Yemen and invaded Afghanistan.[138]

The damage done by disputes over Third World areas was aggravated by each side's propensity to apply a double standard to the actions of the other, imputing offensive motives to actions very similar to its own. The United States violated the BPA in the Middle East; the Soviet Union did the same in Africa. Kissinger and Nixon had encouraged President Sadat of Egypt to expel Soviet advisers, then excluded the Soviet Union from participation in the Middle East peace negotiations, contrary to the prohibition against seeking unilateral advantage.[139]

Neither side understood how the other might be responding to its own actions. Instead, foreign policymakers attributed the other's hostility to internal causes. Moscow did not understand that its behavior in the Third World both undermined Western trust in the Soviets' good faith and exacerbated suspicions about their intentions. When the United States expressed fear of Soviet expansionism, the Soviets derided American imperialism.[140]

When President Nixon took office in 1969, U.S. and Soviet interests were aligned in favor of cooperation on security issues. With Congress agitating for reductions in defense spending, Nixon had an incentive to negotiate arms control agreements with the Soviets that would ratify the balance between the two sides' nuclear forces. Nixon needed a breathing space in order to disengage from Vietnam and develop a more differentiated foreign policy to meet the challenges of the pluralistic world that emerged since the early Cold War period. Soviet border disputes with China helped motivate the Soviets to stabilize their relations with countries in the West. The lackluster performance of the Soviet economy encouraged Brezhnev to consider Western trade, technology, and capital as a possible solution.

Although the structure of incentives favored cooperation, the process of interaction was halting and ragged and could have been aborted at several points. Nixon and Brezhnev agreed to limitations on ABMs but not on the more significant MIRVs. The failure to restrain the installation of MIRVs produced an explosion in the number of nuclear warheads and, ultimately, led to concern in the Reagan administration about the vulnerability of U.S. land-based ICBMs. If the superpowers had been able to agree on a MIRV ban together with the ABM Treaty, they could have significantly restrained the nuclear arms race. The intensity of later U.S. concerns that the Soviets were seeking a first-strike capability might then have been lower, because it was Soviet heavy missiles with multiple warheads that constituted the greatest threat to the U.S. land-based missile force.

Most analysts have blamed the bureaucratic interests of the Pentagon for Nixon's unwillingness to propose a ban on MIRV testing to the Soviets. But neither Kissinger nor Nixon ever expressed any interest in limiting MIRVs, either to their staff members or those in the State Department and the Arms Control and Disarmament Agency (ACDA) who urgently sought at least a temporary moratorium on U.S. testing and deployment. Instead, Nixon and Brezhnev settled for an ABM treaty coupled with a five-year freeze on ICBMs and SLBMs.[141]

While the president and his national security adviser doubted whether a MIRV ban could be verified by satellite surveillance, Nixon's major concern was that the Soviets would nibble away at peripheral areas, acquiring marginal gains too insignificant to be challenged, until they had succeeded in overturning the balance of power.[142] Nixon's mistrust was more fundamental than his worries about Soviet cheating. Judging from the Soviets' insistence that peaceful coexistence did not mean an end to support for national liberation movements, and given Moscow's later intervention in Africa, Nixon had reason to be wary. As a result, Nixon and Kissinger were highly disturbed by evidence of Soviet meddling or complicity in conflicts in the Middle East, South Asia, and Vietnam because of what that portended for future Soviet behavior. Whereas Nixon quickly abandoned the negotiating tactic of linking SALT to Soviet concessions in the Middle East and Vietnam, he and Kissinger saw connections between Soviet actions across widely different issues and areas of the world. In September 1970, Nixon and Kissinger interpreted events in Cuba, Jordan, and Egypt as a pattern of Soviet testing of American resolve. For their part, the Soviets viewed Nixon's escalation in Vietnam, accusations of bad faith, and frequent use of military force demonstrations as inconsistent with a policy of seeking "negotiation rather than confrontation."

The turning point in U.S.-Soviet relations was Brezhnev's May 1971 offer to negotiate on mutual balanced force reductions and Soviet concessions in the Berlin and SALT negotiations. Through these actions, Brezhnev demonstrated that he was serious about cooperating with the United States on security questions. Brezhnev and Nixon embarked on a personal correspondence that allowed them to communicate their interests and concerns to each other, while bypassing the bureaucracy and the need to adhere to formal diplomatic positions.

Even so, Nixon remained distrustful and dubious about cooperating with the Soviets, given what he perceived as their efforts to gain unilateral advantage in the Indo-Pakistani War and their aid to the North Vietnamese. Nixon and Kissinger risked their foreign policy accomplishments—détente and SALT—to end the war in Vietnam without a loss of prestige. After Brezhnev made the costly gesture of celebrating U.S.-Soviet good relations at the Moscow summit while U.S. planes were bombing an important Soviet ally, Nixon and Kissinger concluded that the Soviets were serious about cooperating with the United States. The 1972–73 détente between the United States and the Soviet Union marked the beginning of a working relationship; the two superpowers were engaged in cooperative activities in a variety of issue areas. Ideology and psychological mistrust impeded further progress despite the existence of a shared interest in collaboration.

[6]

The Allure of Defense

No one predicted that Ronald Reagan, the most fervently anticommunist U.S. president, would engage in a process of accommodation culminating in the end of the Cold War. Reagan launched the largest peacetime military buildup in history, and denounced the Soviet Union at his first press conference, saying that "the only morality they recognize is what will further their cause, meaning they reserve unto themselves the right to commit any crime, to lie, to cheat."[1] Actually, Reagan was not as anti-Soviet as his public rhetoric suggested. While he abhorred the communist system, Reagan came to admire the Russian people. The president also had great faith in face-to-face contacts, and he was confident in his skills as a negotiator. He believed that if he could just get a Soviet leader in the same room, he could persuade him that the United States was not out to destroy the USSR. Reagan was receptive to cooperation with the Soviets if they proved their good intentions by deeds as well as words.[2] Reagan's efforts to communicate with the Soviets were strongly encouraged by Secretary of State George P. Shultz, who believed that the Soviets would cooperate with the United States when it was in their interest to do so and that Washington could influence the incentives and penalties for Soviet international conduct.[3] By 1983, American and Soviet leaders had begun to engage in efforts to restore good relations.

The shift to a new generation of Soviet leadership after Brezhnev, Andropov, and Chernenko presented an opportunity for change. Mikhail S. Gorbachev, although he was initially suspicious of the United States, wanted arms control agreements so that he could shift economic resources from defense into civilian high-technology sectors and consumer enterprises. Just as Gorbachev's conception of *perestroika* changed from reform to revolution when he realized the depth of the Soviet economic crisis, so too the Soviet leader recognized that public relations gestures would not suffice to gain Western trust or help to modernize Soviet society. More than any Soviet leader, Gorbachev successfully communicated his intentions and goals through words and deeds.

Despite Gorbachev's heroic efforts, Reagan's deep mistrust of the Soviets resulted in a missed opportunity to conclude an agreement that would slash both sides' strategic arsenals in return for limits on space-based defenses. The West was also slow to respond to Gorbachev or to reciprocate his startling concessions. Then the Bush administration wasted an entire year reviewing previous policy and imposing various tests for Gorbachev to pass as a condition for serious negotiations. While the United States cannot be blamed for the failure of *perestroika*, a more generous response by the West might have saved Gorbachev some humiliation and forestalled some of the bitterness that many Russian people feel toward the United States.

EARLY PROBES

The change in Reagan's beliefs about the Soviet Union was slow in coming. In the first year of the Reagan administration, Washington focused on a military buildup. Secretary of State Alexander Haig made it clear to Anatoly Dobrynin that the United States had no interest in arms control negotiations with the Soviet Union.[4] Possibilities for constructive change emerged in June 1982, however, when Reagan replaced Haig with Shultz, who was a conservative pragmatist. Unlike other members of the Reagan administration, Shultz had negotiated with the Soviets as secretary of the treasury in the Nixon administration. Shultz respected the Soviets as tough, well-prepared, and able negotiators, and he believed that once they had made a deal, they would stick to it. The new secretary of state was convinced that the Soviets would cooperate if the United States was not only strong but prepared to strike agreements that were mutually advantageous. Not everyone in the Reagan administration, though, shared Shultz's optimism. The national security adviser William Clark, Secretary of Defense Caspar Weinberger, the head of the CIA William Casey, and the NSC staff fundamentally distrusted the Soviet Union and opposed any diplomatic contacts. But Shultz worked slowly and patiently to bring Ronald Reagan around to his views on the usefulness of negotiations with the Soviets. In January 1983, Shultz sent a memorandum to the president titled "U.S.-Soviet Relations in 1983," in which he urged that the United States put Soviet intentions to the test. The secretary of state outlined a four-part agenda, including human rights, arms control, regional issues, and bilateral relations.[5]

In his 25 January State of the Union address, President Reagan declared that he was prepared for a positive change in Soviet-American relations. "But the Soviet Union must show by deeds as well as words a sincere commitment to respect the rights and sovereignty of the family of nations."[6]

Reagan had not yet committed himself to Shultz's strategy of testing Soviet intentions through small agreements. Shultz though, got an unexpected opportunity to argue his views before Reagan in private—without interference from the White House staff—when a heavy snowfall on 12 February prevented the Reagans from going to Camp David, and Nancy Reagan asked Shultz and his wife, O'Bie, over to the White House for dinner. Reagan expressed interest to Shultz in visiting the Soviet Union and China. In order to have a meaningful summit, Shultz replied, step-by-step improvements in relations were necessary. President Reagan said that he recognized it would be difficult to move forward in dealing with either of the two communist countries. As Reagan admitted, his path was blocked not only by his own White House staff, the Defense Department, and Casey in the CIA but by his own previous anticommunist rhetoric.[7]

The secretary of state had not realized that Reagan was eager to meet with Soviet leaders. Shultz told Reagan that he was scheduled to meet with Ambassador Dobrynin three days later, on 15 February. "What would you think about my bringing Dobrynin over to the White House for a private chat?" Shultz suggested.[8]

Reagan agreed to see Dobrynin, so long as the meeting was kept secret. He intended to tell the Soviet ambassador that "if Andropov is willing to do business, so am I."[9]

On 15 February, when Dobrynin arrived at the State Department for a routine talk with Shultz, he was ushered quietly to the White House. In the president's family quarters, Reagan spoke freely and eloquently about his concerns with respect to U.S.-Soviet relations. The president noted that Andropov was committed to the maxim "More deeds, less words." Reagan said that it would be easier for a newcomer, who was not so burdened by the weight of the past, to make the first step, even if it was a symbolic one. As just such a symbolic gesture, President Reagan asked the Soviet Union to grant exit visas for seven Pentecostal Christians who had been living in the American embassy in Moscow since 1978, when they had pushed their way past Soviet guards. Reagan's focus on the Pentecostal Christians fit with his propensity to view complex issues in terms of personal and vivid anecdotes. If the Soviets would do something about the Pentecostals or some other human rights issue, Reagan promised that he would not embarrass the Soviets with undue publicity, claims of credit, or "crowing."[10]

[192]

Ambassador Dobrynin reported the conversation to Moscow and recommended that the Soviet government grant Reagan's request. Dobrynin advised that small, inch-by-inch steps toward establishing a personal relationship with Reagan were more likely to be successful than any major projects for which the president was psychologically unprepared. The Soviet leadership regarded Reagan's request as odd, even suspicious; with all the major issues at stake in U.S.-Soviet relations, that the U.S. president had chosen the Pentecostals as a test case was disappointing. Nevertheless, Moscow decided to take action on Reagan's request. Two weeks after Dobrynin's meeting with Reagan, the Soviet government sent a message that the Pentecostals could leave the embassy without fear of persecution, and that the authorities would then consider the question of their leaving the Soviet Union.[11]

In his diary, Reagan reflected that "some of the NSC staff are too hard line and don't think any approach should be made to the Soviets." Reagan wrote that he, too, was hard-line and would never appease. "But I do want to try to let them see there is a better world if they'll show *by deed* they want to get along with the free world.[12] That statement summed up Reagan's attitude toward the Soviets. He was deeply distrustful, but ready to negotiate strategic arms reduction *if* the Soviets proved their good intentions.

Reagan regarded the release of the Pentecostals as a sign that the Soviets were ready to meet his request for "deeds not words." To reciprocate, President Reagan agreed on 22 April to resume negotiations on a long-term grain agreement, thereby lifting the embargo on grain sales he had imposed in December 1981 in retaliation for the Soviet crackdown on the Solidarity movement. Shultz did not consider this to be a quid pro quo, because the Reagan administration had been under substantial pressure from farmers to sell their surplus grain. On 26 June 1983, Soviet authorities announced that the seven Pentecostal Christians would be allowed to leave the Soviet Union.[13]

Yet despite his cordial meeting with Dobrynin, President Reagan warned in a speech before the National Association of Evangelicals on 8 March that the United States must guard against the temptation to "label both sides equally at fault, to ignore the facts of history and the aggressive impulses of an evil empire, to simply call the arms race a giant misunderstanding and thereby remove yourself from the struggle between right and wrong and good and evil." The speech had not been cleared with State Department officials, who did not even know there were any references in it to the Soviet Union. Reagan was trying to counter the appeal of the nuclear freeze movement, which had substantial support from clerics. In addition, the president was trying to recapture his support from the radical right by using harsh anti-Soviet language. Nevertheless, the memorable phrase "evil empire" seemed to encapsulate the Reagan administration's attitude toward the Soviet government, and almost immediately the president's address was viewed as a major policy statement.[14]

According to Dobrynin, Moscow was greatly angered by the contradictions between Reagan's words and deeds. Reagan, however, seemed to see no contradiction between publicly condemning the morality of Soviet leaders and engaging in negotiations with them. Of course, Soviet leaders themselves had indulged in polemical excesses, but they applied a double standard to their own use of invective.[15]

REAGAN'S STRATEGIC DEFENSE INITIATIVE

Even worse, from the Soviets' perspective, was Reagan's announcement on 23 March 1983 of the Strategic Defense Initiative (SDI), known popularly as "Star Wars." In the speech, Reagan reviewed the Soviets' accumulation of military power. The president declared that "the Soviet Union is acquiring what can only be considered an offensive military force." Reagan reported that in recent months, his advisers, including the Joint Chiefs of Staff, had underscored the need to break out of a future "that relies solely on offensive retaliation for our security." In a turn of phrase that he had borrowed from a Joint Chiefs briefing, Reagan asked: "Wouldn't it be better to save lives than to avenge them?" He asked the scientific community to use their talents to find a "means of rendering these nuclear weapons impotent and obsolete." Despite the glowing rhetoric, Reagan's immediate recommendation was more modest: he called for a research-and-development program on strategic defenses "consistent with our obligations of the ABM Treaty and recognizing the need for closer consultation with our allies."[16]

Reagan's announcement suggested that the United States was moving away from a reliance on mutual deterrence to prevent nuclear war. Moscow regarded Reagan's initiative as intended to develop a defensive system to protect American territory against Soviet retaliation for a U.S. nuclear attack. Soviet physicists were skeptical about the feasibility of such a system, but their views did not influence the Soviet leadership, which was convinced that the Americans had scored another technological breakthrough and therefore saw Reagan's statement as a threat. The Soviet leader Yuri Andropov charged that Reagan's new concept would extend the arms race into outer space and warned that the United States had embarked on "an extremely dangerous path." The Soviet news agency *Tass* called the speech an attempt to violate the ABM Treaty and achieve strategic superiority for the United States.[17]

[194]

Although Reagan's speech had been under consideration for only a month, a small, informal group of Reagan administration officials, conservatives, and close friends of the president had been meeting secretly since 1981 in the White House to plan for a transition from deterrence to defense. Despite the 1972 ABM Treaty, the scientific infrastructure for ballistic missile defense—the U.S. Army Ballistic Missile Defense System Command, Huntsville, Alabama; the U.S. Air Force Space Command, Colorado Springs, Colorado; and the weapons laboratories at Lawrence Livermore, Sandia, and Los Alamos—received annual funding. By the end of the 1970s, with the decline of détente, public support for ballistic missile defense grew as conservatives sought a technical or military solution to the problem of preventing nuclear war as an alternative to détente. Members of the group included Reagan's domestic policy adviser Martin Anderson; the businessman Karl Bendetsen; Lieutenant General Daniel Graham, U.S. Army (Ret.), who had formed a group called High Frontier to lobby for orbiting battle stations; California businessman Jacquelin Hume and oil magnate William Wilson; and Jim Jenkins and Edwin Thomas, who were assistants to Attorney General Edwin Meese and William Clark. Physicist Edward Teller, who had played a role in the development of the hydrogen bomb, was an influential member of the group as well.[18]

On 11 February 1983, the Joint Chiefs reported to Reagan that strategic defense was technically feasible and merited a strong research effort. Teller (an anticommunist who had opposed the nuclear test ban in the 1950s) and the president's scientific adviser George Keyworth II had informed the president about new technological advances in ballistic missile defense. Laser beams, aimed from outer space and reaching their targets with the speed of light, might be able to shoot down enemy missiles at the beginning of their flight. In the early 1980s, as part of a program called Excalibur, directed by Teller, scientists at Lawrence Livermore Laboratory had tested nuclear-powered X-ray laser beams that could be directed at enemy missiles. Even the Joint Chiefs, however, were surprised by the timing of Reagan's initiative and its scope.[19]

On 23 March, Reagan was scheduled to give a speech to justify the MX missile program and a 10 percent increase in the defense budget. His deputy national security assistant Robert C. McFarlane added to the end of a "standard threat speech" Reagan's bid to make nuclear weapons obsolete. This "annex" was a tightly guarded secret, known only to a small group of officials.[20]

The various domestic groups that favored ballistic missile defense—defense contractors, conservatives, proponents of space defense, and arms control opponents—would not have achieved such success if they had not had a fervent supporter in the White House. When Shultz, Weinberger, Assistant Secretary of Defense Richard Perle, and Undersecretary of Defense Fred Iklé found out about the speech a few days before its delivery, they were horrified and tried to persuade the president to moderate his rhetoric. Shultz was worried about the reaction of the Soviets, who had only recently been labeled an "evil empire," and of the allies, who might begin to question the reliability of the U.S. promise to launch a nuclear attack in response to a Soviet invasion of Western Europe. Shultz expressed concern about U.S. obligations under the ABM Treaty. What Reagan had proposed would amount to a "revolution" in U.S. strategic doctrine, upon which U.S. allies depended.[21]

For all his reputation as a conservative, when it came to nuclear weapons Ronald Reagan was a visionary, a radical who wished to abolish the doctrine of "mutual assured destruction" (MAD), which he regarded as immoral. In his memoirs, Reagan recalls that deterrence "didn't seem to me to be something that would send you to bed feeling safe. It was like having two westerners standing in a saloon aiming their guns at each other's head—permanently."[22]

Reagan's interest in defensive systems dated back to 1967, when Teller gave him a tour of Lawrence Livermore Laboratory and described the scientists' research using nuclear explosives to defend against nuclear weapons. Then, in 1979, Reagan visited the North American Aerospace Defense Command (NORAD) at Cheyenne Mountain, Colorado. Reagan asked the commanding general what would happen if a Soviet SS-18 hit within a few hundred yards of the massive steel front doors at the entrance of what was an underground city carved into the mountain. The general answered, "It would blow us away." Reagan was shocked. "What can we do about it?" he asked. "Nothing," was the response. Reagan was deeply disturbed that the United States had no means of defense against a nuclear attack. Thus, as Reagan recalled it, "after the Joint Chiefs of Staff returned to me with their collective judgment that development of a shield against nuclear missiles might be feasible, I decided to make public my dream and move ahead with the Strategic Defense Initiative."[23]

IMPERCEPTIBLE PROGRESS

Within the Reagan administration, mistrust of Soviet intentions was so intense that Shultz could make only slow and halting progress in his effort to negotiate small, step-by-step agreements with the Soviet Union. Shultz even had difficulty gaining Reagan's permission to propose to the Soviets that they open discussions on cultural exchanges and new consulates in Kiev and New York. A series of large interagency meetings

[196]

was held to debate what would seem to be trivial questions, but the NSC staff was opposed to any contacts with the Soviet Union. According to Vice-President George Bush, the NSC staff countered Shultz's papers to Reagan concerning policy toward the Soviet Union with "absolutely vicious" memos.[24]

Finally, in the summer of 1983, there was a slight thaw in U.S.-Soviet relations. In May 1983, the experienced diplomat Jack F. Matlock had replaced the hard-liner Richard Pipes as the Soviet expert on the NSC staff. Now President Reagan authorized Shultz to propose to Dobrynin an agreement on cultural exchanges and the opening of new consulates. One month later, on 15 July, Dobrynin notified Shultz that the Soviets were ready to begin negotiations on these two subjects. On 28 July, the United States and the Soviet Union concluded a grain agreement under which the Soviets agreed to purchase from 9 to 12 billion metric tons of grain in each of the next five years. U.S. and Soviet officials were also conducting talks on modernizing the hot line, keeping nuclear weapons out of terrorist hands, and nuclear nonproliferation. The Soviets also agreed to more moderate language at the Madrid talks on European security and human rights.[25]

This brief interlude, however, was abruptly ended by the tensions created when the Soviets downed a Korean Airlines passenger flight, KAL 007, which had strayed over Soviet territory. On 1 September 1983, Shultz held an emotional press conference at which he announced that the United States reacted with revulsion against the attack and saw no excuse whatsoever for this "appalling act." The impassioned statement had been hastily drafted by Undersecretary of State Lawrence S. Eagleburger and Assistant Secretary of State Richard R. Burt so that Shultz could take credit for the first, tough statement. In so doing, however, Shultz acted before the U.S. government had received and analyzed intelligence on the circumstances surrounding the attack, such as the presence of a U.S. reconnaissance airplane in the area shortly before the Korean airliner crossed into Soviet airspace. The Soviets, too, mishandled the tragedy at first, denying that they had any knowledge concerning the airliner's disappearance. Reagan later claimed that there was no way a Soviet pilot could have mistaken a civilian airliner for a military reconnaissance aircraft, and charged that the attack was deliberate.[26]

According to Dobrynin, the Soviet leadership was convinced that the Korean airliner was an American reconnaissance operation. The Politburo had not been consulted until after the plane had been shot down. When informed about the intrusion, Moscow Air-Defense Command probably told the regional air-defense command to follow standard operating procedures. In 1993, the International Civil Aviation Organization conducted an investigation making use of the airliner's flight recorder, and concluded that there was no evidence that the Soviet fighter pilot knew he was attacking a passenger airplane.[27]

Andropov lashed back on 28 September with a formal denunciation of U.S. militarism. "If anybody ever had any illusions about the possibility of an evolution to the better in the policy of the present American administration, these illusions are completely dispelled now." The Politburo had collectively decided that it was impossible to reach an agreement with Reagan.[28]

When the United States went ahead with the deployment of new intermediate-range missiles in Europe, in November 1983, the Soviets walked out of both the intermediate-range and the strategic weapons talks. Moscow placed short-range missiles in Czechoslovakia and East Germany to counter the new American intermediate-range missiles and stationed Soviet submarines close to the U.S. coast. The Kremlin had deprived itself of a voice in arms control and an opportunity to stabilize the arms race.[29]

Almost immediately, the Soviets pulled back. In December 1983, Defense Minister Dmitri Ustinov said that it was unnecessary to "overdramatize" the situation and that Soviet power was strong enough to deal with any contingency. The Soviets also agreed to resume technical talks on upgrading the hot line and delimiting the Soviet-U.S. maritime boundary between Siberia and Alaska.[30]

Ronald Reagan's address to the United Nations on 16 January 1984 was described by the president's advisers as signaling a turning point in his policy toward the Soviets. Reagan called for a "constructive working relationship" with the Soviets. More specifically, the president proposed that the United States and the Soviet Union cooperate to reduce their nuclear arsenals and try to manage regional conflicts so as to reduce the risk of a U.S.-Soviet confrontation. Given Reagan's previous shifts from private conciliation to public condemnation, the Soviets suspected that the president's speech was merely election-year rhetoric. Also conveying a possible lack of seriousness was Reagan's failure to propose any concrete solutions to the Soviets through private diplomatic channels.[31]

When Chernenko succeeded Andropov in February 1984, he was already wheezing with emphysema. Given Chernenko's ill health and lack of knowledge about foreign issues, Gromyko recaptured the control over foreign policymaking that he had briefly lost to Andropov, who did have his own ideas on the subject. Chernenko simply wanted to reestablish the détente of the 1970s. So it was that Reagan met with Gromyko in September 1984, the first time that the Soviet foreign minister had been invited to the White House since the 1979 Soviet invasion of Afghanistan. A more important breakthrough occurred in January 1985, when Gromyko and Shultz agreed to resume arms control negotiations, divided into three sets of talks: strategic arms, intermediate nuclear missiles, and space-based defensive systems. After a year of wrangling over whether the talks should try to prevent militarization of space, and whether offensive as well as defensive weapons should be included, the Soviets had dropped their four preconditions for resuming negotiations: a nuclear freeze, a declaration of "no first use" of nuclear weapons, ratification of the 1974 and 1976 nuclear testing and peaceful nuclear explosion treaties, and renunciation of the militarization of outer space. Reagan's landslide election in November 1984 had convinced the Soviet leadership that they had no choice now but to deal with the president.[32]

Thus, despite Shultz's efforts and Reagan's receptiveness to personal contacts and arms control agreements, U.S.-Soviet cooperation made imperceptible progress until Gorbachev came to power. The Reagan administration's policy proposals toward the Soviet Union had consisted of a mishmash of agreements and issues, including confidence-building measures, regional conflicts, and human rights. The policy had no underlying vision, which might have imbued these small initiatives with some coherence and direction.[33]

The earlier contacts are important largely because, through them, Reagan gradually became committed to improving U.S.-Soviet relations and negotiating arms control agreements. The president had taken the first steps toward resuming talks with the Soviets, over the active opposition of the NSC staff. Over the next two years, Gorbachev's bold initiatives and Reagan's continuing personal engagement would help create an atmosphere of mutual trust.

A New Leader with New Initiatives

When Gorbachev succeeded Chernenko as general secretary of the Communist Party after his death in March 1985, the new leader faced international isolation and stagnating economic growth rates. Brezhnev's extension of Soviet involvement in the Third World and his buildup of Soviet strategic forces had undermined proponents of détente in the United States and indirectly contributed to the election of Ronald Reagan, who rebuilt and modernized America's strategic forces. A Soviet campaign of war threats and bullying tactics against the U.S. deployment of Pershing 2s and cruise missiles in Europe had backfired, uniting the NATO allies rather than intimidating them.[34]

In the early 1980s, the Soviet economy was falling behind the West in the key economic indicators. The technology gap was growing wider, as the Soviets had failed to participate in the revolution in microelectronics, computers, and lasers. The Soviet gross national product had increased by only 2 percent in 1984, and agriculture showed no growth at all, which meant that the Soviet Union was steadily falling behind the United States. The Soviet standard of living was at only 40 percent of the American level.[35]

In a December 1984 speech at a Communist Party conference on ideology, Gorbachev had warned that the Soviet Union could not continue to be a superpower unless it had a highly developed economy. Early on, he had decided to pursue arms control agreements with the West, to create a peaceful international environment that would allow him to restructure the Soviet economy and divert resources away from the military. In a speech to British members of Parliament, also in December 1984, Gorbachev declared that the Soviet Union needed peace in order to achieve its "truly breathtaking creative plans."[36]

Gorbachev and his advisers were "men of the sixties," part of a generation that experienced the shock of Khrushchev's 1956 secret speech, exulted in the liberalization of thought, became excited by the reforms in Czechoslovakia which became known as the Prague Spring, and grew disillusioned with the 1968 invasion of Czechoslovakia. These men had bided their time, waiting for the next "Great Reformer." They had for the most part not become dissidents, but had tried to avoid being sullied by the worst excesses of the communist system. They often wrote within the ideological conventions of the day, but thought differently. Gorbachev gathered many such men around him as his advisers, installed them as heads of academic institutes, allowed them to edit key newspapers and journals. The "men of the sixties" included the Americanist Georgi Arbatov, the policy advisers Anatoly Chernyaev, Georgi Shakhnazarov, and Oleg Bogomolov, the journalists Aleksandr Bovin and Fedor Burlatsky. Initially, Gorbachev merely wanted to "cleanse" socialism, to return to the original vision expressed by Lenin before it became muddied by Stalinism.[37]

When Shultz visited the Soviet embassy on 11 March to sign the condolence book for Chernenko, he informed Dobrynin that President Reagan believed a new situation with new opportunities was emerging in Soviet-American relations; it would be unforgivable not to take advantage of it. Just as Reagan was beginning his second term as president, the Soviet Union had a new leader who would manage domestic and foreign affairs energetically. Reagan wanted to start a dialogue at the highest level from the very beginning, and with that objective the president had decided to send a personal letter to Gorbachev. Thus Shultz reported that Reagan planned to send Vice-President George Bush to Chernenko's funeral with a letter inviting Gorbachev to a summit in Washington. Dobrynin was excited because, for the first time, Reagan had openly expressed interest in a summit with a Soviet leader.[38]

Gorbachev received Reagan's letter but had to consult with the Politburo before answering. The Soviet leadership actively debated whether or not to participate in a summit with Reagan without first achieving a major agreement. Gorbachev argued that "if you make it a rule, the summit will not be held earlier than in two or three years." It might not even be held at all. "Now, time is short," he said. "We need a summit to get to know Reagan and his plans and, most important, to launch a personal dialogue with the American president." In his reply, which was delivered to Reagan on 24 March, the Soviet leader wrote that their first priority should be to conduct business in such a way as to make clear that the two countries were not trying to deepen their differences and whip up animosity. Such a businesslike approach, he asserted, "would help create an atmosphere of trust between our countries," which was not an easy task. "For trust is an especially sensitive thing, keenly receptive to both deeds and words. It will not be enhanced if, for example, one were to talk as if in two languages: one—for private contacts, and the other . . . for the audience." Gorbachev affirmed that he had a "positive attitude" with respect to a meeting between himself and the president, although he was not yet ready to set a date. And such a meeting need not conclude with the signing of a major document. The main thing was that they should search for mutual understanding on the basis of equality and take into account each other's legitimate interests.[39]

On 8 April 1985, Gorbachev came out publicly in favor of a summit in *Pravda*. He also announced a freeze on the deployment of intermediate-range SS-20s in Europe until November, a freeze that could be extended if the United States followed suit. The Reagan administration immediately rejected the freeze because it would perpetuate a ten-to-one Soviet advantage in European missiles.[40]

In his reply to Gorbachev's letter, Reagan proposed businesslike contacts and reviewed a range of issues. Among these issues were human rights, curbs on chemical weapons, cooperation on regional conflicts, and the nonproliferation of nuclear weapons.[41]

Gorbachev, for his part, did not want to meet in Washington, because that would make him look like a supplicant. He suggested that they meet in November in Moscow. In May, Reagan almost backed out of the proposed meeting. Finally, Shultz informed Dobrynin that the president had reluctantly accepted Geneva.[42]

On 1 July, Ambassador Dobrynin reported that Gorbachev had agreed to a summit in Geneva on 19 and 20 November 1985. Two days later, when the Soviets made a public announcement, they also disclosed that Eduard Shevardnadze, a former party boss of Georgia who had no foreign policy experience, would replace Gromyko as foreign minister. Shevardnadze was personable and warm, a master politician able to win the confidence of others, in marked contrast to the dour Gromyko, who seemed incapable of humor or warmth. Most important, Shevardnadze was an intelligent man, unburdened by ideological stereotypes. Gorbachev had long wished to get rid of Gromyko, whose conservative and dogmatic approach to policy bothered him. Gorbachev could trust Shevardnadze to share his own views on foreign policy toward the United States. They had known each other since their membership in the Young Communist League and had become friends when they were Communist Party secretaries of neighboring regions, Gorbachev in Stavropol and Shevardnadze in Georgia.[43]

Shevardnadze's appointment signaled a new, more flexible, and less conventional Soviet foreign policy. Then, on 30 July 1985, Gorbachev announced that he was unilaterally suspending nuclear tests until the end of the year, and he offered to extend the moratorium if the United States reciprocated. In an interview with *Time* magazine, the Soviet leader noted that "we do not simply limit ourselves to appeals, mere appeals for disarmament and improved relations. We act likewise."[44]

Gorbachev's unilateral halt in testing had little impact on Reagan administration attitudes. One senior official accused the Soviets of conducting accelerated tests before the moratorium began so that they would not need to test over the next five months anyway. Others maintained that a temporary Soviet moratorium would cost little in terms of weapons development and could be followed by more intensive testing after it expired. It was recalled that the Soviet moratorium of 1958–1961 was followed by the "largest series of high-yield explosions in history."[45]

Indeed, the Reagan administration now took action to show that the United States could not be manipulated by Gorbachev's sophisticated public relations strategy. Reagan's national security adviser Robert McFarlane labeled the Soviet Union's arguments about arms control a "masterpiece of chutzpah," and the administration announced that it planned to test an antisatellite weapon—in violation of a tacit U.S.-Soviet convention not to target satellites, which were indispensable for arms control verification and the prevention of surprise attack.[46]

On 20 August, the United States accused the Soviet Union of using a cancer-causing chemical powder to track the movements of Americans in Moscow. Concerns about the health hazards of this "spy dust" were later shown to be unfounded. Calling the accusations "absurd," "outrageous," and a "gross falsehood," the Kremlin denounced Washington for trying to "poison" U.S.-Soviet relations.[47]

Gorbachev became frustrated at the failure of the United States to present any concrete proposals for a summit agenda or expected agreements. On 27 September 1985 with Gorbachev's approval, Shevardnadze presented to the White House a radical proposal to reduce by 50 percent all nuclear missiles that could strike the other side's territory—a reduction to about 6,000 warheads. Moscow proposed to limit the number of warheads that either side could place on any one "delivery means," such as land-based ICBMs to 3,600, an important concession to American concerns that Soviet heavy missiles could give them a first-strike capability. The United States had 2,125 warheads on land-based missiles, the Soviets 6,400. The Soviet proposal was less than it appeared, though, because the criterion of "weapons that could hit the other side's territory" would include U.S. intermediate-range missiles based in Europe, cruise missiles, and weapons carried by bombers but not Soviet intermediate-range missiles targeted on U.S. allies in Europe. A more serious problem, from Reagan's perspective, was that the offer was contingent on a U.S. agreement not to deploy "space attack" weapons, the Soviet term for SDI.[48]

Secretary of State Shultz and his special arms control adviser Paul Nitze favored making a "grand compromise," trading major reductions in Soviet offensive forces in return for restraints on the deployment of U.S. strategic defenses. Other U.S. officials such as Kenneth Adelman (the head of ACDA), Defense Secretary Weinberger, and Deputy Defense Secretary Perle strongly objected to an "offense–defense" trade-off. In their view, the United States had tried this approach in the 1972 SALT agreement, in which the Nixon administration had relinquished its ABM system in return for the promise of Soviet restraint in building offensive weapons, but the Soviets had not carried out their part of the bargain. President Reagan was adamantly opposed to trading SDI for Soviet weapons reductions.[49]

The debate within the Reagan administration over whether to limit or delay SDI deployment then shifted to the question of what sort of research and development was permitted by the 1972 ABM Treaty. The State Department's legal counsel Abraham Sofaer reviewed the classified records of the negotiations and concluded that Article 5 of the SALT I Treaty, which states that "each party undertakes not to develop, test, or deploy ABM systems or components" referred only to components that were "current" at the time the treaty was written. This so-called broad interpretation meant that the Reagan administration could test and develop ABM systems based on new technologies without violating the ABM Treaty.[50]

On 6 October, in a broadcast of the television program *Meet the Press*, Robert McFarlane stated that the ABM Treaty did not prohibit testing and development of space-based ABM systems but only their deployment, implying that the broad interpretation was official policy. McFarlane had exceeded his authority, however, because the Reagan administration was deeply divided over whether to accept the more permissive reading of the treaty, and the president had not yet made a decision.[51]

Secretary Shultz was appalled by McFarlane's gaffe. He tried to finesse the issue by saying that while the permissive interpretation was "fully justified," as a matter of policy the administration would conduct its SDI research in accordance with the restrictive view of the treaty.[52]

Yet this compromise did not end the dispute within the Reagan administration over what types of SDI research and testing were legally permitted by the ABM Treaty. From time to time the Defense Department, in proposals to the Soviets for cooperation on arms reductions, would insert language implying that the Reagan administration had accepted the broad interpretation as official policy. Nor did Shultz's disclaimer satisfy the Soviets, who had closely followed the Washington debate. Marshal Sergei F. Akhromeyev, chief of the Soviet General Staff, was quoted in *Pravda* as commenting that recent efforts by the Reagan administration to reinterpret the ABM Treaty were a "deliberate deceit" that "distorted the essence of the treaty." In a 5 November meeting with Shultz to prepare for the summit, Gorbachev objected vigorously to the broad interpretation of the ABM Treaty, saying that SDI was an attempt to justify an ABM system by "unworthy means."[53]

THE BEGINNING OF A RELATIONSHIP

At their first meeting in Geneva, on 19 November 1985, Reagan told Gorbachev that they had a historic opportunity to free the world from the "uncivilized doctrine" of assured destruction. Anticipating Gorbachev's objections that the defensive system would be used to prevent the Soviets from retaliating against a first strike, Reagan reassured the Soviet leader that the United States would negotiate a transition to a defense-dominant world and would share defensive technology with the Soviets.[54]

Gorbachev objected that "what you call research" on SDI could produce "offensive nuclear weapons circling the earth." He charged that the United States was "plotting" to use SDI to reestablish a "one-sided advantage" over the USSR. Reagan reminded Gorbachev that the United States had a monopoly in atomic weapons after World War II but had not used them for aggressive purposes. "Why don't you trust me?" Reagan asked.

Gorbachev asked why Reagan did not trust him. The president replied that any American leader must plan based on the other side's capabilities. That was precisely the point, Gorbachev replied. SDI had the capability of upsetting parity and the strategic balance.

At Reagan's suggestion, the two men continued their discussion in a nearby pool house, where a fire had been prepared by the president's "advance men" for just such a "spontaneous" occasion. Reagan took out a manila envelope and showed him an arms control proposal that called for a 50 percent cut in strategic weapons and for research on strategic defense in compliance with the ABM Treaty. But the proposal also suggested that both sides immediately begin exploring means for a cooperative transition to greater reliance on defensive systems, an endorsement of SDI. The blatant contradiction reflected differences between the Defense Department and State over whether the United States should observe the ABM Treaty.[55]

Gorbachev objected that the paper allowed SDI to continue. It must continue, Reagan replied. "Then we just disagree," the Soviet leader replied.[56]

As the two men walked back to the chateau on Lake Geneva where the plenary sessions were held, Reagan invited Gorbachev to Washington for another summit. Gorbachev accepted and asked the president to Moscow for a third summit.[57] This was one of the major achievements of the Geneva summit—to restore regular meetings and open the channels of communication that had been disrupted in the early Reagan term.

Their session on the second day proved to be the most heated. President Reagan argued vehemently that SDI was not an offensive system: "I am talking about a shield, not a spear." Gorbachev retorted, "The reality is that SDI would open a new arms race."

The Soviet leader pressed Reagan: "Why don't you believe me when I say the Soviet Union will never attack?" Why, then, should he accept Reagan's stated willingness to share SDI research when the United States did not even share its advanced technology with its allies? The Soviets, Gorbachev said, would agree to restraints on intermediate-range missiles. They would talk about deep cuts in strategic missiles. "But SDI has got to come to an end." Finally, seeing that Reagan was very angry, Gorbachev said calmly: "Mr. President, I disagree with you, but I can see you really believe it."[58]

In an agreed statement at the end of the meeting, Gorbachev and Reagan declared that "a nuclear war can never be won and must never be fought," and each promised that his country would not seek superiority over the other. Both sides stressed the importance of preventing any war between the United States and the Soviet Union, whether nuclear or conventional. This was a Soviet proposal. Before the summit, the Politburo had agreed: "The best we can expect is a joint statement that both sides will proceed from the assumption that nuclear war is unacceptable and unwinnable." In addition, the two leaders committed themselves to achieve a 50 percent reduction in nuclear arms and an interim agreement on intermediate-range nuclear forces (INF). Shultz and Shevardnadze also signed a cultural, scientific, and educational exchange agreement, the result of some two hundred hours of previous negotiations, and an agreement setting up consulates in Kiev and New York.[59]

After the summit, Gorbachev held a press conference at which he declared that "trust is not restored right away. It is a difficult process." He had heeded Reagan's statements that the United States was not seeking superiority and did not want nuclear war. "We sincerely want these statements to be confirmed by deeds."[60]

The Geneva meeting had convinced Gorbachev that Reagan was sincere about wanting to abolish nuclear weapons. In their one-to-one conversation in the pool house, Reagan had commented to Gorbachev that if they could agree to eliminate nuclear missiles, then there would be no need for defenses against them. The Soviet leader therefore sought to go over the heads of Reagan's advisers and appeal directly to the president and American public opinion.[61]

On 15 January 1986, Gorbachev proposed a three-stage program to eliminate nuclear weapons entirely by the end of the century. In the first phase, the superpowers would eliminate all medium-range missiles, as in Reagan's 1981 "zero option," and would reduce their strategic arms by 50 percent within five to eight years. For the first time, Gorbachev agreed to exclude British and French missiles from an INF agreement. In this initial stage when strategic arsenals were to be reduced, there must be a ban on development, testing, and deployment of "space strike" (SDI) weapons. In the second phase, beginning in 1990, other nuclear powers would join the process, and battlefield (i.e., tactical) nuclear weapons would be eliminated. The third phase, beginning in 1995, would witness the destruction of all remaining nuclear weapons. Anticipating U.S. objections, Gorbachev said that "special procedures" could be worked out for verification, including on-site inspection. Finally, the Soviet leader extended the nuclear test moratorium three months, despite the U.S. refusal to reciprocate.[62]

The 15 January disarmament proposal had been written by First Deputy Foreign Minister Georgi Kornienko and by Marshal Akhromeyev sometime before the Geneva conference. Kornienko and Akhromeyev had decided that the United States and the Soviet Union would be just as secure—and safer—with much smaller stockpiles of nuclear weapons. When Gorbachev found out about their plan, he enthusiastically supported it. Gaining the support of the Politburo was more difficult, but Gorbachev already had the support of the Foreign Ministry, and Akhromeyev's role helped to offset military opposition.[63]

Secretary Shultz pointed out to President Reagan that "this is our first indication that the Soviets are interested in a staged program toward zero." Shultz advised Reagan not to reject the Soviet proposal, "since it contains certain steps which we earlier set forth," such as the concept of massive reductions in nuclear arms.[64]

Reagan agreed. "Why wait until the end of the century for a world without nuclear weapons?" he asked. At a press conference, President Reagan observed that the plan was "different from the things that we have heard in the past from leaders in the Soviet Union" and that his administration was "grateful."[65] For the first time, Reagan spoke favorably about a Soviet arms control proposal.

Shultz attributed the Soviet willingness to reduce nuclear weapons down to zero to a concern about stopping SDI. The secretary of state therefore wanted to preserve the early phases of U.S. research on strategic defenses as an inducement for the Soviets to agree to reductions in their strategic forces. Shultz believed that in order to give drive and momentum to the arms control process, it was important to maintain Reagan's goal of a world without nuclear weapons. Distrustful of the Soviets, however, he favored starting with an INF agreement.[66]

Most State Department and Defense officials did not share Reagan's vision of a "nuclear-free world" as either desirable or feasible. Without nuclear weapons, the United States could not defend Europe against a Soviet conventional attack. Nuclear weapons had maintained the peace in Europe for more than forty years. In a world without nuclear weapons, the Soviet Union would have the world's largest conventional military force. The Defense Department wanted to "pick out the raisin" of Gorbachev's acceptance of on-site inspection and reject everything else. Perle said that the NSC should not discuss the idea of abolishing nuclear weapons because Reagan might actually direct U.S. officials to come up with a program to achieve that objective.[67]

On 23 February, Reagan sent Gorbachev a handwritten letter, drafted by the State Department, saying that many aspects of the Soviet plan could not be considered without first addressing such issues as conventional forces, verification, and regional conflicts. Reagan welcomed Gorbachev's proposal for an agreement to eliminate all INF missiles in Europe, but maintained that Soviet missiles in Asia should be destroyed as well.[68]

Most Western observers regarded Gorbachev's proposal on 15 January as a public relations gimmick, but the Soviet leader apparently took it very seriously. Dobrynin labeled Reagan's response a "pick-and-choose strategy." In other words, the Reagan administration would negotiate on those aspects of Gorbachev's program which it found attractive, while ignoring the elements it did not like. At the Twenty-seventh Party Congress, Gorbachev read Reagan's reply, noting that while it agreed in general with some Soviet positions on disarmament and security, "these positive pronouncements [were] lost in various kinds of reservations."[69]

The United States had passed up an opportunity to engage the Soviets in negotiations for major reductions in nuclear weapons. Granted, there were propagandistic elements in Gorbachev's proposal. But it was a sincere effort to meet U.S. concerns, and American and Soviet negotiators might have been able to work out some of their differences. Most notable was Gorbachev's acceptance of on-site inspection for the purpose of verification. Gorbachev also had accepted the "zero option" for intermediate-range nuclear forces, a proposal that previous Soviet officials had regarded as unacceptable. The Soviet leader had called for speeding up negotiations on mutual and balanced force reductions in Europe. Not only did Moscow propose to destroy chemical weapons, but it would eliminate their production facilities as well.[70]

"NEW THINKING" IN SOVIET FOREIGN POLICY

At the Twenty-seventh Party Congress, Gorbachev began to develop some concepts of "new thinking" in Soviet foreign policy. The "new thinking" gave coherence and meaning to isolated Soviet acts of cooperation, placing them within an intellectual framework that allowed Western observers to understand Gorbachev's actions. Similar foreign policy ideas had been circulating among Soviet security specialists and academics since the 1970s, especially since the decline of détente in the early Reagan administration. Nevertheless, these new conceptions of international relations might have remained quiescent had Gorbachev not had the insight and sophistication to seize upon them.[71]

In the nuclear age, Gorbachev said, no country could hope to safeguard itself solely with military-technical means. "Ensuring security is increasingly seen as a political problem," he said, "and it can only be resolved by political means." Security could not be built on fear of retaliation. Among other things, deterrence merely encouraged an arms race that sooner or later could go out of control. In relations between the USSR and the United States, he said, "security can only be mutual." It was vital that all should feel equally secure, because fears and anxieties could generate unpredictable actions. In the nuclear age, Gorbachev said, "the aspiration to win military superiority can, speaking in objective terms, bring no political gain to anybody."[72]

Gorbachev cautioned against expecting immediate results, and called for greater consistency in Soviet foreign policy. "The problem of international security cannot be resolved by one or two, even very intensive, peace campaigns," he said. "Success can only be achieved by consistent, methodical, and persevering effort." Continuity, however, did not mean endless repetition of the same positions. Gorbachev said that what was needed was firmness in upholding principles and standards combined with tactical flexibility and a readiness for mutually acceptable compromises.[73]

Mutual security suggested that the Soviets should be more aware of how their military doctrine might be perceived by others. "We intend to act in such a way as to give nobody grounds for fears, even imagined ones, about their security," Gorbachev promised. He was the first Soviet leader to acknowledge that Soviet weapons programs could conceivably be viewed as threatening by other states. Just as Richard Nixon had said that the United States should try for sufficiency rather than superiority when he realized that the latter was no longer achievable, so Gorbachev declared that Soviet defense forces should aim at "reasonable sufficiency." Like Nixon, Gorbachev articulated the idea of "sufficiency" with only a vague idea of what it would imply in practice for Soviet defense policy. Soviet defense analysts and military officials did not begin to debate "reasonable sufficiency" until well into 1986 and 1987.[74]

Again, at the time, most Western analysts regarded Gorbachev's "new thinking" as a sophisticated public relations strategy or an attempt to gain a breathing spell before confronting the West.[75] Gorbachev therefore had to follow up his words with concrete deeds in order to give substance to the "new thinking."

It is well that Gorbachev did not expect immediate success, for the Reagan administration soon initiated several belligerent actions. On 7 March 1986, the U.S. government demanded that the Soviet mission to the United Nations be reduced from 320 to 170 over the period of a year, because many Soviet employees were working for the KGB. Moscow protested that "such actions reinforce distrust toward [U.S.] policies and by no means create a favorable background for a summit meeting."[76]

On 13 March, two U.S. naval ships equipped with extensive, sophisticated electronic gear moved within six miles of the Black Sea to establish the right of U.S. warships to cross territorial waters in a straight line. That Gorbachev happened to be at his dacha in the area conveyed the impression that the naval exercise was a deliberate insult to the general secretary.[77]

Then, by conducting a test on 22 March, the Reagan administration flouted Gorbachev's effort to obtain a comprehensive test ban.[78] Next the U.S. Air Force bombed Libya (14 April), after which the Soviets canceled a scheduled visit of Foreign Minister Shevardnadze to Washington.[79]

Finally, on 27 May 1986, Reagan announced that the United States would no longer base its weapons programs on the standards of the "flawed" SALT II Treaty. Although the treaty was never ratified by the United States, both sides had been observing it. Reagan noted that two Poseidon submarines would be dismantled as called for by the SALT II Treaty—but only for budgetary reasons, not to remain in compliance.[80]

Meanwhile, concerned that the United States was not responding to his 15 January disarmament proposal, Gorbachev told the diplomats at a closed meeting at the Ministry of Foreign Affairs on 23 May that he was serious about his arms control proposals and expected them to work for their implementation. The strategic goals developed at the Twenty-seventh Party Congress should be converted into the "language of concrete foreign policy acts." In disarmament, he said, one could not "allow a rupture between words and deeds."[81]

On 29 May, the Soviets presented a new START proposal in which they offered a one-third cut in nuclear warheads (to 8,000). This time, the Soviets had abandoned their "reach criterion" by which any weapon that could reach Soviet territory counted as strategic. Instead of insisting on a ban against "space-strike weapons," the Soviets offered to allow SDI research, testing, and deployment so long as it was conducted in the laboratory. In return, the Soviets wanted a U.S. commitment not to withdraw from the ABM Treaty for fifteen to twenty years.[82]

Shultz regarded the Soviet proposal as highly promising, the first real opening since the Geneva summit. Shultz favored proposing a 50 percent cut in strategic weapons together with a shorter period of enforced compliance with the ABM Treaty that would not place any significant practical restrictions on the SDI program. In this way, they could get the Soviets to make significant reductions in their most accurate and dangerous missiles without affecting the U.S. ability to deploy SDI in the future. As Shultz told Reagan, the United States could trade away the sleeves of its vest, having convinced the Soviets that they were getting the overcoat. Reagan was convinced, however, that the Soviets would use any negotiations to kill SDI.[83]

On 25 July, instead of proposing some changes in the Soviet offer, President Reagan sent Gorbachev a letter (inspired by Weinberger) proposing that the United States and the Soviet Union observe the ABM Treaty for seven and a half years. During the first five years, both states would confine their research, development, and testing to whatever was permitted by the ABM Treaty. If either side then decided to deploy strategic defenses, it should offer a plan for sharing "the benefits of strategic defense" and for eliminating all ballistic missiles. If the two superpowers could not agree on how to destroy ballistic missiles and make a cooperative transition to strategic defenses by the end of the seven-and-a-half-year period, each would be free to deploy SDI after six months notice. Although Reagan took it seriously, the proposal was pure propaganda, designed to counter the appeal of Gorbachev's 15 January proposal for nuclear disarmament. *Pravda* replied that Reagan's letter was not "constructive."[84]

On 18 August, Gorbachev announced that he was extending the nuclear test moratorium until the end of the year, much to the displeasure of the Soviet military. By the time the moratorium was scheduled to expire, seventeen months down the road, the Soviet Union would normally have conducted twenty to thirty tests. Gorbachev contended that the moratorium would improve the Soviet image and build trust by showing that the Soviet Union "not only makes proposals but acts on them, too." Reagan administration officials rejected a comprehensive test ban on the grounds that the Soviets could cheat and the United States needed additional testing to develop more sophisticated weapons.[85]

Once again, Soviet-American relations were derailed by accusations of spying. On 23 August 1986, FBI agents arrested a Soviet U.N. employee, Gennadi F. Zakharov, after he paid for classified documents provided to him by a student who was helping the FBI. One week later the Soviet KGB arrested Nicholas Daniloff, a journalist for *U.S. News & World Report*, after having planted phony documents on him in what appeared to be a transparent gambit to acquire trading stock for their own employee.[86]

At first, Reagan was adamant against trading Zakharov, a supposed spy, for Daniloff, an innocent journalist. Despite President Reagan's personal intervention, Gorbachev maintained that Daniloff had long been engaged in illegal activities, and asserted that the Soviets would conduct their own investigation.[87]

When Shevardnadze arrived in Washington to resolve the Daniloff-Zakharov imbroglio, he brought with him a letter from Gorbachev inviting Reagan to a mini-summit in London or Iceland to give "impulse" to the arms control negotiations. Gorbachev offered to discuss reducing medium-range missiles in Asia as well as in Europe, thus creating expectations for a breakthrough in the INF negotiations. In his own words, Reagan "opted for Iceland."[88]

Before they could announce the summit, Shultz and Shevardnadze had to work out a deal with respect to Zakharov-Daniloff that would satisfy American public opinion, particularly conservatives who opposed a trade. Shultz had changed his mind about a trade when he learned that the CIA had used Daniloff as a courier and that the Soviets had a strong legal case against him. The Soviets freed Daniloff, and the following day Zakharov was sent back to the Soviet Union. Moscow then released the Soviet dissident Yuri Orlov and his wife.[89]

On 22 September 1986, at the thirty-five-nation security conference in Stockholm, the United States and the Soviet Union signed a major agreement on confidence-building measures to reduce fears of surprise attack in Europe. In line with Gorbachev's 15 January pledge to accept intrusive forms of verification, the Soviets agreed to on-site inspection of military exercises involving more than 17,000 troops, thus creating a break-through in the talks which had been stalemated since January 1984. When the Stockholm conference first opened, Foreign Minister Gromyko had said that Western demands for inspection were "an excuse to peek through the neighbor's fence."[90]

REYKJAVIK: A FAILURE LEADING TO SUCCESS

The meeting of Gorbachev and Reagan at Reykjavik, Iceland, was a stunning missed opportunity for an agreement on comprehensive arms reduction, but it did make possible later successes.[91] The two leaders agreed on major principles that would be carried out subsequently in other agreements. Each developed the impression that the other was se-rious about eliminating nuclear weapons. Indeed, it was at Reykjavik that Gorbachev decided he could work with Reagan. Back in Moscow, the Soviet leader confided to Dobrynin that Reagan was capable of making great decisions.[92]

At their first private meeting, on 11 October, Reagan told Gorbachev: "There is a Russian saying: *doveryai no proveryai*, trust but verify. How will we know that you'll get rid of your missiles as you say you will?" Gorbachev replied that he accepted strict verification, including on-site inspection.[93]

Later, with Shultz and Shevardnadze present, Gorbachev proposed a 50 percent cut in all strategic nuclear forces, including Soviet heavy mis-siles and bombers. American and Soviet intermediate nuclear forces in Europe should be eliminated. This, Gorbachev told Reagan, is "your own zero option." In return for these concessions, the Soviet leader proposed that both sides agree to observe the ABM Treaty for ten instead of fifteen years, followed by a three- to five-year period of negotiations about how to proceed next. Research and testing of "space-strike weapons" should be confined to the laboratory.[94] Reagan later told Shultz, "He's brought a whole lot of proposals, but I'm afraid he's going after SDI."[95]

At the afternoon session, Reagan argued that SDI would eventually make possible the elimination of ballistic missiles. If tests showed that SDI worked, Reagan said, the United States would be obligated to share it with the Soviet Union. "If you will not share oil-drilling equipment or even milk-processing factories," Gorbachev scoffed, "I do not believe that you will share SDI."[96]

Reagan retorted, "We are willing to eliminate all ballistic missiles before SDI is deployed, so a first strike would be impossible."[97]

Turning to human rights and regional conflicts, Reagan explained that "we arm because we don't trust each other, so we must get at the human rights problems and regional disputes that are the sources of distrust."[98] Several months later, Gorbachev inaugurated a human rights policy to win the confidence of the West.

Two working groups were set up to negotiate on (a) human rights and bilateral issues and (b) arms control. The arms control group made more progress in one night than in the entire previous history of U.S.-Soviet arms control talks. Working late into Saturday night, this working group—under Paul Nitze and Marshal Akhromeyev—agreed in principle to reduce nuclear warheads by 50 percent and to arrive at equal outcomes of 6,000 warheads and 1,600 strategic delivery vehicles.[99]

At the Sunday morning session, Gorbachev agreed to limit intermediate-range missiles in Asia to 100 warheads. The United States would have the right to deploy 100 missiles on its territory.[100]

But on Sunday afternoon, Shevardnadze complained that the Soviets had made all the concessions. Everything depended on Washington's agreement to a ten-year period of nonwithdrawal from the ABM Treaty and strict adherence to the treaty during that period.[101]

Assistant Secretary of Defense Perle and Colonel Robert Linhard, an NSC arms control expert, quickly jotted down a proposal by which both sides would observe the ABM treaty for ten years—if strategic weapons were reduced 50 percent in the first five years, and if ballistic missiles were eliminated during the second five years. After ten years, with all their ballistic missiles gone, either side could deploy a strategic defense system as insurance against accidents or a third-party attack.[102] In other words, in order to induce the United States to observe the ABM Treaty for ten years, Gorbachev would have to give up the Soviet advantage in land-based missiles while leaving untouched the U.S. lead in bombers and air-launched cruise missiles. After ten years, the United States would be free to deploy SDI, while the Soviets would be vulnerable to a first strike.

Gorbachev countered with the proposal that the United States and the Soviet Union reduce their strategic arms by 50 percent during the first five years and eliminate all their remaining nuclear weapons by the end of the following five years. During this time, testing of space-based ABM components should be confined to the laboratory. After ten years, both sides should enter into negotiations on what to do regarding space defenses.[103]

Reagan replied that "this seems only slightly different from the U.S. position." Reagan's advisers tried to explain to him the difference between ballistic missiles and strategic nuclear weapons.[104]

The president then argued that an agreement to eliminate nuclear weapons should remove any worries that Gorbachev might have about the first-strike potential of SDI. The United States should be free to test during that ten-year period and deploy at the end. "Who knows when the world will see another Hitler. We need to be able to defend ourselves."[105]

To this the Soviet leader replied, "Leave open for negotiation what would happen at the end of ten years, prohibit testing in space, and confine research and testing to the laboratory." Gorbachev insisted that the ABM Treaty should be observed for at least ten years; thus there could be no defensive deployments in space while offensive weapons were being eliminated.[106]

"If we both eliminate nuclear weapons, why would there be a concern if one side wants to build defensive systems just in case?" Reagan asked. "Are you considering starting up again with weapons after ten years?"[107]

Gorbachev: "Mr. President, we are close to a mutually acceptable formula. Don't think we have evil designs. We don't."[108]

This exchange between Gorbachev and Reagan exemplifies the dilemma facing the two leaders. Neither understood how the other could perceive his position as threatening. Reagan did not really believe that the Soviets would destroy all their ballistic missiles, and he wanted to have strategic defenses as insurance in case the Soviets decided to deploy nuclear weapons after the United States had disarmed. That Gorbachev would not allow him to have this protection suggested to Reagan that the Soviets must indeed have such intentions. Gorbachev, on the other hand, did not see why the United States would want to deploy a defensive shield in a nuclear-free world unless Washington was planning a first strike with a hidden cache of nuclear weapons. In February 1986, Gorbachev had asked some of his assistants whether it was time to stop being afraid of SDI. His scientists had informed him that they could destroy or neutralize an American SDI system by spending only 10 percent of what the Americans planned to spend. But Gorbachev had been persuaded by representatives of the Soviet military-industrial complex that he must obtain Reagan's withdrawal from SDI because such a system would give the United States a first-strike advantage. Besides, Gorbachev did not believe that Reagan would share SDI technology with the Soviet Union. Gorbachev said: "I may believe you, Mr. President, but would your successors repeat the offer?"[109]

At one point, Reagan replied that "it would be fine with me if we eliminated all nuclear weapons."[110]

What was not so fine was Gorbachev's insistence on confining SDI research to the laboratory. "It is a question of one word," Reagan said.[111]

Gorbachev said he would be viewed as a "dummy" if he accepted cuts in offensive weapons while allowing the United States to continue to do research, testing, and development that would enable it to create a large-scale space-defense system in ten years. "You are asking me to allow you to develop a system that will permit the U.S. to destroy the Soviet Union's offensive nuclear potential." This was unacceptable.[112]

After Gorbachev refused his request to "give me this one thing," Reagan closed his briefing book and stood up, ending the summit. "The meeting is over," he said. "Let's go, George, we're leaving." Reagan was disappointed and very angry.[113]

Reykjavik was a missed opportunity for a breathtaking arms reduction agreement that might have reduced strategic weapons by 50 percent and eliminated intermediate-range missiles in Europe. The two men came very close and their differences were over trivial nonessentials. Granted, the proposal to eliminate all nuclear weapons or even ballistic missiles would never have survived military scrutiny, allied protests, or congressional concerns. The Joint Chiefs were known to be unhappy about the proposal to eliminate all ballistic missiles, a notion they had originally approved only because they regarded it as nonnegotiable. But Gorbachev's proposals for START were both feasible and unprecedented. "The best Soviet proposal we have received in twenty-five years," commented Nitze[114]—this from the author of NSC 68 and an outspoken opponent of SALT II. If the two leaders had been able to sign such an ambitious agreement, with constraints on SDI research and testing, it would have contributed to greater trust on both sides and enhanced Gorbachev's political prestige. The Cold War might have ended sooner, with less economic burden placed on the American people for costly weapon systems.

Both men could have compromised without affecting the essence of their positions. At that early stage of the Strategic Defense Initiative, testing could have been confined to the laboratory without impeding progress. The United States was far from ready to deploy a space-based defensive system. Similarly, Gorbachev could have agreed to put aside the question of space-based defenses for later discussion, as he did at the Washington summit.[115] But Reagan feared that the Soviets were trying to kill SDI, and Gorbachev believed that SDI would give the U.S. a first-strike advantage.

Finally, continued U.S. nonreciprocity became too much for Gorbachev and, on 18 December 1986, the Soviet Union announced that it would discontinue its test moratorium at whatever time the United States conducted another test. Such a U.S. test would occur in February 1987.[116]

However, on 19 December 1986, Gorbachev disarmed foreign critics and appealed to the Soviet intelligentsia by releasing the famous dissident Andrei Sakharov, a nuclear physicist and Nobel Peace Prize laureate who had been sent into exile in Gorky for his criticism of the Soviet invasion of Afghanistan. In a symbolic act of contrition, Gorbachev telephoned Sakharov and invited him to return to Moscow. It was risky for Gorbachev to release such an outspoken critic as Sakharov, who spoke out against the war in Afghanistan the same day that he was released. Soon, though, Sakharov became a prominent supporter of Gorbachev's reforms.[117]

DEMOCRACY, HUMAN RIGHTS, AND BOLD INITIATIVES

In the two years since he had taken office, Gorbachev had made more than twenty-five unreciprocated arms control concessions. On the other hand, none of Gorbachev's concessions was very costly; all were either contingent on a reciprocal response from the United States or reversible. For example, Gorbachev's acceptance of the "zero option" was conditional on other concessions, such as restraints on British and French forces, causing many Westerners to have doubts about Soviet motives. The stunning cuts that Gorbachev had proposed to make in strategic weapons were linked to negotiated limits on SDI testing, development, and deployment.[118]

Gorbachev had been reluctant to take major risks because he feared that the United States would view Soviet initiatives as forced by the weak Soviet economy. He was deeply distrustful of the Reagan administration, and frequently made speeches attacking the right-wing militarists who wanted to drive the Soviets into bankruptcy through arms racing.[119]

Indeed, the Reagan administration had responded with provocative, hostile actions. Reagan maintained an unshakable commitment to deploying a strategic defense system, refusing to accept any constraints on testing and development, or even to stay within the bounds of the ABM Treaty. U.S. officials had belittled Gorbachev's seventeen-month unilateral nuclear test moratorium. Refusing to negotiate any limits on antisatellite systems, the United States tested an antisatellite weapon. The U.S. Navy, moreover, had dispatched warships to the Black Sea coast of the Soviet Union. Finally, in November 1986, the Reagan administration deliberately exceeded the SALT II limits.[120]

Beginning in late 1986 and continuing through the early part of the following year, Shevardnadze conducted a thorough review of Soviet policy toward the United States to determine if it was worthwhile to continue trying to do business with the Reagan administration. Discouraged at the hostile reaction to his overtures, Gorbachev could have adopted a traditional Soviet dual-track foreign policy—competition for geopolitical influence and negotiations with the United States—or he could have adopted a "Europe first" policy of trying to drive a wedge between the United States and its NATO allies. Instead, Gorbachev and his closest advisers apparently decided on a radical strategy to undermine the Western "devil" image of the Soviet Union.[121]

The year 1987 was a turning point in U.S.-Soviet relations. Beginning with the January 1987 Central Committee Plenum, Gorbachev tried to implement the principles of democracy and human rights in both his domestic and his foreign policy. In a September 1986 speech, Gorbachev had called for "democratization" of Soviet society and all spheres of life. Shortly after making this speech, Gorbachev tried to schedule a plenum on political democratization, but he was unable to persuade other members of the Soviet leadership. The conference was postponed three times before it was finally held on 27–28 January 1987. Gorbachev argued that economic reforms would not be effective unless the public was fully engaged; the Soviet people would not be motivated unless they had some voice in their destiny. "A house can be put in order," said the general secretary, "only by a person who feels that he owns this house." Accordingly, Gorbachev called for secret elections and multiple candidacies at all levels of the party, in local government and in factories and farms. He encountered strong opposition from the Central Committee, and the plenum adopted a vague resolution on improving the mechanism of party elections. On the other hand, steps toward implementing Gorbachev's wishes were taken gradually over subsequent months. Gorbachev also proposed another party conference the following year, to complete his envisioned political reforms. When the plenum failed to approve another party conference, Gorbachev decided to announce on television that members of the Central Committee had spoken in favor of it.[122]

Democratic reforms would inevitably destabilize the Soviet system, making it even more essential for Gorbachev to have a peaceful international environment. The Soviet leader had long ago decided to end the Cold War, but he had intended to do so through arms control agreements. Gorbachev now realized that he would get nowhere unless he assuaged the West's concerns about democracy and human rights. He had come into office with no blueprint for reform, other than improving the efficiency of the communist system, but he was determined to achieve *perestroika*, or "restructuring," and he was willing to pursue the logical and practical implications of his initial ideas as far as they took him, including greater freedom within the Soviet Union.[123]

In February 1987, Gorbachev announced that 140 dissidents and political prisoners would be freed; the cases of another group of dissidents would be reconsidered. Books such as *Doctor Zhivago* which had formerly been banned were now published. The film *Repentance*, never released because of its symbolic depiction of Stalin's crimes, received its premiere. The new rector of the Moscow State Institute of Historian-Archivists, Yuri Afanasyev, called for historians to investigate Stalin's crimes against the Soviet people.[124]

On 16 February, to win Western support for his reforms, Gorbachev convened an international group of about one thousand intellectuals and celebrities at a forum in Moscow called "For a Nuclear-Free World, For the Survival of Humanity." In his address to this distinguished audience, Gorbachev asserted that confidence had to be built up through experience with cooperation. He criticized the doctrine of nuclear deterrence because it required the use of military force to make nuclear threats credible and did not allow for human irrationality and the dangers of accidental war. He declared that the Soviet Union was willing to renounce its nuclear power status and reduce all other armaments to a "minimal reasonable" amount. While scaling down arms, he said, it was important to lessen the risk of surprise attack by eliminating the most dangerous offensive arms and adopting purely defensive military doctrines. Gorbachev also emphasized the need to settle regional conflicts, an issue that the Reagan administration had stressed.[125]

Gorbachev's shift from the reform of communism to its democratic transformation presaged bolder initiatives in foreign policy that would overcome the resistance of the Reagan administration to better relations. On 28 February 1987, the Soviet leader announced that the problem of medium-range missiles in Europe should be "singled out from the package of issues," and a separate agreement concluded "without delay," thus reversing his decision after Reykjavik to link an INF treaty to restraints on SDI. Gorbachev decoupled INF from SDI because a Soviet-American agreement on medium-range missiles would "create an atmosphere of greater trust," which could lead to further arms control agreements.[126]

Of course the Soviet leader may have been motivated by such narrower strategic considerations as eliminating the highly accurate Pershing 2 missiles, which could reach the Soviet Union in minutes from West German territory, or decoupling American and European defenses. On the other hand, Moscow had never before offered to relinquish existing Soviet missiles in order to remove an American weapon system. Further, if the military advantages of the zero option were so compelling, then why did no Soviet leader before Gorbachev accept it?[127]

Gorbachev then made a series of concessions on inspections, short-range systems, and the geographic scope of the treaty. Reflecting continuing skepticism about Soviet cheating, U.S. negotiators proposed that inspectors witness the destruction of the missiles as well as the launchers, that inspectors be stationed at missile production sites, and that each side have the right to make spur-of-the moment challenge inspections, "any time, any place."[128] The Soviets accepted these intrusive verification requirements, forcing Reagan administration hard-liners to take yes for an answer. Indeed, First Deputy Foreign Minister Yuli Vorontsov proposed that each side be able to go inside factories owned by private American military contractors in order to make sure those companies were not building missiles to replace the ones destroyed in Europe.[129]

The Soviets' unexpected acceptance of the U.S. inspection proposals aroused the anxiety of defense contractors, the CIA, and FBI officials, who did not want to give the Soviets access to military production facilities where sensitive information might be revealed. The Reagan administration retreated in September to a much less ambitious plan for on-site inspection.[130]

In mid-April, Gorbachev adopted the "double zero" option. That is to say, he agreed to eliminate all shorter-range intermediate nuclear forces in Europe: those with a range from 300 to 1,000 miles. West Europeans had feared that withdrawal of medium-range missiles would still leave them vulnerable to the remaining Soviet shorter-range systems. Yet this, too, was an asymmetric concession because the United States had no shorter-range INF missiles.[131] In July, Gorbachev agreed that the ban on medium- and short-range missiles would apply to Asia as well, alleviating fears that the Soviets would transfer missiles from Asia to Europe in a crisis.[132]

At about this time, several personnel changes occurred in the Reagan administration that, by removing several important hard-liners, would serve to facilitate an agreement. The moderate Frank Carlucci replaced Vice-Admiral John Poindexter as national security adviser in late 1986. In March 1987, William Casey, stricken by brain cancer, was replaced as director of the CIA by William Webster. A month later, Richard Perle left the administration. Then, in October, Caspar Weinberger resigned as secretary of defense because of his wife's ill health. He was replaced by Carlucci; and Carlucci's assistant, General Colin Powell, became national security adviser. For the first time, then, the officials within the Reagan administration who worked on foreign policy and security issues were functioning as a cohesive team.[133]

On 8 December 1987, Reagan and Gorbachev signed the INF Treaty at a summit in Washington. The treaty was the first to eliminate an entire category of weapons—all medium-range missiles in Europe as well as the shorter-range systems. Further, the Soviets would eliminate more missiles than the United States—1,752 missiles with a range of 300 to 3,400 miles as opposed to only 859 U.S. missiles.[134]

The intrusive verification provisions were critical in winning the support of the Reagan administration. Reagan said that conservatives who opposed the INF Treaty were "ignorant of the advances that had been made in verification." For thirteen years, American inspectors would be stationed outside a Soviet factory in Votkinsk that once produced SS-20s and SS-25s, while Soviet inspectors would be based outside a plant in Utah that manufactured components of the MX missile. Both sides would have the right to inspect factories that produced the launchers for ground-launched cruise missiles. During the first thirteen years of the treaty, U.S. and Soviet officials were authorized to conduct an annual quota of challenge inspections at any site where missiles had been stored, based, repaired, or deployed.[135]

President Reagan told the press that Gorbachev was a new kind of Soviet leader, the first who did not talk about world domination: he was truly willing to coexist with other philosophies. The president observed that he and Gorbachev had established "an entirely different relationship from what existed previously."[136]

The American people overwhelmingly favored both the INF Treaty and Gorbachev himself. In a *New York Times*–CBS News poll, 62 percent expressed approval of the treaty, including 55 percent who called themselves conservatives. Of those who had formed an opinion, respondents had a favorable view of Gorbachev by a margin of more than two to one. More than 60 percent believed that Gorbachev was different from previous Soviet leaders. In a mid-October poll conducted by Martilla & Kiley Inc. of Boston, 70 percent then felt that the Kremlin was "more serious about arms control and more willing to make compromises than it has been in a long time."[137]

The INF Treaty, however, was no substitute for a START agreement: it covered no weapons that could reach U.S. territory. Gorbachev had made numerous concessions in an effort to achieve a START agreement. He had agreed to cut back from 10,500 to 6,000 nuclear warheads (down to 4,900 ballistic missile warheads and 1,600 delivery systems) and to reduce Moscow's 308 SS-18 missiles to 154. On SDI, Gorbachev was now willing to permit some testing in space of exotic laser and particle beam weapons (that shot subatomic particles at objects). The major outstanding issues recapitulated the dispute between Gorbachev and Reagan at Reykjavik: namely, how long the two sides should commit themselves to observe the ABM Treaty, what kind of tests should be permitted, and whether either side would have an automatic right to deploy. Both sides agreed to defer the issue of compliance with the ABM Treaty while negotiating a START treaty.[138] Once again, Gorbachev delinked offensive weapons limitations from SDI.

AFGHANISTAN AND MORE "NEW THINKING"

Still, many U.S. officials and experts on Soviet policy remained skeptical and mistrustful about Gorbachev's commitment to cooperation with the West, for his arms control concessions could have been motivated by the traditional Soviet goal of minimizing the U.S. nuclear advantage. Again, reducing the number of nuclear weapons in Europe played to the Soviet advantage in conventional forces. The INF Treaty reduced Soviet vulnerability by removing the highly accurate Pershing 2 missiles while leaving Western Europe exposed to Soviet conventional forces, ICBMs, and short-range missiles.[139]

If the Soviets had truly decided to become a status quo power, skeptics argued, they should prove that they had ceased trying to impose their domestic system on others by withdrawing from Afghanistan and Eastern Europe. In a speech in Los Angeles in late August 1987, the president pointed out that "while talking about reform at home, the Soviet Union has stepped up its efforts to impose a failed system on others." He accused the Soviets of engaging in "indiscriminate bombing and civilian massacre in Afghanistan."[140]

Gorbachev had long regarded the Soviet entanglement in Afghanistan as a mistake. He had not been consulted about the decision to move into Afghanistan, a decision that had been taken when he was a junior member of the Politburo. The human and financial cost of the war now impeded his economic, social, and political reforms. As early as December 1985, the Politburo had decided "in principle" to withdraw from Afghanistan. At the Twenty-seventh Party Congress in February 1986, Gorbachev referred to Afghanistan as a "bleeding wound" and promised that the Soviet Union would bring its troops home "in the nearest future." In December of that year, the Afghan president Najibullah Ahmadzai was invited to Moscow and informed by Gorbachev that Soviet troops would be withdrawn within eighteen months to two years. The problem that Gorbachev faced was how to pull out troops without damaging Soviet credibility or abandoning a Soviet client government to a bloodbath of retaliation and reprisals.[141]

On 8 February 1988, Gorbachev announced that the Soviet Union would start pulling out its troops from Afghanistan on 15 May, and that all troops would be home by 25 February 1989. Representatives of Afghanistan, Pakistan, the Soviet Union, and the United States signed a series of agreements on 14 April 1988 that provided a cover for Soviet troop withdrawal, but without resolving the conflict or ending outside intervention.[142]

Secretary Shultz favored making a major push to achieve a START agreement by the Moscow summit, but Reagan decided that such a complex issue as strategic arms control needed more leisurely consideration. The Joint Chiefs wanted to slow the pace of negotiation so that they could decide on future U.S. military programs. Further discouraging a last-minute push was the unexpectedly intense domestic debate over ratifying INF.[143]

During the president's visit to Moscow from 29 May to 2 June 1988, Reagan and Gorbachev concluded two arms control agreements—one providing for advance notice of ballistic missile tests, the other establishing experimental procedures for test ban verification—which were so minor that Shultz and Shevardnadze were authorized to sign them. Representatives from the two states also signed numerous small agreements on such subjects as fishing rights, cooperation in maritime search-and-rescue operations, extension of the 1973 agreement on peaceful uses of nuclear energy, cooperation in transportation technology, expanded civilian cooperation in space, and an extension of the general agreement on cultural exchange. These accords were the fruits of the Shultz-Dobrynin strategy of small steps.[144]

The real significance of the Moscow summit was that Reagan, the most conservative president in history, had visited the "evil empire" and called Gorbachev his friend. When Reagan was asked if he still thought of the Soviet Union as the "evil empire," the president shook his head and said: "No, I was talking about another time, another era." President Reagan attributed the change to General Secretary Gorbachev, who he said was different from previous Soviet leaders.[145]

Major developments in this "new thinking" within the Soviet Union were presented at a special conference on foreign policy, held at the Ministry of Foreign Affairs from 25 to 28 July and attended by academics, officials, and Foreign Ministry officials. In his speech, Shevardnadze criticized past Soviet foreign policy as counterproductive and contrary to the national interest, for it had provoked a hostile reaction from the West. The Soviet foreign minister repudiated "peaceful coexistence as a form of class struggle," a line that had been promoted during the 1970s détente. Equating peaceful coexistence with the class struggle was hard to reconcile with peaceful coexistence as a universal principle, referring to mutually beneficial cooperation among states with different social systems. Dialogue and lowering the level of military confrontation had helped to "break what seemed to be a hopelessly closed circle," he said. Shevardnadze reported that "trust, which is solidly being promoted by *glasnost* and *perestroika*, has increased manyfold."[146]

Finally, Shevardnadze argued for the importance of a "country's reputation as a significant element of foreign policy, as a component of state interests and national security." In order to be accepted, he argued, a state had to observe the norms of "what is called civilized conduct in the world community."[147]

Shevardnadze's renunciation of the class struggle was quite controversial within the Soviet Union. Indeed, it provoked an attack from one member of the Politburo, Yegor Ligachev, who was subsequently demoted from responsibility for ideology to party secretary for agriculture. The repudiation of class struggle was important because the Soviets had used "peaceful coexistence" as a rationalization for supporting national liberation movements in the Third World while pursuing détente and cooperation with the United States.[148]

Gorbachev's address to the United Nations on 7 December 1988 was another watershed in Soviet policy toward the United States and in the formulation of the "new thinking." Gorbachev declared that "the use or threat of force can no longer be, and should not be instruments of foreign policy," and he ruled out any outward-oriented use of force.[149]

The Soviet leader declared categorically that "freedom of choice is a general principle to which there should be no exceptions." So that there would be no ambiguity about the application to Eastern Europe, he later added that "this relates to both the capitalist and to the socialist system."[150]

Gorbachev exhorted his audience to "look [at] how our relations with the United States have changed." He pointed out that "elements of trust," without which it was "very difficult to move forward in politics," had arisen in U.S.-Soviet relations.[151]

In addition, Gorbachev announced that he was cutting Soviet military forces unilaterally by 500,000 men before the end of 1990. Six tank divisions, or about 50,000 Soviet troops, were to be withdrawn from Czechoslovakia, East Germany, and Hungary. Also, the Soviets would pull out 5,000 tanks from the three Eastern bloc countries and 5,000 from the European portion of the Soviet Union. This withdrawal included roughly half the Soviet tanks based in those satellite nations, and such a move would seriously impair the Soviet offensive capability. Gorbachev declared as well that he was withdrawing 800 combat aircraft and 8,500 artillery systems from the same area. The aircraft amounted to 10 percent of the Warsaw Pact's European theater airplanes, and the cut in artillery would reduce Warsaw Pact firepower along the central front by 20 percent.[152]

Just as important as the numerical reductions, Gorbachev promised to reconfigure remaining Soviet forces for defensive purposes—for example, by withdrawing assault landing troops and bridge-crossing equipment from Soviet divisions. In case of a NATO invasion, Soviet forces would be trained to fight defensively and then to reestablish the status quo, rather than to carry the war immediately to Western territory. Gorbachev had laid the basis for restructuring and reducing Soviet forces at a May 1987 Warsaw Pact conference which formally adopted a defensive doctrine. Western observers did not take the conference communiqué or the Soviet academic writings on "defensive defense" seriously, however, because there had been no observable changes in Soviet force deployment and structure or in defense procurement. Gorbachev's troop cuts and restructuring provided the first hard evidence that the Soviet military had abandoned the offensive posture that so frightened the West.[153]

"Is the Soviet leader committed to reform merely to become a stronger enemy?" *U.S. News & World Report* asked. "A surprisingly broad consensus emerged from the speech that it does not seem so." As Walter Isaacson noted in *Time*, "With every Gorbachev move, the evidence mounts that he is seeking not just a breathing space but a fundamental change in the Soviet system."[154]

The Soviet Foreign Ministry spokesman Gennadi Gerasimov observed that "through this decision, we are finally doing away with the endlessly repeated myth of the Soviet threat to Western Europe." Gorbachev had realized that he could not expect major improvements in relations with the West until he had redressed the source of Western fears: the conventional imbalance and the Red Army's offensive doctrine.[155]

Nonetheless, the newly elected President George Bush was both skeptical about Gorbachev's sincerity and determined not to be stampeded into a summit meeting or arms control negotiation with the Soviet leader. The Soviet Union was still a formidable military power. Bush believed that it was too soon to say the Cold War was over. In some ways, he felt the Soviet challenge might be even greater than before, because it was buried.[156]

Bush's national security team shared a distrust of Gorbachev's intentions. The national security adviser Brent Scowcroft feared that the Soviets were trying to lull the United States while pursuing expansionist objectives, as Brezhnev had done in the 1970s. Gorbachev's foreign policy might be intended to give the Soviet Union a breathing spell in which to restore its economy and prepare for the next offensive. Even if Gorbachev were sincere, he might be replaced by a hard-liner who would renew domestic repression and foreign expansion. Secretary of State James Baker had no experience in foreign policy, and closely followed the position papers prepared for him by the State Department.[157]

A year passed before U.S.-Soviet cooperation recovered some of the momentum of the latter part of the Reagan administration, and even then it was only because of the startling developments in Eastern Europe.

During this time, the Bush administration lost an opportunity to develop an economic relationship with the Soviet Union, to help Gorbachev make the transition from a centralized, militaristic system to one based on market principles and oriented toward the consumer.[158]

THE (FORMER) SOVIET SPHERE OF INFLUENCE

By far the most costly concession that Gorbachev made was to renounce the Soviet sphere of influence in Eastern Europe, which the Soviets had maintained for forty years through troops, aid, and intimidation. Some analysts have speculated that Gorbachev did not intend to unleash anticommunist forces in Eastern Europe, that events there developed a momentum which the Soviet leader was powerless to reverse.[159]

This argument fails to acknowledge, however, that the Soviet Union remained a military superpower and could have used its troops stationed in Eastern Europe to halt any realignment of its allies. To do so, though, would conflict with *perestroika* and the new image that Gorbachev had been trying to create for the Soviet Union in the West. By 1988, Gorbachev highly valued his relationship with the United States; he valued the prospect of negotiated arms reductions that would allow diversion of resources from investment in defense to investment in consumer goods, Western economic assistance, and a stable international environment in which to pursue reform in the Soviet Union. He had embraced the principles of "freedom of choice" and noninterference in other countries' internal affairs, and he was prepared to follow these ideas to their logical conclusions, however unpleasant the prospect. Thus, the Soviet Union's declining international power position and its economic crisis cannot explain Gorbachev's policies unless we take into consideration the "new thinking" that security must be mutual and can only be achieved by political means. According to his foreign policy adviser Anatoly Chernyaev, Gorbachev "succeeded in carrying out an '*ideological revolution*' within himself and [in] turning 'new thinking' from an emotional impulse and tactical concept into a real world policy." The process of transformation of Gorbachev's beliefs was by no means straightforward or linear, but proceeded by zigzags, fallbacks and delays, doubts, and emotional outbursts. An important contribution to his desire to allow Eastern Europe to slip away was the reassurance he received from West German Chancellor Helmut Kohl and President Bush that the United States would not take advantage of the situation.[160]

When he took office, Gorbachev pursued an orthodox policy of promoting greater unity and integration among the Eastern bloc countries, but by 1986 he had shifted toward encouraging them to exercise greater autonomy in their domestic affairs. Gorbachev stressed that there were many paths to socialism, but he clearly showed his preference for more reformist leaders such as Polish communist leader Wojciech Jaruzelski. Gorbachev envisioned that East European countries might adopt some form of reformist socialism, as a "third road" between pluralist, social-democratic Western capitalism and Stalinist centralized communism.[161]

In 1988, however, Gorbachev began to emphasize that East European countries should be allowed "freedom of choice." He could not very well democratize the Soviet Union while failing to allow the satellite regimes to follow suit. Gorbachev's domestic policies legitimized change in Eastern Europe and undermined the authority of the aging conservative leaders, who could no longer blame the Soviets for their economies' poor performance or for their repression of domestic dissent.[162]

European reformers in Poland and Hungary were inspired by the example that Gorbachev set in the Soviet Union and took him at his word. In January 1989, the Hungarian parliament authorized freedom of assembly and freedom of association. One month later, the Hungarian Communist Party's Central Committee legalized a multiparty system and freedom of association. In February 1989, the Polish President General Wojciech Jaruzelski opened up "round table" talks with the labor union Solidarity, which he had banned in 1981, to persuade union members to participate in a Communist-led coalition government. Solidarity members refused to accept minority status, but they induced the Communists to agree to free elections for a new upper house in the Polish parliament.[163]

On 2 May 1989, Hungarian soldiers began cutting the barbed wire separating their country from Austria, the first breach in the Iron Curtain. Hungarians had long had the right to travel to the West. East Germans, however, soon realized that they could escape to West Germany by going through Hungary. Under a 1968 treaty with East Germany, Hungary was supposed to send would-be emigrés back to East Germany. The Hungarian government returned hundreds of asylum-seekers to East Germany. Some East Germans managed to cross the border to Austria, others sought asylum at the West German embassy in Budapest, and still others were detained by the Hungarian government. At the same time, Hungary had already allowed thousands of Romanian refugees to escape to the West. How could Hungary treat Romanians differently from East Germans?[164]

Despite the stunning developments in Poland and Hungary, Secretary of State James Baker declared in a major foreign policy address that the United States must "test the application of Soviet 'new thinking' again and again" to determine the reality behind the slogans.[165]

As the process of reform unfolded, Bush's response lagged behind each development in Eastern Europe and the Soviet Union. In a major policy address at Texas A & M University on 12 May, Bush insisted that the Soviet Union must pass additional tests before being allowed "back into the world order." He cautioned that a new relationship with the United States could not be declared by Moscow, but had to be earned because "promises are never enough. The Soviet Union has promised a more cooperative relationship before, only to reverse course and return to militarism." Bush declared that U.S. national security was not based on hope. "It must be based on deeds." As examples of the deeds he had in mind, Bush called on the Soviets to "tear down the Iron Curtain," cooperate with the United States in solving regional conflicts, and achieve "lasting political pluralism and respect for human rights." Just as President Eisenhower had come up with the "Open Skies" proposal because he felt the need to respond to changes in the Soviet Union yet did not fully trust Khrushchev to observe agreements, so Bush resurrected Ike's plan to allow surveillance planes to fly over each other's territory, even though such a right of overhead inspection was mainly symbolic in an age of satellite reconnaissance.[166] So, too, Marlin Fitzwater, the White House press secretary, described the Soviet leader as a "drug-store cowboy," a pretentious imposter, "throwing out one arms control proposal after another," who had not matched "words with deeds."[167]

Disgruntled by the tepid reception to his proposal of "Open Skies," and stung by criticism that he was relinquishing world leadership to Gorbachev, Bush called on his staff for a bolder arms control proposal. On 29 May, Bush proposed reducing Soviet and American troops in Europe by 20 percent and conventional arms by 15 percent, an initiative that was well received by the press and the public in the United States, Western Europe, and the Soviet Union.[168]

Internal politics in Eastern Europe outpaced both U.S. and Soviet policy. In June, the Poles held a free election for the upper house of the Polish parliament in which the independent union Solidarity won 99 out of 100 seats, a disaster for the Communist Party. The Soviet spokesman Gerasimov quipped to news correspondents that Moscow had supplanted the Brezhnev Doctrine with the Frank Sinatra Doctrine: "I do it my way."[169]

In his July 1989 speech before the twenty-three-nation Council of Europe at Strasbourg, Gorbachev suggested that the Soviet Union would not use force to preserve Communist rule in Eastern Europe. He acknowledged that "social and political orders in one country or another [have] changed in the past and may change in the future." But this was "the exclusive affair of the people in that country and is their choice." Gorbachev said that the idea of the "common European home" ruled out the "very possibility of the use of force or threat of force—alliance against alliance, inside the alliances, wherever."[170]

Impressed by the evidence of change when he visited Poland and Hungary in early July, Bush decided to sent a secret letter inviting Gorbachev to an informal, get-acquainted meeting. Baker and Shevardnadze then embarked on a series of diplomatic exchanges that culminated with the Malta summit.[171]

In Poland, the rules for forming a new government that had been drafted during the roundtable talks broke down. After the Communists' electoral defeat in June, President Jaruzelski tried unsuccessfully to form a government. Finally, Jaruzelski approached a Solidarity member to lead the effort to establish a new cabinet. On 24 August, Gorbachev telephoned the Polish Communist leader Mieczyslaw Rakowski and advised him to join a Solidarity-led coalition government. Subsequently, the Polish Communists voluntarily gave up power, the first time ever by a communist party.[172]

On 10 September, Hungary announced that it was reneging on the 1968 treaty with the GDR and that East Germans would be allowed to enter Austria through Hungary. By the end of September, forty thousand more East Germans had emigrated to the West via that route.[173]

Gorbachev's visit to East Germany (6–7 October) catalyzed the end of the communist regime. Large crowds greeted Gorbachev, shouting "Freedom! Freedom!" or "Gorby! Gorby! Help us!" Gorbachev advised the East German leader Erich Honecker not to postpone needed reforms. He also told Honecker privately that Soviet troops would not be used to quell disorders—then allowed this news to be leaked to the press.[174]

The day after Gorbachev left, more than fifty thousand people demonstrated in Leipzig. Although many expected another bloody repression in the fashion of the Tiananmen Square incident, the East German authorities made no attempt to interfere. The Soviet ambassador had advised the East German Politburo member Egon Krenz against using the army. On 17 October, the East German Politburo voted Honecker out of office.[175]

The newly elected head of the East German Communist Party, Egon Krenz, traveled to Moscow to ask Gorbachev for advice. There Gorbachev approved Krenz's plans to enact a new travel law that would allow East Germans to travel anywhere, but without foreign exchange.[176]

The East German authorities hastily drafted a new and liberal travel law, but they failed to make clear that the policy of allowing East Germans to travel abroad did not apply to trips between East and West Berlin. When the East Berlin party leader read a draft of the law at a press conference on 9 November, both the press and the public were confused and uncertain about what it meant. Crowds of people gathered

[228]

at the Berlin Wall. Finally, on the evening of 9 November, without any instructions, border guards allowed crowds to pass through into West Berlin. The Berlin Wall had been opened—by mistake.[177] Other East European regimes fell in close succession. On 10 November, the Bulgarian Politburo chose the reformer Petar Mladenov to replace the Stalinist leader Todor Zhivkov.[178]

These East European revolutions at last convinced President Bush that he should give Gorbachev some tangible signs of support. He could not very well continue to argue that changes in the Soviet Union were cosmetic and easily reversible, or that U.S.-Soviet relations could revert to the ways of the Cold War.[179]

At the summit in Malta (2–3 December 1989), Bush agreed to a series of measures that, in the words of the Soviet analyst Georgi Arbatov, the director of Moscow's Institute for the Study of the USA and Canada, ended "the economic Cold War." Bush proposed negotiations on a U.S.-Soviet trade agreement to be completed by the superpower summit in Washington, which the president proposed to be held in June 1990. He also offered to lift the Jackson-Vanik amendment, to increase U.S. technical economic assistance, and to support Soviet observer status in the General Agreement on Tariffs and Trade (GATT). While these concessions were incremental, they were also, at Bush's insistence, without "strings"—that is to say, they were noncontingent on any action by Gorbachev, such as increasing Jewish emigration or reforming the Soviet price system.[180]

Gorbachev replied that, until then, he had been looking for a tangible demonstration that Bush supported *perestroika*. "I was going to ask you today to go beyond words. But you have done so."[181]

The Soviet leader assured President Bush that the Soviets would not use force to prevent changes in Eastern Europe: he was aware that Soviet troops would have to be withdrawn, and he would allow the East Europeans to choose their own political and economic system. For his part, Bush informed Gorbachev that, so long as the Soviets did not use force, the United States would not try to take advantage of the changes in Eastern Europe.[182]

The collapse of the East German regime galvanized changes in the remaining communist countries of Eastern Europe. In December 1989, the first non-Communist cabinet took office in Czechoslovakia, and the Communist hard-liner President Gustav Husák resigned to make way for the election of Václav Havel, the playwright and former dissident. On 22 December, the Romanian dictator Nicolae Ceaușescu and his wife were forced to flee the capital and were later executed by a firing squad.[183]

The revolutions in Eastern Europe convinced the American people that democratic reform in the Soviet Union and a cooperative foreign policy were irreversible. An NBC News/*Wall Street Journal* public opinion poll found that 52 percent of those surveyed saw the events in Germany and Eastern Europe as "the beginning of a long-term positive relationship" with the Soviet Union, as opposed to 37 percent who regarded it as "temporary and easily changed." A focus group in San Francisco interviewed by the Public Agenda Foundation reached a consensus that the changes in Europe were irreversible, the Soviets would not intervene, and the reunification of Germany was likely.[184]

By January 1990, Gorbachev was resigned to the reunification of Germany. On 26 January, Gorbachev convened an ad hoc group of advisers to discuss policy toward Germany: Shevardnadze, Prime Minister Nikolai Ryzhkov, the Politburo member Aleksandr Yakovlev, the head of the Communist Party's International Department Valentin Falin, the KGB chief Vladimir Kryuchkov, Marshal Akhromeyev, Anatoly Chernyaev, and Gorbachev's adviser Georgi Shakhnazarov. Gorbachev said that all premises were open for discussion except the use of armed force. Everyone seemed to accept German unification; the question was on what terms. Summing up the consensus of the group, Gorbachev said that the Soviet Union would have to deal more with Chancellor Kohl. It would be unacceptable for a united Germany to be part of NATO. Gorbachev asked Akhromeyev to look into possible plans for withdrawal of Soviet troops from East Germany.[185]

When Helmut Kohl visited Moscow in February 1990, Gorbachev assured him that the Germans could decide for themselves the timing and structure of reunification. Even then, however, the Soviet leader was opposed to full membership for a united Germany in NATO. Gorbachev proposed numerous alternatives to German membership in NATO— neutrality, continued four-power responsibility, integration of Germany into both alliances, a European security system based on the Conference for Security and Cooperation in Europe (CSCE) and, finally, a "French" solution whereby Germany would participate in NATO but not in its military command.[186]

The turning point came during Gorbachev's meeting with Bush in Washington on 31 May 1990. Gorbachev began by arguing that Germany could not be a member of NATO because that would "unbalance" Europe. He suggested instead that Germany could be a member of both alliances. Bush argued that Germany had the right to decide for itself which alliance it would join under the Helsinki agreements. Gorbachev agreed. The Soviet delegation was surprised and disconcerted. Chernyaev later recalled that Gorbachev could not logically advocate "freedom of choice" while denying Germany the right to choose its own alliance. Gorbachev would not, however, make the change in his position public.[187]

Gorbachev's reluctance to accept Germany's readmission to NATO was motivated by domestic political considerations. The Twenty-eighth Party Congress would meet in July 1990, and Gorbachev faced charges of having "lost" Eastern Europe. German unification was particularly contentious. Already the Politburo member Yegor Ligachev had warned against a "new Munich." For many Soviets, East Germany was the principal achievement of the "Great Patriotic War."[188]

Important as a face-saver was the NATO summit in London, where the allies formally agreed that the Cold War was over and that they would restructure NATO forces defensively so that nuclear weapons would only be used as a "last resort." The NATO declaration allowed Gorbachev to claim that Moscow was not giving up positions won through great sacrifice, but moving to a new stage of cooperation and development.[189]

The Soviets received notification of the London communiqué during the Twenty-eighth Party Congress, where representatives from the Soviet military and the military-industrial complex were protesting that Gorbachev's acquiescence in the loss of Eastern Europe had destroyed parity. Shevardnadze recalled that in the inflamed atmosphere of the party congress, he and Gorbachev needed a favorable sign from the West: "When the news came out about the NATO session in London, I knew there had been a reponse."[190]

In talks with Gorbachev in mid-July, Chancellor Kohl of West Germany promised to reduce a united Germany's armed forces by 40 percent to 370,000 men, and that Germany would not try to acquire nuclear, biological, or chemical weapons. Gorbachev then announced that Germany was free to join NATO.[191] On 3 October 1990, a copy of the Liberty Bell rang out in front of the Berlin Reichstag to signal that Germany had been reunited.

Gorbachev was not compelled to agree to an immediate German reunification. In spring 1990 he still had more than 364,000 troops in East Germany as well as occupation rights and continuing four-power responsibility. Gorbachev realized, though, that the Soviet Union would be less threatened by friendly neighbors than by countries it tried to dominate by force—a logical derivation of the "new thinking" that security could best be achieved by political rather than military means.[192]

Reagan's dream of a nuclear-free world warred with his distrust of Soviet duplicity. He originally conceived of SDI as a means to achieve his goal of eliminating nuclear weapons. While it is true that the prospect of a race in high-technology weapons motivated the Soviets to offer offensive weapons reductions, ultimately SDI proved to be an obstacle to agreement, as Gorbachev viewed the program as threatening while Reagan refused to place any restraints on research. This might appear to be inconsequential, because the United States and the Soviet Union finally did sign START I and II agreements in 1991 and 1993. On the other hand, the conclusion of such an agreement during the Reagan administration would have had a greater impact on each side's perceptions of the other and could have resulted in substantial savings to the American taxpayer. In addition, if Gorbachev had been able to achieve an agreement reducing American weapons, he would have come under less criticism at home for making too many concessions to the West.

The two leaders came very close to a major arms reduction agreement at Reykjavik, excluding the unrealistic last-minute provision to eliminate ballistic missiles or nuclear weapons. The major obstacle to an agreement was mistrust. Even if nuclear weapons were drastically cut, Reagan insisted on having the option to deploy a defensive system because he feared that the Soviets might cheat or adopt an aggressive policy. Gorbachev, on the other hand, linked an offensive agreement to restraints on SDI, which was technically infeasible and, in the remote possibility that it worked, could have been outflanked by relatively cheap offensive measures.

Then, the Bush administration's delays and caution meant that Gorbachev did not achieve a major foreign policy success in 1989 or 1990, when it might have helped him politically. Largely because of lingering Cold War attitudes about trade, the Bush administration did not take advantage of an opportunity to develop a broader economic relationship with the Soviet Union and to help Gorbachev guide his reforms in the direction of a market economy.

Gorbachev's foreign policy was shaped by his domestic political strategy: he needed a peaceful international environment in which to carry out economic reforms. Soviet economic stagnation initially stimulated Gorbachev to seek arms control agreements with the Reagan administration so that the Soviets could reduce their military spending. But the relationship between domestic politics and foreign policy is a two-way relationship. Gorbachev's desire to lessen the West's perception of a threat induced him to release Soviet dissidents and demonstrate respect for human rights. Gorbachev's domestic political reforms, such as *glasnost*, freedom for dissidents, and free elections, improved the Soviet image so that it would be a more acceptable partner with the West. Thus, at the Twenty-eighth Party Congress in July 1990, Shevardnadze defended the "democratization of society, humanization of the country's legislation, the granting of rights to citizens, [and of redress] to the unjustly imprisoned" on the grounds that "from such gestures, a new image of our country is being shaped which is respected by the whole world."[193]

Other Soviet leaders—Georgi Malenkov and Nikita Khrushchev—had advocated both an end to the military blocs in Europe and an effort to cooperate with the United States on a basis of reciprocity. But there was always a disjuncture between the Soviets' public statements (which were utopian and designed to "expose" Western pretensions) and their private, more conservative negotiating positions.[194] Gorbachev's actions and foreign policy statements, on the other hand, had a philosophical coherence that made his expressed intentions more believable. Gorbachev's withdrawal from Eastern Europe was not a "costly signal," as conceived of in game theory; it was an expression of the principle of "free choice." It would have been more costly in the long run for the Soviet Union to use force to restrain national aspirations in Eastern Europe, because Gorbachev would have forfeited his slowly nurtured partnership with the West along with the benefits of economic assistance and a peaceful international environment.

Soviet-American cooperation did not arise through a tit-for-tat process. Far from it. In his first two years in office, Gorbachev made more than twenty-five concessions which not only were not reciprocated but frequently were met with unnecessary belligerence.

Contrary to the tenets of realism, Gorbachev allowed the balance of power in Europe to be upset. Without Soviet troops, Moscow's alliance withered away; NATO was made even more rich and powerful with Germany's admission. Instead of competing for strategic advantage, Gorbachev accepted treaties obligating the Soviets to make heavier reductions in troops and weapons than the United States.

Gorbachev and his advisers had learned from the Cold War that the race to acquire more arms only stimulated Western efforts to surpass the Soviet Union, that Soviet security could be more economically achieved through political cooperation with the West. Unlike Brezhnev, Gorbachev realized that sizable Soviet military capabilities would impede U.S.-Soviet cooperation on arms control and security issues.

Reagan adopted a new attitude toward Gorbachev as a result of the Soviet leader's one-sided concessions with respect to INF and his acceptance of on-site inspection—"Trust but verify." Still, even Gorbachev's acceptance of the U.S. position on all disputed issues in INF was not sufficient to undermine Western suspicions, because the Soviet leader was making changes that were arguably in the Soviet Union's long-term strategic interests, such as removing the American Pershing 2 missiles from Europe and settling the Afghanistan conflict.

It was only when Gorbachev made concessions that were noncontingent, irrevocable, and deleterious to Soviet vulnerability—his December 1988 unilateral troop reductions and shift to a defensive posture, the Soviet withdrawal from Eastern Europe—that the West declared an end to the Cold War.

[7]

Missed Opportunities, Conflict Spirals, and History

Why did the United States and the Soviet Union fail to cooperate more in order to prevent wasteful and extravagant arms competition when each side had more than enough weapons to destroy the other many times over? Why could the superpowers not agree on at least a temporary resolution of the German question before 1970?

THE INSUFFICIENCY OF REALIST EXPLANATIONS

Many realists argue that arms races reflect underlying conflicts of interest.[1] In hindsight, though, one is hard-pressed to find any underlying material or geopolitical conflicts of interest between the former superpowers that would explain their failure to reach particular arms control agreements. The Soviet Union and the United States did not share a common frontier, nor did the two states claim the same territory. Their vital strategic interests conflicted at no point. The Soviet Union was a land power, the United States a sea power. Both states had an abundance of natural resources, raw materials, and food-producing areas; each could acquire whatever materials they lacked from adjacent countries.[2]

Instead, the main sources of conflict were ideological and psychological. As Eduard Shevardnadze recalled, "We and the Americans were divided by walls built out of the rubble of distrust and the stones of ideology."[3] Ideological blinders, derived from different domestic systems, often prevented the United States and the Soviet Union from recognizing their shared interests. For example, both states wanted to prevent Germany from ever again endangering world peace, but the Soviets ultimately tried to impose their political and economic system on the eastern half of the country, thus repressing the aspirations of its people for a unified Germany. The superpowers shared an interest in preventing a nuclear war, but some military and political officials believed that the other side might resort to war to preserve or expand its economic system. The Soviets would have benefited from helping the United States disengage from the Vietnam War, which enhanced the influence of China and impeded U.S.-Soviet cooperation on arms control, but some Soviet officials believed that they had to show support for "proletarian internationalism."

Perhaps the superpowers did not attain more arms control agreements because the bipolar distribution of power made it prudent for each state to acquire additional weapons to ensure against attack or blackmail. Yet competition for relative advantage was not responsible for their failure to achieve several agreements in areas of common interest. Some proposals would have affected both sides about equally. In 1953, for example, the United States could have traded the West German military contribution to NATO in return for a Soviet withdrawal of forces from East Germany. The Soviet disarmament proposal of 10 May 1955 called for the United States and the Soviet Union to have equal numbers of troops. The revised Rapacki Plan for a nuclear-free zone in Central Europe also included reductions in conventional forces so that the West would not be vulnerable to Soviet conventional superiority. In 1986, the Soviets proposed to trade their advantage in heavy missiles for restraints on the U.S. testing and deployment of a strategic defense system.

The failure of the United States to propose limits on MIRVs in 1969–70 might possibly be viewed as illustrating how the desire to maintain a technological advantage and overall military superiority can block cooperation between states on arms control. Richard Nixon did not seem to have been motivated by such considerations: he believed that both sides had more than enough weapons. But Nixon did not want to give up any weapon system unilaterally because to do so might convey an image of weakness and invite Soviet probes in the Third World.

Nuclear weapons in fact facilitated cooperation by allowing each state to be secure from attack despite the other state's advantage in some area. In 1955, Dwight David Eisenhower decided on a criterion of sufficiency for U.S. defense programs—i.e., having enough warheads and varied delivery systems to retaliate against a Soviet attack—and he maintained this policy despite congressional pressure after *Sputnik*. In 1969, Nixon renounced the effort to regain strategic superiority, adopting instead a policy of sufficiency that made it possible to negotiate limits on delivery systems with the Soviet Union.

Nor was the inability of the United States and the Soviet Union to cooperate in areas of common interest merely a matter of Soviet unwillingness to allow on-site inspection or a matter of not having adequate means to monitor compliance. There is no absolute level of verification that is necessary or sufficient for an arms control agreement. Just how confident political leaders must be in their ability to detect the other's cheating depends on their beliefs about the other side's motives and intentions as well as on their estimate of the potential strategic consequences of being betrayed. John F. Kennedy believed that the Eisenhower administration had made too much of the risks of clandestine Soviet testing underground. Eisenhower himself admitted that the number of on-site inspections required for a test ban treaty was a political issue, not a scientific one.

As mentioned above, sometimes the term "trust" is used to refer to the belief that the other side has good intentions and motives, not merely that it will carry out an agreement or commitment. American leaders fundamentally distrusted the Soviets because they were communists. Often, what U.S. officials feared was not principally that the Soviets might cheat on any particular arms control agreement, for most violations would have had inconsequential effects on the strategic balance. Rather, policymakers such as John Foster Dulles believed that the Soviets would lull Western public opinion into complacency and reduce public support for defense spending. The Soviets might also take advantage of an atmosphere of good feeling to subvert democratic governments.

Despite the ideological differences, U.S. and Soviet preferences concerning specific arms control issues were often complementary or overlapping. By the late 1950s, Dwight Eisenhower and Nikita Khrushchev, for example, both wanted to sign a comprehensive test ban. In addition to achieving a test ban, Khrushchev and Kennedy shared an interest in stabilizing the refugee crisis in Berlin and in recognizing the division of Germany. Nixon correctly assessed that, largely for domestic political reasons, the superpowers shared an interest in controlling defense spending and ending U.S. involvement in the Vietnam War. Ronald Reagan and Mikhail Gorbachev both wanted to reduce or eliminate the reliance on nuclear deterrence.

SOURCES OF MISTRUST

If U.S. and Soviet leaders were reasonable, they should have tried to assess each other's interest in stabilizing the balance of power in Europe and in controlling the arms race as a basis for deciding whether they could trust each other to observe an arms control agreement. Instead, these leaders often quickly dismissed proposals for cooperation as deceptive or disingenuous. When Georgi Malenkov proposed a summit meeting in 1953, Eisenhower and Dulles never considered whether Soviet leaders might have an interest in ridding themselves of their weak, unstable East German ally in return for preventing West Germany from rearming. When policymakers did recognize issues on which both sides could benefit from cooperating, they were often inhibited from acting on this insight by a fear of appearing weak or being tricked. Nevertheless, sensible leaders would have adjusted their beliefs in response to unambiguous conciliatory moves from the other side. Instead, U.S. policymakers were slow to respond to major "peace offensives" by Soviet leaders, and discounted a great deal of evidence before finally changing their attitudes.

Given the advantages of having a reputation for carrying out commitments, one would expect U.S. and Soviet leaders to have been concerned with maintaining an image of reliability. Instead, U.S. leaders often abandoned arms control positions after the Soviet Union had indicated its willingness to accept them. For example, the United States reconsidered its position when the Soviets adopted language very similar to that of the West in their 10 May 1955 disarmament proposal, and this reaction was inexplicable to the Soviet officials who had drawn up the offer precisely to achieve an agreement. In January 1958, Eisenhower reneged on a previous U.S. agreement to the Geneva inspection system for a test ban, for scientists had discovered that it would be more difficult to identify underground tests than they had previously believed.

Domestic political conditions often motivated U.S. and Soviet leaders to seek cooperative agreements on arms control. Malenkov, Khrushchev, and Gorbachev sought to reduce the crushing burden of the arms race on the Soviet economy by negotiating arms control agreements and reducing the threat posed by the external political environment. Similarly, electoral considerations sometimes encouraged U.S. leaders to seek a summit meeting or an arms control agreement. In 1971, Nixon strongly desired a summit before the November 1972 elections so that he could portray himself as a "man of peace." Similarly, in 1984 Reagan had the forthcoming elections in mind when he made a major speech offering the Soviets a constructive working relationship.

Counteracting this positive influence of domestic politics was the tendency to interpret the other's actions through the lens of ideology—to perceive peaceful gestures by the Soviets as mere tactical shifts in pursuit of world conquest; or, from the Soviet perspective, to infer that U.S. opposition to Soviet military policies was an outgrowth of monopoly capitalism. The Cold War could not have ended if Gorbachev had not freed Soviet foreign policy from its deformation by ideology. The "new thinking" provided a new foundation for Soviet policy, which now renounced the threat of force and started with the premise that the United States and the Soviet Union shared an interest in each other's security.

A shared interest in collaboration was not sufficient; the identity of individual leaders also mattered. If Eisenhower had been as inflexible as Dulles, or if Reagan had been as intransigent as Caspar Weinberger, U.S.-Soviet cooperation might never have occurred. Dulles and Weinberger regarded the Soviets as invariably malevolent, deceitful, and expansionist.

In general, policymakers' beliefs strongly influenced their interpretation of each other's negotiating proposals and actions. Thus the Eisenhower administration quickly dismissed as propaganda the Rapacki Plan for a nuclear-free zone, even though the proposal also included troop reductions and inspections in East Central Europe. When Khrushchev unilaterally cut Soviet troops in 1958, U.S. State Department officials inferred that he did so because he was not interested in negotiated reductions.

Policymakers also failed to see how the other's intransigent or competitive behavior might be a reaction to the external environment. The Eisenhower administration did not consider that Khrushchev might have resorted to threats to cut off access to Berlin out of sheer desperation after the United States refused to reconsider its plans to provide nuclear weapons to West Germany. For his part, Khrushchev seemed not to understand how his threatening of U.S. allies with nuclear war or his issuing of ultimatums damaged his reputation and made the Eisenhower and Kennedy administrations less inclined to cooperate with him on arms control and the German question.

Although I began with the puzzle of why the United States and the Soviet Union failed to cooperate when they would have benefited by doing so, the results of this inquiry have wider implications. Several findings suggest areas where further research would be worthwhile.

IMPLICATIONS FOR INTERNATIONAL RELATIONS THEORY AND RESEARCH

The Need for First Steps

Even when a favorable balance of incentives is obvious to both, states may not be able to reach an agreement if they distrust each other. Each may hesitate to take the initiative, fearing that the other side may exploit any move to achieve a cooperative solution. For example: Syria has been unwilling to reveal its conception of peace with Israel until assured that its sovereignty over the Golan Heights will be restored; Israel has been reluctant to offer any commitment to withdraw from the area until Syria has explained what it means by "peace."

As each side waits for the other to make the first move and break the deadlock, both parties become increasingly sure that the other side is recalcitrant, and the conflict becomes more difficult to resolve. Thus, for example, after Khrushchev threatened to allow East Germany to control communications with West Berlin, he and Kennedy both waited for the other to make a bona fide, concrete diplomatic proposal; as neither did, each became more strongly convinced that the other was not serious about negotiations.

When relations between two states are unusually tense or hostile, as they were in 1983, even minor symbolic gestures—as when the Soviets allowed the Pentecostal Christians to leave the USSR—can have a major impact because they affect attitudes or beliefs on the other side. Small, step-by-step agreements are one way that enemies can break the ice and develop sufficient confidence to go on to more consequential issues. In general, what was feasible in U.S.-Soviet relations depended on the stage of the relationship. Successful collaboration on arms control agreements gave U.S. and Soviet leaders greater confidence in each other's reliability and enabled them to go on to more ambitious cooperative arrangements. The limited test ban was indeed a first step, as Kennedy had predicted.

On the other hand, because our images of other states tend to lag behind changes in their behavior, policymakers may not develop sufficient trust from small agreements to take a larger leap. Psychological theory suggests that beliefs do not change incrementally in response to each new piece of evidence, but all at once as in a religious conversion. Then, too, a step-by-step process can easily be wrecked by unpredictable events, such as when the Soviets shot down the Korean airliner KAL 007 in 1983. The negotiations in which the United States and the Soviet Union engaged beginning in 1983 yielded several small agreements, such as the establishment of two new consulates and a cultural exchange agreement. But the step-by-step process did not make real progress until Gorbachev appeared and carried out bold moves.

The Need for Trust-Building Moves

The tit-for-tat strategy deals with the problem of who goes first by assumption: it begins with a cooperative move, then mirrors what the other did in the previous round. But if two states acutely distrust each other, a single cooperative action may not be enough to elicit a reciprocal response. Throughout the history of U.S.-Soviet relations, the theme of "words versus deeds" has recurred as each side challenged the other to prove its sincerity. A state will usually discount the enemy's conciliatory gesture as a trick or a propaganda ploy. It is more difficult, however, for a state's leaders to scoff at or dismiss a costly or risky concession from the other side, especially when that concession is part of a series of co-operative acts.

Where the superpowers successfully reached cooperative agreements—the Limited Test Ban Treaty, SALT I, the INF Treaty—one side demonstrated its good intentions through several conciliatory actions, and it is difficult to envision how a cooperative outcome could have been achieved otherwise. In 1955, for example, when Khrushchev agreed to withdraw from Eastern Austria, recognized the West German government, and apologized to the Yugoslav leader Marshal Tito, Eisenhower concluded that he should probe Soviet intentions more thoroughly at a summit meeting, the first since Potsdam in 1945. By removing Soviet troops from Austria, Khrushchev gave up territory occupied at the end of World War II which served as a forward strategic base. Given Dulles's reluctance to engage in negotiations that might legitimize the Soviet regime and its domination of Eastern Europe, it is hard to imagine Eisenhower agreeing to a summit in return for anything less. Two years previously, when Malenkov had carried out numerous but relatively minor initiatives—such as agreeing to the nomination of Dag Hammarskjöld as U.N. secretary-general, assisting in the Korean armistice negotiations, and easing the occupation regime in Austria—Eisenhower did not regard his peace offensive as entirely credible and called for Soviet "deeds not words."

While no agreement was reached at Geneva in 1955, that meeting was important because it greatly reduced tensions and convinced both sides that the enemy did not want to fight a nuclear war. Thus, the Geneva summit laid the basis for subsequent diplomatic contacts between U.S. and Soviet leaders.

In 1957–58, Khrushchev vigorously advocated the Rapacki Plan and the disengagement of foreign troops from Europe, but he took no costly actions to prove his good faith. It would have been very difficult for Khrushchev to convince the West that his proposal for mutual reduction of U.S. and Soviet forces was not a trick to undermine NATO and expose West Germany to Soviet conventional superiority. When it came to Germany, the stakes were too high for the United States or the Soviet Union to assume any risk. In contrast, Khrushchev successfully proved his interest in a test ban by unilaterally halting nuclear testing even though the Soviets had carried out far fewer tests than the United States and still lagged in nuclear weapons design. If Khrushchev had not taken the initiative by ceasing to test in April 1958, it is doubtful that Eisenhower would have been able to overcome bureaucratic inertia or the Defense

Department's opposition to any restraints on U.S. nuclear testing. The longer the moratorium continued, the more confident Eisenhower became that the Soviet leader was serious about a test ban and negotiated arms reductions. By February 1960, Eisenhower was willing to agree to a two-year, unpoliced moratorium on small underground tests, which could not be reliably distinguished from earthquakes by existing methods of verification.

Often, what one state regards as a significant concession by the other depends on the context. In June 1963, Kennedy's speech at American University was a beacon of rationality and civility in an era of high tension and ideological rhetoric. In that speech, Kennedy asked Americans to reexamine their attitudes toward the Soviet Union and to consider the two countries' common interest in avoiding a nuclear war and halting the arms race. Before the speech, the United States and the Soviet Union had reached a deadlock in the test ban negotiations, and an agreement appeared increasingly unlikely. Khrushchev, however, was impressed by Kennedy's speech, which he called the greatest by any American president since Franklin D. Roosevelt, and he agreed to accept a limited test ban, although the Soviets did not have much experience in underground nuclear testing.

In 1969, some Soviet officials were eager for SALT, but the leadership was divided. The Soviets made only token gestures toward improving relations; Nixon and Kissinger, who wanted substance, not "atmospherics," were not impressed. After emerging preeminent in the Soviet leadership struggle, Leonid Brezhnev made several concessions. The Soviet leader offered negotiations on mutual and balanced force reductions, thereby dooming the chances for congressional passage of the Mansfield amendment, which would have withdrawn U.S. troops unilaterally. The Soviets got rid of their old East German ally Walter Ulbricht in order to achieve a Berlin agreement. In the 20 May 1971 agreement, the Soviets committed themselves to a temporary freeze on offensive weapons as well as limitations on ABMs. Most important, Brezhnev did not cancel the summit despite the U.S. bombing of Hanoi and mining of Haiphong harbor. Nixon was deeply suspicious, and prone to see the Soviets as guiding the offending parties in such regional conflicts as the Indo-Pakistani War and Vietnam. Brezhnev's concessions made it easier for Nixon to justify going to a summit. At the May 1972 summit, not only did Brezhnev and Nixon sign the SALT I agreements and the BPA, but U.S. and Soviet officials concluded several economic, scientific, and cultural agreements that promoted a working partnership between the United States and the Soviet Union.

The turning point in U.S.-Soviet relations during the Reagan administration came when President Reagan and Gorbachev signed the treaty on intermediate nuclear forces. Previous Soviet leaders had wanted détente with the West, but only Gorbachev was willing to pay the price of removing Soviet medium-range missiles targeted at NATO and agreeing to on-site inspection. In December 1988, moreover, Gorbachev reduced the Soviet ability to invade Western Europe by reducing Soviet military forces by 500,000 and implementing a defensive military doctrine.

Of course, even the best-designed conciliatory strategy will not always be successful. Trust may be a necessary condition but it is not sufficient: something more is needed to achieve cooperative agreements between states. For example, despite the positive experiences of the Washington and Moscow summits, and the precedent set at Reykjavik, Reagan did not try for a START agreement during the remainder of his term in office, largely because of domestic political concerns and the opposition of the Joint Chiefs.

In retrospect, potential opportunities for cooperation have a lower probability of success if their fulfillment would have required the acquiescence of outside parties not under the leaders' control. Allied opposition, particularly from France and West Germany, played a major role in the inability of Kennedy and Khrushchev to come to an agreement on Berlin. In general, it was more difficult for the superpowers to resolve the German question because a solution entailed influencing the policies of the two German states, France, and Britain. President Eisenhower and Khrushchev were more likely to have reached an agreement clearing the way to a test ban at the Paris summit than they were to have settled Berlin's status.

Finally, one state's leaders may dismiss the other's concession as easily reversed or discontinued. Once demobilized, troops can be called back into service. Cease-fires can be violated. A moratorium on nuclear tests can be broken without notice. Even if the other side's current leadership genuinely wishes to collaborate, that leadership might later be replaced by a more aggressive regime. One reason why states are reluctant to take advantage of the enemy's offer to cooperate is that no one can predict who will come to power in the future or what they might do. At the beginning of the Bush administration, for example, the president's advisers suspected that Gorbachev was trying to win a breathing spell in order to build up Soviet power for a renewed competition; even if Gorbachev himself was sincere about wanting to cooperate with the West, it was felt, he would soon be succeeded by a more conventional communist leader. Gorbachev's acceptance of sovereignty for the East European states and their right to choose noncommunist regimes resulted in the loss of the Soviet empire and was irreversible, except at great cost in Soviet lives and reputation. Consequently, the revolutions of 1989 in Eastern Europe convinced Bush that Gorbachev's efforts at reform were sincere and worthy of U.S. support.

We should not view these successful examples of U.S.-Soviet cooperation as merely one state's submission to the demands of the other. U.S. leaders developed a sense of trust that enabled them to take actions that previously they would never have considered. Reagan called Gorbachev "my friend" and repudiated his earlier characterization of the Soviet Union as the "evil empire." Bush ended the economic embargo against the Soviet Union at the Malta summit.

Nonevents

In cases of missed opportunity, one must study nonevents—things that did not happen. We often fail to notice forgone possibilities for cooperation precisely because they were not actualized; then we infer that the failure must have been inevitable.

To explain the causes of a nonevent, the analyst will have to vary initial conditions mentally. Would the two states have been able to reach an agreement if condition A or condition B had been different? Political scientists have generally shied away from the explicit use of counterfactual analysis, but they may not be able to continue doing so if we are to understand better the failure by states to resolve conflicts or to achieve common interests.

In order to see whether a particular condition or event was a sufficient cause of the breakdown of state efforts to cooperate, one should identify the critical turning points and consider whether alternative actions might have made a difference, rather than assuming that the events which did occur were inevitable. As the evolutionary biologist Stephen Jay Gould suggests, we need to rewind the tape of history at a particular juncture.[4] In hindsight, despite bipolarity, alliance constraints, and differing domestic political systems, diplomacy might have made a difference in several instances.

Thus the best opportunity to reunify Germany was in 1953–54, before West Germany was admitted into NATO and when East Germany was still not fully integrated into the socialist bloc. The prospect of West German rearmament was a powerful incentive for the Soviets to make concessions with respect to German unity, but the United States did not try to use this lever. Similarly, a MIRV ban could have been more easily verified if it were concluded in 1969, before either state had completed testing. If Nixon had proposed such an agreement, Soviet leaders might well have agreed to a ban on MIRVs in order to contain a perceived U.S. technological advantage, just as they in fact did with respect to ABMs.

Self-Fulfilling Prophecies

Distrust is not only difficult to disconfirm but can create a supportive reality. The beliefs that actors bring to any social encounter help to shape and guide the interaction. In psychological experiments, for example, people assume that a physically attractive individual is friendly, sociable, and outgoing and that an unattractive person is shy, withdrawn, and aloof. People behave more warmly toward attractive individuals, bringing out outgoing qualities in the other that confirm their original belief that handsome people are more extroverted.[5]

In the same way, policymakers' beliefs and assumptions often shape their dealings with other states in such a way as to support their preconceptions. Distrust of another state is apt to be self-fulfilling. A state that fears another will engage in hostile actions, such as refusing to enter into long-term credit or trade arrangements, increasing armaments, conducting military maneuvers, issuing threats, or organizing an opposing alliance. Such unfriendly acts arouse the suspicions of the feared state, which will take countermeasures to protect itself. Compounding the misperception, the state whose suspicions activated the spiral may not understand that the other state's military measures are reactions to its own unfriendly behavior.[6]

This phenomenon is no less evident in the case of authoritarian states, such as Wilhelmine Germany or the Soviet Union, whose leaders may deliberately create a war scare to achieve domestic or foreign policy objectives. Their hostile rhetoric and belligerent actions may create external enemies where there were none before.

Indeed, this cycle may be starting again in U.S. relations with Russia. Referring to NATO's plans to expand its membership to include Hungary, Czechoslovakia, and Poland, President Boris Yeltsin asked: "Why are you sowing the seeds of mistrust?" From the Russians' perspective, if there are no blocs, alliances, or enemies in Europe, why does the West still need NATO? The Russians suspect that the effort to move NATO alliance boundaries eastward constitutes an attempt to isolate Russia in case it veers away from democracy. In reality, the United States is considering expanding NATO to include the Baltic states and the states of East Central Europe because it still does not trust Russia fully. As President Bill Clinton acknowledged in January 1994, attempts to "draw a new line between East and West . . . could create a self-fulfilling prophecy of future confrontation."[7]

[245]

The state that is the target of efforts to reduce tensions may not understand the meaning of a signal or may dismiss it as not credible when it is embedded in hostile, threatening rhetoric or masked by competitive actions in peripheral areas. Two issues are involved in the reception of signals: What is the sender trying to say, and does he mean what he is saying?[8]

Where communication between two states is difficult—because of differing cultures, opposing ideologies, or mistrust—a state may not take the other side's words at face value. Rather, foreign policy officials may examine the situational and behavioral context of the state's language in order to determine what the words really mean, how they make sense in light of the state's other actions. Inconsistent or contradictory actions create "noise," which debases the quality of the sending state's signals.

Even if they correctly understand what a state is trying to say, observers may regard the message as deceptive or disingenuous. States usually suspect the credibility of an adversary's conciliatory gestures. They may test the sincerity of the enemy's desire for cooperation by looking at its actions in other contexts or issues. Consequently, a great power's actions in one part of the world have repercussions elsewhere, for they become linked in observers' minds as indicators of national goals or resolve.[9] The Nixon administration could not separate Soviet offers to control the arms race from Soviet support for clients in the Third World who opposed American policies by force. Gorbachev gradually came to realize that U.S.-Soviet arms control could not be insulated from the political aspects of the relationship, such as human rights and Soviet support for national liberation movements in the Third World. Because state actions in different areas are interconnected, states may be unable to exclude disputed questions in order to reach agreements.

Contradictory statements by officials from different agencies or branches of the same government can also hurt the credibility of a state's conciliatory policy. For example, a few days after Eisenhower tried to encourage the Soviets with his "Chance for Peace" speech, John Foster Dulles gave a speech before the same audience in which he claimed that recent positive changes in Soviet foreign policy were a defensive response to U.S. military strength.

In order to build greater trust, a state should demonstrate its reliability by behaving consistently across issues as well as over time. Kennedy's 1961 buildup of U.S. strategic and conventional forces undercut the credibility of his offer to cooperate with Khrushchev on the test ban and Berlin. In contrast, Gorbachev made concessions to the West on a wide variety of issues, from human rights in the Soviet Union and acceptance of on-site inspection to unilateral troop reductions and withdrawal of Soviet support for guerrilla movements in the Third World.[10]

Time Lags

Foreign policymakers' beliefs about a state usually lag behind changes in its behavior. The conciliatory side may not, however, be able to determine why the other state is so slow to respond to its well-meaning gestures. Lack of reciprocity could mean that the other state has no interest in cooperative arrangements or that it is fearful of being exploited.

Convinced that its efforts are futile at best, a state may prematurely halt its efforts to achieve a cooperative agreement, efforts that might eventually have borne fruit. For example, Khrushchev's good intentions were undone by his impatience for quick results. If Gorbachev had not maintained a steady, consistent course despite provocations from the Reagan administration, his efforts at establishing U.S.-Soviet cooperation would not have been taken seriously and might never have produced results.

Thus, time lags themselves may lead to missed opportunities, simply because the other side responds too late. In 1953–54, Dulles and Eisenhower assumed that the Soviets were using the lure of negotiations on German reunification to delay ratification of the EDC Treaty. Their sluggish, grudging response to Malenkov's overtures decreased the chances for negotiations on German reunification, because no Soviet official had any reason to believe that Eisenhower might forgo arming West Germany in return for reunifying that country.

Washington was also caught off guard by Khrushchev's initiation of a policy of détente with the United States in 1955. Although Khrushchev signed the Austrian State Treaty, accepted important provisions of the Anglo-French disarmament proposal, and recognized West Germany, Dulles believed that the Soviets were in fact trying to win a breathing spell, not a disarmament agreement. Dulles's failure to reciprocate meant that a promising moment in U.S.-Soviet relations passed with no concrete achievements.

The Importance of Sequence

In short, the sequence of a state's actions is extremely important in shaping the other side's inferences about its intentions and preferences. Each side is apt to accuse the other of cheating first, or having first provoked the conflict. Since the interaction is continually in process, it is difficult to tell who was at fault. Kennedy's military buildup, for example, was a response to Khrushchev's boasts about Soviet rocket capabilities during the Eisenhower administration.

If state actions A, B, C, D, and E led to conflict, then changes in the order of state actions to, say, E, C, A, B, and D might have produced a different outcome. Not just the first and last moves, but the entire sequence helps to determine whether states escalate a conflict or resolve their differences.

In U.S.-Soviet relations, there were several junctures at which the superpowers had a chance to mitigate or resolve their differences: after Stalin's death in 1953; Khrushchev's accession to power in 1955; Khrushchev's peace offensive after *Sputnik*; the early months of the Kennedy administration; the initial months of the Nixon administration, before the United States had completed its testing of MIRVs; and Gorbachev's rise to power in the Soviet Union. Whether the relationship took on a cooperative or a competitive path was influenced by whether one state took the initiative and accompanied negotiating proposals with supportive actions. As Secretary of State George Shultz informed Reagan, it is sometimes necessary, before making a major arms reduction offer, to create the right background music.[11]

Kennedy and Khrushchev, for example, initially sought to improve U.S.-Soviet relations by exchanging symbolic concessions. After JFK initiated his buildup of U.S. strategic and conventional capabilities, however, Khrushchev responded by resuming atmospheric nuclear testing, renewing the Berlin crisis and, finally, installing missiles in Cuba, leaving both men bewildered in retrospect about what had happened. If Kennedy had delayed his military buildup until after he had better information about Soviet deployments, he might not have built so many missiles, and the total numbers of weapons on both sides might not have reached such absurd heights. Khrushchev might have accepted an interim agreement on Berlin, similar to one he had planned to conclude with Eisenhower at the Paris summit.

Some state rivalries seem to be preordained by geography or religion. Nevertheless, in many instances, whether a relationship eventuates in cooperation, peaceful competition, or armed conflict depends on the process of state interaction over time. The analyst should try to reconstruct the sequence of communication and action between states. For conflict is about history—about who did what to whom and when. The chronology of events is also critical for making counterfactual arguments (if, for example, one state had taken another specified action somewhere in the progression of events, then the other state might well have responded differently).

In various areas of the world, from Northern Ireland to the Middle East, mutual mistrust between states or factions may inhibit either side from taking the initiative to resolve a conflict, thus leading to missed opportunities for diplomacy. When small agreements are themselves difficult to initiate, or when they seem to go nowhere, a state may have to take unilateral action to overcome the psychological barriers to cooperating with the enemy. That even heroic efforts at de-escalating conflict have a delayed impact increases the intractability of such conflicts as the Arab-Israeli confrontation and the "trouble" in Northern Ireland. Democratic governments, which are subject to public pressure to show that they have received something tangible in return for making concessions, find it difficult to carry out trust-building actions. Thus, it is not surprising that the Soviet Union carried out most of the peace initiatives during the postwar era.

The noise of domestic politics often interferes with efforts to establish cooperation between states. The more conservative or hard-line factions within a state may seek to block the development of better relations with an adversary, holding up necessary legislation or even engaging in terrorist acts. Because states look for consistency between word and deed, such hostile acts, even when unauthorized, can undermine the development of trust.

Trust is also germane to the new issues raised by nationalism and nuclear proliferation. The ideal of "liberal nationalism" suggests that different ethnic groups can live together peaceably within the same territorial boundaries. The chief obstacle to realizing this ideal in the real world, however, is that minority ethnic groups, recalling past inequities and atrocities, distrust the majority group. The majority may have to make unilateral concessions in order to instill greater confidence among minority groups that their rights will be respected.

Maintaining the trust of Russia in the good intentions of the West will also be a difficult task, one requiring that the U.S. president balance the understandable security needs of the East European countries and the former republics of the Soviet Union against the suspicions of Russian political leaders. Trust grows when states draw on it to engage in collaborative activities, and it is easier to destroy than to reestablish. As President Nixon commented to Henry Kissinger, "Trust is like a thin thread: once you break it, it's very hard to splice together again."[12] Yet trust is necessary if leaders are to achieve cooperative agreements in international relations, and so the task for leadership is to reestablish former congruences, to weave together words and deeds in a stronger skein.

Notes

1. Distrust and Missed Opportunities in Foreign Policy

1. Eisenhower to General Alfred M. Gruenther, 25 July 1955, Ann C. Whitman File, DDE Diary Series, "DDE Diary, July 1955 (1)," Dwight David Eisenhower Library (DDEL), Abilene, Kans.; Secretary of State to Department of State, 21 July 1955, in U.S. Department of State, *Foreign Relations of the United States: 1955–1957* (Washington, D.C.: Government Printing Office, 1988) 5:464 (hereafter cited as *FR*).

2. Nikita S. Khrushchev, *Khrushchev Remembers*, trans. and ed. Strobe Talbott (Boston: Little, Brown, 1970), 519–20.

3. George B. Kistiakowsky, *A Scientist at the White House. The Private Diary of President Eisenhower's Special Assistant for Science and Technology* (Cambridge: Harvard University Press, 1976), 375.

4. Glenn T. Seaborg, *Kennedy, Khrushchev, and the Test Ban* (Berkeley: University of California Press, 1981), 128, 134 (quotation).

5. The United States and the Soviet Union also signed many less consequential agreements on security issues. See Alexander L. George, Philip J. Farley, and Alexander Dallin, eds., *U.S.-Soviet Security Cooperation: Achievements, Failures, Lessons* (New York: Oxford University Press, 1988), esp. the list of security agreements on pp. 619–20.

6. Peter D. McClelland, *Causal Explanation and Model Building in History, Economics, and the New Economic History* (Ithaca: Cornell University Press, 1975), 163–64.

7. Hans J. Morgenthau and Kenneth W. Thompson, *Politics among Nations: The Struggle for Power and Peace*, 6th ed. (New York: Alfred A. Knopf, 1985), 424–45; Kenneth N. Waltz, *Theory of International Politics* (Reading, Mass.: Addison-Wesley, 1979), 103–5, 174.

8. Robert Axelrod, *Evolution of Cooperation* (New York: Basic Books, 1984); Charles Lipson, "International Cooperation in Economic and Security Affairs," *World Politics* 37 (1984): 1–23; Harrison Wagner, "The Theory of Games and the

Problem of International Cooperation," *American Political Science Review* 70 (1983): 336–46; Kenneth A. Oye, ed., *Cooperation under Anarchy*, special issue of *World Politics*, vol. 38 (October 1985); Arthur A. Stein, *Why Nations Cooperate: Circumstance and Choice in International Relations* (Ithaca: Cornell University Press, 1990), chap. 2.

9. Nelson Goodman, *Fact, Fiction, and Forecast* (Cambridge: Harvard University Press, 1955), 24–25; Jon Elster, *Logic and Society: Contradictions and Possible Worlds* (New York: John Wiley, 1978), 182; J. D. Gould, "Hypothetical History," *Economic History Review* 22 (1969): 196–97; Philip E. Tetlock and Aaron Belkin, eds., *Counterfactual Thought Experiments in World Politics* (Princeton: Princeton University Press, 1996).

10. Charles E. Osgood, "Suggestions for Winning the Real War with Communism," *Journal of Conflict Resolution* 3 (1959): 295–325; idem, *An Alternative to War or Surrender* (Urbana: University of Illinois Press, 1962), 26–33, 84–124.

11. Morgenthau and Thompson, *Politics among Nations*, 439; Waltz, *Theory of International Politics*, 105–6, 165–67, 170–72, 175.

12. Morgenthau and Thompson, *Politics among Nations*, 439–40, 442; Waltz, *Theory of International Politics*, 195.

13. "Cold War Foes Forge Warm Ties," *Los Angeles Times*, 23 June 1995; Matthew L. Wald, "Today's Drama: Twilight of the Nukes," *New York Times*, 16 July 1995. For different rationales offered to explain wasteful competition between the superpowers, see Morgenthau and Thompson, *Politics among Nations*; Hans J. Morgenthau, *In Defense of the National Interest: A Critical Examination of American Foreign Policy* (New York: Alfred A. Knopf, 1952), 136, 138; Waltz, *Theory of International Politics*; Stephen M. Walt, *The Origins of Alliances* (Ithaca: Cornell University Press, 1987); and Jack Snyder, *Myths of Empire: Domestic Politics and International Ambition* (Ithaca: Cornell University Press, 1991).

14. John H. Herz, "Idealist Internationalism and the Security Dilemma," *World Politics* 2 (1950): 15; idem, *Political Realism and Political Idealism: A Study in Theories and Realities* (Chicago: University of Chicago Press, 1951), 3–4, 14–15, 239; Robert Jervis, *Perception and Misperception in International Politics* (Princeton: Princeton University Press, 1976), 65–66, 76–77; idem, "Cooperation under the Security Dilemma," *World Politics* 30 (1978): 167–214; idem, "Security Regimes," in *International Regimes*, ed. Stephen D. Krasner (Ithaca: Cornell University Press, 1983), 362.

15. On the difficulties that states face in cooperating on security issues as opposed to economic issues, see Charles Lipson, "International Cooperation," *World Politics* 37 (1984): 1–23; and Jervis, "Security Regimes," 358–59.

16. Robert Axelrod, *The Evolution of Cooperation* (New York: Basic Books, 1984); Martin Shubik, "Game Theory, Behavior, and the Paradox of the Prisoner's Dilemma: Three Solutions," *Journal of Conflict Resolution* 14 (1970): 181–93; Michael Taylor, *Anarchy and Cooperation* (London: John Wiley, 1976); Russell Hardin, *Collective Action* (Baltimore: Johns Hopkins University Press, for Resources for the Future, 1982).

17. Axelrod, *Evolution of Cooperation*, 139–40, 173 (quotation).

18. Diego Gambetta, "Can We Trust Trust?" in *Trust: Making and Breaking Cooperative Relations*, ed. Diego Gambetta (New York: Basil Blackwell, 1988),

229; Charles S. Maier, "Introduction," in Kistiakowsky, *A Scientist at the White House*, xlvii; Michael R. Beschloss and Strobe Talbott, *At the Highest Levels: The Inside Story of the End of the Cold War* (Boston: Little, Brown, 1993), 120, 370–73.

19. Fred Charles Iklé, "After Detection—What?" *Foreign Affairs* 39 (1961): 208–20. For a recent statement of the argument that verification does not promote compliance, see Colin S. Gray, *House of Cards: Why Arms Control Must Fail* (Ithaca: Cornell University Press, 1992), chap. 6; Kenneth L. Adelman, "Why Verification Is More Difficult (and Less Important)," *International Security* 14 (1990): 141–46.

20. Axelrod, *Evolution of Cooperation*, 84–85, 170, 182; David Hume, *A Treatise of Human Nature* (London: Longmans, Green, 1898) 2: 288–89.

21. On this point, see John Lewis Gaddis, "The Long Peace: Elements of Stability in the Postwar International System," in *The Long Peace: Inquiries into the History of the Cold War* (New York: Oxford University Press, 1987), 243.

22. The seminal work on what is now known as the "lemon problem" is George A. Akerlof, "The Market for 'Lemons': Quality Uncertainty and the Market Mechanism," *Quarterly Journal of Economics* 84 (1970): 488–500. Robert Keohane first applied the lemon problem to international cooperation in *After Hegemony: Cooperation and Discord in the World Political Economy* (Princeton: Princeton University Press, 1984), 93–95. On opportunism, see Oliver E. Williamson, *The Economic Institutions of Capitalism: Firms, Markets, Relational Contracting* (New York: Free Press, 1985), 47–48.

23. Robert Jervis, *The Logic of Images in International Relations* (Princeton: Princeton University Press, 1970), 66.

24. For the argument that economists have neglected trust, see Mark Granovetter, "Economic Action and Social Structure: The Problem of Embeddedness," *American Journal of Sociology* 91 (1985): 481–510; and Partha Dasgupta, "Trust as a Commodity," in *Trust*, ed. Gambetta, 49. Exceptions to this pattern of neglect include Gambetta, ed., *Trust*; Kenneth J. Arrow, *The Limits of Organization* (New York: Norton, 1974); idem, "Gifts and Exchanges," *Philosophy and Public Affairs* 1 (1972): 343–62; and Fred Hirsch, *Social Limits to Growth* (Cambridge: Harvard University Press, 1976), chap. 6. James S. Coleman is a sociologist, but he uses economic theory in his *Foundations of Social Theory* (Cambridge: Harvard University Press, 1990). On the role of trust in continuing business relationships, see Stewart Macaulay, "Non-Contractual Relations in Business: A Preliminary Survey," *American Sociological Review* 28 (1955): 55–67; Bernard Barber, *The Logic and Limits of Trust* (New Brunswick: Rutgers University Press, 1983), 129–30; and Francis Fukuyama, *Trust: The Social Virtues and the Creation of Prosperity* (New York: Free Press, 1995).

25. Gambetta, "Can We Trust Trust?" 217–18, 222; Edward H. Lorenz, "Neither Friends nor Strangers: Informal Networks of Subcontracting in French Industry," in *Trust*, ed. Gambetta, 197.

26. Dasgupta, "Trust as a Commodity," 53–54; Gambetta, "Can We Trust Trust?" 222; Russell Hardin, "Trusting Persons, Trusting Institutions," in *Strategy and Choice*, ed. Richard J. Zeckhauser (Cambridge: MIT Press, 1991), 189; Russell Hardin, "The Street-Level Epistemology of Trust," *Politics & Society* 21 (1993): 505, 525–26; Henry Raymond, "Rusk Will Start Atom Pact Drive in Senate Today," *New York Times*, 12 August 1963.

27. Thomas C. Schelling, *The Strategy of Conflict* (New York: Oxford University Press, 1963; Cambridge: Harvard University Press, 1960), 45–46, 134 (page citations are to the reprint edition); Jervis, "Cooperation under the Security Dilemma," 181; Axelrod, *Evolution of Cooperation*, 131–32.

28. Carl Shapiro, "Premiums for High Quality Products as Returns to Reputations," *Quarterly Journal of Economics* 98 (1983): 659–79; Keohane, *After Hegemony*, 105–6; Thompson to Secretary of State, 3 December 1958, President's Office File, Countries, "USSR-Vienna Meeting, Background Documents, 1953–1961, Previous Khrushchev Conversations," John F. Kennedy Library (JFKL), Boston, Mass.

29. Paul Milgrom and John Roberts, "Predation, Reputation, and Entry Deterrence," *Journal of Economic Theory* 27 (1982): 280–312; David M. Kreps and Robert Wilson, "Reputation and Imperfect Information," *Journal of Economic Theory* 27 (1982): 253–79; Robert Wilson, "Deterrence in Oligopolistic Competition," in *Perspectives on Deterrence*, ed. Paul C. Stern, Robert Axelrod, Robert Jervis, and Roy Radner (New York: Oxford University Press, 1989), 163, 171; A. Michael Spence, *Market Signaling: Informational Transfer in Hiring and Related Screening Processes* (Cambridge: Harvard University Press, 1974), 88–89; Benjamin Klein and Keith B. Leffler, "The Role of Market Forces in Assuring Contractual Performance," *Journal of Political Economy* 89 (1981): 630–31; Dasgupta, "Trust as a Commodity," 70; Thomas C. Schelling, *Arms and Influence* (New Haven: Yale University Press, 1966), 150; Jervis, *Logic of Images*, 28, 46; *New York Times*, 19 May 1955.

30. Jervis, *Logic of Images*, 20; Kreps and Wilson, "Reputation and Imperfect Information," 266–75; Dasgupta, "Trust as a Commodity," 69; Joel Sobel, "Theory of Credibility," *Review of Economic Studies* 52 (1985): 557–73.

31. On legitimation, see B. Thomas Trout, "Rhetoric Revisited: Political Legitimation and the Cold War," *International Studies Quarterly* 19 (1975): 251–84; Alexander L. George, "Domestic Constraints on Regime Change in U.S. Foreign Policy: The Need for Policy Legitimacy," in *Change in the International System*, ed. Ole R. Holsti, Randolph M. Siverson, and Alexander L. George (Boulder, Colo.: Westview Press, 1980), 233–59.

32. Reo M. Christenson et al., *Ideologies and Modern Politics*, 2d ed. (New York: Dodd, Mead, 1977), 6; Alexander L. George, "Ideology and International Relations: A Conceptual Analysis," *Jerusalem Journal of International Relations* 9 (1987): 1–20; idem, "Psychological Dimensions of the U.S.-Soviet Conflict," in *Reexamining the Soviet Experience: Essays in Honor of Alexander Dallin*, ed. David Holloway and Norman Naimark (Boulder, Colo.: Westview Press, 1996), 101–18; Trout, "Rhetoric Revisited."

33. Stephen F. Cohen, *Rethinking the Soviet Experience: Politics and History since 1917* (New York: Oxford University Press, 1985), 152–53; Georgi Arbatov, *The System: An Insider's Life in Soviet Politics* (New York: Times Books, 1992), 169–70, 172, 189.

34. Trout, "Rhetoric Revisited"; William E. Odom, "The 'Militarization' of Soviet Society," *Problems of Communism* 25 (1976): 34–51; David Holloway, "War, Militarism, and the Soviet State," *Alternatives* 6 (1980): 59–62; Robert C. Tucker, *Stalin in Power: The Revolution from Above, 1928–1941* (New York: W. W. Norton, 1990), 70, 74–75; idem, *The Soviet Political Mind: Stalinism and Post-*

Stalin Change (New York: W. W. Norton, 1971), 192; Arbatov, *The System*, 52–53, 106–7.

35. Holloway, "War, Militarism, and the Soviet State," 85; Snyder, *Myths of Empire*, 237–38; Thomas M. Nichols, *The Sacred Cause: Civil-Military Conflict over Soviet National Security, 1917–1992* (Ithaca: Cornell University Press, 1993), 1–20.

36. Steven E. Miller, "Politics over Promise," *International Security* 8 (1984): 79–82.

37. Joseph S. Nye Jr., "Can America Manage Its Soviet Policy?" in *The Making of America's Soviet Policy*, ed. Nye (New Haven: Yale University Press, 1984), 331–32.

38. Theodore J. Lowi, *The End of Liberalism: Ideology, Policy, and the Crisis of Public Authority* (New York: W. W. Norton, 1969), 157–88; Joseph S. Nye Jr., "The Domestic Root of American Policy," in *The Making of America's Soviet Policy*, ed. Nye, 6–7.

39. James Richter, *Khrushchev's Double Bind: International Pressures and Domestic Coalition Politics* (Baltimore: Johns Hopkins University Press, 1994), 19–20; Dmitri Volkogonov, *Lenin: A New Biography*, trans. and ed. Harold Shukman (New York: Free Press, 1994), 306, 313, 321–22 (Volkogonov, a director of the Institute for Military History and a colonel-general, was given access to secret party archives during the Gorbachev era); McGeorge Bundy, "To Cap the Volcano," *Foreign Affairs* 48 (1969): 17; Louis Kriesberg, *International Conflict Resolution: The U.S.-USSR and Middle East Cases* (New Haven: Yale University Press, 1992), 56, 77–78 (also 43–49, where Kriesberg presents a list of peace initiatives in U.S.-Soviet relations from 1948 to 1989).

40. Holloway, "War, Militarism, and the Soviet State," 74, 83–84; Timothy J. Colton, "Perspectives on Civil-Military Relations in the Soviet Union," in *Soldiers and the Soviet State: Civil-Military Relations from Brezhnev to Gorbachev*, ed. Timothy J. Colton and Thane Gustafson (Princeton: Princeton University Press, 1990), 23–24; Nichols, *Sacred Cause*, 32; Arbatov, *The System*, 200–201; Thane Gustafson, "Conclusions: Toward a Crisis in Civil-Military Relations," in *Soldiers and the Soviet State*, ed. Colton and Gustafson, 343.

41. Bernard J. Firestone, *The Quest for Nuclear Stability: John F. Kennedy and the Soviet Union* (Westport, Conn.: Greenwood Press, 1982), 134; Miller, "Politics over Promise," 82–83.

42. Morton Deutsch, "Trust and Suspicion," *Journal of Conflict Resolution* 22 (1958): 266; idem, *The Resolution of Conflict: Constructive and Destructive Processes* (New Haven: Yale University Press, 1973), 152; Niklas Luhmann, *Trust and Power* (New York: John Wiley & Sons, 1979), 25; Barry R. Schlenker, Bob Helm, and James T. Tedeschi, "The Effects of Personality and Situational Variables on Behavioral Trust," *Journal of Personality and Social Psychology* 25 (1973): 419–27; Khrushchev, *Khrushchev Remembers*, trans. and ed. Talbott, 307.

43. Deutsch, "Trust and Suspicion," 265; Niklas Luhmann, "Familiarity, Confidence, Trust: Problems and Alternatives," in *Trust*, ed. Gambetta, 97–98.

44. J. David Lewis and Andrew Weigert, "Trust as a Social Reality," *Social Forces* 63 (1985): 971; Harold Macmillan, *Pointing the Way: 1959–1961* (London: Macmillan, 1972), 202–3.

45. I am indebted to Robert Jervis for this observation.

46. Barber, *The Logic and Limits of Trust*, 9; Luhmann, *Trust and Power*, 25, 27.

47. J. B. Rotter, "Generalized Expectancies for Interpersonal Trust," *American Psychologist* 26 (1971): 443–52.

48. Dean G. Pruitt, "Definition of the Situation as a Determinant of International Action," in *International Behavior: A Social-Psychological Analysis*, ed. Herbert C. Kelman (New York: Holt, Rinehart & Winston, 1965), 397.

49. Pruitt, "Definition of the Situation," 413; Barber, *The Logic and Limits of Trust*, 17–18; Luhmann, *Trust and Power*, 92; William M. Webb and Philip Worchel, "Trust and Distrust," in *Psychology of Intergroup Relations*, ed. Stephen Worchel and William G. Austin (Chicago: Nelson-Hall, 1986), 224–25.

50. Deutsch, *Resolution of Conflict*, 152, 153–54; Luhmann, *Trust and Power*, 42, 73.

51. Schelling, *Strategy of Conflict*, 45; Steven Greenhouse, "Administration Defends North Korea Accord," *New York Times*, 25 January 1995.

52. E. W. Kenworthy, "Rusk's Assurance on Nuclear Pact Pleases Senators," *New York Times*, 13 August 1963.

53. Richard Nisbett and Lee Ross, *Human Inference: Strategies and Shortcomings of Social Judgment* (Englewood Cliffs, N.J.: Prentice-Hall, 1980); Ole R. Holsti, "Cognitive Dynamics and Images of the Enemy: Dulles and Russia," in *Enemies in Politics*, ed. David J. Finlay, Ole R. Holsti, and Richard R. Fagen (Chicago: Rand McNally, 1967), 25–96.

54. Philip Kitcher, "The Evolution of Human Altruism," *Journal of Philosophy* 10 (1993): 497–516; Thomas L. Friedman, "An American's Respite from Disillusionment," *New York Times*, 19 September 1993.

55. Minutes, NSC Meeting, 26 January 1956, Whitman File, NSC Series, DDEL, Abilene, Kans.

56. For reviews of the extensive psychological literature on self-fulfilling prophecies, see John M. Darley and Russell H. Fazio, "Expectancy Confirmation Processes Arising in the Social Interaction Sequence," *American Psychologist* 35 (1980): 867–81; Dale T. Miller and William Turnbull, "Expectancies and Interpersonal Processes," *Annual Review of Psychology* 37 (1986): 233–56; and Mark Snyder, "Motivational Foundations of Behavioral Confirmation," in *Advances in Experimental Social Psychology*, ed. Mark P. Zanna (New York: Academic Press, 1992), 25: 67–114. Also see C. O. Word, M. P. Zanna, and J. Cooper, "The Nonverbal Mediation of Self-fulfilling Prophecies in Interracial Interaction," *Journal of Experimental Social Psychology* 31 (1974): 109–20; Harold H. Kelley and Anthony J. Stahelski, "Social Interaction Basis of Cooperators' and Competitors' Beliefs about Others," *Journal of Personality and Social Psychology* 16 (1970): 66–91; Charles D. McClintock and Steven P. McNeel, "Reward and Score Feedback as Determinants of Cooperative Game Behavior," *Journal of Personality and Social Psychology* 4 (1966): 606–13; and Charles D. McClintock and Steven P. McNeel, "Reward Level and Game Playing Behavior," *Journal of Conflict Resolution* 10 (1966): 98–102.

57. George A. Quattrone, "Overattribution and Unit Formation: When Behavior Engulfs the Person," *Journal of Personality and Social Psychology* 42 (1982): 593–607; Lee Ross, "The Intuitive Psychologist and His Shortcomings: Distortions in the Attribution Process," in *Advances in Experimental Social Psychology*, vol. 10, ed. Leonard Berkowitz (New York: Academic Press, 1977); Arbatov,

The System, 193–96, 203; Archive of the President of the Russian Federation, "Special File" Minutes of Politburo, 4 August 1983, p. 66, cited in Volkogonov, *Lenin*, 463.

58. Edward E. Jones and Richard E. Nisbett, "The Actor and the Observer: Divergent Perceptions of the Causes of Behavior," in *Attribution: Perceiving the Causes of Behavior*, ed. Edward E. Jones, David E. Kanouse, Harold H. Kelley, Richard E. Nisbett, Stuart Valins, and Bernard Weiner (Morristown, N.J.: General Learning Press, 1971); Robert J. Robinson, Dacher Keltner, Andrew Ward, and Lee Ross, "Actual versus Assumed Differences in Construal: 'Naive Realism' in Intergroup Perception and Conflict," *Journal of Personality and Social Psychology* 68 (1991): 404–17; Stuart Oskamp, "Attitudes toward U.S. and Russian Actions: A Double Standard," *Psychological Reports* 16 (1965): 43–46; Stuart Oskamp and A. Harty, "A Factor-Analytic Study of the Double Standard in Attitudes toward U.S. and Russian Actions," *Behavioral Science* 13 (1968): 178–88.

59. Daniel T. Gilbert, Brett W. Pelham, and Douglas S. Krull, "On Cognitive Busyness: When Person Perceivers Meet Persons Perceived," *Journal of Personality and Social Psychology* 54 (1988): 733–40.

60. Dennis T. Regan and Judith Totten, "Empathy and Attribution: Turning Observers into Actors," *Journal of Personality and Social Psychology* 32 (1975): 850–56; B. S. Moore, D. R. Sherrod, T. J. Liu, and B. Underwood, "The Dispositional Shift in Attribution over Time," *Journal of Experimental Social Psychology* 15 (1979): 553–69.

61. Albert Michotte, *The Perception of Causality* (New York: Basic Books, 1963); Harold H. Kelley and Anthony J. Stahelski, "The Inference of Intentions from Moves in the Prisoner's Dilemma Game," *Journal of Experimental Social Psychology* 6 (1970): 401–19.

62. Arbatov, *The System*, 187; Raymond L. Garthoff, *Detente and Confrontation: American-Soviet Relations from Nixon to Reagan*, rev. ed. (Washington, DC: Brookings, 1994), 519, 733–35.

63. Stuart Oskamp, "Effects of Programmed Strategies on Cooperation in the Prisoner's Dilemma and Other Mixed-Motive Games," *Journal of Conflict Resolution* 15 (1971): 225–59.

64. Webb and Worchel, "Trust and Distrust," 224.

65. G. Marwell, K. Ratcliff, and D. R. Schmitt, "Minimizing Differences in a Maximizing Difference Game," *Journal of Personality and Social Psychology* 12 (1969): 158–63; Harold H. Kelley and John W. Thibaut, *Interpersonal Relations: A Theory of Interdependence* (New York: John Wiley, 1978), 186–87; Nikita S. Khrushchev, *Khrushchev Remembers: The Glasnost Tapes*, trans. and ed. Jerold L. Schecter and Vyacheslav V. Luchkov (Boston: Little, Brown, 1990), 71–72.

66. Glenn H. Snyder and Paul Diesing, *Conflict among Nations: Bargaining, Decision Making, and System Structure in International Crises* (Princeton: Princeton University Press, 1977).

67. Kriesberg, *International Conflict Resolution*, 114.

68. On the utility of positive inducements, see David A. Baldwin, "The Power of Positive Sanctions," *World Politics* 24 (1971): 19–38.

69. Osgood, "Suggestions for Winning the Real War," 295–325; idem, *An Alternative to War or Surrender*, 26–33, 84–124.

70. Osgood, "Suggestions for Winning the Real War," 321–22; Alexander L.

George, "Strategies for Facilitating Cooperation," in *U.S.-Soviet Security Cooperation*, ed. George, Farley, and Dallin, 703–4.

71. C. R. Mitchell, "A Willingness to Talk: Conciliatory Gestures and Deescalation," *Negotiation Journal* 7 (1991): 408.

72. Dean G. Pruitt, "Reciprocity and Credit Building in a Laboratory Dyad," *Journal of Personality and Social Psychology* 8 (1968): 143; Harold H. Kelley, "Processes of Causal Attribution," *American Psychologist* 28 (1973): 113–14.

73. Abraham Tesser, Robert Gatewood, and Michael Driver, "Some Determinants of Gratitude," *Journal of Personality and Social Psychology* 9 (1968): 233–36; Kenneth J. Gergen, Phoebe Ellsworth, Christina Maslach, and Magnus Seipel, "Obligation, Donor Resources, and Reactions to Aid in Three Cultures," *Journal of Personality and Social Psychology* 31 (1975): 390–400; Stuart Komorita, "Concession-Making and Conflict Resolution," *Journal of Conflict Resolution* 17 (1973): 745–62; Dean G. Pruitt, *Negotiation Behavior* (New York: Academic Press, 1981), 124–25; M. S. Gorbachev, "The Reality and Guarantees of a Secure World," *Pravda*, trans. Foreign Broadcast Information Service, *FBIS Daily Report-Soviet Union*, 17 September 1987 (PrEx 7.10: FBIS-SOV-87-180), 23; Raymond L. Garthoff, *The Great Transition: American-Soviet Relations and the End of the Cold War* (Washington, D.C.: Brookings, 1994), 366.

74. Theodore C. Sorensen, *Kennedy* (New York: Harper & Row, 1965), 733. In a psychological experiment, subjects attributed greater honesty to a speaker who argued in favor of higher licensing fees for truck trailers before a group of truckers (who would presumably be opposed) than other subjects attributed to the speaker when he argued before an audience of railroad union men (who agreed with his views). See J. Mills and J. M. Jellison, "Effect on Opinion Change of How Desirable the Communication Is to the Audience the Communicator Addressed," *Journal of Personality and Social Psychology* 6 (1967): 98–101. In another experiment, a prosecutor who argued in favor of reducing the power of the police and of the public prosecutor was judged to be more sincere than a criminal who made similar arguments. See Elaine Walster, Elliot Aronson, and Darcy Abrahams, "On Increasing the Persuasiveness of a Low Prestige Communicator," *Journal of Experimental Social Psychology* 2 (1966): 325–42.

75. Harold H. Kelley, "Attribution in Social Interactions," in *Attribution*, ed. Kelley, Nisbett, Valins, and Weiner, 12; Jack M. Feldman, "Stimulus Characteristics and Subject Prejudice as Determinants of Stereotype Attribution," *Journal of Personality and Social Psychology* 21 (1972): 333–40.

76. Mitchell, "A Willingness to Talk," 405–30.

77. Ibid., 420–21; Barry Schlenker, Bob Helm, and James T. Tedeschi, "The Effects of Personality and Situational Variables on Behavioral Trust," *Journal of Personality and Social Psychology* 23 (1973): 419–27; Svenn Lindskold, "Trust Development, the GRIT Proposal, and the Effects of Conciliatory Acts on Conflict and Cooperation," *Psychological Bulletin* 95 (1978): 773.

78. Mitchell, "A Willingness to Talk," 418–19; Michael Parks and Mark Fineman, "Peace a Hard Sell to Many Palestinians," *Los Angeles Times*, 6 September 1993.

79. Verbatim Minutes of the Western European Chiefs of Mission Conference, Paris, 6 May 1957, *FR: 1955–1957*, 4:597.

80. Bruce Parrott, "Soviet National Security under Gorbachev," *Problems of Communism* 37 (1988): 12, 30; Beschloss and Talbott, *At the Highest Levels*, 324.

81. Robert L. Swinth, "The Establishment of the Trust Relationship," *Journal of Conflict Resolution* 11 (1967): 335–44.

82. Zeev Maoz and Dan S. Felsenthal, "Self-Binding Commitments, the Inducement of Trust, Social Choice, and the Theory of International Cooperation," *International Studies Quarterly* 31 (1987): 177–200.

83. George P. Shultz, *Turmoil and Triumph: My Years as Secretary of State* (New York: Charles Scribner's Sons, 1993), 534.

84. Kelley, "Attribution in Social Interaction," 1–26; Teresa Hayden and Walter Mischel, "Maintaining Trait Consistency in the Resolution of Behavioral Inconsistency: The Wolf in Sheep's Clothing," *Journal of Personality* 44 (1976): 109–32; George Bunn and Roger A. Payne, "Tit-for-Tat and the Negotiation of Nuclear Arms Control," *Arms Control* 9 (1988): 215.

85. Kriesberg, *International Conflict Resolution*, 111–12. An incidental, accidental mixing of cooperative and coercive signals should not be confused with a deliberate bargaining *strategy* involving the sequencing of carrots and sticks. Often, leaders may wish to begin with coercive moves to establish their resolve, but may then offer the other side inducements in order to increase its incentives to concede.

86. Charlan Nemeth, "Bargaining and Reciprocity," *Psychological Bulletin* 74 (1970): 297–308; John Schopler and Vaida Diller Thompson, "Rule of Attribution Process in Mediating Amount of Reciprocity for a Favor," *Journal of Personality and Social Psychology* 10 (1968): 243–50; Jack W. Brehm and Ann Himelick Cole, "Effect of a Favor Which Reduces Freedom," *Journal of Personality and Social Psychology* 3 (1966): 420–26.

87. Shultz, *Turmoil and Triumph*, 711; Robert Gates, deputy director for intelligence, still maintains that Gorbachev's rhetoric was not matched by his actions, and that the Soviet Union continued its vast military programs. See *From the Shadows: The Ultimate Insider's Story of Five Presidents and How They Won the Cold War* (New York: Simon & Schuster, 1996), 381–82.

88. R. E. Goranson and Leonard Berkowitz, "Reciprocity and Responsibility Reactions to Prior Help," *Journal of Personality and Social Psychology* 3 (1966): 227–32.

89. Joshua S. Goldstein and John R. Freeman found that the target's response lagged in six cases of initiatives effected by the United States, China, and the Soviet Union: see *Three-Way Street* (Chicago: University of Chicago Press, 1990), 127–28. Also see Holsti, "Cognitive Dynamics and Images of the Enemy"; Beschloss and Talbott, *At the Highest Levels*.

90. Edward E. Jones and K. E. Davis, "From Acts to Dispositions: The Attribution Process in Person Perception," in *Advances in Experimental Social Psychology*, ed. Leonard Berkowitz (New York: Academic Press, 1965), 2:227; Robert Axelrod, "The Rational Timing of Surprise," *World Politics* 31 (1979): 244; Joel Sobel, "A Theory of Credibility," *Review of Economic Studies* 52 (1985): 557.

91. Glenn D. Reeder and Marilyn B. Brewer, "A Schematic Model of Dispositional Attribution in Interpersonal Perception," *Psychological Review* 86 (1979): 68; Glenn D. Reeder, D. J. Henderson, and J. J. Sullivan, "From Dispositions to Behaviors: The Flip Side of Attribution," *Journal of Research in Personality* 16 (1982): 355–75; Michael H. Birnbaum, "Morality Judgments: Test of an Averaging Model," *Journal of Experimental Psychology* 93 (1972): 35–42; idem, "Morality Judgments: Test of an Averaging Model with Differential Weights,"

Journal of Experimental Psychology 99 (1973): 395–99; John J. Skowronski and Donal E. Carlston, "Negativity and Extremity Biases in Impression Formation: A Review of Explanations," *Psychological Bulletin* 105 (1989): 131–42; John J. Skowronski and Donal E. Carlston, "Social Judgment and Social Memory: The Role of Cue Diagnosticity in Negativity, Positivity, and Extremity Biases," *Journal of Personality and Social Psychology* 52 (1987): 688–99; Jeffrey Schmalz, "Words on Bush's Lips in '88 Now Stick in Voters' Craw," *New York Times*, 14 June 1992; Myron Rothbart and Bernadette Park, "On the Confirmability and Disconfirmability of Trait Concepts," *Journal of Personality and Social Psychology* 50 (1986): 137–38; Luhmann, *Trust and Power*, 28–29.

92. Alexander L. George, "U.S.-Soviet Efforts to Cooperate in Crisis Management and Crisis Avoidance," in *U.S.-Soviet Security Cooperation*, ed. George, Farley, and Dallin, 588–89; Garthoff, *Detente and Confrontation*, 434–41.

93. Evidence suggests that people are far more conservative about modifying their beliefs in response to incoming information than one would predict from Bayesian models. In fact, psychological experiments show that it takes seven to ten times as many observations to get subjects to change their beliefs about probabilities as the Bayesian rules would prescribe. See Paul Slovic and Sarah Lichtenstein, "Comparison of Bayesian and Regression Approaches to the Study of Information Processing in Judgment," *Organizational Behavior and Human Performance* 6 (1971): 693, 705. These data, moreover, probably underestimate the extent of conservatism in international relations, because the beliefs that people hold about enemies are far stronger than their convictions about the distribution of white and black balls in an urn. See Thomas Gilovich, *How We Know What Isn't So: The Fallibility of Human Reason in Everyday Life* (New York: Free Press, 1991), 53–54; Nisbett and Ross, *Human Inference*.

94. Luhmann, *Trust and Power*, 40–41.

95. Geoffrey Hawthorn, *Plausible Worlds: Possibility and Understanding in History and the Social Sciences* (Cambridge: Cambridge University Press, 1991), 79–80.

96. Alexander L. George, " 'Missed Opportunities' in Preventive Diplomacy" (draft manuscript, June 1995); Hawthorn, *Plausible Worlds*, 164.

97. J. L. Mackie, *The Cement of the Universe: A Study of Causation* (Oxford: Clarendon Press, 1974), 34–35.

98. William Taubman, *Stalin's American Policy: From Entente to Detente to Cold War* (New York: W. W. Norton, 1982), 184–87; Bennett Kovrig, *Of Walls and Bridges: The United States and Eastern Europe* (New York: New York University Press, 1991), 109; Richard E. Neustadt and Ernest R. May, *Thinking in Time: The Uses of History for Decision-Makers* (New York: Free Press, 1986), 111–33.

99. G. M. Korniyenko, "A 'Missed Opportunity'—Carter, Brezhnev, SALT II, and the Vance Mission to Moscow, November 1976–March 1977," in Woodrow Wilson International Center for Scholars, *Cold War International History Project Bulletin* (Spring 1995), 141–43. See also Strobe Talbott, *Endgame: The Inside Story of SALT II* (New York: Harper & Row, 1979); Garthoff, *Detente and Confrontation*, 883–94.

100. Steven Lukes, "Elster on Counterfactuals," *Inquiry* 23 (1980): 150–51.

101. This is John Stuart Mill's method of agreement, described in *A System of Logic* (London: Longmans, Green, 1949), chap. 8. The investigator tries to find similar causes in cases that are quite different except for the outcome to be

explained. Whatever factors the two cases share could be necessary conditions for the phenomenon in question. Mill's method has many problems, not the least of which is that social phenomena can have complex causation or multiple causal paths. But since some version of Mill's method is commonly used in comparative case analysis, the investigator must try somehow to cope with possible pitfalls (e.g., by use of "process tracing," discussed below). For a discussion, see Alexander L. George and Timothy J. McKeown, "Case Studies and Theories of Organizational Decision Making," in *Advances in Information Processing in Organizations*, ed. Robert J. Coulam and Richard A. Smith (Greenwich, Conn.: JAI Press, 1985), 2:26–27; Daniel Little, "Evidence and Objectivity in the Social Sciences," *Social Research* 60 (1993): 381–84.

102. Mackie, *Cement of the Universe*, 78; McClelland, *Causal Explanation and Model Building*, 82; Alexander L. George, "Case Studies" (draft manuscript, March 1994); Little, "Evidence and Objectivity in the Social Sciences," 383–84.

103. David Collier, "The Comparative Method: Two Decades of Change," in *Comparative Political Dynamics: Global Research Perspectives*, ed. Dankwart A. Rustow and Kenneth Paul Erickson (New York: Harper Collins, 1991), 19.

104. George and McKeown, "Case Studies and Theories of Organizational Decision Making," 34–41; Alexander L. George, "The Causal Nexus between Cognitive Beliefs and Decisionmaking Behavior: The 'Operational Code' Belief System," in *Psychological Models and International Politics*, ed. Lawrence Falkowski (Boulder, Colo.: Westview Press, 1979), 95–124; idem, "Case Studies and Theory Development: The Method of Structured Focused Comparison," in *Diplomatic History: New Approaches in History, Theory, and Policy*, ed. Paul G. Lauren (New York: Free Press, 1979).

105. Serge Schmemann, "Soviet Archives Provide Missing Pieces of History's Puzzles," *New York Times*, 8 February 1993.

106. Alexander L. George, *Propaganda Analysis* (Evanston, Ill.: Row, Peterson, 1959; Westport, Conn.: Greenwood Press, 1973), 37–44 (page citations are to the reprint edition); Deborah Welch Larson, "Problems of Content Analysis in Foreign Policy Research: Notes from the Study of the Origins of Cold War Belief Systems," *International Studies Quarterly* 32 (1988): 249.

2. German Reunification and Disarmament

1. George W. Breslauer, *Khrushchev and Brezhnev as Leaders: Building Authority in Soviet Politics* (London: Allen & Unwin, 1982), 23; James G. Richter, *Khrushchev's Double Bind: International Pressures and Domestic Coalition Politics* (Baltimore: Johns Hopkins University Press, 1994), 30.

2. Dietrich Staritz, "The SED, Stalin, and the German Question: Interests and Decision-Making in the Light of New Sources," *German History* 10 (1992): 274–89; Victor Baras, "Beria's Fall and Ulbricht's Survival," *Soviet Studies* 27 (1975): 381–82; Arnulf Baring, *Uprising in East Germany: June 17, 1953*, trans. Gerald Onn (Ithaca: Cornell University Press, 1972), 20; Jerry F. Hough and Merle Fainsod, *How the Soviet Union Is Governed* (Cambridge: Harvard University Press, 1979), 192–93.

3. In 1958, Eisenhower said he was appalled that Walter Lippmann was ready to "acquiesce" in the status quo with respect to Germany (quoted in

Marc Trachtenberg, *History and Strategy* [Princeton: Princeton University Press, 1991], 176). Dulles had complained in 1956 that the allies were not clearly dedicated "to the policy of bringing about the unity of one of the most important members of NATO, i.e., Germany. Its continued division carries a threat to the wholehearted and lasting identification of Western Germany with the fortunes of the West" (quoted ibid., 178; for other citations, see p. 174). According to a State Department policy statement on Germany, "while such a united Germany would probably ally itself with the West, it might choose to remain neutral or to retain freedom of action. Under present conditions, such a risk must be accepted" (NSC 160/1, "United States Position with Respect to Germany," 17 August 1953, in U.S. Department of State, *Foreign Relations of the United States: 1952–1954* [Washington, D.C.: Government Printing Office, 1986], 7[1]:517 [hereafter cited as *FR*]).

4. For the argument that the Eisenhower administration wanted the arms race to continue and had no interest in a disarmament agreement, see Matthew Evangelista, "Cooperation Theory and Disarmament: Negotiations in the 1950s," *World Politics* 42 (1990): 502–28.

5. Memorandum from President to Secretary of State, 8 September 1953, *FR: 1952–1954*, 2(1):461; Memorandum from Secretary of State to President, 6 September 1953, ibid., 458.

6. Those who argue that the West missed an opportunity for German reunification include Richard Lowenthal, "Foreword," in Baring, *Uprising in East Germany*; Ann L. Phillips, *Soviet Foreign Policy toward East Germany Reconsidered: The Postwar Decade* (New York: Greenwood Press, 1986), 130–35; and Rolf Steininger, *The German Question: The Stalin Note of 1953 and the Problem of Reunification*, trans. Jane T. Hedges (New York: Columbia University Press, 1990). Notable among scholars who contend that the Soviets never intended to give up East Germany is James Richter, "Re-examining Soviet Policy towards Germany in 1953," *Europe-Asia Studies* 45 (1993): 671–91.

7. See, for example, Secretary of State to Foreign Minister Schuman, 18 March 1952, *FR: 1952–1954*, 7(1):185. Acheson states: "Our main purpose sh[ou]ld be to drive ahead with the signature and ratification of the EDC and the contractual relations with Ger[many] and that we sh[ou]ld not permit the Russians to accomplish their obvious purpose of frustrating both by delay."

8. David Holloway, *Stalin and the Bomb: The Soviet Union and Atomic Energy, 1939–1946* (New Haven: Yale University Press, 1994), 268–70; Robert C. Tucker, *The Soviet Political Mind: Stalinism and Post-Stalin Change* (New York: W. W. Norton, 1971), 94–95, 100–102; Amy Knight, *Beria: Stalin's First Lieutenant* (Princeton: Princeton University Press, 1993), 182, 184–85; William J. Tompson, *Khrushchev: A Political Life* (New York: St. Martin's Press, 1995), 118–19.

9. Chargé in the Soviet Union Beam to Department of State, 18 March 1953, *FR: 1952–1954*, 8:1131n.

10. Hughes Diary, 11 March 1953, Emmet J. Hughes Papers, Seeley G. Mudd Manuscript Library (SGMML), Princeton, N.J.; Minutes, NSC Meeting, 11 March 1953, *FR: 1952–1954*, 8:1121.

11. Minutes, NSC Meeting, 11 March 1953, *FR: 1952–1954*, 8:1122.

12. The following account of Eisenhower's meeting with Hughes is taken from the Hughes Diary, 16 March 1953, Hughes Papers, SGMML, Princeton, N.J.

13. Hughes Diary, 17 March 1953, Hughes Papers, SGMML, Princeton, N.J.

14. Herbert S. Parmet, *Eisenhower and the American Crusades* (New York: Macmillan, 1972), 277.

15. Townsend Hoopes, *The Devil and John Foster Dulles* (Boston: Little, Brown, 1973), 170–71.

16. Minutes, NSC Meeting, 11 March 1953, Ann C. Whitman File, NSC Series, Dwight David Eisenhower Library (DDEL), Abilene, Kans.

17. Ole R. Holsti, "Cognitive Dynamics and Images of the Enemy: Dulles and Russia," in *Enemies in Politics*, ed. David J. Finlay et al. (Chicago: Rand McNally, 1967), 25–96; John Lewis Gaddis, *Strategies of Containment* (New York: Oxford University Press, 1982), 137–38; Hoopes, *The Devil and John Foster Dulles*, 170–71; Ronald W. Pruessen, *John Foster Dulles: The Road to Power* (New York: Free Press, 1982), 286–88, 290; Anthony Clark Arend, *Pursuing a Just and Durable Peace: John Foster Dulles and International Organization* (New York: Greenwood Press, 1988), 228–29.

18. Hughes Diary, 27 March and 1 April 1953, Hughes Papers, SGMML, Princeton, N.J.; David J. Dallin, *Soviet Foreign Policy after Stalin* (Philadelphia: J. B. Lippincott, 1962), 126–27.

19. Albert Resis, ed., *Molotov Remembers: Inside Kremlin Politics, Conversations with Felix Chuev* (Chicago: Ivan R. Dee, 1993), 75; Richard P. Stebbins, *The United States in World Affairs: 1953* (New York: Harper & Brothers, 1955), 120–21; Holloway, *Stalin and the Bomb*, 333–34.

20. Hughes Diary, 2 April 1953, Hughes Papers, SGMML, Princeton, N.J.; Stebbins, *The United States in World Affairs: 1953*, 123; Memorandum by Carlton Savage of the Policy Planning Staff to the Director of the Staff (Nitze), 1 April 1953, *FR: 1952–1954*, 8:1138.

21. W. W. Rostow, *Europe after Stalin: Eisenhower's Three Decisions of March 11, 1953* (Austin: University of Texas Press, 1982), 48; Nitze to Dulles, 2 April 1953, John Foster Dulles Papers, Draft Correspondence and Speech Series, "President's Speech April 1953 (1)," DDEL, Abilene, Kans.; Minutes, NSC Meeting, 8 April 1953, Whitman File, NSC Series, DDEL, Abilene, Kans.

22. Stebbins, *The United States in World Affairs: 1953*, 125; Hughes Diary, 9 April 1953, Hughes Papers, SGMML, Princeton, N.J.

23. Hughes Diary, 28 March 1953, Hughes Papers, SGMML, Princeton, N.J. See also Dulles's comments at a 31 March NSC meeting: "The current peace offensive is designed by the Soviets to relieve the ever-increasing pressure upon their regime. Accordingly, we must not relax this pressure until the Soviets give promise of ending the struggle" (*FR: 1952–1954*, 2[1]:268).

24. Hughes Diary, 29 March and 3 April 1953, Hughes Papers, SGMML, Princeton, N.J.

25. When Undersecretary of State Walter Bedell Smith confided to Eisenhower that the State Department was opposed to the speech, the president was shocked: "I just don't understand what the hell you mean. Why the State Department has been present at every meeting of the NSC when this has been discussed, and they've never said they're opposed" (Hughes Diary, 11 April 1953, Hughes Papers, SGMML, Princeton, N.J.).

26. Dulles to Hughes, 10 April 1953, Dulles Papers, Draft Correspondence and Speech Series, "President's Speech April 1953 (1)," DDEL, Abilene, Kans.; Hughes Diary, 11 April 1953, Hughes Papers, SGMML, Princeton, N.J.

27. Dallin, *Soviet Foreign Policy after Stalin*, 249.

28. Hoopes, *The Devil and John Foster Dulles*, 172; Hughes Diary, 12 April 1953, Hughes Papers, SGMML, Princeton, N.J.

29. Hughes Diary, 11 April 1953, Hughes Papers, SGMML, Princeton, N.J.

30. Hughes Diary, 6 April 1953, Hughes Papers, SGMML, Princeton, N.J.

31. Address by President Eisenhower, 16 April 1953, reprinted in *FR: 1952–1954*, 8:1151–52.

32. Dulles, "The Eisenhower Foreign Policy: A World-wide Peace Offensive," in Rostow, *Europe after Stalin*, 130; Hoopes, *The Devil and John Foster Dulles*, 173.

33. Bohlen to Washington, 25 April 1953, *FR: 1952–1954*, 8:1162–63; Georgi Arbatov, *The System: An Insider's Life in Soviet Politics* (New York: Times Books, 1992), 43–44.

34. Rostow, *Europe after Stalin*, 74–75; Piers Brendon, *Ike: His Life and Times* (New York: Harper & Row, 1986), 250; Parmet, *Eisenhower*, 242; Richard I. Immerman, "Eisenhower and Dulles: Who Made the Decisions?" *Political Psychology* 1 (1979): 16; Coral Bell, *Negotiation from Strength: A Study in the Politics of Power* (New York: Alfred A. Knopf, 1963; Westport, Conn.: Greenwood Press, 1977), 109 (page citations are to the reprint edition); Minutes, Cabinet Meeting, Hughes Diary, 16 March 1953, Hughes Papers, SGMML, Princeton, N.J.

35. For a discussion of the historiographic debate over Eisenhower, see Vincent De Santis, "Eisenhower Revisionism," *Review of Politics* 38 (1976): 190–207; Gary Reichard, "Eisenhower as President: The Changing View," *South Atlantic Quarterly* 77 (1979): 265–81; Mary McAuliff, "Commentary: Eisenhower, the President," *Journal of American History* 68 (1981): 625–31; Arthur M. Schlesinger Jr., "The Ike Age Revisited," *Reviews in American History* 11 (1983): 1–11; and Stephen G. Rabe, "Eisenhower Revisionism," *Diplomatic History* 17 (1993): 97–115. Prominent Eisenhower revisionists include Immerman, "Eisenhower and Dulles," 21–38; Fred I. Greenstein, "Eisenhower as an Activist President: A New Look at the Evidence," *Political Science Quarterly* 94 (1979–80): 575–99; idem, *The Hidden Hand Presidency: Eisenhower as Leader* (New York: Basic Books, 1982); Blanche Wiesen Cook, *Declassified Eisenhower: A Divided Legacy of Peace and Political Warfare* (Garden City, N.Y.: Doubleday, 1981); Stephen E. Ambrose, *Eisenhower: The President*, vol. 2 (New York: Simon & Schuster, 1984); and Robert A. Divine, *Eisenhower and the Cold War* (Oxford: Oxford University Press, 1981).

36. Rostow, *Europe after Stalin*, 74, 80.

37. Philip E. Mosely, "The Kremlin's Foreign Policy since Stalin," *Foreign Affairs* 32 (1953): 21.

38. Ibid., 21–22; Boris I. Nicolaevsky, *Power and the Soviet Elite: 'The Letter of an Old Bolshevik' and Other Essays by Boris I. Nicolaevsky*, ed. Janet D. Zagoria (New York: Frederick A. Praeger, 1965), 146.

39. Hughes Diary, 1 April 1953, Hughes Papers, SGMML, Princeton, N.J.; Peter Lyon, *Eisenhower: Portrait of the Hero* (Boston: Little, Brown, 1974), 537.

40. Baras, "Beria's Fall and Ulbricht's Survival," 383–84; Baring, *Uprising in East Germany*, 20–21; Christian Ostermann, "New Documents on the East German Uprising of 1953," in Woodrow Wilson International Center for Scholars, *Cold War International History Project Bulletin* (Spring 1995), 10–11.

41. Resis, ed., *Molotov Remembers*, 334.

42. Ibid., 334–35, 336–37.

43. Richter, "Re-examining Soviet Policy towards Germany in 1953," 682.

44. Resis, ed., *Molotov Remembers,* 335–36.

45. Baras, "Beria's Fall and Ulbricht's Survival," 385; Baring, *Uprising in East Germany,* 26; Ostermann, "New Documents," 12.

46. Steininger, *The German Question,* 110–11.

47. Heinz Brandt, *The Search for a Third Way: My Path between East and West,* trans. Salvator Attanasio (Garden City, N.Y.: Doubleday, 1970), 200.

48. Steininger, *The German Question,* 110–11.

49. Acting U.S. High Commissioner for Germany Reber to the Department of State, 16 June 1953, *FR: 1952–1954,* 7(1):471.

50. Baring, *Uprising in East Germany,* 33, 67, 72–73; Ostermann, "New Documents," 13.

51. Nikita S. Khrushchev, *Khrushchev Remembers,* trans. and ed. Strobe Talbott (Boston: Little, Brown, 1970), 331–38; Resis, ed., *Molotov Remembers,* 343–45; Knight, *Beria,* 191–99.

52. Rachel A. Connell, "New Evidence on Beria's Downfall," in Woodrow Wilson International Center for Scholars, *Cold War International History Project Bulletin* (Spring 1992), 17, 27.

53. Richter, "Re-examining Soviet Policy towards Germany in 1953," 678–80; Ostermann, "New Documents," 16; Brandt, *The Search for a Third Way,* 230–31, 241. The new documentary evidence supports the interpretation in Baras, "Beria's Fall and Ulbricht's Survival," 390–95.

54. Andrei Gromyko, *Memories,* trans. Harold Shukman (London: Hutchinson, 1989), 316–17; N. S. Khrushchev, "Aktskii," in *Beria: Konets kar'ery* (Moscow: Politizdat, 1991), 262, cited in Richter, "Re-examining Soviet Policy towards Germany in 1953," 683.

55. A transcript of the July 1953 Central Committee Plenum held to discuss the crimes of Beria was printed in *Izvestia CC-CPSU: 1991,* 1:140–214 and 2:141–208. The Central Committee of the Communist Party sponsored publication of party documents in *Izvestia CC CPSU,* a specialized journal. An English translation was later published as D. M. Stickle, ed., *The Beria Affair: The Secret Transcripts of the Meetings Signaling the End of Stalinism* (New York: Nova Science Publishers, 1992); the quotation from Malenkov is on p. 7. Also see Richter, "Re-examining Soviet Policy towards Germany in 1953," 684.

56. Stickle, ed., *The Beria Affair,* 28.

57. Stickle, ed., *The Beria Affair,* 22.

58. Resis, ed., *Molotov Remembers,* 337–38, 338–39; Khrushchev, *Khrushchev Remembers,* trans. and ed. Talbott, 393, 546.

59. The 24 June 1953 Russian Foreign Ministry document written by Sokolovsky, Semenov, and Yudin is translated and reprinted in Woodrow Wilson International Center for Scholars, *Cold War International History Project Bulletin* (Spring 1995), 10ff.; Richard Lowenthal, "Foreword," in Baring, *Uprising in East Germany,* xxv; Steininger, *The German Question,* 111.

60. Telephone Conversation with Allen Dulles, 10 July 1953, Dulles Papers, Telephone Conversations Series, "July 1953–October 31, 1953 (5)," DDEL, Abilene, Kans.; Bohlen to Department of State, 7 July 1953, *FR: 1952–1954,* 8:1195–96.

61. Gerhard Wettig, "Stalin and German Reunification: Archival Evidence on Soviet Foreign Policy in Spring 1952," *Historical Journal* 37 (1994): 411–19; Staritz, "The SED, Stalin, and the German Question."

62. Brandt, *The Search for a Third Way*, 189–90, 198–99.

63. Minutes, NSC Meeting, 7 July 1955, *FR: 1955–1957*, 5:276–77; M. S. Handler, "Bonn to Expedite Arms Bills to Bar Neutrality Move," *New York Times*, 21 May 1955; "Peace Maneuvers" (editorial), *New York Times*, 22 May 1955; and James Reston, "A Problem in Publicity," *New York Times*, 25 May 1955.

64. Minutes, NSC Meeting, 13 August 1953, *FR: 1952–1954*, 7(1):504; NSC 160/1, "United States Position with Respect to Germany," 17 August 1953, ibid., 516; Brian R. Duchin, "The 'Agonizing Reappraisal': Eisenhower, Dulles, and the EDC," *Diplomatic History* 16 (1992): 208–9, 215.

65. NSC 160/1, 17 August 1953, *FR: 1952–1954*, 7(1):515, 517–18.

66. At an NSC meeting, for example, Eisenhower stated that "we should look on the presence of U.S. armed forces in friendly countries abroad as invariably an emergency measure rather than as a normal aspect of United States policy" (Minutes, NSC Meeting, 7 July 1955, *FR: 1955–1957*, 5:274).

67. Bennett Kovrig, *Of Walls and Bridges: The United States and Eastern Europe* (New York: New York University Press, 1991), 55.

68. Hughes Diary, 7 April 1953, Hughes Papers, SGMML, Princeton, N.J.

69. Dulles observed that Molotov, who was "undoubtedly the ablest and shrewdest diplomat since Machiavelli," was "determined to defeat and destroy European unity at this moment when it seemed on the very point of consummation" (Minutes, NSC Meeting, 18 June 1953, *FR: 1952–1954*, 7(2):1588).

70. Stebbins, *The United States in World Affairs: 1953*, 188; Department of State to the Embassy of the Soviet Union, 15 July 1953, *FR: 1952–1954*, 7(1): 601–2; Rostow, *Europe after Stalin*, 65.

71. Soviet Ministry for Foreign Affairs to the Embassy of the United States, 4 August 1953, *FR: 1952–1954*, 7(1):604–7.

72. Editorial Note, ibid., 8:1184–85.

73. Georgi M. Malenkov, "We Will Never Step Aside" (speech delivered to the Supreme Soviet of the USSR, 8 August 1953), *Vital Speeches* 19 (1953): 679–91.

74. Bohlen to Department of State, 10 August 1953, *FR: 1952–1954*, 8:1212.

75. Tompson, *Khrushchev*, 127–28, 135–36.

76. Vladislav Zubok, "Soviet Intelligence and the Cold War: The 'Small' Committee of Information, 1952–1954," *Diplomatic History* 19 (1995): 469–70.

77. Stebbins, *The United States in World Affairs: 1953*, 382–83; Soviet Ministry of Foreign Affairs to the Embassy of the United States, 26 November 1953, *FR: 1952–1954*, 7(1):673–77.

78. Ann C. Whitman Diary, 2 December 1953, Whitman File, "Ann C. Whitman Diary Nov.–Dec. 1953 (2)," DDEL, Abilene, Kans; Minutes, NSC Meeting, 21 January 1954, *FR: 1952–1954*, 7(1):781.

79. Memorandum by Secretary of State, 6 September 1953, *FR: 1952–1954*, 2(1):457–60; Memorandum by President to Secretary of State, 8 September 1953, ibid., 458, 460–61.

80. NSC 162/2, 30 October 1953, *FR: 1952–1954*, 2(1):579; Stebbins, *The United States in World Affairs: 1953*, 124.

81. U.S. Delegation at the Berlin Conference to Department of State, 25 January 1954, *FR: 1952–1954*, 7(1):813; U.S. Delegation at Berlin to Department of State, 3 February 1954, ibid., 937; U.S. Delegation at Berlin Conference to De-

partment of State, 5–6 February 1954, ibid., 956–57, 966–67, 981; Berlin to Washington, 13 February 1954, Whitman File, Dulles-Herter Series, "Dulles, John Foster, Feb. 1954 (1)," DDEL, Abilene, Kans.

82. Arnold L. Horelick and Myron Rush, *Strategic Power and Soviet Foreign Policy* (Chicago: University of Chicago Press, 1966), 30–31; John Foster Dulles, *Evolution of Foreign Policy*, a speech to the Council on Foreign Relations, 12 January 1954 (Washington, D.C.: Government Printing Office, 1954), 3–4.

83. Herbert S. Dinerstein, *War and the Soviet Union: Nuclear Weapons and the Revolution in Soviet Military and Political Thinking*, rev. ed. (New York: Praeger, 1962), 101–2; Horelick and Rush, *Strategic Power and Soviet Foreign Policy*, 19; Holloway, *Stalin and the Bomb*, 336.

84. Richter, *Khrushchev's Double Bind*, 38–39; Charles E. Bohlen, *Witness to History* (New York: W. W. Norton, 1971), 370; Holloway, *Stalin and the Bomb*, 337.

85. Dinerstein, *War and the Soviet Union*, 100, 104.

86. Hough and Fainsod, *How the Soviet Union Is Governed*, 208.

87. Dinerstein, *War and the Soviet Union*, 110–11; Richter, *Khrushchev's Double Bind*, 48.

88. Dinerstein, *War and the Soviet Union*, 73, 112–13; Holloway, *Stalin and the Bomb*, 338.

89. Adam B. Ulam, *Expansion and Coexistence: Soviet Foreign Policy, 1917–73*, 2d ed. (New York: Holt, Rinehart & Winston, 1974), 554–55; Tompson, *Khrushchev*, 139; Richter, *Khrushchev's Double Bind*, 49–50.

90. Bohlen, *Witness to History*, 367, 369; Dinerstein, *War and the Soviet Union*, 125; Jonathan Haslam, "Soviet Policy toward Western Europe since World War II," in *Learning in U.S. and Soviet Foreign Policy*, ed. George W. Breslauer and Philip E. Tetlock (Boulder, Colo.: Westview Press, 1991), 480.

91. Dinerstein, *War and the Soviet Union*, 116–17; Robert Conquest, *Power and Policy in the U.S.S.R.: The Struggle for Stalin's Succession, 1945–1960* (London: Macmillan, 1961; New York: Harper & Row, Harper Torchbooks, 1967), 245–55 (page citations are to the reprint edition).

92. Bohlen, *Witness to History*, 371; Khrushchev, *Khrushchev Remembers*, trans. and ed. Talbott, 393.

93. Tompson, *Khrushchev*, 141; Holloway, *Stalin and the Bomb*, 338–39.

94. Dinerstein, *War and the Soviet Union*, 144–45; Tompson, *Khrushchev*, 143. Bulganin, for example, in his first speech as premier, stated: "We believe that there are healthy forces in the capitalist countries who will find the means to improve relations between countries in the interests of peace and the security of the peoples" (*Pravda*, 10 February 1955, quoted in Richter, *Khrushchev's Double Bind*, 67).

95. Nikita S. Khrushchev, *Khrushchev Remembers: The Glasnost Tapes*, trans. and ed. Jerrold L. Schecter and Vyacheslav V. Luchkov (Boston: Little, Brown, 1990), 69, 71, 78; Richter, *Khrushchev's Double Bind*, 44, 70; Holloway, *Stalin and the Bomb*, 340; Anatoly Dobrynin, *In Confidence: Moscow's Ambassador to America's Six Cold War Presidents (1962–1986)* (New York: Random House, Times Books, 1995), 32.

96. Audrey Kurth Cronin, *Great Power Politics and the Struggle over Austria, 1945–1955* (Ithaca: Cornell University Press, 1986), 145, 148–50; Deborah Welch

Larson, "Crisis Prevention and the Austrian State Treaty," *International Organization* 41 (1987): 44, 46–47.

97. Cronin, *Great Power Politics and the Struggle over Austria*, 151; *New York Times*, 10 May 1955; "The 'Deed' We Wanted?" *Nation*, 23 April 1955, 339; Alexander Kendrick, "Fishing for Germany with Austrian Bait," *New Republic*, 2 May 1955, 11–12. The Soviets relinquished their right under the previous treaty draft to 60 percent of Austrian oil production, 420,000 tons of Austrian refinery capacity, concessions for oil exploration and exploitation for thirty-five years, and title to the Danube Shipping Company. In return, Austria promised it would pay the Soviets $150 million in goods as compensation for former German assets and $2 million for the Danube Shipping Company. In addition, the Austrians agreed to provide the Soviet Union with 10 million tons of oil over ten years in payment for the Soviet share of Austrian oil enterprises. See John MacCormack, "Austrian Treaty Set for Signing as Soviet Yields," *New York Times*, 13 May 1955; William Lloyd Stearman, *The Soviet Union and the Occupation of Austria* (Bonn: Siegler, 1961), 150.

98. Stearman, *The Soviet Union and the Occupation of Austria*, 162; James Reston, "Soviet's New Tactics," *New York Times*, 21 April 1955; Dallin, *Soviet Foreign Policy after Stalin*, 262–65, 278–79; Wolfram F. Hanrieder, *The Stable Crisis: Two Decades of German Foreign Policy* (New York: Harper & Row, 1970), 92–95; Michael Balfour, *West Germany* (New York: Praeger, 1968), 217.

99. *New York Times*, 19 May 1955; Khrushchev, *Khrushchev Remembers: The Glasnost Tapes*, trans. and ed. Schecter and Luchkov, 80.

100. *New York Times*, 17 April and 12 May 1955; Dwight D. Eisenhower, *Mandate for Change: 1953–1956* (Garden City, N.Y.: Doubleday, 1963), 505–6.

101. Eisenhower to Churchill, 1 December 1954, Whitman File, DDE Diary Series, "December 1954 (1)," DDEL, Abilene, Kans.

102. "When the Big Four Meet," *New Republic*, 23 May 1955, 8; Bernhard G. Bechhoefer, *Postwar Negotiations for Arms Control* (Washington: Brookings, 1961), 291–95.

103. Progress Report Prepared by Stassen, 26 May 1955, *FR: 1955–1957*, 20: 96–97; Richter, *Khrushchev's Double Bind*, 70; Roschin quoted in Holloway, *Stalin and the Bomb*, 340–41.

104. Minutes, NSC Meeting, 19 May 1955, Whitman File, NSC Series, DDEL, Abilene, Kans. At a June 1955 NSC meeting, Dulles again stated that "he believed that the Soviets genuinely wanted some reduction in the armament burdens in order to be able to deal more effectively with their severe internal problems. Accordingly, the Soviet Union may be prepared to make concessions." See Minutes, NSC Meeting, 30 June 1955, *FR: 1955–1957*, 20: 150–51.

105. Bechhoefer, *Postwar Negotiations for Arms Control*, 312–14.

106. Jerome H. Kahan, *Security in the Nuclear Age: Developing U.S. Strategic Arms Policy* (Washington: Brookings, 1975), 31; Minutes, NSC Meeting, 30 June 1955, *FR: 1955–1957*, 20:148.

107. Kenneth W. Thompson, "The Strengths and Weaknesses of Eisenhower's Leadership," in *Reevaluating Eisenhower: American Foreign Policy in the 1950s*, ed. Richard A. Melanson and David Mayers (Urbana: University of Illinois Press, 1987), 22; Richard A. Melanson, "The Foundations of Eisenhower's Foreign Policy: Continuity, Community, and Consensus," ibid., 58; Douglas

Kinnard, *President Eisenhower and Strategy Management: A Study in Defense Politics* (Lexington: University Press of Kentucky, 1977).

108. Memorandum of Conversation, 4 January 1955, *FR: 1955–1957*, 20:5; Draft Memorandum by the Secretary of State, 29 June 1955, ibid., 141.

109. Roschin quoted in Holloway, *Stalin and the Bomb*, 341; Minutes, NSC Meeting, 21 November 1955, *FR: 1955–1957*, 5:804–5.

110. "Toward 'Active Coexistence,'" *Nation*, 11 June 1955, 493; Khrushchev, *Khrushchev Remembers: The Glasnost Tapes*, trans and ed. Schecter and Luchkov, 103–4; Tompson, *Khrushchev*, 144–46; Hollis W. Barber, *The United States in World Affairs: 1955* (New York: Harper & Brothers, 1956), 68, 70.

111. Notes on a Bipartisan Conference, 12 July 1955, *FR: 1955–1957*, 5:307; Remarks of Secretary Dulles at Magazine Editors and Publishers Meeting, Greenbrier Hotel, White Sulphur Springs, W.Va., 23 May 1955, John Foster Dulles Papers, Box 98, SGMML, Princeton, N.J.; Eisenhower to Swede Hazlett, 15 August 1955, Whitman File, DDE Diary Series, "DDE Diary August 1955 (1)," DDEL, Abilene, Kans.

112. Eisenhower, *Mandate for Change*, 508; Barber, *The United States in World Affairs: 1955*, 60.

113. Minutes, NSC Meeting, 19 May 1955, Whitman File, NSC Series, DDEL, Abilene, Kans.; Notes on a Bipartisan Conference, 12 July 1955, *FR: 1955–1957*, 5:307.

114. Barber, *The United States in World Affairs: 1955*, 61; Livingston T. Merchant, "Recollections of the Summit Conference: Geneva July 1955," Livingston T. Merchant Papers, "Re Geneva Conference 1955 [Summit]," SGMML, Princeton, N.J., reprinted in *FR: 1955–1957*, 5:368–79.

115. John Eisenhower Diary, 21 July 1955, Whitman File, International Meetings Series, "Geneva Notes—Goodpaster, ACCO," DDEL, Abilene, Kans.; Delegation at the Geneva Conference to the Department of State, 21 July 1955, *FR: 1955 1957*, 5:452 53; Livingston T. Merchant, "Recollections of the Summit Conference," Merchant Papers, "Re Geneva Conference [Summit], SGMML, Princeton, N.J.

116. Memorandum of Conversation at Buffet, 21 July 1955, *FR: 1955–1957*, 5: 456 57; Memorandum of Conversation, Zhukov with Chief of Staff of the USAF, General N. F. Twining, 25 June 1956, Whitman File, International Series, "USSR 1956–1957," DDEL, Abilene, Kans.

117. See Lyon, *Eisenhower*, 663–64; Parmet, *Eisenhower*, 406; Evangelista, "Cooperation Theory and Disarmament," 521; and Memorandum of Meeting of Delegation at Geneva, 20 July 1955, *FR: 1955–1957*, 5:427.

118. Telephone Conversation Memorandum, 6 July 1955, Dulles Papers, Telephone Conversations Series, "March 7, 1955–August 17, 1955 (1)," DDEL, Abilene, Kans.

119. Memorandum of Meeting of Delegation at Geneva, 20 July 1955, *FR: 1955–1957*, 5:428.

120. Memorandum of Conversation, 17 July 1955, ibid., 350.

121. Eisenhower to General Alfred M. Gruenther, 25 July 1955, Whitman File, DDE Diary Series, "DDE Diary, July 1955 (1)," DDEL, Abilene, Kans.

122. Livingston T. Merchant, "Recollections of the Summit Conference," Merchant Papers, "Re Geneva Conference [Summit]," SGMML, Princeton, N.J.; Memorandum of Conversation, 21 July 1955, *FR: 1955–1957*, 5:456–57.

123. Barber, *The United States in World Affairs: 1955*, 74.

124. Raymond L. Garthoff, *Soviet Strategy in the Nuclear Age* (New York: Frederick A. Praeger, 1958), 150–51; Barber, *The United States in World Affairs: 1955*, 40–41.

125. Raymond L. Garthoff, "Estimating Soviet Military Levels: Some Light from the Past," *International Security* 14 (1990): 93–109; idem, *Soviet Strategy in the Nuclear Age*, 150–51; Nikita S. Khrushchev, *Khrushchev Remembers: The Last Testament*, trans. and ed. Strobe Talbott (Boston: Little, Brown, 1974), 220–21; idem, *Khrushchev Remembers*, trans. and ed. Talbott (see n. 51 above), 515–16; Richter, *Khrushchev's Double Bind*, 82.

126. Minutes, NSC Meeting, 11 May 1956, Whitman File, NSC Series, DDEL, Abilene, Kans.

127. Tompson, *Khrushchev*, 159–60; Tucker, *The Soviet Political Mind*, 245.

128. Khrushchev, *Khrushchev Remembers: The Glasnost Tapes*, trans. and ed. Schecter and Luchkov, 122; Veljko Micunovic, *Moscow Diary*, trans. David Floyd (Garden City, N.Y.: Doubleday, 1980), 133–34; Arbatov, *The System*, 60.

3. Disengagement, German Nuclear Weapons, and the Test Ban

1. Peter Lyon, *Eisenhower: Portrait of the Hero* (Boston: Little, Brown, 1974), 806; Piers Brendon, *Ike: His Life and Times* (New York: Harper & Row, 1986), 12, 387.

2. Stephen Ambrose, *Eisenhower*, vol. 2: *The President* (New York: Simon & Schuster, 1984), 621.

3. Minutes, NSC Meeting, 23 May 1957, Ann C. Whitman File, NSC Series, "NSC Summaries of Discussion," Dwight David Eisenhower Library (DDEL), Abilene, Kans.; DDE to Dulles, 26 March 1958, Whitman File, DDE Diary Series, "DDE Dictation March 1958," DDEL, Abilene, Kans.

4. Thomas W. Wolfe, *Soviet Power and Europe: 1945–1970* (Baltimore: Johns Hopkins University Press, 1970); Hans Speier, *Divided Berlin: The Anatomy of Soviet Political Blackmail* (New York: Frederick A. Praeger, 1961), 28–29; Jack Snyder, *Myths of Empire: Domestic Politics and International Ambition* (Ithaca: Cornell University Press, 1991), 232.

5. Carl A. Linden, *Khrushchev and the Soviet Leadership: With an Epilogue on Gorbachev*, rev. ed. (Baltimore: Johns Hopkins University Press, 1990); Roman Kolkowicz, *The Soviet Military and the Communist Party* (Princeton: Princeton University Press, 1967), 284–86; Christer Jonsson, *Soviet Bargaining Behavior: The Nuclear Test Ban Case* (New York: Columbia University Press, 1979); Lincoln P. Bloomfield, Walter C. Clemens Jr., and Franklyn Griffiths, *Khrushchev and the Arms Race* (Cambridge: MIT Press, 1966), 153–55, 174; Bruce Parrott, *Politics and Technology in the Soviet Union* (Cambridge: MIT Press, 1983), 137. Linden and Kolkowicz are part of the "conflict school" of Sovietologists who, in contradistinction to the older "totalitarian school," saw conflict among Soviet leaders as enduring and not confined to the period of leadership succession. In their view, Soviet leaders competed over policy issues, not merely over power. Other scholars who are part of this tradition include Robert Conquest, Robert Tucker, Sidney Ploss, and Wolfgang Leonhard. The totalitarian school of Soviet politics

embraces the works of Merle Fainsod, Thomas Rigby, and Myron Rush. For a discussion, see Linden, *Khrushchev and the Soviet Leadership*, 2–7.

6. Eugene J. Rosi, "Mass and Attentive Opinion on Nuclear Weapons Tests and Fallout, 1945–1963," *Public Opinion Quarterly* 29 (1965): 280–97; William J. Tompson, *Khrushchev: A Political Life* (New York: St. Martin's Press, 1995), 182, 189.

7. Memorandum of Conversation, 5 October 1957, in U.S. Department of State, *Foreign Relations of the United States: 1955–1957* (Washington, D.C.: Government Printing Office, 1990), 20:732–33 (hereafter cited as *FR*).

8. James Reston, "Approach to Russia Raises Serious Problems for U.S.," *New York Times*, 5 January 1958; Arnold Horelick and Myron Rush, *Strategic Power and Soviet Foreign Policy* (Chicago: University of Chicago Press, 1965), 42–45; Herbert S. Parmet, *Eisenhower and the American Crusades* (New York: Macmillan, 1972); Robert Osgood, *NATO: The Entangling Alliance* (Chicago: University of Chicago Press, 1962), 174–75; Ambrose, *Eisenhower*, 2:429–30.

9. Quoted in Horelick and Rush, *Strategic Power and Soviet Foreign Policy*, 43, italics omitted.

10. Ibid., 47–48; William C. Wohlforth, *The Elusive Balance: Power and Perceptions during the Cold War* (Ithaca: Cornell University Press, 1993), 52–53.

11. Richard P. Stebbins, *The United States in World Affairs: 1958* (New York: Harper & Brothers, 1959), 42–43; Coral Bell, *Negotiation from Strength: A Study in the Politics of Power* (New York: Alfred A. Knopf, 1963; Westport, Conn.: Greenwood, 1977), 185 (page citations are to the reprint edition).

12. Stebbins, *The United States in World Affairs: 1958*, 42–43; Richard G. Hewlett and Jack M. Holl, *Atoms for Peace and War, 1953–1961: Eisenhower and the Atomic Energy Commission* (Berkeley: University of California Press, 1989), 468.

13. Stebbins, *The United States in World Affairs: 1958*, 66–68; Robert Divine, *Blowing on the Wind: The Nuclear Test Ban Debate, 1954–1960* (New York: Oxford University Press, 1978), 175, Elmer Plishke, "Eisenhower's 'Correspondence Diplomacy' with the Kremlin—Case Study in Summit Diplomatics," *Journal of Politics* 30 (1968): 145–48.

14. Ambrose, *Eisenhower*, 2:439–40; Memorandum of Conversation, 4 November 1957, *FR: 1955–1957*, 19:621; Michael H. Armacost, *Politics of Weapons Innovation: The Thor-Jupiter Controversy* (New York: Columbia University Press, 1969), 188–89; David N. Schwartz, *NATO's Nuclear Dilemmas* (Washington, D.C.: Brookings, 1983), 70–71; Memorandum of Conversation, 22 November 1957, *FR: 1955–1957*, 19:691, 697.

15. Armacost, *Politics of Weapons Innovation*, 188; Harold Macmillan, *Riding the Storm: 1956–1959* (New York: Harper & Row, 1971), 334–35; Catherine McArdle Kelleher, *Germany and the Politics of Nuclear Weapons* (New York: Columbia University Press, 1975), 130–31; Schwartz, *NATO's Nuclear Dilemmas*, 70–71.

16. Telegram from the U.S. Delegation at the NATO Heads of Government Meeting to the Department of State, 17 December 1957, *FR: 1955–1957*, 4:234.

17. Telegram from U.S. Delegation at the NATO Heads of Government Meeting to the Department of State, 17 December 1957, *FR: 1955–1957*, 4:245–46.

18. Armacost, *Politics of Weapons Innovation*, 184, 187; Bell, *Negotiation from*

Strength, 192–93; Macmillan, *Riding the Storm*, 337; Richard Goold-Adams, *The Time of Power: A Reappraisal of John Foster Dulles* (London: Weidenfeld & Nichols, 1962), 270; Townsend Hoopes, *The Devil and John Foster Dulles* (Boston: Little, Brown, 1973), 430.

19. Bernhard G. Bechhoefer, *Postwar Negotiations for Arms Control* (Washington, D.C.: Brookings, 1961), 449; Memorandum from the Director of Intelligence and Research Cumming to the Secretary of State, 21 December 1957, *FR: 1955–1957*, 24:190.

20. "Red Aim: 'Summit of Summits,'" *Newsweek*, 13 January 1958, 34. See also Veljko Micunovic, *Moscow Diary*, trans. David Floyd (Garden City, N.Y.: Doubleday, 1980), 335–36; *New York Times*, 2 January 1958.

21. William J. Jorden, "Soviet Announces a Cut of 300,000 in Armed Forces," *New York Times*, 7 January 1958; J. M. Mackintosh, *Strategy and Tactics of Soviet Foreign Policy* (New York: Oxford University Press, 1963), 207.

22. Department of State to the Mission to the North Atlantic Treaty Organization, 9 January 1958, *FR: 1958–1960*, 10(1):146–48.

23. William J. Jorden, "Russian Insistent," *New York Times*, 10 January 1958; Stebbins, *The United States in World Affairs: 1958*, 45; Bechhoefer, *Postwar Negotiations for Arms Control*, 449.

24. "Red Aim: 'Summit of Summits,'" 34.

25. Macmillan, *Riding the Storm*, 467.

26. Dana Adams Schmidt, "Eisenhower Bids Soviet Join a Ban on Space War," *New York Times*, 13 January 1958.

27. Max Frankel, "Khrushchev Sets Atom Ban as Price of Curbs on ICBM," *New York Times*, 26 January 1958; Micunovic, *Moscow Diary*, 26 January 1958, 337–38.

28. *New York Times*, 1 February 1958; "Soviet Concedes a Need for Talks Prior to Summit," *New York Times*, 4 February 1958.

29. Russell Baker, "Eisenhower Urges Soviet Stop Talk, Work for Parley," *New York Times*, 18 February 1958; E. W. Kenworthy, "Eisenhower Seeks Accord by Soviet on Envoys' Talks," *New York Times*, 6 February 1958.

30. Macmillan, *Riding the Storm*, 470; E. W. Kenworthy, "U.S. Drops Demand Ministers Gather as Step to Summit," *New York Times*, 12 February 1958; idem, "Soviet, in Shift, Proposes Foreign Ministers Meet to Arrange Summit Talk," *New York Times*, 2 March 1958; Dana Adams Schmidt, "Dulles Rules Out Ministers' Talks on Soviet Terms," *New York Times*, 5 March 1958; Max Frankel, "Moscow Rejects U.S. Summit Ideas as Disappointing," *New York Times*, 25 March 1958; Dana Adams Schmidt, "Dulles Says Soviet Perils Peace by Debauching Usual Diplomacy," *New York Times*, 16 April 1958.

31. Dana Adams Schmidt, "Atom-Free Zone Rejected by U.S.," *New York Times*, 5 May 1958; Note of U.S. Ambassador to Poland, Jacob D. Bream, 3 May 1958, reprinted in Hansjakov Stehle, *The Independent Satellite: Society and Politics in Poland since 1945* (New York: Praeger, 1965), 328–29; Kenworthy, "Eisenhower Seeks Accord by Soviet on Envoys' Talks"; idem, "Soviet Envoy Sees Dulles," *New York Times*, 8 February 1958; Department of State to the Mission to the North Atlantic Treaty Organization, 21 January 1958, *FR: 1958–1960*, 10(1):1–4.

32. Osgood, *NATO*, 321; Henry A. Kissinger, *The Necessity for Choice: Prospects of American Foreign Policy* (Garden City, N.Y.: Doubleday, 1962), 160–61.

33. Adam B. Ulam, *The Rivals: America and Russia since World War II* (New York: Viking, 1971; New York: Penguin Books, 1976), 250–51 (page citations are to the reprint edition).

34. Kelleher, *Germany and the Politics of Nuclear Weapons*, 111; M. S. Handler, "All-German Talk on Unity Backed," *New York Times*, 25 February 1958; *New York Times*, 5 January 1958; M. S. Handler, "Opposition Stirs Debate," *New York Times*, 9 February 1958; Harry Gilroy, "Germans Critical of U.S. on Talks," *New York Times*, 15 February 1958.

35. Stehle, *The Independent Satellite*, 222–23, 225–26.

36. George F. Kennan, *Russia, the Atom, and the West* (New York: Harper & Brothers, 1958), 36, 38, 41–43, 45; for a summary of various proposals for disengagement, see Eugene Hinterhoff, *Disengagement* (London: Stevens & Sons, 1959).

37. Kissinger, *Necessity for Choice*, 163–64; Bloomfield, Clemens, and Griffiths, *Khrushchev and the Arms Race*, 150–51; Osgood, *NATO*, 319–21; George F. Kennan, "Disengagement Revisited," *Foreign Affairs* 37 (1959):200.

38. In December 1958, Eisenhower complained that other countries were "withdrawing forces, in spite of the fact that they are doing better financially than we at the moment; and yet when we mention withdrawing any portion of our forces, they protest vehemently." See Memorandum of Conversation with the President, 12 December 1958, Whitman File, DDE Diary Series, "Staff Notes Dec. 1958 (1)," DDEL, Abilene, Kans. For other citations, see Marc Trachtenberg, *History and Strategy* (Princeton: Princeton University Press, 1991), 160–68, 185–86. In a 9 November 1956 phone call to Secretary George Humphrey, Eisenhower said that he was interested in a mutually negotiated withdrawal of Soviet and American troops from Europe (Phone Calls, 9 November 1956, Whitman File, DDE Diary Series, "Nov. '56 Diary Staff Memos," DDEL, Abilene, Kans.). In May 1957, in response to a question from a journalist about the Soviet revival of the Eden Plan for a demilitarized zone in West and East Germany, Eisenhower replied that he would be sympathetic to such proposals for test areas of disarmament. See Goold-Adams, *The Time of Power*, 256.

39. Dana Adams Schmidt, "U.S. Insists Soviet Clarify Its Stand," *New York Times*, 4 February 1958.

40. Osgood, *NATO*, 315–16; Kennan, "Disengagement Revisited," 193.

41. William J. Jorden, "Soviet Announces Atom-Test Halt with Conditions," *New York Times*, 1 April 1958; Stebbins, *The United States in World Affairs: 1958*, 52.

42. James Reston, "Propaganda Tragedy," *New York Times*, 1 April 1958; Elie Abel, "Khrushchev Bids West Halt Tests," *New York Times*, 5 April 1958; *New York Times*, 6 April 1958; Micunovic, *Moscow Diary*, 17 February 1958, 342–43.

43. James Reston, "The Ordeal of Dulles," *New York Times*, 2 April 1958; Stebbins, *The United States in World Affairs: 1958*, 53; Divine, *Blowing on the Wind*, 200–201; E. W. Kenworthy, "Eisenhower Calls Soviet Atom Halt Just 'a Gimmick,' " *New York Times*, 3 April 1958.

44. "It Won't Wash, Mr. President," *Nation*, 12 April 1958, 305; "Costly," *Newsweek*, 14 April 1958, 32; "Mr. Gromyko's Timing," *New Republic*, 7 April 1958, 4; *New York Times*, 6 April 1958.

45. David Lawrence, "Why Suspend Only Bomb 'Tests'?" *U.S. News & World Report*, 11 April 1958, 112; "Offensive Weapon," *Time*, 7 April 1958, 15.

46. E. W. Kenworthy, "U.S. Dropped Plan to Beat Russians to Ban on H-Tests," *New York Times*, 2 April 1958; James Reston, "Propaganda Tragedy."

47. Memorandum of Conference with the President, 24 March 1958, Whitman File, DDE Diary Series, "Staff Notes March 1958 (1)," DDEL, Abilene, Kans.

48. Memorandum of Conference with the President, 24 March 1958, Whitman File, DDE Diary Series, "Staff Notes March 1958 (1)," DDEL, Abilene, Kans.

49. Memorandum of Conference with the President, 24 March 1958, Whitman File, DDE Diary Series, "Staff Notes March 1958 (1)," DDEL, Abilene, Kans.

50. Dana Adams Schmidt, "President Urges Soviet to Study Arms Inspection," *New York Times*, 9 April 1958; E. W. Kenworthy, " 'Real Reasons' for U.S. Test Stand," *New York Times*, 13 April 1958; Pre–Press Conference, 9 April 1958, Whitman File, DDE Diary Series, "Staff Notes April 1958 (2)," DDEL, Abilene, Kans.; Stebbins, *The United States in World Affairs: 1958*; Harold Jacobson and Eric Stein, *Diplomats, Scientists, and Politicians: The United States and the Nuclear Test Ban Negotiations* (Ann Arbor: University of Michigan Press, 1966), 48–49; Bechhoefer, *Postwar Negotiations for Arms Control*, 351–52. On 8 July 1957, the Soviet negotiator on the U.N. Disarmament Subcommittee, Valerian Zorin, had said that a cessation in the production of nuclear material involved a degree of outside control that no state could accept. See ibid., 362.

51. E. W. Kenworthy, "Khrushchev Note Rejects U.S. Plan for Arms Study," *New York Times*, 24 April 1958; Jacobson and Stein, *Diplomats, Scientists, and Politicians*, 49.

52. Divine, *Blowing on the Wind*, 210–11; Felix Belair, "Eisenhower Note to Khrushchev on Arms Ready," *New York Times*, 28 April 1958.

53. Memorandum for the President, 30 April 1958, John Foster Dulles Papers, White House Memoranda Series, "White House—General Correspondence 1958 (3)," DDEL, Abilene, Kans.

54. Memorandum of Conference with the President, 17 April 1958, Whitman File, DDE Diary Series, "Staff Notes April 1958 (1)," DDEL, Abilene, Kans.; Memorandum of Conference with the President, 14 May 1958, Whitman File, DDE Diary Series, "May 1958 Staff Notes (2)," DDEL, Abilene, Kans.; Donald A. Quarles, Deputy Secretary of Defense, 9 May 1958, White House Office, Staff Secretary, Subject Series, Department of Defense Subseries, "Joint Chiefs of Staff," DDEL, Abilene, Kans.

55. Divine, *Blowing on the Wind*, 215; Max Frankel, "Soviet to Attend Parley on Atoms," *New York Times*, 14 June 1958; William J. Jorden, "Soviet Requests Talk on Barring Surprise Attack," *New York Times*, 4 July 1958; Thomas J. Hamilton, "Soviet Again Shifts Approach to Summit," *New York Times*, 6 July 1958.

56. William J. Jorden, "Moscow Begins Peace Offensive," *New York Times*, 28 May 1958.

57. "Warsaw Pact Propaganda" (editorial), *New York Times*, 28 May 1958.

58. Stebbins, *The United States in World Affairs: 1958*, 64–65.

59. Felix Belair, "U.S. and Britain Give Plan to Halt A-tests if Soviet Will

Confer on Controls," *New York Times*, 23 August 1958; Stebbins, *The United States in World Affairs: 1958*, 65–66; William J. Jorden, "Moscow Accepts Oct. 31 Meeting on Atom Test Ban," *New York Times*, 31 August 1958.

60. Quoted in Divine, *Blowing on the Wind*, 238.

61. Macmillan, *Riding the Storm*, 562; Divine, *Blowing on the Wind*, 231.

62. Johan J. Holst, "Strategic Arms Control and Stability: A Retrospective Look," in *Why ABM? Policy Issues in the Missile Defense Controversy*, ed. Johan J. Holst and William Schneider (New York: Pergamon Press, 1969), 267–68, 274–75; Osgood, *NATO*, 204–5; Bechhoefer, *Postwar Negotiations for Arms Control*, 476, 478–84; "Reds Offer Plan to Curb Attacks," *New York Times*, 29 November 1958.

63. Stebbins, *The United States in World Affairs: 1958*, 86–87; Osgood, *NATO*, 210.

64. Jack M. Schick, *The Berlin Crisis: 1958–1962* (Philadelphia: University of Pennsylvania Press, 1971), 10–11.

65. Max Frankel, "Moscow Proposes West Berlin Be Free City," *New York Times*, 28 November 1958; Dana Adams Schmidt, "U.S. Refuses to Yield Its Rights," *New York Times*, 28 November 1958; Schick, *The Berlin Crisis*, 12–14, 34.

66. Linden, *Khrushchev and the Soviet Leadership*, 82; Ulam, *The Rivals*, 299–300; Pre–Press Notes, 6 August 1958, Whitman File, DDE Diary Series, "August 1958 Staff Notes (3)," DDEL, Abilene, Kans.; Harrison E. Salisbury, "Tensions Mount for Khrushchev, Too," *New York Times Magazine*, 24 August 1958; Memorandum of Conversation between Senator Humphrey and Acting Secretary of State Herter, 8 December 1958, President's Office File, Countries, "USSR-Vienna Meetings, Background Documents 1953–1961 (d) Previous Khrushchev Conversations," John F. Kennedy Library (JFKL), Boston, Mass.

67. Sydney Gruson, "Russian Implies Berlin Deadline Can Be Extended," *New York Times*, 29 November 1958; Max Frankel, "Khrushchev Hints Talk Might Delay Action on Berlin," *New York Times*, 30 November 1958; Speier, *Divided Berlin*, 11; Schick, *The Berlin Crisis*, 16–17.

68. Writers who emphasize Soviet fear of German nuclear weapons as the motivation for Khrushchev's ultimatum include Adam B. Ulam, *Expansion and Coexistence: Soviet Foreign Policy, 1917–1973*, 2d ed. (New York: Holt, Rinehart & Winston, 1974), 619–20; Schick, *The Berlin Crisis*; and Trachtenberg, *History and Strategy*, 169–234. Other scholars have suggested that Khrushchev provoked the Berlin crisis in order to get a summit. See Mackintosh, *Strategy and Tactics of Soviet Foreign Policy*, 211–12; Linden, *Khrushchev and the Soviet Leadership*, 82. Some writers have argued that Khrushchev used Berlin as a lever to obtain international recognition of the GDR and to stabilize the division of Europe. See Hannes Adomeit, *Soviet Risk-Taking and Crisis Behavior: A Theoretical and Empirical Analysis* (London: George Allen & Unwin, 1982), 306–7. More recent scholarship argues that Khrushchev was motivated both by fear of German nuclear weapons and by a desire to increase the status of the East German regime. See Hope M. Harrison, "Ulbricht and the Concrete 'Rose': New Archival Evidence on the Dynamics of Soviet East–German Relations and the Berlin Crisis, 1958–1961," Working Paper no. 5, Cold War International History Project (Woodrow Wilson International Center for Scholars, Washington, D.C., May 1993, mimeograph); Vladislav M. Zubok, "Khrushchev and the Berlin Crisis

(1958–1962)," Working Paper no. 6, Cold War International History Project (Woodrow Wilson International Center for Scholars, Washington, D.C., May 1993, mimeograph). For an analysis of alternative interpretations of Khrushchev's motives in provoking the Berlin Crisis, see Adomeit, *Soviet Risk-Taking and Crisis Behavior*, 188–94.

69. Schick, *The Berlin Crisis*, 16. At his February 1959 meeting with Khrushchev, Prime Minister Macmillan inferred that "what the Russians really wanted was for us to accept the existence of Eastern Germany with its existing frontiers." If the West preferred not to sign a peace treaty with the German Democratic Republic, Khrushchev suggested that they find some formula recognizing the frontiers de facto (Macmillan, *Riding the Storm*, 624–25). In his memoirs, Khrushchev recalls that "the international system throughout Europe was highly unstable, and therefore internal stabilization was impossible for the German Democratic Republic." The only way to relieve the dangerous tension that was building up in regard to West Berlin, Khrushchev claimed, was to conclude a peace treaty with the West. See Nikita S. Khrushchev, *Khrushchev Remembers*, trans. and ed. Strobe Talbott (Boston: Little Brown, 1970), 453.

70. James Richter, *Khrushchev's Double Bind: International Pressures and Domestic Coalition Politics* (Baltimore: Johns Hopkins University Press, 1994).

71. Harrison, "Ulbricht and the Concrete 'Rose,' " 6–7, 19–20. On Khrushchev's desire to avoid war over Berlin, see Fedor Burlatsky, *Khrushchev and the First Russian Spring*, trans. Daphne Skillen (London: Weidenfeld & Nicolson, 1991), 166–67.

72. Stehle, *The Independent Satellite*, 39; Schick, *The Berlin Crisis*, 8, 16; Ulam, *Expansion and Coexistence*, 620; Mackintosh, *Strategy and Tactics of Soviet Foreign Policy*, 205–12, 214; Trachtenberg, *History and Strategy*, 191; George F. Kennan, "Proposal for Western Survival," *New Leader*, 16 November 1959, 10.

73. Trachtenberg, *History and Strategy*, 180–91; Kelleher, *Germany and the Politics of Nuclear Weapons*, 92–93; Osgood, *NATO*, 221, 402n.

74. Harrison, "Ulbricht and the Concrete 'Rose,' " 12.

75. Trachtenberg, *History and Strategy*, 207.

76. James L. Richardson, *Germany and the Atlantic Alliance: The Interaction of Strategy and Politics* (Cambridge: Harvard University Press, 1966), 276–77, 303–4; Horelick and Rush, *Strategic Power and Soviet Foreign Policy*, 117; Wolfe, *Soviet Power and Europe*, 89; Speier, *Divided Berlin*, 28–29.

77. Horelick and Rush, *Strategic Power and Soviet Foreign Policy*, 50.

78. Linden, *Khrushchev and the Soviet Leadership*, 83–87; Jonsson, *Soviet Bargaining Behavior*, 154; Ulam, *Expansion and Coexistence*, 621; Parrott, *Politics and Technology in the Soviet Union*, 141; Tompson, *Khrushchev*, 202; Richter, *Khrushchev's Double Bind*, 109.

79. Snyder, *Myths of Empire*, 247; Richter, *Khrushchev's Double Bind*, 106–8, 117–18.

80. Telephone Calls, 27 November 1958, Whitman File, DDE Diary Series, "Telephone Nov. 1958," DDEL, Abilene Kans.; Dwight D. Eisenhower, *Waging Peace: 1956–1961* (Garden City, N.Y.: Doubleday, 1965), 333–34; Schick, *The Berlin Crisis*, 12–14.

81. Telephone Call from the President, 13 January 1959, Dulles Papers, Telephone Conversations Series, "Memoranda of Telephone Conversations—White

House, Jan. 4, 1959 to April 13, 1959," DDEL, Abilene, Kans. (quoted in Trachtenberg, *History and Strategy*, 204); E. W. Kenworthy, "Washington Relieved at Delay in a Showdown on West Berlin," *New York Times*, 29 November 1958.

82. Whitman Diary, 6 December 1958, Whitman File, DDE Diary Series, "DDE Diary Dec. 1958," DDEL, Abilene, Kans.; Hoopes, *The Devil and John Foster Dulles*, 467.

83. Richard P. Stebbins, *The United States in World Affairs: 1959* (New York: Harper & Brothers, 1960), 88–89, 144–45; Schick, *The Berlin Crisis*, 20, 34–36; Note from the United States to the Soviet Union on the Status of Berlin and the Potsdam Agreements, 31 December 1958, U.S. Department of State, *Documents on Germany: 1944–1985* (Washington, D.C.: Government Printing Office, 1985), 576.

84. Stebbins, *The United States in World Affairs: 1959*, 145–46; Schick, *The Berlin Crisis*, 20, 36–37; "A Question of Sincerity," *Newsweek*, 19 January 1959, 17.

85. Schick, *The Berlin Crisis*, 29–30, 36–39; Hoopes, *The Devil and John Foster Dulles*, 468–69.

86. At a meeting of State and Defense Department representatives at the end of January, Eisenhower decided that the United States should propose a foreign ministers' meeting on the German question to "provide a cover which would facilitate the indefinite postponement or modification by the Soviet Union of their present 'ultimatum' as regards Berlin" without Khrushchev's losing face. See Memorandum of Conclusions of White House Conference re Berlin, 29 January 1959, Dulles Papers, White House Memoranda Series, "Meetings with the President—1959 (2)," DDEL, Abilene, Kans.; Eisenhower, *Waging Peace*, 341. In March, Eisenhower told congressional leaders that the "chief advantage to negotiation" was that it would "continue the status quo past the artificial deadline laid down by the Soviets" (Memorandum of Conference with the President, 6 March 1959, Whitman File, DDE Diary Series, "Staff Notes March 1–15, 1959 (2)," DDEL, Abilene, Kans.). Also see "Comment on Khrushchev Speech of February 24," White House Office, Staff Secretary, International Series, "Khrushchev—Vol. 1 of III (3)," DDEL, Abilene, Kans.; Macmillan, *Riding the Storm*, 601, 605, 623–24; and Schick, *The Berlin Crisis*, 59.

87. Memorandum for the Record, 10 March 1959, Whitman File, DDE Diary Series, "Staff Notes March 1–15, 1959 (1)," DDEL, Abilene, Kans.; Memorandum of Conference with President Eisenhower, 6 March 1959, *FR: 1958–1960*, 8:431; Telephone Call from Dulles to Mr. Greene, 13 March 1959, Dulles Papers, Telephone Conversations Series, "January 4, 1959–May 8, 1959 (1)," DDEL, Abilene, Kans.; Telephone call from Dulles to Mr. Greene, 24 March 1959, Dulles Papers, Telephone Conversations Series, "January 4, 1959–May 8, 1959 (1)," DDEL, Abilene, Kans.; Memorandum of Conversation, Walter Reed Hospital, 20 March 1959, White House Office, Staff Secretary, International Trips and Meetings Series, "Macmillan Talks, Friday March 20, 1959," DDEL, Abilene, Kans.; Macmillan, *Riding the Storm*, 643–44.

88. Memorandum of Conversation between President Eisenhower and Secretary of State Dulles, 19 March 1959, *FR: 1958–1960*, 8:508.

89. Jacobson and Stein, *Diplomats, Scientists, and Politicians*, 136; Divine, *Blowing on the Wind*, 245–46.

90. John Lewis Gaddis, *Strategies of Containment: A Critical Appraisal of Postwar American National Security Policy* (New York: Oxford University Press, 1982), 192–93; Memorandum of Conversation, 16 January 1959, *FR: 1958–1960*, 10(1): 235.

91. Jacobson and Stein, *Diplomats, Scientists, and Politicians*, 136–37, 162–63; Divine, *Blowing on the Wind*, 251; Robert Owen to State Department, 26 June 1959, "Conversation between N. S. Khrushchev and Governor Harriman," 23 June 1959, President's Office File, Countries, "USSR-Vienna Meetings, Background Documents 1953–1961 (d) Previous Khrushchev Conversations," JFKL, Boston, Mass.

92. Memorandum of Conversation with the President, 18 February 1959, Whitman File, DDE Diary Series, "Staff Notes February 1959 (1)," DDEL, Abilene, Kans.; Memorandum of Conversation, 17 March 1959, Whitman File, DDE Diary Series, "Staff Notes, March 15–31, 1959," DDEL, Abilene, Kans.; Ambrose, *Eisenhower*, 2:522.

93. Memorandum of Conversation with the President, 19 March 1959, Whitman File, DDE Diary Series, "Staff Notes, March 15–31, 1959," DDEL, Abilene, Kans.

94. Memorandum of Conversation with the President, 25 February 1959, Whitman File, DDE Diary Series, "Staff Notes February 1959 (1)," DDEL, Abilene, Kans.; Divine, *Blowing on the Wind*, 252–53.

95. Jacobson and Stein, *Diplomats, Scientists, and Politicians*, 159–61, 166; Divine, *Blowing on the Wind*, 254; Memorandum for Dr. J. R. Killian Jr., 24 March 1959, by Lloyd V. Berkner Panel, Office of Special Assistant for Science and Technology, "Nuclear Test Suspension-Seismic Data (3)," DDEL, Abilene, Kans.; Memorandum of Conference with the President, 13 March 1959, Whitman File, DDE Diary Series, "Staff Notes, March 1–15, 1959 (1)," DDEL, Abilene, Kans.

96. Stebbins, *The United States in World Affairs: 1959*, 160–61; Jacobson and Stein, *Diplomats, Scientists, and Politicians*, 171–72; Divine, *Blowing on the Wind*, 256–57.

97. Jacobson and Stein, *Diplomats, Scientists, and Politicians*, 176–77.

98. Ibid., 181; Memorandum of Conversation with the President, 5 May 1959, Whitman File, DDE Diary Series, "Staff Notes May 1959 (3)," DDEL, Abilene, Kans.

99. Schick, *The Berlin Crisis*, 72, 78; Stebbins, *The United States in World Affairs: 1959*, 152–54.

100. Schick, *The Berlin Crisis*, 79; Memorandum of Conversation with the President, 15 June 1959, Whitman File, DDE Diary Series, "Staff Notes, June 1–15, 1959 (1)," DDEL, Abilene, Kans.

101. Memorandum of Telephone Conversation with the President, 8 July 1959, Christian A. Herter Papers, "Presidential Telephone Calls 1959 (2)," DDEL, Abilene, Kans.; Memorandum of Conversation with the President, 9 July 1959, Whitman File, DDE Diary Series, "Staff Notes 1959 (4)," DDEL, Abilene, Kans.; Memorandum of Conversation with the President, 10 July 1959, Whitman File, DDE Diary Series, "Staff Notes July 1959 (3)," DDEL, Abilene, Kans.

102. Ann C. Whitman Diary, 13 July 1959, Whitman File, "July 1959 (2)," DDEL, Abilene, Kans.; Eisenhower, *Waging Peace*, 407.

103. Memorandum of Conversation with the President, 22 July 1959, Whitman File, DDE Diary Series, "Staff Notes July 1959 (2)," DDEL, Abilene, Kans.

104. Nikita S. Khrushchev, *Khrushchev Remembers: The Last Testament*, trans. and ed. Strobe Talbott (Boston: Little, Brown, 1974), 369; Arkady N. Shevchenko, *Breaking with Moscow* (New York: Alfred A. Knopf, 1989), 92; Thompson to Dulles, 30 July 1959, White House Office, Staff Secretary, International Trips and Meetings Series, "Khrushchev Exchange of Visits, Vol. 1," DDEL, Abilene, Kans.

105. Jacobson and Stein, *Diplomats, Scientists, and Politicians*, 202–3; George B. Kistiakowsky, *A Scientist at the White House: The Private Diary of President Eisenhower's Special Assistant for Science and Technology* (Cambridge: Harvard University Press, 1976), 36; Divine, *Blowing on the Wind*, 286; Memorandum of Conversation, Meeting of Principals—Geneva Test Negotiations, 13 August 1959, Office of Special Assistant for National Security Affairs, NSC Series, Briefing Notes Subseries, "[Atomic Testing] Suspension of Nuclear Testing and Surprise Attack (4)," DDEL, Abilene, Kans.

106. Henry A. Kissinger, "The Khrushchev Visit—Dangers and Hopes," *New York Times Magazine*, 6 September 1959; "Surrender Is Not Peace" (editorial), *New York Times*, 10 August 1959; "The 'New Diplomacy'," *New Republic*, 24 August 1959, 3–4; C. L. Sulzberger, "Some Sobering Aspects of Summitry" (editorial), *New York Times*, 8 August 1959; "Cold Thaw," *Time*, 17 August 1959, 17; "The Visit—the Visitors," *Newsweek*, 17 August 1959, 21–22.

107. "Truman Would Not Have Dared Invite Stalin, Symington Says," *New York Times*, 28 September 1959; William J. Jorden, "Most in Capital Welcome Visits," *New York Times*, 4 August 1959.

108. "Not Everybody Favors Khrushchev's Visit," *U.S. News & World Report*, 17 August 1959, 65; "Spellman Warns of Soviet Threat," *New York Times*, 21 September 1959; Peter Kihss, "2,500 Anti-Communists Rally; Mayor and President Scored," *New York Times*, 18 September 1959.

109. Memorandum of Conversation, 15 September 1959, President's Office File, Countries, "USSR-Vienna Meeting, Background Documents, 1953–1961 (c) Reading Material," JFKL, Boston, Mass.

110. Memorandum of Conversation, Khrushchev-Eisenhower, 15 September 1959, President's Office File, Countries, "USSR-Vienna Meeting, Background Documents, 1953–1961 (c) Reading Material," JFKL, Boston, Mass.

111. Ann C. Whitman Diary, 16 September 1959, Whitman File, "September 1959," DDEL, Abilene, Kans.

112. Bell, *Negotiation from Strength*, 202n; Report on Khrushchev Visit to the United States, 15–27 September 1959, White House Office, Staff Secretary, International Trips and Meetings Series, "Khrushchev Visit, Sept. 1959 (5)," DDEL, Abilene, Kans.; "The Elemental Force," *Time*, 28 September 1959, 16.

113. Los Angeles to Secretary of State, from Lodge, 20 September 1959, Whitman File, International Series, "Khrushchev Visit 9/15–27/59 (1)," DDEL, Abilene, Kans.

114. Memorandum of Conversation, 21 September 1959, White House Office, Staff Secretary, International Trips and Meetings Series, "Khrushchev Exchange of Visits, Vol. 2," DDEL, Abilene, Kans.; Osgood Caruthers, "Premier at Rally," *New York Times*, 29 September 1958; Jonsson, *Soviet Bargaining Behavior*, 158.

115. Memorandum of Conversation, 27 September 1959, White House Office, Staff Secretary, International Trips and Meetings Series, "Khrushchev Visit, Sept. 1959 (3)," DDEL, Abilene, Kans.

116. Memorandum of Conversation, 27 September 1959, White House Office, Staff Secretary, International Trips and Meetings Series, "Khrushchev Visit, Sept. 1959 (3)," DDEL, Abilene, Kans.; Stebbins, *The United States in World Affairs: 1959*, 171.

117. Kolkowicz, *The Soviet Military and the Communist Party*, 149–54, 157–58, 260; Richter, *Khrushchev's Double Bind*, 121; Tompson, *Khrushchev*, 216–17.

118. Kolkowicz, *The Soviet Military and the Communist Party*, 151; Tompson, *Khrushchev*, 217.

119. Horelick and Rush, *Strategic Power and Soviet Foreign Policy*, 59.

120. Robert Gilpin, *American Scientists and Nuclear Weapons Policy* (Princeton: Princeton University Press, 1962), 246–47; Jacobson and Stein, *Diplomats, Scientists, and Politicians*, 236; Divine, *Blowing on the Wind*, 297–98.

121. Memorandum of Conference with the President, 16 October 1959, Whitman File, DDE Diary Series, "Staff Notes October 1959 (1)," DDEL, Abilene, Kans.; Kistiakowsky Diary, 11 November 1959, in Kistiakowsky, *A Scientist at the White House*, 150; Memorandum of Meeting with the Vice-President, 11 December 1959, Office of Special Assistant for National Security Affairs, NSC Series, Briefing Notes Subseries, DDEL, Abilene, Kans.

122. Divine, *Blowing on the Wind*, 299; Jacobson and Stein, *Diplomats, Scientists, and Politicians*, 240; Gilpin, *American Scientists and Nuclear Weapons Policy*, 248–49.

123. Kistiakowsky Diary, 24 March 1960, in Kistiakowsky, *A Scientist at the White House*, 282; Memorandum of Conference with the President, 24 March 1960, Whitman File, DDE Diary Series, "Staff Notes March 1960 (1)," DDEL, Abilene, Kans.

124. Kistiakowsky Diary, 29 March 1960, in Kistiakowsky, *A Scientist at the White House*, 288–89.

125. Ambrose, *Eisenhower*, 2:567, 570.

126. Michael Tatu, *Power in the Kremlin: From Khrushchev to Kosygin*, trans. Helen Katel (New York: Viking Press, 1967), 50; Jonsson, *Soviet Bargaining Behavior*, 150–51.

127. Memorandum of Conversation with the President, 16 October 1959, White House Office, Staff Secretary, State Department Subseries, DDEL, Abilene, Kans.; Report of the Working Group on Germany Including Berlin, 9 April 1960, *FR: 1958–1960*, 9:281–84; Minutes, NSC Meeting, 14 April 1960, ibid., 322.

128. Jacobson and Stein, *Diplomats, Scientists, and Politicians*, 248–49.

129. Kistiakowsky Diary, 29 March 1960, in Kistiakowsky, *A Scientist at the White House*, 288; Harold Macmillan, *Pointing the Way: 1959–1961* (London: Macmillan, 1972), 191; Charles de Gaulle, *Memoirs of Hope*, trans. Terence Kilmartin (London: Weidenfeld & Nicolson, 1971), 243–44.

130. Ulam, *Expansion and Coexistence*, 628–29. In "On Peaceful Coexistence," *Foreign Affairs* 38 (1959): 1–18, an article appearing at about the time of the Soviet leader's visit to the United States, Khrushchev advocated making progress toward disarmament by concentrating attention on "partial steps," or problems that "lend themselves most easily to a solution," such as the test ban (p. 10).

131. Michael R. Beschloss, *Mayday: Eisenhower, Khrushchev, and the U-2 Affair* (New York: Harper & Row, 1986), 133, 140, 150–51, 161, 173, 233.

132. Ambrose, *Eisenhower*, 2:568.

133. Ibid., 561–63; Kistiakowsky, *A Scientist at the White House*, 219; John Prados, *The Soviet Estimate: U.S. Intelligence Analysis and Soviet Strategic Forces* (Princeton: Princeton University Press, 1986; New York: Dial Press, 1962), 87–88 (page citations are to the reprint edition); Lawrence Freedman, *U.S. Intelligence and the Soviet Strategic Threat*, 2d ed. (Princeton: Princeton University Press, 1986), 71.

134. Ambrose, *Eisenhower*, 2:569; Beschloss, *Mayday*, 237–38.

135. Beschloss, *Mayday*, 241–42. When asked by Senator Lyndon B. Johnson why the U-2 flights were not stopped before the summit, Eisenhower replied that "the ill-fated flight had to take advantage of the weather to get the needed information that would not be available later on." See Memorandum of Conversation, Bipartisan Leaders Breakfast with the President, 26 May 1960, Whitman File, DDE Diary Series, "Staff Notes May 1960 (1)," DDEL, Abilene, Kans.

136. Ambrose, *Eisenhower*, 2:569; Beschloss, *Mayday*, 9–10.

137. Kistiakowsky, *A Scientist at the White House*, 328. See also Eisenhower, *Waging Peace*, 547; Beschloss, *Mayday*, 241.

138. Anatoly Dobrynin, *In Confidence: Moscow's Ambassador to America's Six Cold War Presidents (1962–1986)* (New York: Random House, Times Books, 1995), 39; Beschloss, *Mayday*, 359.

139. Beschloss, *Mayday*, 44; Tatu, *Power in the Kremlin*, 41, 59; Jonsson, *Soviet Bargaining Behavior*, 178; Thompson to Secretary of State, 8 September 1960, White House Office, Staff Secretary, International Series, "USSR—Vol. II of II (5)," DDEL, Abilene, Kans.; Khrushchev, *Khrushchev Remembers: The Last Testament*, trans. and ed. Talbott, 447.

140. Tatu, *Power in the Kremlin*, 42–43, 59; Ambrose, *Eisenhower*, 2:576; Dobrynin, *In Confidence*, 39 40; Beschloss, *Mayday*, 39, 58 59, 247 48; Memorandum of Conversation, Bipartisan Leaders Breakfast with the President, 16 May 1960, Whitman File, DDE Diary Series, "Staff Notes May 1960 (1)," DDEL, Abilene, Kans.

141. Tatu, *Power in the Kremlin*, 77 78.

142. Eisenhower, *Waging Peace*, 553, 555; Macmillan, *Pointing the Way*, 203; Tatu, *Power in the Kremlin*, 43; Ambrose, *Eisenhower*, 2:579; Beschloss, *Mayday*, 285–86; Dobrynin, *In Confidence*, 40–42.

143. Eisenhower, *Waging Peace*, 553–54; Beschloss, *Mayday*, 286.

144. Dobrynin, *In Confidence*, 41.

145. Ibid., 42; Beschloss, *Mayday*, 299–300.

146. Richardson, *Germany and the Atlantic Alliance*, 273; Speier, *Divided Berlin*, 89–90; Tatu, *Power in the Kremlin*, 44–45, 56–57; Richard Ned Lebow and Janice Gross Stein, *We All Lost the Cold War* (Princeton: Princeton University Press, 1994), 58.

147. Schick, *The Berlin Crisis*, 107; Annual Report of KGB Chief Aleksandr Shelepin to the Party Presidium, 14 February 1961, cited in Zubok, "Khrushchev and the Berlin Crisis," 12–13.

148. Jonsson, *Soviet Bargaining Behavior*, 215.

149. Linden, *Khrushchev and the Soviet Leadership*, 94–96; Tatu, *Power in the Kremlin*, 85; Jonsson, *Soviet Bargaining Behavior*, 162–63.

150. Tompson, *Khrushchev*, 221–22; Linden, *Khrushchev and the Soviet Leadership*, 97.

151. Tompson, *Khrushchev*, 222; Beschloss, *Mayday*, 39–40; Glenn T. Seaborg, *Kennedy, Khrushchev, and the Test Ban* (Berkeley: University of California Press, 1981), 24; Kistiakowsky, *A Scientist at the White House*, 311–12; Eisenhower, *Waging Peace*, 481.

152. "Sino-Soviet Problems Accentuated," 16 August 1960, White House Office, Staff Secretary, Subject Series, State Department Subseries, DDEL, Abilene, Kans.; Bloomfield, Clemens, and Griffiths, *Khrushchev and the Arms Race*, 127–28; Linden, *Khrushchev and the Soviet Leadership*, 102.

153. Dobrynin, *In Confidence*, 42; Fedor Burlatsky, *Khrushchev and the First Russian Spring*, trans. Daphne Skillen (London: Weidenfeld & Nicolson, 1991), 156–57.

154. Jonsson, *Soviet Bargaining Behavior*, 31.

155. Kistiakowsky, *A Scientist at the White House*, 375. For the argument that Eisenhower anticipated that the summit would fail, see, for example, Trachtenberg, *History and Strategy*, 208.

156. Richter also argues that Khrushchev might not have provoked the Berlin crisis if Eisenhower had agreed to a summit: see *Khrushchev's Double Bind*, 117.

157. Gaddis, *Strategies of Containment*, 187–88; Jerome H. Kahan, *Security in the Nuclear Age* (Washington, D.C.: Brookings, 1975), 32–33.

4. JFK, Khrushchev, and the German Question

1. Arthur M. Schlesinger Jr., *A Thousand Days: John F. Kennedy in the White House* (New York: Greenwich House, 1983; Boston: Houghton Mifflin, 1965), 345–46, 347–48, 366, 404, 921 (page citations are to the reprint edition); Theodore C. Sorensen, *Kennedy* (New York: Harper & Row, 1965), 516–17, 602–3, 745.

2. James Richter, *Khrushchev's Double Bind: International Pressures and Domestic Coalition Politics* (Baltimore: Johns Hopkins University Press, 1994), 139–40; Vladislav M. Zubok, "Khrushchev and the Berlin Crisis (1958–1962)," Working Paper no. 6, Cold War International History Project (Woodrow Wilson International Center for Scholars, Washington, D.C., May 1993, mimeograph); Hope M. Harrison, "Ulbricht and the Concrete 'Rose': New Archival Evidence on the Dynamics of Soviet–East German Relations and the Berlin Crisis, 1958–1961," Working Paper no. 5, Cold War International History Project (Woodrow Wilson International Center for Scholars, Washington, D.C., May 1993, mimeograph).

3. See, for example, Thomas G. Paterson, "Introduction: John F. Kennedy's Quest for Victory and Global Crisis," in *Kennedy's Quest for Victory: American Foreign Policy, 1961–1963*, ed. Paterson (New York: Oxford University Press, 1989), 22; Bruce Miroff, *Pragmatic Illusions: The Presidential Politics of John F. Kennedy* (New York: McKay, 1976), 12, 16; Louise Fitzsimons, *The Kennedy Doctrine* (New York: Random House, 1972), 13–15, 94–95, 98–99, 236–37; Richard J. Walton, *Cold War and Counterrevolution: The Foreign Policy of John F. Kennedy* (New York: Viking Press, 1972), chaps. 1, 5; and Michael R. Beschloss, *The Crisis Years: Kennedy and Khrushchev, 1960–1963* (New York: Harper Collins, Edward

Burlingame Books, 1991), 232–33. For a summary of the revisionist position, see Thomas Brown, *JFK: History of an Image* (Bloomington: Indiana University Press, 1988), 52–53, 56.

4. Carl A. Linden, *Khrushchev and the Soviet Leadership: With an Epilogue on Gorbachev*, rev. ed. (Baltimore: Johns Hopkins University Press, 1990); Alexander Yanov, "In the Grip of the Adversarial Paradigm: The Case of Nikita Sergeyevich Khrushchev in Retrospect," in *Reform in Russia and the U.S.S.R.*, ed. Robert O. Crummey (Urbana: University of Illinois Press, 1989), 156–81; idem, *The Drama of the Soviet 1960s: A Lost Reform* (Berkeley: University of California Press, 1984); William J. Tompson, *Khrushchev: A Political Life* (New York: St. Martin's Press, 1995); Richter, *Khrushchev's Double Bind*, 83–84, 192.

5. Allan Nevins, ed., *The Strategy of Peace: Senator John F. Kennedy* (New York: Harper & Row, 1960), 212; Jack M. Schick, *The Berlin Crisis: 1958–1962* (Philadelphia: University of Pennsylvania Press, 1971), 144; Schlesinger, *A Thousand Days*, 452; Sorensen, *Kennedy*, 617.

6. Sorensen, *Kennedy*, 511–12; Bernard J. Firestone, *The Quest for Nuclear Stability: John F. Kennedy and the Soviet Union* (Westport, Conn.: Greenwood Press, 1982), 40; Paterson, "Introduction: John F. Kennedy's Quest for Victory and Global Crisis," 5–6; Schick, *The Berlin Crisis*, 148.

7. Osgood Caruthers, "Khrushchev Eases Stand in U-2 Case in Bid to Kennedy," *New York Times*, 1 January 1961; Harry Schwartz, "Russia and Summitry," *New York Times*, 15 January 1961; Beschloss, *The Crisis Years*, 42.

8. "Khrushchev's Two Policies" (editorial), *New York Times*, 5 January 1961; [Nikita S. Khrushchev], "For New Victories of the World Communist Movement," 6 January 1961, in N. S. Khrushchov, *Communism—Peace and Happiness for the Peoples* (Moscow: Foreign Languages Publishing House, 1963), 1:17, 38–39, 41, 43, 46.

9. Osgood Caruthers, "Victory Seen by Russian," *New York Times*, 19 January 1961; "Challenge to a New President" (editorial), *New York Times*, 20 January 1961; Seymour Topping, "2-Hour Talk at Moscow," *New York Times*, 22 January 1961.

10. Schlesinger, *A Thousand Days*, 302–3.

11. W. II. Lawrence, "Nation Exhorted," *New York Times*, 21 January 1961; Dana Adams Schmidt, "U.S. to Ask Delay in Test-Ban Talks," *New York Times*, 25 January 1961; Glenn T. Seaborg, *Kennedy, Khrushchev, and the Test Ban* (Berkeley: University of California Press, 1981), 36; Schlesinger, *A Thousand Days*, 472–73; Jack Raymond, "Pentagon Speeds Rise in Arms, Defense Reappraisal Under Way," *New York Times*, 31 January 1961.

12. "Return to Quiet Diplomacy" (editorial), *New York Times*, 25 January 1961; "Kennedy Prefers Quiet Diplomacy to Summit Talks," *New York Times*, 24 January 1961; Dana Adams Schmidt, "Kennedy Confers with His Top Aides on Foreign Issues," *New York Times*, 31 January 1961.

13. "Khrushchev Sees Hope for Accord," *New York Times*, 21 January 1961.

14. "Kennedy's First News Conference," *New York Times*, 26 January 1961; Thompson to Secretary of State, 21 January 1961, President's Office File, Countries, "USSR Security 1/61–5/61," John F. Kennedy Library (JFKL), Boston, Mass.; Arkady N. Shevchenko, *Breaking with Moscow* (New York: Alfred A. Knopf, 1985), 108–9; Beschloss, *The Crisis Years*, 35–36.

15. "Return of the Airmen," *Time*, 3 February 1961, 2; James Reston, "A Change in Atmosphere," *New York Times*, 26 January 1961.

16. Reston, "A Change in Atmosphere"; Jack Raymond, "Military Curbed on 'Tough' Talks," *New York Times*, 28 January 1961; Richard P. Stebbins, *The United States in World Affairs: 1961* (New York: Harper & Brothers, 1962), 68; Sorensen, *Kennedy*, 517; Schlesinger, *A Thousand Days*, 304.

17. "President's First Report to Congress on the State of the Union," *New York Times*, 31 January 1961; Beschloss, *The Crisis Years*, 63n. For the political debate on the missile gap, see Edgar M. Bottome, *The Missile Gap: A Study of the Formulation of Military and Political Policy* (Rutherford, N.J.: Fairleigh Dickinson University Press, 1971).

18. Felix Belair Jr., "President Urges U.S. Aid to East European Nations," *New York Times*, 31 January 1961; A. Paul Kubricht, "Politics and Foreign Policy: A Brief Look at the Kennedy Administration's Eastern European Diplomacy," *Diplomatic History* 11 (1987): 55–65.

19. Desmond Ball, *Politics and Force Levels: The Strategic Missile Program of the Kennedy Administration* (Berkeley: University of California Press, 1980), 109–10, 269–70.

20. Schlesinger, *A Thousand Days*, 301; Raymond L. Garthoff, *Deterrence and the Revolution in Soviet Military Doctrine* (Washington, D.C.: Brookings, 1990), 9, 13, 16, 50; Thompson to Rusk, 6 February 1961, National Security File, Countries, "USSR General 2/2/61–2/14/61 [with note president has seen]," JFKL, Boston, Mass.

21. Notes on Discussion of the Thinking of the Soviet Leadership, 11 February 1961, National Security File, Countries, "USSR General 2/2/61–2/14/61," JFKL, Boston, Mass.; Schlesinger, *A Thousand Days*, 305; Beschloss, *The Crisis Years*, 78.

22. Stebbins, *The United States in World Affairs: 1961*, 69; Honoré M. Catudal, *Kennedy and the Berlin Wall Crisis: A Case Study in U.S. Decision Making* (Berlin: Berlin-Verlag, 1980), 40–41.

23. Jean Edward Smith, *The Defense of Berlin* (Baltimore: Johns Hopkins University Press, 1963), 230–31; Schlesinger, *A Thousand Days*, 347–48.

24. Telegram from the Embassy in the Soviet Union to the Department of State, 10 March 1961, in U.S. Department of State, *Foreign Relations of the United States: 1961–1963* (Washington, D.C.: Government Printing Office, 1993), 14:18–20 (hereafter cited as *FR*).

25. Thompson to Secretary of State, 10 March 1961, President's Office File, Countries, "USSR Security 1/61–5/61," JFKL, Boston, Mass.; Sydney Gruson, "U.S. and Britain Expect Soviet to Stall in Talk on A-Test Ban," *New York Times*, 20 March 1961; Robert Gilpin, *American Scientists and Nuclear Weapons Policy* (Princeton: Princeton University Press, 1962), 252–53.

26. "Nuclear Tests," Student Convocation at UCLA, Los Angeles, California, 2 November 1959, in *Strategy of Peace*, ed. Nevins, 22; "Disarmament," Washington, D.C., 11 December 1959, ibid., 28–29; Seaborg, *Kennedy, Khrushchev, and the Test Ban*, 36–37.

27. Seaborg, *Kennedy, Khrushchev, and the Test Ban*, 41–44, 48; Seaborg Journal, Presidential Meeting with Officials to Discuss Resumption of Geneva Test Ban Negotiations, 4 March 1961, reprinted in *FR: 1961–1963*, 7:10–11.

28. Seaborg, *Kennedy, Khrushchev, and the Test Ban*, 55–56.

29. Sydney Gruson, "New Soviet Demand Perils Reopened Test-Ban Talks," *New York Times*, 22 March 1961; Seaborg, *Kennedy, Khrushchev, and the Test Ban*, 54–55.

30. Ball, *Politics and Force Levels*, 113–25.

31. Walton, *Cold War and Counterrevolution*, 66.

32. Central Intelligence Agency, Office of Research and Reports, "Visual-Talent Coverage of the USSR in Relation to Soviet ICBM Deployment," 11 July 1960, in *Corona: America's First Satellite Program*, ed. Kevin C. Ruffner (Washington, D.C.: Center for the Study of Intelligence, Central Intelligence Agency, 1995), 107; Kenneth E. Greer, "Corona," *Studies in Intelligence*, supp. 17 (1973): 1–37, ibid., 24, 27.

33. Ball, *Politics and Force Levels*, 90–93.

34. John Prados, *The Soviet Estimate: U.S. Intelligence Analysis and Soviet Strategic Forces* (New York: Dial Press, 1982; Princeton: Princeton University Press, 1986), 117 (page citations are to the reprint edition); Ball, *Politics and Force Levels*, 46–47.

35. National Intelligence Estimate 11–8/1–61, "Strength and Deployment of Soviet Long Range Ballistic Missile Forces," 21 September 1961, in *Corona*, ed. Ruffner, 130.

36. Raymond L. Garthoff, *Intelligence Assessment and Policymaking: A Decision Point in the Kennedy Administration* (Washington, D.C.: Brookings, 1984), 16–17. In reality, as Desmond Ball points out (*Politics and Force Levels*, 156–78, 247), McNamara had privately decided on a Minuteman force of 1,000 missiles, a figure calculated to satisfy the Air Force and the hawks on Capitol Hill.

37. Memorandum for General Clifton from McGeorge Bundy, 2 March 1961, with Attachment (Central Intelligence Agency, "Compendium of Soviet Remarks on Missiles," 28 February 1961), President's Office File, Countries, "USSR General Compendium of Soviet Remarks on Missiles, 2/61," with a note dated 3/3/61: "The President read this with interest" (JFKL, Boston, Mass.).

38. Ball, *Politics and Force Levels*, 58, 121, 125–26, 173; Garthoff, *Intelligence Assessment and Policymaking*, 17–18; John Lewis Gaddis, *Strategies of Containment: A Critical Appraisal of Postwar American National Security Policy* (New York: Oxford University Press, 1982), 219. The NSC document, "Report of the Special Inter-Departmental Committee on Implications of NIE 11–8–62 and Related Intelligence," with a covering 23 August 1962 memo summarizing its content for the president, is reprinted in Garthoff, *Intelligence Assessment and Policymaking*, 37–55.

39. Lawrence Freedman, *U.S. Intelligence and the Soviet Strategic Threat*, 2d ed. (Princeton: Princeton University Press, 1986), 78–79; Ball, *Politics and Force Levels*, 176.

40. Fred Kaplan, *The Wizards of Armageddon* (New York: Simon & Schuster, 1983), 249; Ball, *Politics and Force Levels*, 39–40; John F. Kennedy, "The Missile Gap," speech before the Senate on 14 August 1958, in *Strategy of Peace*, ed. Nevins, 33–45; Albert J. Wohlstetter, "The Delicate Balance of Terror," *Foreign Affairs* 37 (1959): 211–34.

41. Ball, *Politics and Force Levels*, 181–84.

42. JFK Discussion with John Fischer, 9 December 1959, in *Strategy of Peace*, ed. Nevins, 226; Garthoff, *Intelligence Assessment and Policymaking*, 25.

43. Ball, *Politics and Force Levels*, 268; Jerome H. Kahan, *Security in the Nu-*

clear Age: Developing U.S. Strategic Arms Policy (Washington, D.C.: Brookings, 1975), 87.

44. Ball, *Politics and Force Levels*, 86–87, 93–94, 241, 247; Bottome, *The Missile Gap*, 154.

45. Linden, *Khrushchev and the Soviet Leadership*, 106–8; Yanov, "In the Grip of the Adversarial Paradigm," 168–70.

46. Michael MccGwire, *Military Objectives in Soviet Foreign Policy* (Washington, D.C.: Brookings, 1987), 26, 362; Garthoff, *Intelligence Assessment and Policymaking*, 3–4, 362.

47. MccGwire, *Military Objectives in Soviet Foreign Policy*, 361, 483–87.

48. Ibid., 26, 362; Garthoff, *Intelligence Assessment and Policymaking*, 3–4, 13. Khrushchev, and some other Soviet officials, later claimed that the chief objective behind his putting missiles in Cuba was to deter another U.S. invasion of the island. See Nikita S. Khrushchev, *Khrushchev Remembers: The Glasnost Tapes*, trans. and ed. Jerrold L. Schecter and Vyacheslav V. Luchkov (Boston: Little, Brown, 1990), 171; James G. Blight, Bruce J. Allyn, and David A. Welch, *Cuba on the Brink: Castro, the Missile Crisis, and the Soviet Collapse* (New York: Pantheon Books, 1993), 71–72, 77. For further evidence based on memoirs, interviews, and several U.S.-Soviet conferences held to recall the missile crisis, see Richard Ned Lebow and Janice Gross Stein, *We All Lost the Cold War* (Princeton: Princeton University Press, 1994), 29–32. Khrushchev was apparently worried that Kennedy might try again to overthrow Castro. Dobrynin and Burlatsky, however, doubt that the defense of Cuba was Khrushchev's chief motive for emplacing the medium-range missiles. Rather, installing the missiles was part of Khrushchev's long-range strategy to achieve parity with the United States as a basis for negotiations on Berlin and other issues. The Cubans had not requested such protection, and Soviet missiles would certainly increase the attractiveness of the island as a target. See Dobrynin, *In Confidence: Moscow's Ambassador to America's Six Cold War Presidents (1962–1986)* (New York: Random House, Times Books, 1995), 73; Fedor Burlatsky, *Khrushchev and the First Russian Spring*, trans. Daphne Skillen (London: Weidenfeld & Nicolson, 1988), 173–74. Western analysts of the Soviet Union who agree with this assessment include Raymond L. Garthoff, *Reflections on the Cuban Missile Crisis* (Washington, D.C.: Brookings, 1989), 21; and William Taubman, "The Correspondence: Khrushchev's Motives and His Views of Kennedy," *Problems of Communism* 41 (1992): 14–18. At a conference in Havana, Castro remembered that the Cuban leadership regarded the missiles as being intended to "strengthen the socialist camp—something that would, to a certain extent, improve the so-called balance of power." If the purpose of the missiles had been to defend Cuba, Castro states, then the Cubans would not have accepted them, because their presence would have turned Cuba into a "Soviet military base, and that entailed a high political cost for the image of our country" (Blight, Allyn, and Welch, *Cuba on the Brink*, 198–99). Lebow and Stein argue that Khrushchev's first priority was to rescue his domestic reforms by forcing Kennedy to recognize that the Soviet Union was a superpower deserving of respect, a recognition that would lead to negotiations and a détente: see *We All Lost the Cold War*, 61.

49. Shevchenko, *Breaking with Moscow*, 117–18; Thomas M. Nichols, *The Sacred Cause: Civil-Military Conflict over Soviet National Security, 1917–1992* (Ithaca: Cornell University Press, 1993), 73.

50. Schick, *The Berlin Crisis*, 142; Schlesinger, *A Thousand Days*, 343–44; Shevchenko, *Breaking with Moscow*, 110; Dobrynin, *In Confidence*, 44–45.

51. Telegram from the Embassy in the Soviet Union to the Department of State, 24 May 1961, *FR: 1961–1963*, 14:66, 68.

52. W. H. Lawrence, "Kennedy Asks 1.8 Billion This Year to Accelerate Space Exploration, Add Foreign Aid, Bolster Defense," *New York Times*, 26 May 1961; Jack Raymond, "Combat Build-up Set by President," *New York Times*, 26 May 1961; Stebbins, *The United States in World Affairs: 1961*, 37; Schick, *The Berlin Crisis*, 142.

53. Schlesinger, *A Thousand Days*, 347–48.

54. Memorandum of Conversation, 4 June 1961, *FR: 1961–1963*, 7:86–87.

55. Ibid., 88, 91.

56. Ibid., 14:87–88.

57. Ibid., 88–89; Schlesinger, *A Thousand Days*, 370; Sorensen, *Kennedy*, 585.

58. Memorandum of Conversation, 4 June 1961, *FR: 1961–1963*, 14:89–90; Schlesinger, *A Thousand Days*, 370; Sorensen, *Kennedy*, 585.

59. Schlesinger, *A Thousand Days*, 348; Richter, *Khrushchev's Double Bind*, 140–41; Zubok, "Khrushchev and the Berlin Crisis," 19.

60. Memorandum of Conversation, 4 June 1961, *FR: 1961–1963*, 14:90; Schlesinger, *A Thousand Days*, 371.

61. Memorandum of Conversation, 4 June 1963, *FR: 1961–1963*, 14:91.

62. Ibid., 92–93.

63. Ibid., 93–94.

64. Ibid., 94.

65. Ibid., 98.

66. Sydney Gruson, "Blunt Notes Traded by Kennedy and Khrushchev at Conference," *New York Times*, 8 June 1961; idem, "Soviet Proposed Six-Month Delay to U.S. on Berlin," *New York Times*, 11 June 1961; *FR: 1961–1963*, 14:96.

67. Record of Meeting of Comrade N. S. Khrushchev with Comrade W. Ulbricht, 30 November 1960, Russian Foreign Ministry Archives, trans. and reprinted in Harrison, "Ulbricht and the Concrete 'Rose.' "

68. Alexander L. George and Richard Smoke, *Deterrence in American Foreign Policy: Theory and Practice* (New York: Columbia University Press, 1974), 432–33; Memorandum from McGeorge Bundy to Kennedy, 29 May 1961, President's Office File, Countries, "USSR-Vienna Meetings, Background Documents, 1953–1961 (A) General," JFKL, Boston, Mass.

69. Memorandum of Conversation, 31 May 1961, *FR: 1961–1963*, 14:85.

70. Burlatsky, *Khrushchev and the First Russian Spring*, 164.

71. Meeting of Khrushchev with Ulbricht, 30 November 1960, in Harrison, "Ulbricht and the Concrete 'Rose.' " In April 1961, Khrushchev told Walter Lippmann repeatedly that he regarded the threat of war over West Berlin as a bluff. "There are no such stupid statesmen in the West," Khrushchev said, "to unleash a war in which hundreds of millions would perish just because we would sign a peace treaty with the GDR that would stipulate a special status of 'free city' for West Berlin with its 2.5 million population. . . . There are no such idiots or they have not yet been born" (quoted in Zubok, "Khrushchev and the Berlin Crisis," 18).

72. Meeting of Khrushchev with Ulbricht, 30 November 1960, in Harrison, "Ulbricht and the Concrete 'Rose.' "

73. Zubok, "Khrushchev and the Berlin Crisis," 26.

74. William J. Jorden, "Khrushchev Adds to U.S. Pessimism," *New York Times*, 16 June 1961; Osgood Caruthers, "Khrushchev Sets December 31 Deadline for German Pact," *New York Times*, 16 June 1961; idem, "Khrushchev Vows to Renew A-Tests if the West Does," *New York Times*, 22 June 1961.

75. Catudal, *Kennedy and the Berlin Wall Crisis*, 155, 157; [Khrushchev], Speech before Soviet-Vietnamese Friendship Meeting, 28 June 1961, in Khrushchov, *Communism*, 1:251.

76. Catudal, *Kennedy and the Berlin Wall Crisis*, 157; Robert J. Slusser, *The Berlin Crisis of 1961* (Baltimore: Johns Hopkins University Press, 1973), 44.

77. Smith, *The Defense of Berlin*, 293–94, 295–97; George and Smoke, *Deterrence in American Foreign Policy*, 433–34; Catudal, *Kennedy and the Berlin Wall Crisis*, 147–48, 150. For a discussion of how different images of the opponent underlay divisions among Kennedy's advisers, see Alexander L. George, "The Causal Nexus between Cognitive Beliefs and Decision-Making Behavior: The 'Operational Code' Belief System," in *Psychological Models in International Politics*, ed. Lawrence Falkowski (Boulder, Colo.: Westview Press, 1979), 116–18.

78. Catudal, *Kennedy and the Berlin Wall Crisis*, 148.

79. Report by Dean Acheson, 28 June 1961, *FR: 1961–1963*, 14:138–41.

80. Ibid., 148–51.

81. Ibid., 154–59.

82. Minutes, NSC Meeting, 13 July 1961, National Security File, Countries, "Germany Berlin General 7/23/61–7/26/61," JFKL, Boston, Mass.; Minutes, NSC Meeting, 19 July 1961, National Security File, Countries, "Germany: Berlin: Subjects Berlin Steering Group 7/7/61–9/11/61 and Undated," JFKL, Boston, Mass.; Schlesinger, *A Thousand Days*, 389; Sorensen, *Kennedy*, 589.

83. Catudal, *Kennedy and the Berlin Wall Crisis*, 148–49, 150; George, "The Causal Nexus between Cognitive Beliefs and Decision-Making Behavior," 116; Schlesinger, *A Thousand Days*, 383–84.

84. Catudal, *Kennedy and the Berlin Wall Crisis*, 148–49; Memorandum from Henry A. Kissinger to Bundy, 14 July 1961, National Security File, Countries, "Germany Berlin General 7/4/61," JFKL, Boston, Mass.

85. Memorandum from Kissinger to Mr. Bundy, 15 July 1961, National Security File, Meetings and Memoranda, "Henry Kissinger 8/61–7/61," JFKL, Boston, Mass.; Schlesinger, *A Thousand Days*, 389–90; Catudal, *Kennedy and the Berlin Wall Crisis*, 176–77.

86. Schlesinger, *A Thousand Days*, 385.

87. Memorandum from the President's Special Assistant Schlesinger to President Kennedy, 7 July 1961, *FR: 1961–1963*, 14:173–76; Schlesinger, *A Thousand Days*, 387.

88. Memorandum from the President's Special Assistant for National Security Affairs to Secretary of State Rusk, Secretary of Defense McNamara, and Secretary of the Treasury Dillon, 7 July 1961, *FR: 1961–1963*, 14:176–77; Schlesinger, *A Thousand Days*, 388–89.

89. [Khrushchev], Speech at a Reception for Graduates of Military Academies, 8 July 1961, in Khrushchov, *Communism*, 1:291–93, 302–3, 306. Khrushchev suspended troop reductions that were half completed; he did not roll them back. See Raymond L. Garthoff, "Estimating Soviet Military Force Levels: Some Light from the Past," *International Security* 14 (1990): 102.

90. Harry Schwartz, "New Soviet Policy Represents a Shift in Khrushchev's Goals," *New York Times*, 31 July 1961; Slusser, *The Berlin Crisis of 1961*, 57–58; Sidney Ploss, *Conflict and Decisionmaking in Soviet Russia: A Case Study of Agricultural Policy, 1953–1963* (Princeton: Princeton University Press, 1965), 228–31.

91. George and Smoke, *Deterrence in American Foreign Policy*, 436–37; Catudal, *Kennedy and the Berlin Wall Crisis*, 176–77, 180; Sorensen, *Kennedy*, 590; Memorandum from Bundy to Kennedy, 19 July 1961, *FR: 1961–1963*, 14:216–18; Minutes, NSC Meeting, 19 July 1961, ibid., 219–22; Memorandum to Sorensen from McGeorge Bundy, 22 July 1961, National Security File, Countries, "Germany—Berlin General 7/19–61–7/22–61," JFKL, Boston, Mass.; National Security Action Memorandum no. 62, *FR: 1961–1963*, 14:225–26.

92. "Text of Kennedy Appeal to Nation for Increases in Spending and Armed Forces," *New York Times*, 26 July 1961.

93. Schick, *The Berlin Crisis*, 149–50. According to McGeorge Bundy, Kennedy's emphasis on West Berlin was intentional. The president defined U.S. interests in terms of what mattered most to the American government and people; he wanted Khrushchev to know precisely what the United States would defend. See McGeorge Bundy, *Danger and Survival* (New York: Random House, 1988), 367–68.

94. *New York Times*, 26 July 1961; Stebbins, *The United States in World Affairs: 1961*, 41–42; Catudal, *Kennedy and the Berlin Wall Crisis*, 181.

95. *New York Times*, 26 July 1961.

96. Sorensen, *Kennedy*, 590–91; James Reston, "The Question Kennedy Did Not Answer," *New York Times*, 26 July 1961.

97. See Seymour Topping, "Moscow Attacks Kennedy Speech," *New York Times*, 27 June 1961.

98. McCloy to Rusk, 28 July 1961, *FR: 1961–1963*, 14:233–34; McCloy to Rusk, 29 July 1961, ibid., 235.

99. McCloy to Secretary of State, 28 July 1961, ibid., 7:112; Hannes Adomeit, *Soviet Risk-Taking and Crisis Behavior: A Theoretical and Empirical Analysis* (London: George Allen & Unwin, 1982), 252–53.

100. [Khrushchev], Speech over Radio and Television, 7 August 1961, in Khrushchov, *Communism*, 1:378.

101. Ibid., 379.

102. Ibid., 383–84.

103. Ibid., 388.

104. "Khrushchev's Reply" (editorial), *New York Times*, 8 August 1961.

105. Seymour Topping, "Khrushchev Says Monster Missile Backs Peace Aim," *New York Times*, 10 August 1961.

106. [Khrushchev], Speech at Soviet-Rumanian Friendship Meeting, 11 August 1961, in Khrushchov, *Communism*, 1:337, 339, 348.

107. Seymour Topping, "Khrushchev Says Prestige Compels a German Treaty," *New York Times*, 12 August 1961.

108. Schick, *The Berlin Crisis*, 162–63.

109. Catudal, *Kennedy and the Berlin Wall Crisis*, 49–50, 209. Catudal's account of the March 1961 Warsaw Pact conference is based on testimony provided to Western intelligence services by Jan Sejna, the former Czech deputy defense minister.

110. Ibid., 164, 184. As Khrushchev recalled, "the resulting drain of workers

was creating a simply disastrous situation in the GDR, which was already suffering from a shortage of manual labor, not to mention specialized labor" (*Khrushchev Remembers*, trans. and ed. Strobe Talbott [Boston: Little, Brown, 1970], 454).

111. Catudal, *Kennedy and the Berlin Wall Crisis*, 201, 226–27; "Transcript of the President's News Conference on Foreign and Domestic Matters," *New York Times*, 11 August 1961; "Kennedy Pledges 'Every Device' for Peaceful Solution on Berlin," *New York Times*, 11 August 1961.

112. Catudal, *Kennedy and the Berlin Wall Crisis*, 37–38.

113. U.S. Department of State, *Documents on Germany: 1944–1985* (Washington, D.C.: Government Printing Office, 1985), 776–77; Smith, *The Defense of Berlin*, 271–72.

114. Memorandum for the President by McGeorge Bundy, 14 August 1961, National Security File, Countries, "Germany Berlin General 8/11/61–8/15/61," JFKL, Boston, Mass.; Minutes, Berlin Steering Group Meeting, 15 August 1961, *FR: 1961–1963*, 14:334.

115. Schick, *The Berlin Crisis*, 167; Norman Gelb, *The Berlin Wall: Kennedy, Khrushchev, and a Showdown in the Heart of Europe* (New York: Times Books, 1986), 218–19.

116. Minutes, Berlin Steering Group Meeting, 17 August 1961, *FR: 1961–1963*, 14:347–48; Schlesinger, *A Thousand Days*, 395–97; Sorensen, *Kennedy*, 594–95.

117. Memorandum for the Secretary of State, 21 August 1961, National Security File, Countries, "Germany Berlin General 8/21/61," JFKL, Boston, Mass.

118. Memorandum for the Secretary of State, 21 August 1961, National Security File, Countries, "Germany Berlin General 8/21/61," JFKL, Boston, Mass.; Memorandum to the President by McGeorge Bundy, 28 August 1961, National Security File, Countries, "Germany Berlin General 8/26/61–8/28/61," JFKL, Boston, Mass.

119. Stebbins, *The United States in World Affairs: 1961*, 87–88; Schlesinger, *A Thousand Days*, 398; Schick, *The Berlin Crisis*, 168; Richard Rovere, "Letter from Washington," *New Yorker*, 2 September 1961, 64; George and Smoke, *Deterrence in American Foreign Policy*, 440–41; Adomeit, *Soviet Risk-Taking and Crisis Behavior*, 242.

120. Seymour Topping, "Soviet Resuming Atomic Tests," *New York Times*, 31 August 1961; Seaborg, *Kennedy, Khrushchev, and the Test Ban*, 90; *New York Times*, 2 September 1961; "Explosion," *New York Times*, 3 September 1961.

121. Lincoln P. Bloomfield, Walter C. Clemens Jr., and Franklyn Griffiths, *Khrushchev and the Arms Race: Soviet Interests in Arms Control and Disarmament, 1954–1964* (Cambridge: MIT Press, 1966), 156, 267–68; Christer Jonsson, *Soviet Bargaining Behavior: The Nuclear Test Ban Case* (New York: Columbia University Press, 1979), 33; MccGwire, *Military Objectives in Soviet Foreign Policy*, 361, 480–87.

122. Meeting of President Kennedy with Congressional Leaders, 31 August 1961, Seaborg Journal, 2:120, 126–28, reprinted in *FR: 1961–1963*, 7:154–56; Editorial Note, ibid., 158–60; Seaborg, *Kennedy, Khrushchev, and the Test Ban*, 86.

123. Schlesinger, *A Thousand Days*, 482–83; National Security Action Memorandum no. 87, *FR: 1961–1963*, 7:162; Stebbins, *The United States in World Affairs: 1961*, 92; Seymour Topping, "Khrushchev Hints He Wants Respite in Berlin Dispute," *New York Times*, 8 November 1961.

124. James Reston, "A Cool Summer Visitor from Washington," *New York Times*, 6 September 1961.

125. C. L. Sulzberger, "Khrushchev Says in Interview He Is Ready to Meet with Kennedy," *New York Times*, 8 September 1961; *FR: 1961–1963*, 14:401; Slusser, *The Berlin Crisis of 1961*, 207; Pierre Salinger, *With Kennedy* (Garden City, N.Y.: Doubleday, 1966), 191–94.

126. Memorandum from President Kennedy to Secretary of State Rusk, 12 September 1961, *FR: 1961–1963*, 14:403.

127. Sorensen, *Kennedy*, 596; Schlesinger, *A Thousand Days*, 399; Memorandum of Conversation, 15 September 1961, *FR: 1961–1963*, 14:420; Ambassador Kennan to Under Secretary of State Bowles, 22 September 1961, ibid., 435–36; Rusk to the Embassy in France, 28 September 1961, ibid., 441.

128. "U.S. Source Advises Bonn to Talk to East Germany," *New York Times*, 23 September 1961; Gelb, *The Berlin Wall*, 263; "Kennedy Calls for Peace Race," *New York Times*, 26 September 1961; C. L. Sulzberger, "What the President's Speech Means," *New York Times*, 27 September 1961.

129. Khrushchev to Kennedy, 29 September 1961, *FR: 1961–1963*, 14:445. For additional letters in this "pen pal" correspondence, see ibid., 502–8, 567–80, 634–36, 643–46, 681–91, 763–66, and 819–22 as well as other *Foreign Relations* volumes.

130. Khrushchev to Kennedy, 29 September 1961, *FR: 1961–1963*, 14:448, 450.

131. Ibid., 453.

132. Rusk to the Embassy in France, 2 October 1961, ibid., 457–59.

133. Memorandum of Conversation, 6 October 1961, ibid., 471, 475, 476–77; Kennedy to Khrushchev, 16 October 1961, ibid., 506.

134. Khrushchev to Kennedy, 9 November 1961, ibid., 570.

135. "Plans to Explode 50-Megaton Bomb," *New York Times*, 18 October 1961; Max Frankel, "U.S. Believes Moscow Softens Tone, if Not Ideas, on Germany," *New York Times*, 18 October 1961.

136. "Power-Persuasions: A Delicate Balance," *Newsweek*, 30 October 1961, 13–14.

137. Joseph A. Loftus, "Gilpatric Warns U.S. Can Destroy Atom Aggressor," *New York Times*, 22 October 1961; Bundy, *Danger and Survival*, 381–82; Arnold L. Horelick and Myron Rush, *Strategic Power and Soviet Foreign Policy* (Chicago: University of Chicago Press, 1966), 84–85.

138. Schlesinger, *A Thousand Days*, 487; Seaborg, *Kennedy, Khrushchev, and the Test Ban*, 114–15; Memorandum from Bundy to President Kennedy, 9 November 1961, *FR: 1961–1963*, 7:226–27. According to Yuri Smirnov and Viktor Adamsky, two Soviet physicists who worked on the 50-megaton bomb, it was never intended to be a weapon. The 50-megaton device was unique: in effect, it was a test of the design for a 100-megaton bomb, a military force demonstration that was part of the superpower game of mutual intimidation. See Smirnov and Adamsky, "Moscow's Biggest Bomb: The 50-Megaton Test of October 1961," in Woodrow Wilson International Center for Scholars, *Cold War International History Project Bulletin* (Fall 1994), 19.

139. Seaborg, *Kennedy, Khrushchev, and the Test Ban*, 121–22.

140. Memorandum of Conversation Pertaining to Nuclear Matters, 21 December 1961, *FR: 1961–1963*, 7:274, 277.

141. Seaborg, *Kennedy, Khrushchev, and the Test Ban*, 122, 134; "Test Ban Parley

in Geneva Ended," *New York Times*, 30 January 1962; Richard P. Stebbins, *The United States in World Affairs: 1962* (New York: Harper & Row, 1963), 73.

142. Memorandum of Conversation, 21 December 1961, *FR: 1961–1963*, 14: 698–99; Kennan to Thompson, 26 December 1961, ibid., 707.

143. Ibid., 792; *New York Times*, 18 February 1962; E. W. Kenworthy, "President Scores Moscow on Berlin Air Harassment," *New York Times*, 15 March 1962; Schick, *The Berlin Crisis*, 190–91, 196.

144. Max Frankel, "U.S. Doubts Shift in Soviet Policy,"*New York Times*, 11 February 1962; Theodore Shabad, "Soviet Says It Freed Pilot to Improve U.S. Relations," *New York Times*, 11 February 1962; Stebbins, *The United States in World Affairs: 1962*, 62–63.

145. Memorandum from Kohler to Secretary of State Rusk, 10 March 1962, *FR: 1961–1963*, 15:4–5; Rusk to Kennedy and Acting Secretary Ball, 19 March 1962, ibid., 49; Memorandum of Conversation, 22 March 1962, ibid., 67–69; Paper Prepared in the U.S. Delegation, Undated, ibid., 69–71; Memorandum of Conversation, 26 March 1962, ibid., 77, 84.

146. "Draft Principles, Procedures, and Interim Steps," 3 April 1962, ibid., 95–98; Memorandum from Bundy to Rusk, 7 April 1962, ibid., 100; Memorandum of Conversation, 13 April 1962, ibid., 101–5; Sydney Gruson, "New U.S. Plan on Berlin Asks Peace Pledges," *New York Times*, 14 April 1962; "Long Convention Foreseen," *New York Times*, 14 April 1962; Schick, *The Berlin Crisis*, 200–201; Frank A. Mayer, "Adenauer and Kennedy: An Era of Distrust in German-American Relations?" *German Studies Review* 17 (1994): 93; Rusk to West German Foreign Minister Gerhard Schroeder, 14 April 1962, *FR: 1961–1963*, 15:113.

147. "Khrushchev Drops Summit Pressure," *New York Times*, 25 April 1962; Seymour Topping, "Gromyko Detects Glimpse of Hope in Berlin Dispute," *New York Times*, 25 April 1962.

148. Schick, *The Berlin Crisis*, 202–3.

149. Salinger, *With Kennedy*, 252–53; *FR: 1961–1963*, 15:141.

150. New information on Khrushchev's decision has come to light based on the recollections of Sergo Mikoyan (son of Anastas Mikoyan), Fedor Burlatsky, Sergei Khrushchev (son of the Soviet leader), and Aleksandr Alekseyev, ambassador to Cuba. See Garthoff, *Reflections on the Cuban Missile Crisis*, 21; idem, "Cuban Missile Crisis: The Soviet Story," *Foreign Policy* 72 (1988): 61–80; Bruce J. Allyn, James G. Blight, and David A. Welch, *Back to the Brink: Proceedings of the Moscow Conference on the Cuban Missile Crisis* (Lanham, Md.: University Press of America, 1992), 46, 129–30; Fedor Burlatsky, "The Lessons of Personal Diplomacy," *Problems of Communism*, special issue, 41 (1992): 9; James G. Blight, Bruce J. Allyn, and David A. Welch, *Cuba on the Brink: Castro, the Missile Crisis, and the Soviet Collapse* (New York: Pantheon Books, 1993), 77; Dobrynin, *In Confidence*, 72.

151. Garthoff, "Cuban Missile Crisis," 66; Garthoff, *Reflections on the Cuban Missile Crisis*, 21; Burlatsky, *Khrushchev and the First Russian Spring*, 164; Dobrynin, *In Confidence*, 73; Richter, *Khrushchev's Double Bind*, 150. Burlatsky bases his judgment concerning Khrushchev's intent to use the missiles to back up his position on the German question on a still-classified letter that Khrushchev wrote to Castro: see Burlatsky, "The Lessons of Personal Diplomacy," 10.

152. "Russians Resume Berlin Air Forays," *New York Times*, 24 July 1962.

153. Sydney Gruson, "2 Western Plans to Curb A-Tests Given to Soviet," *New York Times*, 28 August 1962; Stebbins, *The United States in World Affairs: 1962*, 78; Schlesinger, *A Thousand Days*, 894.

154. Sydney Gruson, "Moscow Rejects U.S.-British Plans on Nuclear Tests," *New York Times*, 29 August 1962; idem, "Soviet Again Asks Unchecked A-Ban," *New York Times*, 30 August 1962.

155. E. W. Kenworthy, "Kennedy Rejects Proposal," *New York Times*, 30 August 1962; Stebbins, *The United States in World Affairs: 1962*, 78.

156. Khrushchev to Kennedy, Undated, *FR: 1961–1963*, 15:338; Kohler to Rusk, 16 October 1962, ibid., 361; Max Frankel, "Capital Ponders Why Khrushchev Would Visit U.S.," *New York Times*, 20 October 1962; Memorandum of Conversation, 17 October 1962, *FR: 1961–1963*, 15:367; Bruce J. Allyn et al., "Essence of Revision: Moscow, Havana, and the Cuban Missile Crisis, *International Security* 14 (1989–90): 150–51.

157. Stebbins, *The United States in World Affairs: 1962*, 105–6, 110–11; Seaborg, *Kennedy, Khrushchev, and the Test Ban*, 206–7; Dobrynin, *In Confidence*, 96–97.

158. Stebbins, *The United States in World Affairs: 1962*, 97–98; Dobrynin to the USSR Ministry of Foreign Affairs, 24 October 1962, translated and reprinted in Woodrow Wilson International Center for Scholars, *Cold War International History Project Bulletin* (Spring 1995), 72–73; Sorensen, *Kennedy*, 726; Joseph Alsop, "The Soviet Deception Plan," *Washington Post*, 5 November 1962.

159. Khrushchev, *Khrushchev Remembers: The Glasnost Tapes*, trans. and ed. Schecter and Luchkov, 174.

160. Garthoff, *Reflections on the Cuban Missile Crisis*, 24, 27; idem, "Cuban Missile Crisis," 65.

161. Max Frankel, "Soviet Proffers On-Site Checking in an Atom Pact," *New York Times*, 21 January 1963; Richard P. Stebbins, *The United States in World Affairs: 1963* (New York: Harper & Row, 1964), 68; Sorensen, *Kennedy*, 728; Schlesinger, *A Thousand Days*, 895–96; Seaborg, *Kennedy, Khrushchev, and the Test Ban*, 178–80.

162. John W. Finney, "U.S. Is Encouraged," *New York Times*, 22 January 1963; Seaborg, *Kennedy, Khrushchev, and the Test Ban*, 181; Schlesinger, *A Thousand Days*, 896.

163. Hedrick Smith, "President Is Ready to Resume Tests as Parley Halts," *New York Times*, 2 February 1963; Dobrynin, *In Confidence*, 100, 103; Schlesinger, *A Thousand Days*, 897; Seaborg, *Kennedy, Khrushchev, and the Test Ban*, 184–85; Sorensen, *Kennedy*, 728.

164. Paper Prepared for the Kennedy-Macmillan Talks, 30 June 1963, *FR: 1961–1963*, 7:756.

165. Dobrynin, *In Confidence*, 104.

166. Seaborg, *Kennedy, Khrushchev, and the Test Ban*, 188–89.

167. Norman Cousins, "Notes on a 1963 Visit with Khrushchev," *Saturday Review*, 7 November 1964, 20–21, 58.

168. Kennedy to Khrushchev, 11 April 1963, *FR: 1961–1963*, 7:672–73; Kennedy and Macmillan to Khrushchev, 15 April 1963, ibid., 676–78; Kohler to Rusk, 24 April 1963, ibid., 686.

169. Khrushchev to Kennedy, 8 May 1963, ibid., 693–99.

170. Sorensen, *Kennedy*, 730–31; Schlesinger, *A Thousand Days*, 900.

171. Commencement Address at American University in Washington, 10 June 1963, *Public Papers of the Presidents: John F. Kennedy, 1963* (Washington, D.C.: Government Printing Office, 1964), 461–62.

172. Ibid., 462.

173. Ibid., 463.

174. "Senators See Possibility of Kennedy-Khrushchev Parley," *New York Times*, 11 June 1963; "An Easing of the Cold War?" *U.S. News & World Report*, 24 June 1963, 8.

175. Sam Pope Brewer, "Watch on Yemen Approved by U.N.," *New York Times*, 12 June 1963; "Giving a Little," *New Republic*, 6 July 1963, 5; Stebbins, *The United States in World Affairs: 1963*, 71; Sorensen, *Kennedy*, 733; Seaborg, *Kennedy, Khrushchev, and the Test Ban*, 218; Seymour Topping, "Detente: Kremlin Reply," *New York Times*, 16 June 1963.

176. Arthur J. Olsen, "Khrushchev Links 2 Treaty Drives," *New York Times*, 3 July 1963; "Strategy of Peace: First, a Test Ban?" *Newsweek*, 15 July 1963, 17.

177. Harriman to Rusk, 15 July 1963, *FR: 1961–1963*, 7:801; Harriman to Rusk, 27 July 1963, ibid., 862; Seaborg, *Kennedy, Khrushchev, and the Test Ban*, 218.

178. Instructions for W. Averell Harriman, 10 July 1963, National Security File, Meetings and Memoranda, "National Security Council Meetings 1963 no. 515, 7/9/63," JFKL, Boston, Mass.; Kennedy to Khrushchev, Undated, *FR: 1961–1963*, 7:798.

179. Minutes, NSC Meeting, 9 July 1963, *FR: 1961–1963*, 7:783.

180. Schlesinger, *A Thousand Days*, 906; Seaborg, *Kennedy, Khrushchev, and the Test Ban*, 241–42.

181. "Treaty Initialed," *New York Times*, 26 July 1963.

182. Tom Wicker, "President on TV, Tells Nation Treaty is 'Victory for Mankind' but Not Millennium," *New York Times*, 27 July 1963; Henry Tanner, "Test Ban Treaty Signed in Moscow," *New York Times*, 6 August 1963; U.S. Senate Committee on Foreign Relations, *Hearings: Nuclear Test Ban Treaty*, 88th Cong., 1st sess., 1963, 27; William W. Kaufman, *The McNamara Strategy* (New York: Harper & Row, 1964), 165.

183. Max Frankel, "Harriman to Lead Test-Ban Mission to Soviet in July," *New York Times*, 12 June 1963; C. L. Sulzberger, "The Cold Armistice—Phase One," *New York Times*, 31 July 1963; Stebbins, *The United States in World Affairs: 1963*, 76–77, 82; "U.S.-Soviet Expedition to Moon Suggested by Kennedy at U.N.," *New York Times*, 21 September 1963; Thomas P. Bonan, "Gromyko Calls Pact to Bar A-Arms in Space 'Possible'" *New York Times*, 3 October 1963; Thomas P. Bonan, "Big 3's Foreign Ministers Agree in Principle to Ban Orbiting of Nuclear Arms," *New York Times*, 4 October 1963; Raymond L. Garthoff, "Banning the Bomb in Outer Space," *International Security* 5 (1980–81): 34–35.

184. Stebbins, *The United States in World Affairs: 1963*, 83–84; Schlesinger, *A Thousand Days*, 920; Sorensen, *Kennedy*, 741–42; Firestone, *The Quest for Nuclear Stability*, 139.

185. Horelick and Rush, *Strategic Power and Soviet Foreign Policy*, 155; Bloomfield, Clemens, and Griffiths, *Khrushchev and the Arms Race*, 199.

186. Nikita S. Khrushchev, *Khrushchev Remembers: The Last Testament*, trans.

and ed. Strobe Talbott (Boston: Little, Brown, 1974), 146; Tompson, *Khrushchev,* 265.

187. For a summary of recent memoir literature, see Werner Hahn, "Note: Who Ousted Nikita Sergeyevich?" *Problems of Communism* 40 (1991): 109–15. See also Tompson, *Khrushchev,* 268, 270–71, 272–73; Sergei Khrushchev, *Khrushchev on Khrushchev: An Inside Account of the Man and His Era* (Boston: Little, Brown, 1990), 156–57.

188. Rusk to Ambassador Dowling, 12 May 1962, *FR: 1961–1963,* 15:144.

189. Vladislav M. Zubok, "The Missile Crisis and the Problem of Soviet Learning," *Problems of Communism,* 41 (1992): 21–22; Dobrynin, *In Confidence,* 113.

5. Success and Failure in SALT

1. For the view that there was a missed opportunity for a MIRV ban, see Seymour M. Hersh, *The Price of Power: Kissinger in the Nixon White House* (New York: Summit Books, 1983), 149; Steve Weber, *Cooperation and Discord in U.S.-Soviet Arms Control* (Princeton: Princeton University Press, 1991); Walter Isaacson, *Kissinger: A Biography* (New York: Simon & Schuster, 1992), 316–17; and Anatoly Dobrynin, *In Confidence: Moscow's Ambassador to America's Cold War Presidents (1962–1986)* (New York: Random House, Times Books, 1995), 212–13.

2. John Lewis Gaddis, *Strategies of Containment: A Critical Appraisal of Postwar American National Security Policy* (New York: Oxford University Press, 1982), chaps. 9–10; Robert S. Litwak, *Detente and the Nixon Doctrine: American Foreign Policy and the Pursuit of Stability, 1969–1976* (Cambridge: Cambridge University Press, 1984); Raymond L. Garthoff, *Detente and Confrontation: American-Soviet Relations from Nixon to Reagan,* rev. ed. (Washington, D.C.: Brookings, 1994), 11–24; Dobrynin, *In Confidence,* 194–95.

3. Garthoff, *Detente and Confrontation,* 14, 16, 28–40, 77–78; Dobrynin, *In Confidence,* 193–95; Georgi Arbatov, *The System: An Insider's Life in Soviet Politics* (New York: Times Books, 1992), 175.

4. Max Frankel, "U.S.-Soviet Ties: An Uncertain Crisis," *New York Times,* 15 October 1970; Garthoff, *Detente and Confrontation,* 29; Henry Kissinger, *Diplomacy* (New York: Simon & Schuster, 1994), 713.

5. Robert P. Semple Jr., "A Role for Disaffected and the Young Pledged," *New York Times,* 21 January 1969; James Reston, "From Partisan to President of All," *New York Times,* 21 January 1969.

6. Theodore Shabad, "Soviet Tells U.S. That It Is Ready for Missile Talks," *New York Times,* 21 January 1969; Garthoff, *Detente and Confrontation,* 19–20, 64–65; Michael MccGwire, *Military Objectives in Soviet Foreign Policy* (Washington, D.C.: Brookings, 1987), 29, 233–36, 242; Raymond L. Garthoff, "Mutual Deterrence and Strategic Arms Limitation in Soviet Policy," *International Security* 3 (1978): 126; idem, *Deterrence and the Revolution in Soviet Military Doctrine* (Washington, D.C.: Brookings, 1990), 52, 76–77; Aleksandr' G. Savel'yev and Nikolay N. Detinov, *The Big Five: Arms Control Decision-Making in the Soviet Union* (Westport, Conn.: Praeger, 1995), 3–4, 7–8; Harry Schwartz, "U.S. and Russia: Some Quiet, Private Sounds," *New York Times,* 28 January 1969.

7. Henry Kissinger, *White House Years* (Boston: Little, Brown, 1979), 143; Dobrynin, *In Confidence*, 198.

8. Kissinger, *White House Years*, 143; Dobrynin, *In Confidence*, 199.

9. Dobrynin, *In Confidence*, 200.

10. John Newhouse, *Cold Dawn: The Story of SALT* (New York: Holt, Rinehart & Winston, 1973), 141–42; Kissinger, *White House Years*, 127, 132.

11. "Text of President Nixon's News Conference on January 27, 1969," *New York Times*, 28 January 1969.

12. Kissinger, *White House Years*, 129.

13. Ibid., 133; Max Frankel, "Nixon Is Hopeful Moscow Will Help in Peacemaking," *New York Times*, 5 March 1969; Max Frankel, "Nixon Foreign-Affairs Gambles," *New York Times*, 16 March 1969.

14. "Soviet Presses U.S. over Nuclear Talks," *New York Times*, 3 February 1969; Juan de Onís, "Malik Rejects Position of U.S. on Linkage of East-West Issues," *New York Times*, 19 February 1969; Kissinger, *White House Years*, 144, 160, 266–68; Garthoff, *Detente and Confrontation*, 282–84; Richard Nixon, *RN: The Memoirs of Richard Nixon* (New York: Grosset & Dunlap, 1978), 391.

15. Dobrynin, *In Confidence*, 143–44, 189; Savel'yev and Detinov, *The Big Five*, 8. Recently, scholars have found a memorandum of a 21 February 1969 conversation between the Soviet ambassador to France, Valerian Zorin, and representatives of North Vietnam and the National Liberation Front. Zorin asked the Vietnamese Communists about the possibility of trying to push the United States toward a political settlement, but the Vietnamese argued that "the proper time" had not arrived for discussions with the Americans. Memorandum of Conversation, 21 February 1969, in Woodrow Wilson International Center for Scholars, *Cold War International History Project Bulletin* (Fall 1993), 61–62.

16. James Reston, "Washington: President Nixon and the New Soviet Line," *New York Times*, 19 March 1969; Peter Grose, "Moscow Proposes New Consulates in U.S. and Soviet," *New York Times*, 18 March 1969; Henry Kamm, "Soviet May Day, Stressing Peace, Omits Arms Show," *New York Times*, 2 May 1969; Bernard Gwertzman, "Gromyko Urges Closer U.S. Ties and Warns China," *New York Times*, 11 July 1969; Garthoff, *Detente and Confrontation*, 82.

17. Bruce Parrott, *Politics and Technology in the Soviet Union* (Cambridge: MIT Press, 1983), 239–40; Garthoff, *Detente and Confrontation*, 82–83; Michael J. Sodaro, *Moscow, Germany, and the West from Khrushchev to Gorbachev* (Ithaca: Cornell University Press, 1990), 163–64.

18. Savel'yev and Detinov, *The Big Five*, 21–22.

19. Benson D. Adams, *Ballistic Missile Defense* (New York: American Elsevier, 1971), 188, 190–93.

20. Ibid., 188–93; Alton Frye, *A Responsible Congress: The Politics of National Security* (New York: McGraw-Hill, 1975), 30, 32; Newhouse, *Cold Dawn*, 150–53.

21. Haldeman Diary, 20 March 1969, in H. R. Haldeman, *The Haldeman Diaries: Inside the Nixon White House* (New York: G. P. Putnam's Sons, 1994), 42.

22. Robert B. Semple Jr., "Nixon Proposes Revisions," *New York Times*, 15 March 1969; John W. Finney, "Nixon Chances of Getting Senate Approval in Doubt," *New York Times*, 15 March 1969; Adams, *Ballistic Missile Defense*, 199–200; James Reston, "Washington: President Nixon's Priorities," *New York Times*, 16 March 1969; Kissinger, *White House Years*, 207–8; Newhouse, *Cold Dawn*, 151.

23. Warren Weaver, "ABM Foes Beaten," *New York Times*, 7 August 1969; idem, "Agnew Acts to Break Tie though Aid Is Unneeded," *New York Times*, 7 August 1969.

24. Frye, *A Responsible Congress*, 51; Hersh, *The Price of Power*, 152.

25. "MIRV Nightmare," *New York Times*, 18 July 1969; Gerard Smith, *Doubletalk: The Story of SALT I by the Chief Negotiator* (Garden City, N.Y.: Doubleday, 1980; Lanham, Md.: University Press of America), 537 (page citations are to the reprint edition); Hersh, *Price of Power*, 150–52.

26. John W. Finney, "Moratorium on Strategic Arms Suggested by Senate ABM Foes," *New York Times*, 25 April 1969; idem, "Missile Testing Divides U.S. Aides," *New York Times*, 22 May 1969; Robert Kleiman, "Nixon Confronts a Momentous Decision on the Hydra-Headed MIRV," *New York Times*, 17 August 1969; Garthoff, *Detente and Confrontation*, 155; Hersh, *The Price of Power*, 150–52.

27. Newhouse, *Cold Dawn*, 164; Smith, *Doubletalk*, 156, 159–60; John W. Finney, "Critic Says Pentagon Chart Shows ABM to be 'Poor Defense,'" *New York Times*, 4 June 1969; idem, "Case Is Critical of Missile Policy," *New York Times*, 6 June 1969; Peter Grose, "U.S. Intelligence Doubts Soviet First-Strike Goal," *New York Times*, 18 June 1969.

28. Smith, *Doubletalk*, 161; Ted Greenwood, *Making the MIRV: A Study of Defense Decision Making* (Cambridge, Mass.: Ballinger, 1975), 139; Hersh, *The Price of Power*, 155.

29. Kissinger, *White House Years*, 138; Robert B. Semple Jr., "Nixon Considers MIRV Tests Move," *New York Times*, 20 June 1969; Hersh, *The Price of Power*, 163; Peter Grose, "U.S. Intends to Continue Missile Tests," *New York Times*, 6 June 1969; "MIRV Madness" (editorial), *New York Times*, 29 June 1969; Frye, *A Responsible Congress*, 65–66.

30. Hersh, *The Price of Power*, 155; Weber, *Cooperation and Discord in U.S.-Soviet Arms Control*, 177; John W. Finney, "U.S. Aide Cautions on MIRV Test Ban," *New York Times*, 2 July 1969; Hedrick Smith, "Nixon's Advisers Divided on Whether to Propose MIRV Test Ban to Soviet," *New York Times*, 20 August 1969; "MIRV Responsibility" (editorial), *New York Times*, 29 July 1969; John W. Finney, "Missile Testing Divides U.S. Aides," *New York Times*, 22 May 1969; Kleiman, "Nixon Confronts a Momentous Decision on the Hydra-Headed MIRV."

31. Robert B. Semple Jr., "Nixon Will Visit Rumania and 5 Countries in Asia," *New York Times*, 29 June 1969; Garthoff, *Detente and Confrontation*, 83, 151, 285–86; Nixon, *RN*, 405; Dobrynin, *In Confidence*, 202.

32. Kissinger, *White House Years*, 149; Smith, *Doubletalk*, 82–83, 90–92; Garthoff, *Detente and Confrontation*, 152–53.

33. Kissinger, *White House Years*, 541; Smith, *Doubletalk*, 119–20; Garthoff, *Detente and Confrontation*, 155, 158.

34. Kissinger, *White House Years*, 544; Garthoff, *Detente and Confrontation*, 155–56, 159.

35. Kissinger, *White House Years*, 538; Smith, *Doubletalk*, 119, 170; Hersh, *The Price of Power*, 153, 158, 166; Garthoff, *Detente and Confrontation*, 154, 165; Isaacson, *Kissinger*, 318; Greenwood, *Making the MIRV*, 133; Dobrynin, *In Confidence*, 213; Weber, *Cooperation and Discord in U.S.-Soviet Arms Control*, 194–99.

36. Smith, *Doubletalk*, 169; Hersh, *The Price of Power*, 163–64.

37. Garthoff, *Detente and Confrontation*, 158; Smith, *Doubletalk*, 170; Hersh, *The Price of Power*, 165–66; Newhouse, *Cold Dawn*, 179–80.

38. Hersh, *The Price of Power*, 163; Greenwood, *Making the MIRV*, 134–35.

39. Smith, *Doubletalk*, 172, 175–76.

40. Garthoff, *Detente and Confrontation*, 160; William Beecher, "Soviet Diplomats Said to Hint Interest in MIRV Curbs," *New York Times*, 12 March 1970; Robert Kleiman, "New Roadblock to Arms Control Progress," *New York Times*, 11 January 1970; Smith, *Doubletalk*, 165–68.

41. Garthoff, *Detente and Confrontation*, 160–61; Hedrick Smith, "President Links Political Issues to Missile Talks," *New York Times*, 28 January 1969; Marvin Kalb and Bernard Kalb, *Kissinger* (Boston: Little, Brown, 1974), 106–7; Smith, *Doubletalk*, 23; Nixon, *RN*, 415; Kissinger, *Diplomacy*, 751. Steve Weber argues that the Nixon administration missed an opportunity for a MIRV ban because U.S. officials were uncertain about the Soviet interest in observing such a ban, and overt Soviet behavior did not allow them to determine whether the Soviets would exploit U.S. restraint: see *Cooperation and Discord in U.S.-Soviet Arms Control*, 177–78, 186–87, 198–201. While our interpretations are not that far apart, my reading of the evidence suggests that opponents of a MIRV ban were not uncertain about Soviet interests; they *knew* the Soviets could not be trusted.

42. Jerome H. Kahan, *Security in the Nuclear Age* (Washington, D.C.: Brookings, 1975), 138; Weber, *Cooperation and Discord in U.S.-Soviet Arms Control*, 176, 200.

43. Kissinger, *White House Years*, 541, 544; Garthoff, *Detente and Confrontation*, 161.

44. Smith, *Doubletalk*, 125–26; Newhouse, *Cold Dawn*, 183–84.

45. Newhouse, *Cold Dawn*, 184–85; Raymond L. Garthoff, "Negotiating with the Russians: Some Lessons from SALT," *International Security* 1 (1977): 10; idem, *Detente and Confrontation*, 162–63.

46. Kissinger, *White House Years*, 547–48; Smith, *Doubletalk*, 147.

47. Kissinger, *White House Years*, 546, 548–49; Smith, *Doubletalk*, 146, 149–51; Newhouse, *Cold Dawn*, 185–86; Garthoff, *Detente and Confrontation*, 162, 165.

48. Smith, *Doubletalk*, 152; Newhouse, *Cold Dawn*, 190–91, 192; Garthoff, "Negotiating with the Russians: Some Lessons from SALT," 11; idem, *Detente and Confrontation*, 165.

49. Kalb and Kalb, *Kissinger*, 195–96; Hersh, *The Price of Power*, 230–31; Tad Szulc, *The Illusion of Peace: Foreign Policy in the Nixon Years* (New York: Viking Press, 1978), 318–19; William B. Quandt, *Decade of Decisions: American Policy toward the Arab-Israeli Conflict, 1967–1976* (Berkeley: University of California Press, 1977), 108; Kissinger, *White House Years*, 585–92.

50. Kissinger, *White House Years*, 612, 614; Hersh, *The Price of Power*, 237–38; Isaacson, *Kissinger*, 294.

51. Kissinger, *White House Years*, 635, 637–39; Garthoff, *Detente and Confrontation*, 89; Isaacson, *Kissinger*, 295–96.

52. Kissinger, *White House Years*, 641–42; Isaacson, *Kissinger*, 298.

53. Kalb and Kalb, *Kissinger*, 200–201; Kissinger, *White House Years*, 617–22; Isaacson, *Kissinger*, 299–300. Nixon's account varies on some details. According to Nixon, 300 Syrian tanks invaded Jordan on 21 September: see *RN*, 485. For a discussion of the conflicting versions, see Hersh, *The Price of Power*, 241–42.

54. Kissinger, *White House Years*, 627.

55. Kalb and Kalb, *Kissinger*, 207; Quandt, *Decade of Decisions*, 124–25; Kissinger, *White House Years*, 628–30; Isaacson, *Kissinger*, 304.

56. Quandt, *Decade of Decisions*, 124–25; Hersh, *The Price of Power*, 246–47; Isaacson, *Kissinger*, 312.

57. Kissinger, *White House Years*, 645–46; Garthoff, *Detente and Confrontation*, 89–90.

58. Kissinger, *White House Years*, 646.

59. Ibid., 646–47.

60. Ibid., 649; Garthoff, *Detente and Confrontation*, 90.

61. Terence Smith, "Denial by Moscow of Suez Violations," *New York Times*, 10 October 1970; Harry Schwartz, "Soviet Stakes in the Middle East," *New York Times*, 12 October 1970; Hedrick Smith, "U.S. and Russia: Chill in the Air Again," *New York Times*, 18 October 1970; "The Rogers-Gromyko Talks" (editorial), *New York Times*, 12 October 1970; Max Frankel, "U.S.-Soviet Ties: An Uncertain Crisis," *New York Times*, 15 October 1970.

62. Tad Szulc, "U.S. Sees Big Rise in Defense Costs if Arms Talks Fail," *New York Times*, 12 October 1970; *New York Times*, 26 September 1970.

63. "Text of Nixon's Speech to the United Nations," *New York Times*, 23 October 1970; "Action, Not Atmospherics" (editorial), *New York Times*, 21 October 1970.

64. Hedrick Smith, "U.S. and Russia: The Mood Is a Bit Warmer," *New York Times*, 25 October 1970; Bernard Gwertzman, "Kosygin Forgoes Visit to the U.N.," *New York Times*, 10 October 1970; James Reston, "Nixon and Brezhnev," *New York Times*, 20 December 1970.

65. Smith, *Doubletalk*, 192; Garthoff, *Detente and Confrontation*, 166, 170.

66. Smith, *Doubletalk*, 194–95; Garthoff, *Detente and Confrontation*, 168.

67. Dobrynin, *In Confidence*, 209.

68. Ibid.

69. Kissinger, *White House Years*, 802–3; Dobrynin, *In Confidence*, 210–11.

70. Bernard Gwertzman, "Peace and Consumer Gain Stressed at Soviet Parley," *New York Times*, 31 March 1971; David Holloway, *The Soviet Union and the Arms Race* (New Haven: Yale University Press, 1983), 88–89; Samuel B. Payne, *The Soviet Union and SALT* (Cambridge: MIT Press, 1980), 75; Dobrynin, *In Confidence*, 218.

71. Arbatov, *The System*, 171; Dobrynin, *In Confidence*, 192–93.

72. Peter M. Volten, *Brezhnev's Peace Program: A Study of Soviet Domestic Political Process and Power* (Boulder, Colo.: Westview Press, 1982), 58–63.

73. Gwertzman, "Peace and Consumer Gain Stressed at Soviet Parley"; idem, "Gromyko Urges Serious Effort to Ease Tensions," *New York Times*, 4 April 1971.

74. Dobrynin, *In Confidence*, 216–18.

75. Ibid., 219–20.

76. Victor Lusinchi, "Russian Move Opens Way for Biological Arms Ban," *New York Times*, 31 March 1971.

77. Kissinger, *White House Years*, 938–39, 946–47; Garthoff, *Detente and Confrontation*, 133. In his memoirs, Kissinger argues that Brezhnev had inadvertently reiterated previous Soviet policy without being aware of how his offer

would affect congressional politics in the United States. "Nothing illustrates better the inflexibility of the Soviets' cumbersome policymaking machinery than their decision to stick to their game plan even when confronted with the Mansfield windfall" (Kissinger, *White House Years,* 947). One statement by Brezhnev might be deemed unintentional, but it is less likely that subsequent Soviet efforts to call attention to the speech were accidental. Four Politburo members— Alexei Kosygin, Andrei P. Kirilenko, Nikolai V. Podgorny, and Kyril T. Mazurov—referred to Brezhnev's speech as a basis for negotiations. On 11 June, Brezhnev clarified that the Soviet Union was willing to discuss reductions of foreign as well as indigenous troops. See Garthoff, *Detente and Confrontation,* 133n.

78. Dobrynin, *In Confidence,* 146.

79. Max Frankel, "Compromise Set," *New York Times,* 21 May 1971; Garthoff, *Detente and Confrontation,* 167; Smith, *Doubletalk,* 225; Newhouse, *Cold Dawn,* 214.

80. William E. Griffith, *The Ostpolitik of the Federal Republic of Germany* (Cambridge: MIT Press, 1978), 205; Garthoff, *Detente and Confrontation,* 138; Karl E. Birnbaum, *East and West Germany: A Modus Vivendi* (Lexington, Mass.: Lexington Books, 1973), 15–16; Timothy Garton Ash, *In Europe's Name: Germany and the Divided Continent* (New York: Random House, 1993), 77–78.

81. Birnbaum, *East and West Germany,* 15–16, 39–40; Bernard Gwertzman, "Treaty Initialed by Moscow and Bonn," *New York Times,* 8 August 1970; Griffith, *The Ostpolitik of the Federal Republic of Germany,* 191–93; Sodaro, *Moscow, Germany, and the West,* 185; Ash, *In Europe's Name,* 75.

82. Bernard Gwertzman, "Kremlin Viewed as Stunned by Move," *New York Times,* 17 July 1971; Dobrynin, *In Confidence,* 225; Arbatov, *The System,* 179–80, 182.

83. Dobrynin, *In Confidence,* 227.

84. Ibid., 228; Smith, *Doubletalk,* 294–95, 297; Tad Szulc, "Accord Reported to Prevent War by Atomic Error," *New York Times,* 13 September 1971; *New York Times,* 25 September 1971.

85. Dobrynin, *In Confidence,* 228.

86. Kissinger, *White House Years,* 837–38; Dobrynin, *In Confidence,* 232.

87. Kissinger, *White House Years,* 830–32; Garthoff, *Detente and Confrontation,* 138–39; Birnbaum, *East and West Germany,* 41–42; Griffith, *The Ostpolitik of the Federal Republic of Germany,* 207.

88. Kissinger, *White House Years,* 1133.

89. Robert Jackson, *South Asian Crisis: India–Pakistan–Bangla Desh* (London: Chatto & Windus, 1975), 100–102, 111; Garthoff, *Detente and Confrontation,* 296, 298; Christopher Van Hollen, "The Tilt Policy Revisited: Nixon-Kissinger Geopolitics and South Asia," *Asian Survey* 20 (1980): 350. Van Hollen was deputy assistant secretary of state and was a firsthand participant in U.S. policymaking during the crisis.

90. Kissinger, *White House Years,* 897, 901; Garthoff, *Detente and Confrontation,* 300–301; Van Hollen, "The Tilt Policy Revisited," 351.

91. Kissinger, *White House Years,* 900–901.

92. Ibid., 903.

93. Ibid., 905.

94. Kalb and Kalb, *Kissinger,* 260; Kissinger, *White House Years,* 905; Isaacson, *Kissinger,* 377–78; Garthoff, *Detente and Confrontation,* 304.

95. Kissinger, *White House Years,* 908.

96. Ibid., 909.

97. Ibid., 909–10.

98. Ibid., 912; Nixon, *RN,* 529.

99. Haldeman Diary, 15 December 1971, in Haldeman, *The Haldeman Diaries,* 385.

100. Kissinger, *White House Years,* 913; Nixon, *RN,* 530.

101. Kissinger, *White House Years,* 913.

102. Van Hollen, "The Tilt Policy in South Asia," 352, 356; Jackson, *South Asian Crisis,* 128, 160; Pran Chopra, *India's Second Liberation* (Delhi: Vikas Pub. House, 1973), 212–13.

103. David K. Hall, "The Laotian War of 1962 and the Indo-Pakistani War of 1971," in *Force without War: U.S. Armed Forces as a Political Instrument,* ed. Barry M. Blechman and Stephen S. Kaplan (Washington, D.C.: Brookings, 1978), 189–90.

104. Jackson, *South Asian Crisis,* 153; Hall, "The Indo-Pakistani War of 1971," 196, 202, 216; Van Hollen, "The Tilt Policy in South Asia," 348, 356.

105. Hall, "The Indo-Pakistani War of 1971," 193–94, 201.

106. Smith, *Doubletalk,* 343; Kissinger, *White House Years,* 916.

107. Report to the Congress by Richard Nixon, 9 February 1972, *U.S. Foreign Policy for the 1970s: The Emerging Structure of Peace* (Washington, D.C.: Government Printing Office, 1972), 3:5–6, 17–18; Max Frankel, "Moscow Notes: Trust and Doubt," *New York Times,* 28 May 1972.

108. Kissinger, *White House Years,* 1113–14; Garthoff, *Detente and Confrontation,* 289.

109. Garthoff, *Detente and Confrontation,* 290; Kissinger, *White House Years,* 1120, 1135–37, 1154; Nixon, *RN,* 591–92; Isaacson, *Kissinger,* 408–11.

110. Kissinger, *White House Years,* 1144, 1146, 1147–48; Isaacson, *Kissinger,* 411; Garthoff, *Detente and Confrontation,* 290–91.

111. Newhouse, *Cold Dawn,* 242, 244; Kissinger, *White House Years,* 1148–50, 1159–60; Isaacson, *Kissinger,* 412; Smith, *Doubletalk,* 370–71.

112. Kissinger, *White House Years,* 1132, 1136, 1150–51; Alexander L. George, "The Basic Principles Agreement of 1972," in *Managing U.S.-Soviet Rivalry: Problems of Crisis Prevention,* ed. Alexander L. George (Boulder, Colo.: Westview Press, 1983), 108–9; Garthoff, *Detente and Confrontation,* 111–12.

113. Kissinger, *White House Years,* 1151.

114. ibid., 1162.

115. Dobrynin, *In Confidence,* 245; Nixon, *RN,* 594; Kissinger, *White House Years,* 1168, 1174–75, 1176–77.

116. Haldeman Diary, 3 May 1972, in Haldeman, *The Haldeman Diaries,* 452.

117. Haldeman Diary, 4 May 1972, ibid., 454; Nixon, *RN,* 602.

118. Kissinger, *White House Years,* 1178–79; Haldeman Diary, 4 May 1972, in Haldeman, *The Haldeman Diaries,* 454.

119. Haldeman Diary, 3 May 1972, in Haldeman, *Haldeman Diaries,* 452; Kissinger, *White House Years,* 1177.

120. Kissinger, *White House Years,* 1182; Dobrynin, *In Confidence,* 246.

121. Kissinger, *White House Years*, 1189; Dobrynin, *In Confidence*, 247.

122. Dobrynin, *In Confidence*, 248.

123. Arbatov, *The System*, 184; Dobrynin, *In Confidence*, 248; *New York Times*, 28 April 1972; "Survival at Bonn" (editorial), *New York Times*, 28 April 1972.

124. Garthoff, *Detente and Confrontation*, 114–15; Arbatov, *The System*, 185–86; Dobrynin, *In Confidence*, 249.

125. Smith, *Doubletalk*, 383.

126. Garthoff, *Detente and Confrontation*, 335; Dobrynin, *In Confidence*, 252–53.

127. "President Nixon and Dr. Kissinger Brief Members of Congress on Strategic Arms Limitation Agreements," 15 June, *Department of State Bulletin* 67 (10 July 1972), 42; Garthoff, *Detente and Confrontation*, 326–30, 332–33; George, "The Basic Principles Agreement of 1972," 107–8, 110; Dobrynin, *In Confidence*, 252–53.

128. George, "The Basic Principles Agreement of 1972," 109–10; Garthoff, *Detente and Confrontation*, 45–46.

129. Nixon, *RN*, 618; Garthoff, *Detente and Confrontation*, 325–26; Kalb and Kalb, *Kissinger*, 317–19; Henry Brandon, "Nixon's Way with the Russians," *New York Times Magazine*, 21 January 1973, 36; Szulc, *The Illusion of Peace*, 431; Elmo R. Zumwalt Jr., *On Watch: A Memoir* (New York: Quadrangle/New York Times Book Co., 1976), 391–94.

130. Dobrynin, *In Confidence*, 253, 256.

131. Ibid., 258.

132. Garthoff, *Detente and Confrontation*, 375.

133. George, "The Basic Principles Agreement of 1972," 111; Dobrynin, *In Confidence*, 277–78; Garthoff, *Detente and Confrontation*, 376.

134. Henry Kissinger, *Years of Upheaval* (Boston: Little, Brown, 1982), 276–84; Garthoff, *Detente and Confrontation*, 377–79; Dobrynin, *In Confidence*, 277–78.

135. Dobrynin, *In Confidence*, 278; George, "The Basic Principles Agreement of 1972," 114–15; Litwak, *Detente and the Nixon Doctrine*, 91–92; Garthoff, *Detente and Confrontation*, 380.

136. Garthoff, *Detente and Confrontation*, 347–48, 367–68, 461, 512–13.

137. Thomas M. Nichols, *The Sacred Cause: Civil-Military Conflict over Soviet National Security, 1917–1992* (Ithaca: Cornell University Press, 1993), 91, 94–97, 99, 103–4; Arbatov, *The System*, 189, 191–92, 203–4, 207; Dobrynin, *In Confidence*, 474–75.

138. Arbatov, *The System*, 189, 193–96; Dobrynin, *In Confidence*, 472–73.

139. Alexander L. George, "The Arab-Israeli War of October 1973: Origins and Impact," in *Managing U.S.-Soviet Rivalry*, ed. George, 139–54.

140. Garthoff, *Detente and Confrontation*, 732–43.

141. Ibid., 187.

142. Kissinger, *Diplomacy*, 745, 751.

6. The Allure of Defense

1. Lou Cannon, *President Reagan: The Role of a Lifetime* (New York: Simon & Schuster, 1991), 281–82.

2. Ronald Reagan, *An American Life* (New York: Simon & Schuster, 1990), 567, 589.

3. George P. Shultz, *Turmoil and Triumph: My Years as Secretary of State* (New York: Charles Scribner's Sons, 1993), 277–78.

4. Anatoly Dobrynin, *In Confidence: Moscow's Ambassador to America's Six Cold War Presidents (1962–1986)* (New York: Random House, Times Books, 1995), 484–85.

5. Shultz, *Turmoil and Triumph*, 117–19, 159–60, 162.

6. Ibid., 163.

7. Don Oberdorfer, *The Turn: How the Cold War Came to an End; The United States and the Soviet Union, 1983–1990* (London: Jonathan Cape, 1991), 16–17.

8. Ibid., 17; Shultz, *Turmoil and Triumph*, 164.

9. Shultz, *Turmoil and Triumph*, 164.

10. Dobrynin, *In Confidence*, 517–18; Shultz, *Turmoil and Triumph*, 164–65.

11. Dobrynin, *In Confidence*, 520–21; Shultz, *Turmoil and Triumph*, 167.

12. Reagan, *An American Life*, 572.

13. Ibid., 572–73; Shultz, *Turmoil and Triumph*, 171, 271–72; Oberdorfer, *The Turn*, 21.

14. Shultz, *Turmoil and Triumph*, 266–67; Reagan, *An American Life*, 568–70; "Return of the Cold Warrior?" *Newsweek*, 21 March 1983, 21–22.

15. Dobrynin, *In Confidence*, 526–27.

16. Shultz, *Turmoil and Triumph*, 257–58.

17. Dobrynin, *In Confidence*, 528; Shultz, *Turmoil and Triumph*, 260.

18. Edward Reiss, *The Strategic Defense Initiative* (Cambridge: Cambridge University Press, 1992), 32–33, 39, 42–43; Shultz, *Turmoil and Triumph*, 263; Donald R. Baucom, *The Origins of SDI, 1944–1983* (Lawrence, Kans.: University Press of Kansas, 1992), 146–55.

19. Shultz, *Turmoil and Triumph*, 246, 248–49, 261; Strobe Talbott, *The Master of the Game: Paul Nitze and the Nuclear Peace* (New York: Alfred A. Knopf, 1988), 190–93.

20. Talbott, *Master of the Game*, 193; Reiss, *The Strategic Defense Initiative*, 44, 46.

21. Shultz, *Turmoil and Triumph*, 249–56.

22. John Newhouse, "The Abolitionist—I," *New Yorker*, 2 January 1989, 39; Cannon, *President Reagan*, 740–41; Reagan, *An American Life*, 547.

23. Shultz, *Turmoil and Triumph*, 261–62; Reagan, *An American Life*, 571.

24. Shultz, *Turmoil and Triumph*, 274–76.

25. Oberdorfer, *The Turn*, 35, 46; Shultz, *Turmoil and Triumph*, 275, 281.

26. Shultz, *Turmoil and Triumph*, 361–63, 367; Raymond L. Garthoff, *The Great Transition: American-Soviet Relations and the End of the Cold War* (Washington, D.C.: Brookings, 1994), 118–19; Oberdorfer, *The Turn*, 52–53; Dobrynin, *In Confidence*, 536.

27. Dobrynin, *In Confidence*, 538–39. See also Garthoff, *The Great Transition*, 123–24n.

28. Garthoff, *The Great Transition*, 130; Dobrynin, *In Confidence*, 540–41.

29. Garthoff, *The Great Transition*, 132–33; Hannes Adomeit, "Gorbachev's Policy toward the West: Smiles and Iron Teeth," in *Soviet Foreign Policy*, ed. Robbin F. Laird, Proceedings of the Academy of Political Science, vol. 36 (1987): 100–101; Oberdorfer, *The Turn*, 68.

30. Arnold Horelick, "U.S.-Soviet Relations: The Return of Arms Control," *Foreign Affairs* 63 (1985): 517; Garthoff, *The Great Transition*, 133, 137.

31. Horelick, "U.S.-Soviet Relations," 517; Garthoff, *The Great Transition*, 143–45; Cannon, *President Reagan*, 509–10; Shultz, *Turmoil and Triumph*, 467; Dobrynin, *In Confidence*, 545.

32. Dobrynin, *In Confidence*, 551, 559; Jared Mitchell, "A Cautious Return to the Arms Table," *Maclean's*, 21 January 1985, 30; Garthoff, *The Great Transition*, 168, 171, 184, 197; Shultz, *Turmoil and Triumph*, 514–19.

33. Dobrynin, *In Confidence*, 522, 535; Jack F. Matlock Jr., *Autopsy on an Empire: The American Ambassador's Account of the Collapse of the Soviet Union* (New York: Random House, 1995), 79.

34. Seweryn Bialer, "Gorbachev's Program of Change: Sources, Significance, and Prospects," in *Gorbachev's Russia and American Foreign Policy*, ed. Seweryn Bialer and Michael Mandelbaum (Boulder, Colo.: Westview Press, 1988), 243; Robert Legvold, "War, Weapons, and Soviet Foreign Policy," ibid., 111–12; Georgi Arbatov, *The System: An Insider's Life in Soviet Politics* (New York: Times Books, 1992), 209–10.

35. "Changing the Guard," *Newsweek*, 25 March 1985, 26; Ronald D. Asmus, J. F. Brown, and Keith Crane, *Soviet Foreign Policy and the Revolutions of 1989 in Eastern Europe*, R-3903-USDP (Santa Monica, Calif.: Rand, 1991); "A Model in Trouble," *Newsweek*, 25 March 1985, 52.

36. Anders Aslund, *Gorbachev's Struggle for Economic Reform* (Ithaca: Cornell University Press, 1991), 15, 28; Michael MccGwire, *Perestroika and Soviet National Security* (Washington, D.C.: Brookings, 1991), 241, 243; Stephen White, *Gorbachev and After* (Cambridge: Cambridge University Press, 1991), 186.

37. Robert G. Kaiser, *Why Gorbachev Happened: His Triumphs and His Failure* (New York: Simon & Schuster, 1991), 87–88, 90, 92; David Remnick, *Lenin's Tomb: The Last Days of the Soviet Empire* (New York: Random House, 1993; New York: Vintage Books, 1994), 168 (page citations are to the reprint edition).

38. Dobrynin, *In Confidence*, 566–67.

39. Ibid., 569; Shultz, *Turmoil and Triumph*, 534.

40. "Gorbachev: New Label But Old Message," *U.S. News & World Report*, 22 April 1985, 27; Richard Stengel, "Up in the Air After Moscow's Gambit," *Time*, 22 April 1985, 12; Oberdorfer, *The Turn*, 114–15; Dobrynin, *In Confidence*, 570.

41. Shultz, *Triumph and Turmoil*, 537; Dobrynin, *In Confidence*, 570.

42. Shultz, *Triumph and Turmoil*, 566, 570; Dobrynin, *In Confidence*, 572–73.

43. Shultz, *Turmoil and Triumph*, 571; George Russell, "Winds of Kremlin Change," *Time*, 15 July 1985, 36; Kaiser, *Why Gorbachev Happened*, 105; Dusko Doder and Louise Branson, *Gorbachev: Heretic in the Kremlin* (New York: Viking, 1990), 96; Dobrynin, *In Confidence*, 575–76.

44. Seth Mydans, "Soviet to Stop Atomic Tests; It Bids U.S. Do Same," *New York Times*, 30 July 1985; "An Interview with Gorbachev," *Time*, 9 September 1985, 26.

45. Hedrick Smith, "U.S.-Soviet Summit Parley: Jousting for Position," *New York Times*, 30 July 1985; Gerald M. Boyd, "U.S. and Russians Make New Offers on Nuclear Tests," *New York Times*, 30 July 1985.

46. Hedrick Smith, "U.S. Strategy of Toughness: A Counter to the Russians," *New York Times*, 23 August 1985; Stephen Engelberg, "U.S. Asserts Its Protest Is Not Aimed at Talks," *New York Times*, 23 August 1985; Garthoff, *The*

Great Transition, 224. On the importance of satellites, see John Lewis Gaddis, "Learning to Live with Transparency: The Emergence of a Reconnaissance Satellite Regime," in *The Long Peace: Inquiries into the History of the Cold War* (New York: Oxford University Press, 1987), 195–214.

47. Engelberg, "U.S. Asserts Its Protest Is Not Aimed at Talks"; Smith, "U.S. Strategy of Toughness"; Garthoff, *The Great Transition*, 224.

48. Dobrynin, *In Confidence*, 578–79; Shultz, *Turmoil and Triumph*, 576–77; Talbott, *Master of the Game*, 273; Oberdorfer, *The Turn*, 129–30.

49. Talbott, *Master of the Game*, 250–53; Shultz, *Turmoil and Triumph*, 577; Reagan, *An American Life*, 628–29.

50. R. Jeffrey Smith, "Reagan Reinterprets the ABM Treaty," *Science*, 8 November 1985, 644; Talbott, *Master of the Game*, 242–43; Shultz, *Turmoil and Triumph*, 578–79.

51. Talbott, *Master of the Game*, 246; "ABM: The Shift That Never Was," *Newsweek*, 21 October 1985, 55; Shultz, *Turmoil and Triumph*, 578–79.

52. "Resolving a Star Wars Skirmish," *Time*, 28 October 1985, 45; Talbott, *Master of the Game*, 247; Shultz, *Turmoil and Triumph*, 582.

53. Talbott, *Master of the Game*, 247; Honoré M. Catudal, *Soviet Nuclear Strategy from Stalin to Gorbachev* (Atlantic Highlands, N.J: Humanities Press International, 1989), 221; Shultz, *Turmoil and Triumph*, 592.

54. Talbott, *Master of the Game*, 285.

55. Ibid., 286.

56. Ibid, 287.

57. Reagan, *An American Life*, 637; Cannon, *President Reagan*, 752; Shultz, *Turmoil and Triumph*, 601. Dobrynin has revealed that President Reagan had proposed reciprocal summits to Gorbachev through the Soviet ambassador before the summit, and that the Politburo had agreed: see *In Confidence*, 584, 589.

58. Dobrynin, *In Confidence*, 589–90; Oberdorfer, *The Turn*, 148–49. See also Shultz, *Turmoil and Triumph*, 603.

59. Dobrynin, *In Confidence*, 586, 591; Garthoff, *The Great Transition*, 240, 246.

60. Garthoff, *The Great Transition*, 241.

61. Shultz, *Turmoil and Triumph*, 700; John Newhouse, "The Abolitionist—II," *New Yorker*, 9 January 1989, 58.

62. Serge Schemann, "Gorbachev Offers to Scrap A-Arms within 15 Years," *New York Times*, 16 January 1986. Shevardnadze declared bluntly that verification was no longer a problem. "[The] Soviet Union is prepared to use any form of verification—national technical means, international mechanisms, and on-site inspections," he said. See U.S. House Committee on Foreign Affairs, *Verifying Arms Control Agreements: The Soviet View*, report prepared for the Subcommittee on Arms Control International Security and Science, 100th Cong., 1st sess., 1987, 21.

63. Dobrynin, *In Confidence*, 596–97.

64. Shultz, *Turmoil and Triumph*, 700.

65. Ibid.; Bernard Weinraub, "Reagan 'Grateful' for Soviet Plan on Nuclear Arms," *New York Times*, 17 January 1986.

66. Shultz, *Turmoil and Triumph*, 699–706.

67. Ibid., 701, 704; John Newhouse, "Summiteering," *New Yorker*, 8 September 1986, 45.

68. MccGwire, *Perestroika and Soviet National Security*, 195; Shultz, *Turmoil and Triumph*, 706–7, 708–9.

69. Garthoff, *The Great Transition*, 252–53; Dobrynin, *In Confidence*, 599; MccGwire, *Perestroika and Soviet National Security*, 195.

70. "A Farewell to Arms?" *Time*, 26 January 1986, 20.

71. Matthew Evangelista, "Sources of Moderation in Soviet Security Policy," in *Behavior, Society, and Nuclear War*, ed. Philip E. Tetlock et al. (New York: Oxford University Press, 1991), 2:327–28; Garthoff, *The Great Transition*, 261–62.

72. Political Report to the 27th Party Congress, 25 February 1986, in Mikhail Gorbachev, *Selected Speeches and Articles*, 2d ed. (Moscow: Progress Publishers, 1987), 419–21. After the Geneva summit, Gorbachev had told a press conference that "a lower level of security on the part of the United States of America as compared with that of the Soviet Union would not benefit us because this would lead to mistrust and generate instability" (Press Conference in the Soviet Press Center in Geneva, 22 November 1985, ibid., 264–65).

73. Political Report to the 27th Party Congress, ibid., 422.

74. Ibid., 423; Bruce Parrott, "Soviet National Security under Gorbachev," *Problems of Communism* 37 (1988): 10; Raymond L. Garthoff, *Deterrence and the Revolution in Soviet Military Doctrine* (Washington, D.C.: Brookings, 1990), 86.

75. See, for example, Gerhard Wettig, "New Thinking on Security and East-West Relations," *Problems of Communism* 37 (1988): 1–14; Matlock, *Autopsy on an Empire*, 94.

76. Shultz, *Turmoil and Triumph*, 713.

77. Ibid.; Newhouse, "Summiteering," 47; Garthoff, *The Great Transition*, 269–70, 273–74.

78. Newhouse, "Summiteering," 47.

79. MccGwire, *Perestroika and Soviet National Security*, 214–15; Oberdorfer, *The Turn*, 167; Shultz, *Turmoil and Triumph*, 713; Garthoff, *The Great Transition*, 270, 274.

80. Cannon, *President Reagan*, 758–59; Talbott, *Master of the Game*, 288; Shultz, *Turmoil and Triumph*, 717.

81. Gorbachev's speech was published a year later in the first issue of a new foreign ministry publication of official documents, such as the text of treaties. See Mikhail S. Gorbachev, "Time of Perestroika," 23 May 1986 Speech at the Ministry of Foreign Affairs, in *Vestnik Ministerstva innostrannykh del SSSR* (Bulletin of the Ministry of Foreign Affairs of the USSR) (5 August 1987), 4–5, trans. Kristen Williams.

82. Newhouse, "The Abolitionist—II," 60; Jacob V. Lamar Jr., "Overtures in Glassboro," *Time*, 30 June 1986, 38; "A Sudden Thaw in the Cold War," *U.S. News & World Report*, 30 June 1986, 8; Shultz, *Turmoil and Triumph*, 718.

83. Shultz, *Turmoil and Triumph*, 718.

84. Oberdorfer, *The Turn*, 169–74; Shultz, *Turmoil and Triumph*, 719–20, 723–24; Talbott, *Master of the Game*, 307–8; "Soviet Assails Reagan Letter," *New York Times*, 9 August 1986.

85. Philip Taubman, "Gorbachev Says Soviet Test Halt Is Again Extended," *New York Times*, 19 August 1986; Michael R. Gordon, "U.S. Again Says It Won't Join Soviet Moratorium," *New York Times*, 19 August 1986; Franklyn Griffiths, " 'New Thinking' in the Kremlin," *Bulletin of the Atomic Scientists* 43 (April 1987): 23.

86. Anthony Lewis, "The Stupidity Factor," *New York Times*, 18 September 1986; Nicholas Daniloff, *Two Lives, One Russia* (Boston: Houghton Mifflin, 1988), 292–93; Cannon, *President Reagan*, 762.

87. Daniloff, *Two Lives, One Russia*, 176–78; Bernard Gwertzman, "Russians Set Daniloff Free," *New York Times*, 30 September 1986, 10; Shultz, *Turmoil and Triumph*, 730.

88. Talbott, *Master of the Game*, 314–15; Shultz, *Turmoil and Triumph*, 743; Reagan, *An American Life*, 669, 671; P. Edward Haley, " 'You Could Have Said Yes': Lessons from Reykjavik," *Orbis* 31 (1987): 81.

89. Leslie H. Gelb, "Daniloff and the Summit: A New Test for Reagan," *New York Times*, 17 September 1986; Shultz, *Turmoil and Triumph*, 730–31, 733–34; Garthoff, *The Great Transition*, 282–83; Daniloff, *Two Lives, One Russia*, 286–87; Gwertzman, "Russians Set Daniloff Free."

90. "Soviet in a Shift on Troop Checks," *New York Times*, 20 August 1986; Paul Lewis, "East-West Accord Reached on a Plan to Cut Risk of War," *New York Times*, 22 September 1986.

91. Garthoff, *The Great Transition*, 252, 291; Matlock, *Autopsy on an Empire*, 97.

92. Dobrynin, *In Confidence*, 610.

93. Shultz, *Turmoil and Triumph*, 758.

94. Ibid., 758–59.

95. Talbott, *Master of the Game*, 316.

96. Shultz, *Turmoil and Triumph*, 761.

97. Ibid.

98. Ibid., 762.

99. Talbott, *Master of the Game*, 320; Shultz, *Turmoil and Triumph*, 763–64.

100. Shultz, *Turmoil and Triumph*, 765–66.

101. Cannon, *President Reagan*, 766–67; Talbott, *Master of the Game*, 322–23; Shultz, *Turmoil and Triumph*, 768.

102. Newhouse, "The Abolitionist—II," 62; Talbott, *Master of the Game*, 323; Cannon, *President Reagan*, 766.

103. Shultz, *Turmoil and Triumph*, 769–70.

104. Ibid., 769.

105. Ibid., 769–70.

106. Ibid., 770.

107. Ibid., 771.

108. Ibid.

109. Dobrynin, *In Confidence*, 620–21; Pavel Palazchenko, *Interpreting the Whirlwind* (University Park: Pennsylvania State University Press, forthcoming), typescript, 61.

110. Cannon, *President Reagan*, 768; Newhouse, "The Abolitionist—II," 62; Talbott, *Master of the Game*, 324–25; Shultz, *Turmoil and Triumph*, 772.

111. Shultz, *Turmoil and Triumph*, 772.

112. Ibid., 772–73.

113. Reagan, *An American Life*, 679; Cannon, *President Reagan*, 769; Bernard Weinraub, "How Grim Ending in Iceland Followed Hard-Won Gains," *New York Times*, 14 October 1986.

114. Shultz, *Turmoil and Triumph*, 760.

115. Dobrynin, *In Confidence*, 622; Matlock, *Autopsy on an Empire*, 97.

116. Bill Keller, "Moscow, Rebuffed by U.S., Is Planning to Renew A-Tests," *New York Times*, 19 December 1986.

117. Philip Taubman, "Soviet Lifts Sakharov Banishment and Grants a Pardon to Bonner," *New York Times*, 20 December 1986; Doder and Branson, *Gorbachev*, 172–73.

118. Jonathan Dean, "Gorbachev's Arms Control Moves," *Bulletin of the Atomic Scientists* 43 (June 1987): 34; Michael J. Sodaro, *Moscow, Germany, and the West from Khrushchev to Gorbachev* (Ithaca: Cornell University Press, 1990), 323.

119. John Van Oudenaren, *The Role of Shevardnadze and the Ministry of Foreign Affairs in the Making of Soviet Defense and Arms Control Policy*, R-3898-USDP (Santa Monica, Calif.: Rand, 1990), 11–12; MccGwire, *Perestroika and Soviet National Security*, 213–15.

120. Adomeit, "Gorbachev's Policy toward the West," 98–99.

121. Oberdorfer, *The Turn*, 216; Seweryn Bialer and Joan Afferica, "The Genesis of Gorbachev's World," *Foreign Affairs* 64 (1986): 627; Dimitri K. Simes, "Gorbachev: A New Foreign Policy?" *Foreign Affairs* 65 (1987): 478; MccGwire, *Perestroika and Soviet National Security*, 272.

122. Sodaro, *Moscow, Germany, and the West*, 323; Garthoff, *The Great Transition*, 302–3; MccGwire, *Perestroika and Soviet National Security*, 258–66 (quotation on p. 264); Marshall I. Goldman, *What Went Wrong with Perestroika* (New York: W. W. Norton, 1991), 103–4; Kaiser, *Why Gorbachev Happened*, 151–55.

123. MccGwire, *Perestroika and Soviet National Security*, 268–69; Anatoly Chernyaev, "The Phenomenon of Gorbachev in the Context of Leadership," *International Affairs* 6 (1993): 44.

124. David K. Shipler, "State Dept. Gives Moscow a Rare Pat on the Back," *New York Times*, 11 February 1987; Garthoff, *The Great Transition*, 301–2; Doder and Branson, *Gorbachev*, 182–84; Kaiser, *Why Gorbachev Happened*, 156–58.

125. Garthoff, *The Great Transition*, 304–5; Doder and Branson, *Gorbachev*, 209–11; Speech by Mikhail Gorbachev at the Forum "For a Nuclear-Free World, for the Survival of Mankind," Moscow Television Service, 16 February 1987, trans. Foreign Broadcast Information Service, *FBIS Daily Report-Soviet Union*, 17 February 1987 (PrEx 7.10: FBIS-DR-SU), 15–26.

126. Bill Keller, "Moscow, in Reversal, Urges Agreement 'without Delay' to Limit Missiles in Europe," *New York Times*, 1 March 1987; idem, "Gorbachev Looking to More Accords," *New York Times*, 3 March 1987.

127. Robert Legvold, "War, Weapons, and Soviet Foreign Policy," in *Gorbachev's Russia and American Foreign Policy*, ed. Bialer and Mandelbaum, 117–18; Evangelista, "Sources of Moderation in Soviet Security Policy," 321–22.

128. Newhouse, "The Abolitionist—II," 66; Thomas Risse-Kappen, *The Zero Option: INF, West Germany, and Arms Control* (Boulder, Colo.: Westview Press, 1988), 143–44.

129. James M. Markham, "Soviet, in Geneva, Said to Back Idea of Site Inspection," *New York Times*, 5 March 1987; Paul Lewis, "Soviet Aide Sees Arms Pact by Summer," *New York Times*, 7 March 1987.

130. Michael R. Gordon, "Agreeing How to Spy on Each Other," *New York Times*, 28 June 1987; "Closing the Gap," *Time*, 7 September 1987; David Aaron, "Verification: Will It Work?" *New York Times Magazine*, 11 October 1987, 12; Risse-Kappen, *The Zero Option*, 146.

131. Michael R. Gordon, "Soviet Offer Puts U.S. in a Quandary," *New York Times*, 15 April 1987; Risse-Kappen, *The Zero Option*, 123–24; Michael R. Gordon, "Reagan Announces New U.S. Proposal on Mid-Range Arms," *New York Times*, 4 March 1987.

132. Philip Taubman, "A Sense of Strategy," *New York Times*, 24 July 1987.

133. Shultz, *Turmoil and Triumph*, 843, 990–91; Garthoff, *The Great Transition*, 308.

134. Anthony Lewis, "Why the Summit" (editorial), *New York Times*, 6 November 1987; Michael R. Gordon, "How to Destroy the 2,611 Missiles," *New York Times*, 9 December 1987. The total numbers of missiles finally destroyed were slightly different from the figures reported at the time. The Soviet Union had to destroy 889 intermediate-range missiles, and the United States only 677. As for shorter-range systems, the Soviet Union had to destroy 957, while the United States had to eliminate only 169. See Garthoff, *Great Transition*, 327n.

135. Cannon, *President Reagan*, 779; Michael R. Gordon, "Accord Is Reached on Missile Treaty by U.S. and Soviet," *New York Times*, 25 November 1987.

136. David K. Shipler, "The Mood Is Genuinely Hopeful for This Summit," *New York Times*, 6 December 1987; Steven V. Roberts, "President Upbeat over Relationship with Gorbachev," *New York Times*, 12 December 1987.

137. R. W. Apple Jr., "Gorbachev a Hit with the American Public," *New York Times*, 4 December 1987; Hedrick Smith, "Gorbachev's Shrewd Summitry," *New York Times Magazine*, 6 December 1987, 51.

138. Smith, "Gorbachev's Shrewd Summitry," 96; Shultz, *Turmoil and Triumph*, 1013; Michael R. Gordon, "Avoiding the Obstacles," *New York Times*, 11 December 1987; Talbott, *Master of the Game*, 366.

139. Hugh De Santis and Dimitri Simes, "Beware of Wishful Thinking about Gorbachev," *New York Times*, 25 October 1987, 23; Christoph Bertram, "Europe's Security Dilemmas," *Foreign Affairs* 65 (1987), 945; Henry A. Kissinger, "Kissinger: How to Deal with Gorbachev," *Newsweek*, 2 March 1987, 42; R. Craig Nation, *Black Earth, Red Star: A History of Soviet Security Policy, 1917–1991* (Ithaca: Cornell University Press, 1992), 301–2.

140. Charles Krauthammer, "When to Call Off the Cold War," *New Republic*, 16 November 1987, 21; "Closing the Gap," *Time*, 7 September 1987, 12.

141. Oberdorfer, *The Turn*, 238; Doder and Branson, *Gorbachev*, 223; Mcc-Gwire, *Perestroika and Soviet National Security*, 275; Chernyaev, "The Phenomenon of Gorbachev," 43.

142. Philip Taubman, "Soviet Sets May 15 as Goal to Start Afghanistan Exit," *New York Times*, 9 February 1988; Paul Lewis, "Accord Completed on Soviet Pullout," *New York Times*, 9 April 1988; idem, "Four Nations Sign Accords for Soviet Afghan Pullout," *New York Times*, 15 April 1988; Garthoff, *The Great Transition*, 345–46.

143. Newhouse, "The Abolitionist—II," 72; Talbott, *Master of the Game*, 374–76, 382–83, 388; Shultz, *Turmoil and Triumph*, 1085.

144. Michael R. Gordon, "U.S. and Soviet Agree to Widen Student Exchange," *New York Times*, 1 June 1988; Garthoff, *The Great Transition*, 353.

145. "Reagan's 'Moscow Spring,'" *Newsweek*, 13 June 1988, 17; "Text of President Reagan's News Conference at Spaso House," 1 June 1988, *New York Times*, 2 June 1988.

146. "The 19th All-Union CPSU Conference: Foreign Policy and Diplomacy," report by Eduard Shevardnadze at the Scientific and Practical Conference of the USSR Ministry of Foreign Affairs, 25 July 1988, *International Affairs*, no. 10 (1988): 13, 15.

147. Ibid., 23.

148. Garthoff, *The Great Transition*, 362–63.

149. M. S. Gorbachev's United Nations Address, *Pravda*, 8 December 1988, *FBIS Daily Report-Soviet Union*, 7 December 1988 (FBIS-SOV-88-236), 12–13.

150. Ibid., 13.

151. Ibid., 14; Shultz, *Turmoil and Triumph*, 1107.

152. Ibid., 17; Ed Magnuson, "Crunching Gorbachev's Numbers," *Time*, 19 December 1988, 25.

153. F. Stephen Larrabee, "The New Soviet Approach to Europe," in *The New Europe: Revolution in East-West Relations*, Proceedings of the Academy of Political Science, vol. 38 (1991): 16; MccGwire, *Perestroika and Soviet National Security*, 271–72; David Holloway, "Gorbachev's New Thinking," *Foreign Affairs: America & the World* 68 (1988–89): 75.

154. "Responding to Gorbachev," *U.S. News & World Report*, 19 December 1988, 18; Walter Isaacson, "The Gorbachev Challenge," *Time*, 19 December 1988, 20.

155. " 'This Is Not Just a Matter of Tactics,' " *Newsweek*, 19 December 1988, 32; Larrabee, "The New Soviet Approach to Europe," 15.

156. Arnold L. Horelick, "U.S.-Soviet Relations: Threshold of a New Era," *Foreign Affairs: America & the World* 69 (1989–90): 5; Michael R. Beschloss and Strobe Talbott, *At the Highest Levels: The Inside Story of the End of the Cold War* (Boston: Little, Brown, 1993), 9, 11, 24.

157. Beschloss and Talbott, *At the Highest Levels*, 12–13, 17–18, 22–23, 25.

158. Matlock, *Autopsy on an Empire*, 178–81, 196–97.

159. See, for example, Larrabee, "The New Soviet Approach to Europe," 1–25; Coit D. Blacker, "The Collapse of Soviet Power in Europe," *Foreign Affairs: America & the World* 70 (1990–91): 88–102; Goldman, *What Went Wrong with Perestroika*, 197–98.

160. Hannes Adomeit, "Gorbachev and German Unification: Revision of Thinking, Realignment of Power," *Problems of Communism* 39 (1990): 4–5; idem, "Gorbachev, German Unification, and the Collapse of Empire," *Post-Soviet Affairs* 10 (1994): 220; Alexander Dallin, "The Broader Context: A Comment on Adomeit," *Post-Soviet Affairs* 10 (1994): 231–33; Chernyaev, "The Phenomenon of Gorbachev," 45.

161. Larrabee, "The New Soviet Approach to Europe," 6–7; Asmus, Brown, and Crane, *Soviet Foreign Policy and the Revolutions of 1989 in Eastern Europe*, 13, 18–19; Adomeit, "Gorbachev and German Unification," 3; Charles Gati, "Gorbachev and Eastern Europe," *Foreign Affairs* 65 (1987): 970–71.

162. Adomeit, "Gorbachev and German Unification," 5; Asmus, Brown, and Crane, *Soviet Foreign Policy and the Revolutions of 1989*, 20–21.

163. Kaiser, *Why Gorbachev Happened*, 297–98; Gale Stokes, *The Walls Came Tumbling Down: The Collapse of Communism in Eastern Europe* (New York: Oxford University Press, 1993), 124–25; Oberdorfer, *The Turn*, 358.

164. Oberdorfer, *The Turn*, 362–3; Philip Zelikow and Condoleezza Rice, *Ger-*

many Unified and Europe Transformed: A Study in Statecraft (Cambridge: Harvard University Press, 1995), 63–65.

165. George J. Church, "Do-Nothing Detente," *New York Times*, 15 May 1989.

166. Maureen Dowd, "Bush Voices Hope on Soviet Change, But with Caution," *New York Times*, 13 May 1989; Beschloss and Talbott, *At the Highest Levels*, 71.

167. Bernard Weinraub, "U.S. Questions Moscow Pledge on Sandinistas," *New York Times*, 17 May 1989; "Counterpunching Gorbachev," *U.S. News & World Report*, 29 May 1989.

168. Garthoff, *The Great Transition*, 380–81; Oberdorfer, *The Turn*, 349–51; Beschloss and Talbott, *At the Highest Levels*, 75–78.

169. Kaiser, *Why Gorbachev Happened*, 297–98; Oberdorfer, *The Turn*, 359; "Glasnost Innovation: Jokes," *New York Times*, 13 June 1989.

170. James M. Markham, "Gorbachev Spurns the Use of Force in Eastern Europe," *New York Times*, 7 July 1989.

171. Oberdorfer, *The Turn*, 367; Beschloss and Talbott, *At the Highest Levels*, 93–94.

172. Kaiser, *Why Gorbachev Happened*, 298–99; Timothy Garton Ash, *The Magic Lantern: The Revolution of '89 Witnessed in Warsaw, Budapest, Berlin, and Prague* (New York: Random House, 1990), 41; Zelikow and Rice, *Germany Unified and Europe Transformed*, 69–70;

173. Zelikow and Rice, *Germany Unified and Europe Transformed*, 68; Oberdorfer, *The Turn*, 362.

174. Kaiser, *Why Gorbachev Happened*, 302; "Party Coup Turned East German Tide," *New York Times*, 19 November 1989; Ash, *Magic Lantern*, 65; Zelikow and Rice, *Germany Unified and Europe Transformed*, 83–84.

175. Kaiser, *Why Gorbachev Happened*, 302–3; Zelikow and Rice, *Germany Unified and Europe Transformed*, 84–85.

176. Ibid., 90–91.

177. Ibid., 99–101; Elizabeth Pond, *Beyond the Wall: Germany's Road to Unification* (Washington, D.C.: Brookings, 1993), 132–34.

178. Oberdorfer, *The Turn*, 365–66; Stokes, *The Walls Came Tumbling Down*, 147–48.

179. Alan Riding, "Bush Says Soviets Merit West's Help to Foster Reform," *New York Times*, 5 December 1989; Beschloss and Talbott, *At the Highest Levels*, 166.

180. Francis X. Clines, "Economic Pledges Cheer Soviet Aides," *New York Times*, 4 December 1989; Beschloss and Talbott, *At the Highest Levels*, 150–51.

181. Beschloss and Talbott, *At the Highest Levels*, 157.

182. Matlock, *Autopsy on an Empire*, 272–73.

183. Kaiser, *Why Gorbachev Happened*, 313; Oberdorfer, *The Turn*, 366.

184. Oberdorfer, *The Turn*, 365.

185. Zelikow and Rice, *Germany Unified and Europe Transformed*, 162–63; Adomeit, "Gorbachev, German Unification, and the Collapse of Empire," 217–18.

186. Adomeit, "Gorbachev and German Unification," 10–11; Zelikow and Rice, *Germany Unified and Europe Transformed*, 188–89.

187. Zelikow and Rice, *Germany Unified and Europe Transformed*, 275–81;

Adomeit, "Gorbachev, German Unification, and the Collapse of Empire," 220–21.

188. Larrabee, "The New Soviet Approach to Europe," 12; Adomeit, "Gorbachev and German Unification," 20.

189. "NATO Leaders Proclaim End of Cold War, Revise Treaty, Invite Gorbachev to Speak," *New York Times*, 7 July 1990.

190. John-Thor Dahlburg, "Communists Squabble, Assail Leadership," *Los Angeles Times*, 6 July 1990; Eduard Shevardnadze, *The Future Belongs to Freedom* (New York: Free Press, 1991), 141.

191. "Gorbachev Clears the Way to Unification of Germany," *New York Times*, 17 July 1990; Larrabee, "The New Soviet Approach to Europe," 13; Matlock, *Autopsy of an Empire*, 386; Zelikow and Rice, *Germany Unified and Europe Transformed*, 341–42.

192. Adomeit, "Gorbachev and German Unification," 14; Matlock, *Autopsy of an Empire*, 388.

193. John-Thor Dahlburg, "2 Factions Clash at Soviet Congress," *Los Angeles Times*, 4 July 1990.

194. Neil Malcolm, "The 'Common European Home' and Soviet European Policy," *International Affairs* 65 (1989): 675.

7. Missed Opportunities, Conflict Spirals, and History

1. Hans J. Morgenthau and Kenneth W. Thompson, *Politics among Nations: The Struggle for Power and Peace*, 6th ed. (New York: Alfred A. Knopf, 1985), 439.

2. Harold Sprout, "The Role of the Great Powers in the Maintenance of Peace and Security," in *Foundations of National Security: Readings on World Politics and American Security*, ed. Harold and Margaret Sprout (Princeton: Princeton University Press, 1945), 752; Hans W. Weigert, *Generals and Geographers: The Twilight of Geopolitics* (London: Oxford University Press, 1942; Halford J. Mackinder, "The Round World and the Winning of the Peace," in *Compass of the World: A Symposium on Political Geography*, ed. Hans W. Weigert and Vilhjalmur Stefansson (New York: Macmillan, 1945), 168–69.

3. Eduard Shevardnadze, *The Future Belongs to Freedom* (New York: Free Press, 1991), 80.

4. Stephen Jay Gould, *Wonderful Life: The Burgess Shale and the Nature of History* (New York: W. W. Norton, 1989), 283.

5. On such experiments, see Mark Snyder, "When Belief Creates Reality," in *Advances in Experimental Social Psychology*, ed. Leonard Berkowitz (New York: Academic Press, 1984), 18:147–305.

6. Robert Jervis, *Perception and Misperception in International Politics* (Princeton: Princeton University Press, 1976), chap. 3.

7. Elaine Sciolino, "Yeltsin Says NATO Is Trying to Split Continent Again," *New York Times*, 6 December 1994; idem, "Why Russia Still Bangs Its Shoe," *New York Times*, 11 December 1994; Remarks by President Bill Clinton to the Multinational Audience of Future Leaders of Europe, Hôtel de Ville, Brussels, Belgium, 9 January 1994, quoted in Henry Kissinger, *Diplomacy* (New York: Simon & Schuster, 1994), 824.

8. Robert Jervis, *The Logic of Images in International Relations* (Princeton: Princeton University Press, 1970), 24.

9. Teresa Hayden and Walter Mischel, "Maintaining Trait Consistency in the Resolution of Behavioral Inconsistency: The Wolf in Sheep's Clothing?" *Journal of Personality* 44 (1976): 122. See also Beth V. Yarbrough and Robert M. Yarbrough, "Boundary-Maintenance Devices to Assure Contractual Integrity: Identity, Reputation, and the 'Extent of the Market,' " paper prepared for delivery at the 1994 annual meeting of the American Political Science Association.

10. David Baldwin, *Economic Statecraft* (Princeton: Princeton University Press, 1985), 109.

11. George P. Shultz, *Turmoil and Triumph: My Years as Secretary of State* (New York: Charles Scribner's Sons, 1993), 270.

12. Haldeman Diary, 26 May 1971, in H. R. Haldeman, *The Haldeman Diaries: Inside the Nixon White House* (New York: G. P. Putman's Sons, 1994), 292.

Primary Sources

FOREIGN BROADCAST INFORMATION SERVICE

Gorbachev, Mikhail. "For a Nuclear-Free World, For the Survival of Mankind."
Moscow Television Service, 17 February 1987. Translated by Foreign Broad-
cast Information Service. *FBIS Daily Report-Soviet Union,* 17 February 1987
(PrEx 7.10: FBIS-DR-SU), 15–26.
——. "The Reality and Guarantees of a Secure World." *Pravda.* 7 September
1987. Translated by Foreign Broadcast Information Service. *FBIS Daily Report-
Soviet Union,* 7 September 1987 (PrEx 7.10: FBIS-SOV-87-120), 23–28.
——. "United Nations Address." *Pravda.* 8 December 1988. Translated by For-
eign Broadcast Information Service. *FBIS Daily Report-Soviet Union,* 7 December 1988 (PrEx 7.10: FBIS-SOV-88-236), 11–21.

MANUSCRIPTS

Dwight David Eisenhower Library (DDEL), Abilene, Kansas

John Foster Dulles Papers
   Draft Correspondence and Speech Series
   General Correspondence and Memoranda
   JFD Chronological Series
   Subject Series
   Telephone Conversations Series
   White House Memoranda Series
Christian A. Herter Papers
C.D. Jackson Records
John McCone Papers
Office of Special Assistant for Disarmament

Office of Special Assistant for National Security Affairs
  NSC Series
    Administration Subseries
    Briefing Notes Subseries
    Policy Papers Subseries
  Special Assistant Series
    Chronological Subseries
    Subject Series
Office of Special Assistant for Science and Technology
White House Office File
  International Trips and Meetings Series
White House Office, Office of Staff Secretary
  International Series
  International Trips and Meetings Series
  State Department Series
  SubAlpha Series
  Subject Series
    Department of Defense Subseries
    State Department Subseries
Ann C. Whitman File
  DDE Diary Series
  Dulles-Herter Series
  International Meetings Series
  International Series
  NSC Series
  Ann C. Whitman Diary

John F. Kennedy Library (JFKL), Boston, Massachusetts

National Security File
  Countries
  Departments and Agencies
  Meetings and Memoranda
  Subject File
President's Office File
  Countries

Seeley G. Mudd Manuscript Library (SGMML), Princeton, New Jersey

John Foster Dulles Papers
Emmet J. Hughes Papers
Livington T. Merchant Papers

PUBLISHED DOCUMENTS

Gorbachev, Mikhail S. "Time of Perestroika." 23 May 1986 speech at the Ministry of Foreign Affairs. *Vestnik Ministerstva innostrannykh del SSSR* (Bulletin of the Ministry of Foreign Affairs of the USSR), no. 1 (5 August 1986): 4–6.

Primary Sources

Public Papers of the Presidents: John F. Kennedy, 1963. Washington, D.C.: Government Printing Office, 1964.

Ruffner, Kevin C. *Corona: America's First Satellite Program*. Washington, D.C.: Center for the Study of Intelligence, Central Intelligence Agency, 1995.

Stickle, D. M., ed. *The Beria Affair: The Secret Transcripts of the Meetings Signalling the End of Stalinism*. Translated by Jeanne Farrow. New York: Nova Science Publishers, 1992.

U.S. Department of State, *Documents on Germany: 1944–1985*. Washington, D.C.: Government Printing Office, 1985.

U.S. Department of State, *Foreign Relations of the United States, 1952–1963*. Washington, D.C.: Government Printing Office, 1984–1994.

Unpublished Material

Harrison, Hope M. "Ulbricht and the Concrete 'Rose': New Archival Evidence on the Dynamics of Soviet–East German Relations and the Berlin Crisis, 1958–1961." Working Paper no. 5, Cold War International History Project. Woodrow Wilson International Center for Scholars, Washington, D.C., May 1993. Mimeograph.

Zubok, Vladislav M. "Khrushchev and the Berlin Crisis (1958–1962)." Working Paper no. 6, Cold War International History Project. Woodrow Wilson International Center for Scholars, Washington, D.C., May 1993. Mimeograph.

Cornell Studies in Security Affairs

edited by Robert J. Art, Robert Jervis,
and Stephen M. Walt

The Sources of Military Doctrine: France, Britain, and Germany between the World Wars,
    by Barry R. Posen
Dilemmas of Appeasement: British Deterrence and Defense, 1934–1937, by Gaines Post, Jr.
Crucible of Beliefs: Learning, Alliances, and World Wars, by Dan Reiter
Eisenhower and the Missile Gap, by Peter J. Roman
The Domestic Bases of Grand Strategy, edited by Richard Rosecrance and Arthur A. Stein
Societies and Military Power: India and Its Armies, by Stephen Peter Rosen
Winning the Next War: Innovation and the Modern Military, by Stephen Peter Rosen
Israel and Conventional Deterrence: Border Warfare from 1953 to 1970, by Jonathan Shimshoni
Fighting to a Finish: The Politics of War Termination in the United States and Japan, 1945,
    by Leon V. Sigal
The Ideology of the Offensive: Military Decision Making and the Disasters of 1914,
    by Jack Snyder
Myths of Empire: Domestic Politics and International Ambition, by Jack Snyder
The Militarization of Space: U.S. Policy, 1945–1984, by Paul B. Stares
The Nixon Administration and the Making of U.S. Nuclear Strategy, by Terry Terriff
Making the Alliance Work: The United States and Western Europe, by Gregory F. Treverton
The Origins of Alliances, by Stephen M. Walt
Revolution and War, by Stephen M. Walt
The Ultimate Enemy: British Intelligence and Nazi Germany, 1933–1939, by Wesley K. Wark
The Tet Offensive: Intelligence Failure in War, by James J. Wirtz
The Elusive Balance: Power and Perceptions during the Cold War, by William Curti Wohlforth
Deterrence and Strategic Culture: Chinese-American Confrontations, 1949–1958,
    by Shu Guang Zhang